Integrating College Study Skills

Reasoning in Reading, Listening, and Writing

Integrating

College Study Skills

Reasoning

in Reading, Listening, and Writing

Fifth Edition

Peter Elias Sotiriou

Los Angeles City College

Wadsworth Publishing Company

I(T)P® *An International Thomson Publishing Company*

Belmont, CA • Albany, NY • Boston • Cincinnati • Johannesburg • London •
Madrid • Melbourne • Mexico City • New York • Pacific Grove, CA •
Scottsdale, AZ • Singapore • Tokyo • Toronto

Publisher: Karen Allanson
Developmental Editor: Kimberly Johnson
Senior Editorial Assistant: Godwin Chu
Marketing Manager: Jennie Burger
Project Editor: Christal Niederer
Print Buyer: Barbara Britton
Permissions Editor: Susan Walters
Copy Editor: Elliot Simon

Production: Melanie Field/Strawberry Field
  Publishing
Designer: Suzanne Montazer/SLM Graphics
Cover Design: John Odam
Cover Image: Denis Waugh
Compositor: Thompson Type
Printer: Webcom Limited

COPYRIGHT © 1999 by Wadsworth Publishing Company
A Division of International Thomson Publishing Inc.
I(T)P® The ITP logo is a trademark under license.

This book is printed on acid-free, recycled paper.

Printed in Canada
1 2 3 4 5 6 7 8 9 10

For more information, contact Wadsworth Publishing Company, 10 Davis Drive,
Belmont, CA 94002, or electronically at http://www.wadsworth.com

International Thomson Publishing Europe
Berkshire House
168-173 High Holborn
London, WC1V 7AA, United Kingdom

International Thomson Editores
Seneca, 53
Colonia Polanco
11560 México D.F. México

Nelson ITP, Australia
102 Dodds Street
South Melbourne
Victoria 3205 Australia

International Thomson Publishing Asia
60 Albert Street
#15-01 Albert Complex
Singapore 189969

Nelson Canada
1120 Birchmount Road
Scarborough, Ontario
Canada M1K 5G4

International Thomson Publishing Japan
Hirakawa-cho Kyowa Building, 3F
2-2-1 Hirakawa-cho, Chiyoda-ku
Tokyo 102, Japan

International Thomson Publishing Southern Africa
Building 18, Constantia Square
138 Sixteenth Road, P.O. Box 2459
Halfway House, 1685 South Africa

Library of Congress Cataloging-in-Publication Data
Sotiriou, Peter Elias.
    Integrating college study skills : reasoning in reading,
listening, and writing / Peter Elias Sotiriou. — 5th ed.
      p. cm.
    Includes index.
    ISBN 0-534-54990-X
    1. Study skills. 2. Language arts (Higher)   3. Education, Higher—
Computer-assisted instruction.   4. Internet (Computer network) in
education. I. Title.
LB2395.S597 1998
378.1'70281—dc21   98-42488
                               CIP

Contents in Brief

Contents

Part Three   Taking Lecture, Discussion, and Study Notes   213

Chapter 12   Visual Note-taking Techniques: Laddering and Mapping   254

Part Four   Study Skills Systems and Test-Taking Practices   270

Chapter 13   Memory Aids   271

Chapter 14   The SQ3R Study System   283

Part Five   *Applying SQ3R to Textbook Material*   *346*

Preface

<table>
<tr>
<td>New to This Edition</td>
<td>

In this fifth edition of *Integrating College Study Skills,* I have moved this study skills project into the twenty-first century, based on feedback from reviewers. There is a much greater emphasis on study skills and technology in this edition. Each chapter ends with an Internet activity that asks students to access material related to study skills and college topics from Web sites and from InfoTrac College Edition®. These activities will enhance what students learn in each chapter and provide needed practice in accessing information on the Internet. I have also included more material on the computer and its uses in study skills in Chapter 1, "Getting to Know Your College," and in Chapter 3, "Using the Library."

More recent learning research has been incorporated into several chapters. Reference to schemata, or the connections learners make, is made in Chapter 13, "Memory Aids." A greater focus on discussion as a form of learning college material is made in Chapter 10, "Characteristics of Lectures and Discussions." In several exercises throughout the textbook, students are encouraged to work collaboratively to benefit from the social nature of much college learning. And new ways of organizing and retaining material are introduced in Chapter 12, "Visual Notetaking Techniques," with the presentation of the semantic web as a study map. In Chapter 15, "Suggestions for Taking Objective Tests," I have relied on the visual way students can learn in my discussion of visual cards as learning aids, and I have introduced ways that students can integrate what they learn in lecture and reading in my presentation of study sheets and advanced study sheets.

Chapter 8, "Reading and Listening for Inferences," has undergone a major revision with the inclusion of figurative language and the drawing of conclusions from description and action as additional inference practices. Chapter 13, "Memory Aids," now comes *before* "The SQ3R Study System" so that students can apply a variety of memory aids to master the textbook material in Chapter 14.

Fourteen of the textbook readings have been replaced with more recent material. The final part of the book, "Applying SQ3R to Textbook Material," now has three, rather than four, readings, with the last being a full-length textbook chapter.

</td>
</tr>
<tr>
<td>Major Features</td>
<td>

In this fifth edition, I have continued to adapt study skills instruction to include computer technology. I have also retained many features of *Integrating College Study Skills* upon which I conceived the first edition in 1984. The textbook still moves logically, linking one study skill to the next, and the exercises continue to progress incrementally from chal-

</td>
</tr>
</table>

lenging to more challenging activities. Writing still culminates the exercises in most chapters, and a studied focus on integrating the reasoning practices of reading, listening, and writing is evident throughout the textbook. As with editions three and four, I have retained the thematic focus found in most chapters so that students have experience with material they will normally encounter in their college courses.

Integrating College Study Skills, 5th edition, is a challenging study skills textbook that simulates what students need to do as they read, listen, and write in college. It is my hope that with the varied activities and discussions in this textbook, students, in a semester, will find ways to become productive college listeners, readers, and writers as they prepare themselves for the career challenges of the twenty-first century.

Acknowledgments

My thanks go to Karen Allanson, Publisher for College Success, Communications, and Developmental English, who made all the necessary preparations for my writing of this fifth edition; to Kim Johnson, Developmental Editor, who carefully, cheerfully, and promptly followed the development of this fifth edition through its many large and small revisions; to Christal Niederer, the Project Editor, who made sure I met all deadlines; to Melanie Field of Strawberry Field Publishing who was both professional and supportive at every stage of the production process; and, as always, to my wife, Vasi, and my sons Elia and Dimitri, who lovingly made do without me during the many hours I needed to complete this fifth edition. I am also thankful for the comments made by my reviewers.

Fifth Edition Reviewers. Catherine Cavataio, Marygrove College; Katherine H. Clark, Linn-Benton Community College; Susan Crow, Texas Tech University; Mary B. Dorn, SUNY—Oneonta; Carolyn Hopper, Middle Tennessee State University; Virda K. Lester, Tuskegee University; Judith Olson-Fallon, Case Western Reserve University; Martha Risley, Wichita State University; and Faye Z. Ross, Philadelphia College.

Previous Edition Reviewers. Edith Alderson, Joliet Junior College; Janice Beran, McLennan Community College; Jan Bradley, Southwest Missouri State University; Beverly Burch, Vincennes University; Catherine Cavalaio, Marygrove College; Kathy Clark, Linn-Benton Community College; Nancy C. Cook, University of Arkansas; Muriel Davis, San Diego Mesa College; Karen Fenske, Kishwaukee College; Richard D. Grossman, Tompkins-Cortland Community College; Kathryn S. Hawes, Memphis State University; Nancy Hoover, Bellarmine College; Allan Jacobson, Los Angeles Harbor College; Pat John, Lane Community College; Cathy Leist, University of Louisville; Virda K. Lester, Tuskegee University; Lorita Manning, Baylor University; Denise McGinty, University of Texas at Austin; Penney Miller, Clayton Junior College; Thomas Minderman, Vincennes University; Kelli Jayn Nichols, University of Washington; Linda Pounds, Georgia State University; Josef Raab, University of Southern California; Margaret Rauch, St. Cloud State University; Sharon Robertson, University of Tennessee, Martin; Diane Scott, Mesa College; and Melaine Evans Summey, Abraham Baldwin Agricultural College.

To the Student: How to Use This Book

You have no doubt come to a study skills course for several reasons. For one, you probably need to upgrade your textbook reading skills. Two, you may want to improve your note-taking skills to capture the key points your instructors make. And three, you likely want to improve your test-taking skills. If you complete the exercises in this text, you will become a more successful college student—more efficient in reading, note-taking, and taking exams.

How Is This Book Organized?

Before you begin to do the exercises in this text, you need to know how this text is put together. The first part is called "Skills for Beginning Your College Career." Here, you will learn about the basic survival skills that college students need to know: how to use your college's counseling services, what your particular learning style is, when and what to study, how much time to devote to your studies, how to cope with stress in college, and other equally important skills. This first part will carefully point your college career in the right direction.

Part Two, "Basic Reading, Listening, and Writing Skills," is the longest, dealing with the essential reading, listening, and writing skills you will need to practice successfully in college. In this part you will learn several key reasoning skills. You will be shown how to locate the main idea, how to identify and use details, and how to summarize and paraphrase. You will also learn how to read and listen for inferences and how to read graphs, charts, and tables. Throughout this part, you will see how these skills apply to reading, listening, and writing. This is a unique feature of *Integrating College Study Skills*. As the title suggests, you will learn to integrate each study skill into the three activities of reading, listening, and writing. You will also be introduced to material from college subjects. In Chapters 4–8 and in Chapters 11 and 12, the set of exercises for each chapter focus on one college subject.

In Part Three, "Taking Lecture, Discussion, and Study Notes," you will be using the skills learned in the previous part to improve your note-taking skills. You will learn how to condense information and use abbreviations. You will also be introduced to the numeral–letter and Cornell note-taking systems, which will help you organize and remember your lecture, discussion, and study notes. You will also be introduced to laddering and mapping—visual ways of taking notes that are especially helpful when you are studying for exams and you want to organize your study material efficiently.

In Part Four, "Study Skills Systems and Test-Taking Practices," you will be given guidelines for taking various kinds of tests: objective, essay, and math or science. Most importantly, in this part you will learn about the SQ3R study system, a successful method for learning and remembering what you read in textbooks. Finally, in Part Five, "Applying SQ3R to Textbook Material," you will use this method and all the previous study practices you have learned to read and understand two textbook excerpts and one complete textbook chapter.

**How Are the
Chapters Organized?**

Integrating College Study Skills follows a consistent format throughout. Each chapter is divided into two parts: an introduction to the study skills in question, and exercises that allow you to apply these skills. Follow these steps as you work through each chapter:

1. Read the introductions carefully. The information presented in these sections will give you the necessary skills to complete the exercises.

2. Before you begin an exercise, read the directions carefully. Know what you have to do before you begin.

3. Record your answers in the answer box that accompanies most exercises.

4. After you complete the exercise, check your answers. You will find the answers to most odd-numbered exercises at the end of the text. Your instructor will provide the answers to the even-numbered exercises. You will also need to consult your instructor for the correct answers to all exercises involving paragraph writing and to many short answer questions. Finally, your instructor will provide all of the answers for the examinations that follow the study readings in Part Five.

5. Follow the directions for scoring each exercise. Compare your score with that printed directly underneath it. This percentage is the acceptable score, one that shows mastery of the material. If you score below the acceptable one, check your errors to see what went wrong. You may want to ask your instructor for help.

6. Chapters 4–8 and Chapters 11 and 12 have special "Skills Practice Topics," with readings, previews, and follow-up questions and exercises in seven different academic subjects:

   • Chapter 4—Environmental Studies

   • Chapter 5—Business

   • Chapter 6—Sociology

   • Chapter 7—Anthropology

   • Chapter 8—Music History

   • Chapter 11—Consumer Behavior

   • Chapter 12—Early Childhood Development

Internet Activities

Complete the Internet activities, found at the end of each chapter. These exercises will help you to develop your computer research abilities as you learn more about a college discipline or study skills. The Internet activities are identified by the icon at left.

This text contains URLs that were current at the time of printing. If you have difficulty reaching any of the sites mentioned in this text, you may use a search engine such as Yahoo or Alta Vista to look up the new addresses for these sites. You may also find some updates at the Wadsworth College Success Web site at *http://csuccess.wadsworth.com.*

When You Finish the Text

When you have finished *Integrating College Study Skills,* Fifth Edition, you will likely be ready for the demands of college work. You will be able to read textbooks better, take accurate lecture, discussion, and study notes, effectively use test-taking skills, write organized paragraphs and essays explaining what you have learned, and use the Internet as a research tool. Most importantly, when you have completed this text, you will be able to use the same reasoning skills in your college reading, listening, and writing. Rather than completing each assignment in isolation, you will be able to see your work in college as an integrated reasoning activity.

PART ONE

Skills for Beginning Your College Career

In this part of the book, you will become acquainted with the services that your college provides. You will complete schedules for your short- and long-term projects, you will analyze your own learning style, you will learn how to manage your study area, and you will become familiar with the services found in your college library. This information and these skills provide a necessary foundation for your college career.

CHAPTER 1

Getting to Know Your College

In this chapter, you will learn about:

- Services your college or university provides before classes start
- What to do on the first day of class
- Services and centers your college or university provides once you start classes

The first week at a new college is frequently the most hectic. You have to pay tuition and fees, buy books, enroll in your classes, and organize a study and work schedule. Many students find colleges, particularly large ones, impersonal. Yet most every college provides students with materials and services that can make their first semester or their return to college a bit less trying.

College Catalog and Schedule of Classes

Weeks before you enroll in your classes, you can become familiar with your school by obtaining a college catalog and schedule of classes. The catalog is usually published every year. It outlines college policies, gives a short history of the school, lists the services provided to students, names the departments and the courses the college offers, and names the faculty of each department. Reading the catalog is a smart way to begin your college career. Look for services that the college provides: scholarships, financial aid, tutoring, and so on. Read through the course offerings in those departments in which you plan to take classes. You will find out how many courses are offered, what kinds of courses are offered, and when during the calendar year courses are taught.

After most course titles, the catalog will list the prerequisites and the unit value of each course. Prerequisites list the course that you must have taken or the exams that you must have passed in order to enroll. Knowing whether you fulfill the prerequisites is important. An introductory chemistry course may give as one of its prerequisites: "appropriate score on placement test." If you do not take and pass this test before the first meeting, you may not be allowed to enroll. Some students enroll in these courses without being aware of the prerequisites and are turned away the first day of class.

The catalog will also list next to the course title its unit value. A unit is usually equal to one hour per week of lecture or discussion. Many courses are three units, so you attend class three hours a week. Some foreign language and science courses are five units and usually require daily attendance or the equivalent of five hours a week. In most cases, if you are enrolled in fifteen units, you will be attending class fifteen hours a week.

The schedule of classes lists each course that will be offered for that semester, the time it is offered, its unit value, and the instructor of the course. It also provides other important information, like tuition payment and registration deadlines. The schedule of classes is an invaluable tool for you because it provides all the information you will need to set up your study list for the semester and complete all of your registration and financial obligations.

Today most colleges and universities also provide catalog and scheduling information on their Web site, or their specific location on the Internet. If you are familiar with Internet procedures, you can likely access all of this course and scheduling information without having to send for this material or to go to the campus to pick it up. Frequently, each department and service area of the school has its own Web site, so you can find out specific information about the faculty who will be teaching your courses or the staff who can help you with nonacademic support you may need.

Counseling Services

Most colleges and universities offer some sort of counseling services to all their students. If you are new to the college, you need to make an appointment to see a counselor. This meeting with a counselor is often required of students enrolling in two-year colleges. At this meeting, discuss your educational and career goals with your counselor. If you have transcripts of course work completed in high school or at other colleges, bring them to this appointment. Ask your counselor what exactly is required to complete a degree or certificate in your chosen major and what your job opportunities are once you graduate.

Your counselor may advise you to take a battery of tests. The results of these tests will often show you which courses you are qualified to take in English, math, and science. Many colleges also have created career centers where you can go any time during the semester to get information about your intended career or any career you may be interested in. Two-year colleges also often provide transfer centers that answer any questions you may have about the institution you intend to transfer to.

After meeting with your counselor, either alone or with the help of a counselor, you may want to set up your *long-term goals*—that is, the plans you have for the semester, for the year, or for your entire college career. Here are some of the questions that will help you in setting up these goals:

1. Do I know what I want to study? Or do I want to give myself some time to explore various subjects? Do I know how long it will take to complete my studies?

2. Do I know how my college education is going to be paid for, at least for the year?

3. If I am married or have children, do I know how I am going to spend time with my spouse or children and still have time for my studies?

4. If I'm still living with my parents and have obligations at home, can I juggle these obligations and still have time for my studies?

Be sure your goals are both realistic and specific. Finishing a four-year degree in two years is not a realistic goal, and saying that you plan to spend some time with your children each week during the semester is not specific enough. These long-term goals are more effectively stated in the following way: (1) I plan to complete my bachelor's degree in five years, starting this fall semester. (2) I plan to complete all of my homework for the week in order to spend each Sunday this semester with my two children.

Your counselor can also provide you with information about your nonschool concerns, like the day care available to you if you have a child that must be attended to while you are in class, or health and psychological services available to you on or off campus. Discuss these nonacademic issues as well with your counselor. Needing day care assistance or psychological counseling is a problem that occurs during the semester that can interfere with your completing your courses.

Along with or in place of a counselor, your college or university may direct you to an academic advisor, who is usually a faculty member in your major. Along with answering the kinds of questions a college counselor can help you with, your academic advisor will direct you to the courses you must take and their sequence. Often your advisor must approve the courses that you plan to complete for each semester.

Financial Aid

Well before you begin the semester, start planning your finances. This may be one of the long-term goals you considered with your counselor. Many students must drop out of college because they cannot pay all of their school bills. Almost all colleges and universities have a financial aid office. Go to this office before the semester begins to learn of benefits available to you. If you have already been awarded a scholarship or grant, find out when you will be given the stipend and what grade-point average and unit load you need to maintain to keep your funding. Also find out from the financial aid people what the cost of your education will be each semester or quarter. Then determine whether you can afford your education without having to work.

Job Placement Office

Most colleges and universities also provide job placement services. Many students cannot afford to attend college without having to work. If you are a student without a job and need extra money for your school, see what is available at the job placement office.

For most students who are serious about their college studies, being a student is a full-time job. Working full-time and going to school full-time is simply too much for most students. Either school, work, or your health will suffer if you try to do too much. Part-time work of less than twenty hours per week is a reasonable work load for a college student. If you need to work full-time, you may want to delay your full-time education until you have adequate savings. Many full-time workers go to school part-time, often taking one or two courses at night, or during those hours when they are not working. Taking twelve units or more is considered a full load, and you are advised not to work full-time if you are also carrying a full load.

Orientation Activities

Many colleges and universities set aside a day or several days before the semester begins for orientation. At this time, new students are given a tour of the campus and are introduced to the various social and cultural activities that the college provides. Take part in orientation activities, particularly if the college you have chosen is large. At the very least, on your first day of class you will know your way around the campus.

You may also find out about a club or group that may interest you. These student organizations may prove very important to you, particularly if you do not feel that you are an integral part of college life. If you are a commuter, you may want to become a part of a commuters' club. If you are a student of color, you may choose to become active in clubs devoted to concerns for African-Americans, Latinos, Asians, or Native Americans. You may even choose to become active in a religious, political, or social organization on campus. These organizations give you a sense of belonging, which you often need when you are encountering a strange, often large college or university campus for the first time.

The First Class Meeting

The first class meeting for any course is an important one. The instructor officially enrolls you and usually gives you the course requirements: topics you will study, reading materials, exam dates, due dates for essays or projects, and the grading policy. Your instructor will also post office hours—hours when he or she will be able to meet with you outside of class. All of this information is usually presented in a *syllabus,* a calendar of course topics and a statement of class requirements. Save your syllabus, because you will be referring to it all semester. Figure 1-1 presents part of a sample course syllabus.

On your syllabus, your instructor may also provide his or her office phone number or e-mail address. If you are connected to the Internet, you may want to get in contact with your professor via e-mail instead of by phone.

English 103: Critical Thinking, Reading, and Writing
Spring 1998
P. E. Sotiriou
MW 9:30–11:00 ticket no.: 0472
Title of the course: Critical Thinking and Popular Culture

Prerequisite: grade of "C" or better in English 101, or equivalent course; required for transfer to many universities.

Credit: 3 units graded A–F UC:CSU and private colleges and universities

Office Hours: M–Th 8:45–9:30, M–Th 12:30–1:00, or by appointment JH 300, Office D, English/ESL Department. Phone number: (213) 953–4232.

Your grade depends upon completion of:
1) 4 essays (100 points each)   400 points
2) a term paper   200
3) 6 drafts of your essays (10 points each)   60
4) 8 reading quizzes (I drop the lowest one.) 20 points each   140
5) portfolio of essays   30
6) final examination   150
                                                                        980 points total

A = 882–980   (90%)
B = 784–881   (80%)
C = 686–783   (70%)
D = 588–685   (60%)
F = below 587   (59%)

Late Work: I do not accept late work. Work is due on the day assigned, though the assignments I drop may be the ones you do not complete. If you are absent for an assignment, hand in your assignment the day you return from your absence.

Attendance: No more than two absences during the semester; no more than three tardies. If you are absent more than twice or tardy more than three times, you may be excluded from the class.

Texts
Critical Thinking and Popular Culture. Peter Elias Sotiriou. Belmont: Wadsworth, 1998. price: about $25.00
Being There. Jerzy Kosinski. New York: Bantam, 1970. price: about $5.00

Handouts (I provide): advertisements, articles, and student essays.

Media materials (I provide): videos of commercials and television programs that we will view in class and that you can check out to examine out of class.

Description of the Course
This is a second semester composition course that focuses on the critical thinking practices that you use to analyze American popular culture.

Figure 1-1   Sample Syllabus.

Interacting with Your Professor

Make a point of contacting your professor early on in the semester if you don't understand a particular assignment. Make your questions about the assignment clear, and be specific about what it is about the work you do not understand. In contacts with your professor, present your best academic self.

Class Materials

You should take both pens and pencils to class. Take most of your notes in ink, though use pencil or erasable ink in math and science courses, where you will often be recalculating and erasing. Calculators are frequently required in math and science courses. You should have a separate notebook for each class, or at least a separate divider in a three-ring binder. Three-ring notebooks are particularly useful because you can add material for each course at any time during the semester and you can keep your lectures in chronological order.

Buy your books during the first week of the semester or even before the semester begins. Be sure you know which books are required and which are recommended. Your syllabus will carry this information, and the bookstore will probably post "required" and "recommended" after each book title. After the first week of class, the bookstore may run out of some titles, and you may have to wait several weeks for the new order to arrive.

If you can afford it, buy new books; and if you buy used books, try to find those that have few or no markings. If you buy a heavily underlined book, you will be reading someone's else's comments, which may not agree with yours.

Only take those books to class that you will use during lectures or lab or that you will want to study from during the day. Instructors often read from the textbook or refer to specific pages while lecturing. You will want to read along with the instructor or mark those important pages during the lecture. To carry those books that you will need for the day, you will need a briefcase, an attaché case, a large purse or satchel, or a backpack. Backpacks are especially useful when you are carrying several heavy books.

Making Class Contacts

During the first week of class, you should get to know at least one reliable classmate in each class. You should get this student's phone number and give yours to him or her. Whenever you cannot attend lectures or discussions, you can call this student to find out what you missed. You may also want to read over this student's notes whenever your notes are incomplete.

Most students enjoy studying with a classmate and find that they learn more by studying with someone than when they study alone. Often, four to five students form a study group to prepare for a major exam. These groups are especially helpful if your instructor assigns several review questions before an exam. Students in the study group can divide up these questions and then meet to share their answers.

Try working in a study group to see if you learn more easily this way. If you don't find study groups helpful, you may be one of those students who learns best alone. More will be said about various learning styles in Chapter 2.

Tutoring Services and Computer Labs

During the first week of class, you should also be able to find out if there are tutoring services available for that course, either through the department or through the college's learning resources center. Even if you are working in a study group, you may also want to make regular contact with a tutor who can answer those questions that you or your study group cannot answer. Also, ask your tutor if the professor or the tutor will provide a review session before each major examination. These sessions may be scheduled outside of the regular class meeting hours.

Finally, see if there are computer labs available for your use, to write your class assignments and to do Internet research. Many colleges presently provide computer labs in various parts of the campus. Attending these labs is often part of the work requirements for the classes you have chosen.

The Students You Will Meet

You will find that colleges today include a wide variety of people: young and old, rich and poor. These college students now come from all ethnic, racial, and economic groups. Some learners, known as adult students, are over twenty-five. Others are married; some have children. Their needs and time constraints differ from those young, single students who have just finished high school. All come to college with unique desires and interests. As a college student in the 1990s and into the twenty-first century, you need to recognize and appreciate this diversity in the college population and realize that your needs and life circumstances may differ from those of the students you meet, study with, and befriend.

Summary

Preparing for the first day of class takes work. By talking with a counselor or college advisor, taking placement tests, and attending orientation meetings, you will get a clearer picture of your abilities and of the college you have chosen. The first day of class is also important, because you will find out what your instructors expect you to do during the semester or quarter. Finally, getting to know a few fellow classmates early in the semester will help you, so if you cannot attend class, you can call them to find out what you missed. You may also be able to become part of an ongoing study group with them. Also early on, get to know what tutoring and computer lab services are available to you.

Summary Box   *Getting Started in College*

What do you need to do?	Why are these activities important?
Read the catalog and schedule of classes	To learn something about your school
Go to a counselor or academic advisor	To plan your academic and career goals
Establish long-term goals	To have a better sense for what you can accomplish
Attend orientation meetings	To familiarize yourself with the campus
Get the phone number of at least one student in each class	To find out what happened in class should you be absent
Become part of a study group, and get to know tutors for the class and computer lab services	To be well prepared for exams and assignments

Skills Practice

Exercise 1.1
Checklist of Activities
to Complete

Following you will find a list of activities that you need to complete before the semester begins or soon after. Enter the date as you complete each activity. Check the space "Does Not Apply" for those activities that do not concern you.

	Does Not Apply	*Date Completed*	*Activity*
1.	_____	_____	Buy and read through the college catalog.
2.	_____	_____	Buy and read through the schedule of classes.
3.	_____	_____	Make an appointment to see a counselor or college advisor.
4.	_____	_____	Take placement tests.
5.	_____	_____	Make long-term goals.
6.	_____	_____	Go to the financial aid office.
7.	_____	_____	Go to the job placement office.

8. _____   _____   Go to orientation activities.

9. _____   _____   Buy paper, pens, and pencils for classes.

10. _____   _____   Buy textbooks.

11. _____   _____   Get the phone numbers of classmates.

12. _____   _____   Become part of a study group.

13. _____   _____   Additional activities: _____

_____

Exercise 1.2
Setting Goals for the Semester

Answer the following questions pertaining to your plans for the current semester. These answers should help you set reasonable goals for this and later semesters. Write "Does Not Apply" if the question does not pertain to you.

1. After taking the placement tests, what are your strengths and weaknesses?

2. After career testing, what seem to be your academic and vocational interests?

3. After talking to a counselor or college advisor, what courses have you decided to take this semester?

4. What is your intended major?

5. How many units are required for you to complete your major? How many semesters do you need to complete your major?

6. Do you plan to complete all of your course work at your present college, or do you intend to transfer? If you plan to transfer, what school do you intend to transfer to?

7. After meeting with people in the financial aid office, did you learn whether you are eligible for aid? or do you need to work? If you need to work, how many hours a week of work are your planning?

Exercise 1.3
Setting Goals for an
Incoming College
Student

The following is a description of an incoming community college student—Maria. Read over this description of her, and determine the four most important goals she should consider for her first semester of college. Be sure the goals that you set up for Maria are realistic and specific. This activity is best completed in groups of four or five.

Maria is twenty-five years old. She has been a waitress in Hollywood, California, since finishing high school at eighteen. She wants to change careers and has interests in accounting and business management. She thinks that maybe she can be an accountant for a large restaurant one day or manage a restaurant herself. Maria has $10,000 in savings, but she does not know how much money it will take to finish her first year. She still lives at home with her mother and pays her $200 a month for room and board. She also does not know how many courses she should take her first semester or what courses to take. Also, Maria does not know whether she should quit her job as a waitress or simply cut down on her hours. Maria is single and has been going out on the weekends with the same man for over a year.

The four long-term goals Maria should set are:

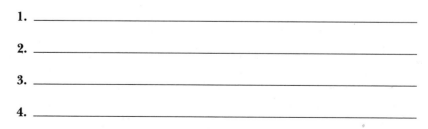

1. _____

2. _____

3. _____

4. _____

Answers will vary. Share your answers with your instructor and your classmates.

Follow-up on Chapter 1

Now that you have studied this introductory chapter and completed the exercises, it may be helpful to consider how your skills for beginning your college career have improved. You may want to go back to this introduction and to the exercises to review what you have learned. Then answer the following questions, either individually or in small groups:

On Getting to Know Your College

1. What information in this introduction proved most helpful to you? How did that information help you during the first weeks of the semester?

2. What are the most important goals you have set for yourself this semester?

3. What parts of this introduction or the exercises you completed are still difficult for you to understand?

4. What areas of your college do you still need more information on?

 **Internet Activity**

Research more about your college through the Internet. Break up into small groups of four or five to locate Web sites concerning various departments and services at your college. If you do not know how to use the Internet, go to your library or computer lab for assistance. After you have done your Internet research, share what you have learned with your group. Answer the following questions:

1. Which Web sites did you find?
2. What information did the Web sites provide you?
3. Describe how you went about locating these Web sites.

CHAPTER 2

Your Learning Inventory: Your Learning Style, Study Time, and Study Area

In this chapter, you will learn about:

- How to manage your time
- Studying and organizing your study area
- Understanding how you learn best

Being a successful student is not unlike being a successful executive. And just as an executive needs a calendar to keep track of business and social appointments, you need to keep track of every hour that you spend in and out of school each day so that you can cut down on the number of wasted hours. Students also need to analyze the kinds of learners they are in order to best devise their study program. In addition, students need to examine where they study to see if these study areas are most conducive to concentration.

Both incoming and returning students will find they have many more hours outside of class than they had in high school, where they often had five to six hours of classes to attend each day. Some days a college student may have only two hours of class, and the rest of the day will be free. For this reason, it is especially important for both incoming and returning students to set up schedules that they can and will follow, that will make the best use of their time, and that will minimize stress.

Getting Motivated

Before you analyze your use of time, your learning style, or your places of study, you need to be *motivated*—to have the desire to do your best. Motivation is central, both as you analyze yourself as a learner and in every activity you complete in college. Staying motivated is not a simple challenge, because very few students get up every morning with a desire to complete all the work that is before them. They often complain of being tired, of assignments being too difficult, or of not having enough time to complete assignments.

One effective way to stay motivated is to set goals. You learned about long-term goals in Chapter 1, when you were analyzing your reasons for attending college. Short-term goals will help you stay motivated. *Short-term goals* are those plans you have for the day, week, or month. They include your plans for studying for a test, completing a homework assignment, or fulfilling the requirements of a longer writing or research project.

To be effective, short-term goals must be specific and reasonable. It would be unreasonable to assume that you could study for your business final in one hour and too vague if you simply said that you planned to study for your business final sometime during the week. A reasonable, short-term goal for studying for your business final would be: "I plan to study for my business final for three hours on Friday and three hours on Saturday; then I plan to review for one hour on Sunday."

Much of the time management material you will read in the following sections and subsections involves writing short-term goals—specific and concise plans. Those goals will help you stay motivated to stay on schedule.

Setting Up a Schedule

Your first job in establishing a study schedule is to determine which hours during the day you cannot study. Be detailed. Include the time that it takes for you to get ready for class in the morning and get ready for bed at night, to eat your meals, and to take care of family and personal matters. List all of these activities and the time allotted to each on a 4 × 6 card, as shown in Figure 2-1.

If you do not already follow a routine of getting up at a certain time, eating at set hours, and exercising regularly, start now. You will not be productive if you do not eat, sleep, and exercise well. Students who don't eat breakfast often become exhausted by midday. Similarly, students who do not exercise feel lethargic as the day wears on. Recent studies have shown that exercise gives your body more energy and fights depression. A half-hour to an hour of jogging, swimming, or brisk walking each day is time well spent. Finally, sleeping at least seven hours a night is important. Staying up late catches up with you. Even though it is tempting to stay up late, particularly if you live on campus, try not to; otherwise you

Time	Activity
6–7 am	Shower, get ready for school, eat breakfast
7–7:30 am	Drive to Campus
12–12:45 pm	Eat lunch on Campus
10–11 pm	Exercise and get ready for bed.

Figure 2-1   *Daily activity card.*

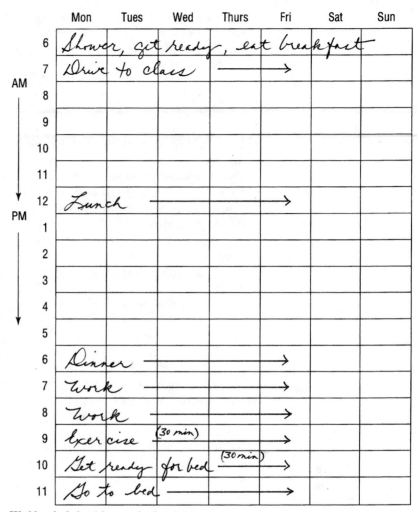

Figure 2-2   *Weekly schedule with nonschool activities.*

will find yourself dozing off in class or sleeping through your morning classes.

You may now want to complete Exercise 2.1 on page 27.

School Activities.   Now that you have established regular times to eat, sleep, and exercise, you are ready to identify those hours you can devote to school. First, enter your hours of nonschool activities on a sheet of paper, listing the days of the week and the hours in each day. Also on this list include those hours that you must work, if part-time work is part of your daily schedule. Your schedule should look something like the one in Figure 2-2. In this schedule, the nonschool activities have been listed in the appropriate hours; for the moment, Saturday and Sunday have been left open. By counting the number of blank spaces in each day, you will find that you can devote ten hours (nine full hours and two half-hours) to school.

You now need to include in this schedule the hours that you spend in class. In Figure 2-3, see how this student has included fifteen hours of class time between Monday and Friday.

You will notice on this schedule that the student has spaced the classes. If you do not have to work, spacing your classes is wise. If you are on campus more hours during the day, you will have more time to study. You will also have time to review your lecture notes right after class. If you check the schedule for Monday, you find that this student has the following hours to study: 9–10 a.m., 11 a.m.–12 p.m., 2–6 p.m., 9–9:30 p.m., and 10:30–11 p.m.—a total of seven hours.

Many instructors will tell you that for every hour of lecture you should spend two hours outside of class studying for that course. This may be true, but a more realistic estimate will have to be made by you. For each course, assess your background knowledge; if your background is limited in a particular course, you may have to devote more time to that course than to your other courses. If you are carrying fifteen units, you may need to study fifteen, thirty, or even more hours during the week to be prepared.

You may now want to complete Exercise 2.2 on page 27.

It is best to write out a study schedule for each day or for each week. Figure 2-4 shows how this same student has completed a schedule for Monday, including three hours of study on campus.

You may now want to complete Exercise 2.3 on page 29.

Daily Assignments. Each day you will have different school tasks to do. The night before, jot down the work you need to complete for the next day. Figure 2-5 is a sample list of short-term goals; note that the activities are specific and that each one can probably be completed in an hour.

When you look at a class syllabus at the beginning of the semester, you may feel overwhelmed, thinking that you can never get through all of the assignments. But breaking up large assignments into smaller tasks of no more than an hour each is an effective way of getting things done and of staying motivated. Psychologists call the breaking up of larger activities into smaller tasks *successive approximations.*

You may now want to complete Exercise 2.4 on page 29.

Long-Term Projects. During the semester, you will probably be assigned large projects—term papers, critical papers, lab reports, and so on. You will also have to prepare for midterms and finals—exams that require more than just a night or two of study. It is best to place the due dates of these larger tasks on a monthly calendar. You may want to buy a large calendar that you can place on your desk or on the wall near where you normally study. On this calendar, enter the dates of the major projects and tests for that month. Look at how the month of May is marked in

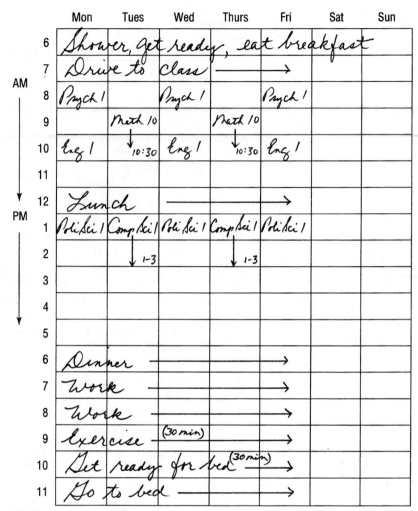

Figure 2-3   *Weekly schedule with school activities.*

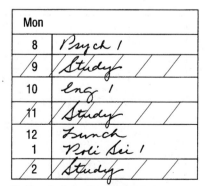

Figure 2-4   *Daily schedule showing study hours.*

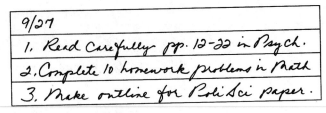

Figure 2-5 *Daily assignment schedule.*

Figure 2-6; on May 1, for example, this student has only eight days to finish a research paper but all month to study for a computer final.

You may want to complete Exercise 2.5 at this time (page 29).

Weekends.   If you keep up during the week, your weekends should not end up as study marathons. On weekends, you should relax as well as study; you should complete any late work, get a jump on assignments for the following week, and work on the larger projects. It is best to set aside three or four hours on a Saturday or Sunday to work on an essay assignment. Writing requires concentrated, uninterrupted time.

If you have to work, weekends are best. With no classes to attend on the weekend, you will be able to work and not feel rushed.

Time for Yourself.   The average student has ample time to study each day. You can therefore set aside some part of each day for fun. Psychologists have shown that students who vary their activities during the day actually

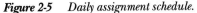

Figure 2-6 *Deadlines marked on the calendar.*

retain more than those who study nonstop. So do not feel that you are wasting your time when you are not doing school work. Give yourself some time each day to relax. On weekends, take advantage of the movies, plays, and concerts available to you on or off campus. If you come back to your studies refreshed, you will have a more positive attitude toward the new material.

What has been said so far about scheduling your time, making lists and noting deadlines on a calendar may seem tedious to you, and some of it is. But being organized is one of the most important characteristics of a successful student. If you stick to your schedules and continue to meet your deadlines, you will begin to enjoy the pleasures of being a successful student. Once being organized becomes a habit for you, you may want to dispense with written lists and goals entirely.

You are now ready to consider specific suggestions about your learning style, managing your time, and setting up your study area. With these suggestions, you will be able to make even better use of each study hour.

Your Particular Learning Style

Before you examine how to effectively complete your work in college and where you learn best, you need to look at the kind of learner you are. Then you can modify the following suggestions on study area and test-taking tips to fit your particular learning needs.

You can generally divide up the world of learners into three categories: (1) those who are verbal, that is, very good with language, (2) those who are quantitative, or very skilled with numbers, and (3) those who are spatial, or talented at visualizing. The English professor, the mathematician, and the artist are, respectively, the most common examples of these three types of learners. A famous Harvard psychologist, Howard Gardner, has identified as many as seven distinct types of intelligence. Along with the three types just mentioned, he includes musical ability, bodily-kinesthetic aptitude, interpersonal intelligence (knowledge of others), and intrapersonal intelligence (knowledge of oneself). For now, consider your abilities in the first three aptitudes mentioned—verbal, quantitative, and visual. You probably have some sense of your strengths in each of these three areas. If not, your counselor can give you more insight into your abilities by analyzing your test scores and previous grades or by giving you a new battery of aptitude tests.

Each of these three aptitudes helps describe a specific kind of learner in college. A verbal learner generally learns best by taking written notes in lecture, by reading, and by responding to his reading in written responses. A student with a mathematical aptitude generally finds numerical facts and figures easy to remember; she also tends to want to organize material into formulas. Finally, a visual thinker remembers material best if it is in picture form and tends to write notes in diagram fashion.

Obviously, very few learners will rely on only one of these three aptitudes. All learners have varying abilities in each of these three types of thinking. Among the various courses you take in college, you will be asked to demonstrate your abilities in each of these three types of thinking.

These three kinds of learners also rely on different ways of remembering information. Some learners remember facts best—dates, numbers, specific details—as they learn a subject; others are much more adept at remembering the concepts in a subject—the larger or global picture: not when the war began but the three major reasons for the war.

Other learners remember what they hear—they are known as *auditory learners*. They retain material merely by listening to a lecture or by reviewing a tape recording of a lecture. Further, they find that by reading material aloud, they remember much more than if they read the same material silently.

Still others retain material best when they are working with others in study groups. They learn by hearing and responding to what others have to say. This type of remembering is known as *collaborative learning*, and it has become a very popular form of instruction, particularly in humanities courses. You will be asked to complete several collaborative assignments in this textbook.

Finally, there are students who learn best not by reading, listening, or working with others, but by doing. Known as *practical learners*, they learn much like apprentices on the job learn. These learners often do well in subjects that require labs or that include on-the-job training.

As you continue to study and learn in college, it is wise to try out all of these learning styles to see which ones work best for you. Remember that you have some sort of aptitude in each, and one of your goals in college is to see just how you can use each aptitude to succeed in your course work.

Also, as you complete your various college courses, you will find that every teacher seems to present information in a different style, comparable to the different learning styles. Some instructors enjoy lecturing, or are *verbal presenters*. Others prefer using graphs and illustrations to explain their material, so they can be considered *visual presenters*. Still others prefer asking questions and listening to their students; they are *auditory presenters*. In each class you take, determine early on what teaching style your instructor prefers, and try to understand the material that way. You will likely master the content more easily.

You may now want to complete Exercise 2.6 on page 29.

Setting Up a Course Priority List

Now that you have been introduced to how students learn, and probably have a better idea of the kind of learner you are, you can more effectively consider the courses you will be taking and the specifics of studying.

At the beginning of each semester, you should look at all your courses and select the one or two that you think are most important. These courses may be the ones in your major or prerequisites to your major. You should list your courses in order of importance and then anticipate the grade you will earn in each. Then you can better predict the time you should devote to each course.

Study the following course priority list, designed by a student majoring in computer science:

Course	Predicted Grade
1. Computer Science	A
2. Mathematics 10	A
3. English 1	B
4. Political Science 1	B
5. Psychology 1	C

It is clear that this student will be exerting more effort in the computer science and math courses. Because this student realizes the need to do very well in the computer science and math courses, the anticipated grade of "C" in psychology is realistic. This student is not being pressured to do exceptionally well in all courses.

If you set up such a priority list, you should be able to establish some realistic goals early in the semester. If, during the semester, you are not doing as well as you had predicted, then you need to determine what is going wrong. Do you need to study more? Do other activities conflict with your studies? Or have you chosen a major that is not well suited for you?

In Exercise 2.7, you will be able to determine your own priority list. You may now want to complete Exercise 2.7 on page 32.

Making the Best Use of Your Study Time

When should you study for each course? You should study for your priority courses when your mind is freshest. Each student's most productive hours vary. Some find the mornings best, others the evenings or late nights. Find out when you work best, and study for your most important courses then.

How to Study.   In this text, you will be introduced to several study hints and learn a successful study reading system called SQ3R, but first consider the following general study hints.

1. Never study with distractions. Music, though soothing, often is distracting. When you are doing concentrated studying, avoid listening to music.

2. Do not begin studying if you are more concerned about something else. Your study hours need to be concentrated ones. A brisk walk, run, or swim before you study can often clear your mind of daily problems.

3. Try to divide your studying into one-hour blocks. You can take a ten-minute break at either the end or the middle of each hour. Gauge your breaks according to the difficulty of the material. The key to a successful study hour, though, is to put in fifty concentrated minutes

of study. For example, if you are worried about your brother, call him. Then, when you feel better, go back to your studying.

4. After your hour is up, do something different. Either study for a course unrelated to what you have just studied, or do something not directly connected to school. Studying during spaced intervals is more productive than cramming your studying into a few days.

5. Devote some time during your study hours to reviewing what you have learned that day. You need to review your lecture notes or the study notes you have taken from your textbooks. You tend to forget more of what you have learned during the first twenty-four hours, so it is important to review soon after you have learned something new. More will be said about how to remember in Chapter 13, "Memory Aids."

6. Be sure to complete your reading assignments when they are assigned. Listening to a lecture on completely new material can confuse and frustrate you. So make your reading assignments a priority study item.

How to Tackle Difficult Assignments.   Sometimes your study material is difficult, and studying for a concentrated hour may be exhausting. If this happens, break your studying into shorter activities, or short-term goals. Write these goals out before you begin studying. For example, if you have five difficult math problems to do, you can write out something like the following:

1. Complete problem #1.
2. Read and think about problem #2.
3. Take a four-minute break.
4. Come back to problem #2.

You will find that such goals are attainable if you make them short and realistic. Instead of focusing on five difficult problems, you reward yourself for completing one problem at a time.

How to Study for Tests.   Much will be said in this textbook on how to study for tests, including objective tests (Chapter 15) as well as essay and math or science tests (Chapter 16). For now, read the following time-management hints that apply to preparing for any test.

1. Before you begin studying for a test, you should have completed all of your reading assignments. In addition, you should have reviewed your notes each day.

2. For a weekly quiz, take two days to study—one day to do your reviewing and a second to let the material settle. If the course is difficult, you may need more days to learn the material.

3. For a midterm test, study for three or four days. On the last night, do not cram; review only the general concepts.

4. For a final examination, reserve about a week to study. As with the midterm, review only the general points the night before.

Analyzing Your Test Results.   You can also learn much about your progress as a student by studying your test results, particularly your first test scores of the semester. Study your errors and try to determine why you made them. You may find that you need to study more or study in a quieter area.

By reviewing your results, you can also determine the kinds of tests your instructor gives and which study materials he emphasizes: lecture notes, textbook material, class discussion, and so on. Does the test emphasize details or concepts? Are any of the questions tricky? If the test is essay, what does the instructor seem to be looking for? an organized essay? accurate details? new ideas? the instructor's ideas? By answering these questions, you will probably do better on the next exam.

If you receive a low or failing score, try to figure out what went wrong. Did you not study enough, or do you need to change your studying style for this course? Or is this course too difficult for you? Do you need tutoring, or should you drop the class? Make an appointment to see your instructor. See what he or she has to say. Take these suggestions seriously.

Remember that a test score is more than a grade. By analyzing it, you will become a more successful student.

Making a Schedule for Your Longer Projects.   Do not wait until the last few days of the semester to complete a project like a term paper. You need to divide these larger assignments into smaller tasks—again, short-term goals—and assign deadlines for completing them.

If, for example, you are assigned a 500-page novel to read in ten days, you need to divide the number of pages by the days you have to complete the reading. In this example, you need to read fifty pages a day.

For a research paper, you can divide your work into several smaller tasks: (1) finding library material, (2) taking notes on this material, (3) writing an outline for the paper, (4) writing a rough draft, and (5) writing a final draft. Look at this sample schedule for completing a research paper on the Hopi Native Americans:

Hopi Culture (30-Day Project)

Task	Number of Days
1. Go to the library; make up a bibliography	5
2. Take notes from the book	8

3. Write an outline	2
4. Write a rough draft	7
5. Type a final draft	4
	Total = 26

You may have noticed in this schedule that, although it is a thirty-day project, the student has estimated twenty-six days for completing the project. The extra four days give him some breathing room in case one task takes longer to complete. Often these projects take longer to finish than you had originally planned. Generally it takes three to four weeks to complete a research paper. Once you complete your first research paper, you will be able to make a more accurate estimate of the time required to complete the next one.

More will be said about the research paper in the next chapter, "Using the Library."

How to Cope with Stress at School

The demands of college work—the tests, the projects, listening attentively in class—all take their toll. Very few students do not complain of stress at some time during the semester. Stress is simply the result of not being able to cope with life's demands, and it often manifests itself in physical symptoms: inability to concentrate, nausea, a fast heartbeat, sweating. These symptoms can occur when you are taking an exam or as you are working on a homework assignment. The symptoms of stress often manifest themselves suddenly and may take you by surprise.

There is no hidden cure for combatting stress. As with our learning styles, each one of us has different coping mechanisms; some of us are naturally more prone to stress than others. But there are some ways to help reduce school stress that apply to us all:

1. Try to control your anxiety. When you feel these symptoms coming on, tell yourself that they will only hinder you, wasting your time in studying or finishing a test.

2. During a difficult exam or a stressful study period, take a break for a minute or two. Think of being in a pleasant, relaxed setting; close your eyes and take deep breaths. With your eyes closed, stretch your back, arms, and neck to relax your muscles. These short breaks can avert a stress attack.

3. During an exam or a study period, reward yourself for completing a problem or section of the assignment. The reward can simply be a mental "pat on the back." Confidence both improves performance and reduces stress.

4. Do what is confidence-building first—the easy test questions, the less difficult part of a homework assignment. With more confidence, you can more easily complete the harder sections of the test or assignment.

5. Set reasonable, short-term goals. Break up difficult assignments into manageable parts—the first three of ten problems on a math exam, a draft of the first paragraph of an extended essay assignment.

For some students, these suggestions do not help overcome stress. Perhaps there are other personal factors causing stress, such as family problems or crises in relationships. If you cannot overcome the stress you experience in school, seek professional help. Your college may have stress counselors or psychologists on their staff, or they may be able to refer you to low-cost professionals if you cannot afford your own private professional. Stress is a psychological problem that can be helped, and only becomes worse if it is not quickly attended to. Psychologists have done extensive research in this field in the last twenty years, and they have devised therapies that frequently offer quick results, such as stress-reducing exercises or biofeedback training involving the monitoring of your brain wave activity.

Setting Up Your Study Area

You may follow all of the previous suggestions and still do poorly in college if you do not have an acceptable study area. Ideally, you should have your own desk in a quiet organized area. On your desk, you need a dictionary, and all the necessary texts and notes that you need to use for a given hour need to be at arm's reach. Your desk should also have scratch paper, lined paper, and typing or computer paper, as well as several pens and pencils. If possible, you should have a typewriter or word processor on your desk. Finally, your chair should not be too comfortable because you want to stay alert while you study. A chair with an upright support for your back is effective. With these materials, you will be able to stay in one place during your study hour.

If these ideal conditions are not possible, you should still be able to create an organized study area. You may be living at home with younger brothers and sisters or with young children of your own often disturbing you. You may be living in a small apartment with several roommates. So your own desk in a quiet area may be an impossibility. But you still can find a large box for all your books and notes for the semester. Keeping all of your material in one area is a must. Students waste precious time looking for books or notes.

If you cannot study without interruption where you live, you need to find a quiet study area, at either a local library or your college library. If you go to the library with friends, sit away from them when you study so that you will not be distracted. If you plan to study in groups, find a quiet area that will encourage your group to get to work and stay focused. All of these activities will encourage you to concentrate, or study intensely. More will be said on concentration in Chapter 13.

You may now want to complete Exercise 2.8 on page 33.

Summary

Setting up schedules is a key to success in and out of school. To organize your time, you must first list those activities not related to school.

Once you have listed nonschool activities, you can then include those hours when you attend school. Try to space your classes throughout the day. On this same schedule, you can then mark those hours that you reserve for studying. You must plan your hours of study the night before and stick to your plan. Finally, you need to place long-term projects on a monthly calendar so that you know how much time you have to complete them.

Also, knowing the kind of learner you are and the sorts of aptitudes you have will greatly assist you in finding the most effective ways to study in college. Once you have assessed your learning styles, you can begin to devise successful study practices. Set up class priorities to determine which courses you need to concentrate on; then project a grade that you intend to receive in each of these courses. During your study hours, you should concentrate only on your school assignments. When you are working on large projects, you should break them up into smaller tasks, then set up a deadline for completing each one. You need to engage in stress-reducing activities whenever college work becomes too demanding. Finally, you need to create a quiet study area for yourself, one that has all the necessary materials you need for your study hours.

Summary Box   *Your Learning Inventory*

What is time and study area management?	*Why should you manage your time and your study area?*
A way of analyzing how you spend your day so that you can set aside certain quiet hours to study Devices to help you manage your time and study area: 1. Nonschool schedules 2. On-campus schedules 3. Daily activity schedules 4. Time schedules for longer projects 5. Course priority lists 6. Stress-reducing exercises 7. Analysis of test results 8. Designing of a study area	To develop order in your life as a student To provide time to complete reading assignments, study for tests, and complete term projects To assess your progress in school To get the most out of college

What are learning styles?	*Why should you be aware of your learning styles?*
1. Verbal, quantitative, and visual 2. Factual and conceptual 3. Auditory, social, and practical	To apply these various styles to understand how you learn best

Skills Practice

Exercise 2.1
Setting Up a
Schedule of
Nonschool Activities

Answer the following questions. Then transfer the answers to these questions to the weekly schedule shown in Figure 2-7.

1. When do you get up each morning for school?

2. When do you eat breakfast, lunch, and dinner during the week (excluding Saturday and Sunday)?

3. When do you exercise?

4. When do you go to bed during the week (excluding Saturday and Sunday)?

5. If you work, what are your hours?

Exercise 2.2
Setting Up a
Schedule of School
Activities

Answer the following questions on your school activities. Then transfer the answers to these questions to Figure 2-7.

1. How many units are you carrying this semester?

2. List your classes and the times they meet.

	Class Name	*Time Class Meets*
a.		
b.		
c.		
d.		
e.		
f.		
g.		

3. When do you study? In Figure 2-7, shade the boxes of those hours you regularly use for study.

4. How many hours have you reserved for study? Do these hours equal or exceed the number of units that you are carrying? Have you reserved enough hours each week for study?

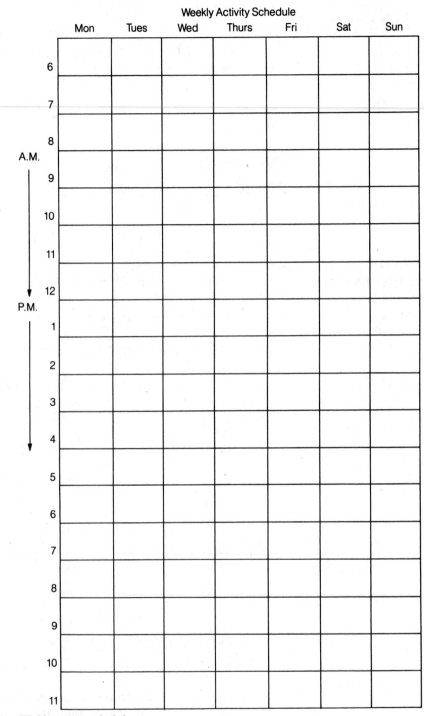

Figure 2-7   *Weekly activity schedule.*

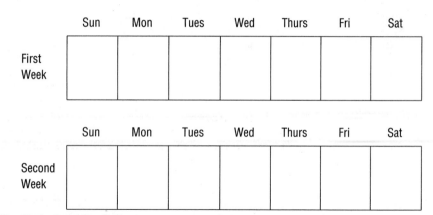

Figure 2-8   *Typical weekly calendar.*

Exercise 2.3
Setting Up Weekly
Schedules

Use the activity reminders shown in Figure 2-8 for the next two weeks. Include no more than two important activities for each day. As with the monthly calendar, include due dates of projects and exam dates. At the end of each week, see how or if the weekly calendar was useful to you.

Exercise 2.4
Setting Up Daily
Schedules

Use the activity reminders depicted in Figure 2-9 for the next three days. Remember to write out each task so that you can complete each one in an hour. At the day's end, see if you have completed each task. If you didn't, try to figure out why.

Exercise 2.5
Making a Calendar
for Long-Term
Projects

In Figure 2-10, you will find a calendar for a typical month. Fill in the current month and the appropriate dates. Then enter the due dates for longer projects and major exams for this month.

Use this calendar to remind yourself of important due dates. At the end of the month, ask yourself whether this calendar was a useful reminder for you. If you found it helpful, continue using it.

Exercise 2.6
Assessing Your
Learning Style

This activity will help you understand the kind of learner you are. It is best completed with your peers in groups of two or three. Answer the following questions as honestly and completely as you can. If you have any questions, discuss them with your peers and share your responses with the group. Once you have answered the questions and shared them in discussion, complete your learning profile. As you work in your groups, ask your instructor for help when you do not understand any part of this activity.

1. If I were assigned the following tasks—(1) read a book, (2) do math problems, and (3) draw a picture—which one would I rather do?

1. First Day   Date: _____
To Do:
1. _____
2. _____
3. _____
4. _____

2. Second Day   Date: _____
To Do:
1. _____
2. _____
3. _____
4. _____

3. Third Day   Date: _____
To Do:
1. _____
2. _____
3. _____
4. _____

Figure 2-9   *Activity reminders for three days.*

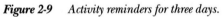

Month:	Sun	Mon	Tues	Wed	Thurs	Fri	Sat
___							

Figure 2-10   *Typical month's calendar.*

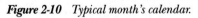

Why? _____

2. Do I take written notes easily when I listen to a lecture? _____

3. Can I complete my reading assignments easily? _____

4. Do I have a difficult time writing essays or essay exams? Or do I

    prefer essay tests to other kinds of tests? _____

5. Has math been an easy subject for me in the past? Am I good at
    making change, doing my checkbook and taxes, and remembering

    sports statistics? _____

6. When I study my notes, is it easy for me to create a diagram of the

    material? _____

7. After I have studied, do I tend to remember the specific facts, or the

    general outlines? _____

8. Do I remember very much when I listen to a discussion or lecture?

    Or do I have to write things down in order to remember them? ____

9. Do I prefer reading silently or orally when I am study reading? ____

10. Do I enjoy using a tape recorder to study? _____

11. Do I learn a lot by watching videos and films and studying photo-

    graphs when I am taking a history course? _____

12. Do I learn very much in study groups? Or do I study best alone?

    _____

13. Am I good at science lab work? _____

14. Do I enjoy hands-on courses like shop? auto mechanics? computer

    processing? _____

    After answering these questions and discussing them in my group,
we have decided that I have strengths in:

1. _____ verbal thinking

2. _____ quantitative thinking

3. _____ visual thinking

4. _____ remembering facts

5. _____ remembering concepts

6. _____ remembering by listening

7. _____ remembering by discussing study material with others

8. _____ learning by doing

Some techniques that we have come up with so that I can study more effectively include:

1. _____

2. _____

3. _____

Exercise 2.7
Setting Up Course
Priorities

In this exercise, set up a priority list of your courses. List the courses in their order of importance. Then predict the grade that you will receive in each.

	Course	*Predicted Grade*
1.		
2.		
3.		
4.		
5.		
6.		
7.		

Save this exercise; then, at the end of the semester, compare your predicted grades with your actual grades. If there were differences, try to figure out why.

Exercise 2.8
Assessing Your Time
Management and
Your Study Area

Below you will find eleven questions about your ability to manage time and your study area. Read each question carefully; then answer it by circling yes or no. After you have answered all eleven questions, you will be asked to use these results to determine where you need to improve your time management and your study area.

1. Yes   No   Does your mind wander when you study?
2. Yes   No   Do you often take study breaks that are too long?
3. Yes   No   Do you often study for the same kinds of courses back to back?
4. Yes   No   Do you frequently fail to review your reading and study notes?
5. Yes   No   Do you often go to a lecture without having completed the reading assignment for it?
6. Yes   No   Do you become frustrated when you read difficult material?
7. Yes   No   Do you wait until the last day to study for your exams?
8. Yes   No   Do you wait until the last days to complete longer projects?
9. Yes   No   Do you look only at your test score when you get an exam back?
10. Yes   No   Do you sometimes feel overwhelmed by the stress school causes?
11. Yes   No   Is your study area disorganized?

If you answered yes to any of these questions, you need to reread the section in this chapter that applies to the skill in question. Now make a list of those skills that you intend to improve during this semester.

Skills Needing Improvement

1. _____

2. _____

3. _____

4. _____

5. _____

6. _____

7. _____

8. _____

9. _____

This semester, make it your goal to sharpen those skills that you have listed.

Exercise 2.9
Analyzing a Student
Learning and Study
Profile

Larry is a nineteen-year-old community college student who wants to major in accounting. He recently graduated from high school in a rural area in Washington State. Following is an excerpt of what Larry shared with his career counselor. Read this excerpt over with a group of four or five students. Then determine the kind of learner Larry is and the sorts of suggestions you may have to improve his success in college.

I've always enjoyed making and saving money. I remember opening up my first savings account at eight years old and watching my account grow each month. I was good in math in high school and finished intermediate algebra. English is another story. I have difficulty understanding poetry and finishing long novels. I also think I read too slowly—only twenty pages an hour. I can write organized essays, and I have no problems locating grammar and spelling errors in the essays I write. I prefer reading the business and sports sections of the newspaper over any other parts. I especially enjoy following the stock market in the newspaper.

This is my first semester away from home, and I'm homesick. I miss my mother and father keeping me on track to finish my homework, and I miss playing basketball with my two younger brothers after school. I need people to push me to get my work done. The dorm I'm in is not the best place to study because there are few quiet places to read, and I'm getting behind in my English and political science classes.

1. Profile of Larry as a learner: _____

   _____

2. Suggestions for organizing Larry's study time and area: _____

   _____

Answers will vary. Ask instructor for suggested answers.

Follow-up on
Chapter 2

Now that you have studied this chapter and completed the exercises, it may be helpful to see how much you have learned about your learning abilities and how much you still need to learn. You may want to review the chapter and the exercises you completed. Then answer the following questions, either individually or in small groups.

On Your Learning Inventory

1. Did you set up schedules of school and nonschool activities? Were these schedules helpful this semester?
2. What did you learn about how you manage your study time and about whether your study area is conducive to learning?
3. What did you learn about your learning style that you did not know before studying this chapter?
4. What is it about you as a learner that you want to improve upon the most during this semester?

Internet Activity

Do research on the Internet to find out more information on learning styles and motivation. You may want to research the following Web sites to gather your information:

Learning Style Inventory:
http://www.hcc.hawaii.edu/hccinfo/facdev/lsi.html

Techniques to Manage Procrastination:
http://128.32.89.153/CalREN/procrastechniques.html

Answer the following questions. Then come back to your group to share what you have learned.

If you cannot access this Web site, research the Internet to find information on learning styles and motivation to answser these questions.

1. What new material have you gathered about learning styles?
2. What new material have you learned about staying motivated?
3. Describe the procedures you followed to access these or other Web sites.

CHAPTER 3

Using the Library

In this chapter, you will learn about:

- Materials in the library
- Computer resources in the library
- How library materials are organized
- How to do library research

In Chapter 2, you learned about the various ways you can study effectively and complete longer projects. An important source of information for your studying and the major resource for your longer projects is the library. In this chapter, you will learn about how libraries are organized, how you can use them to obtain more information for your courses and projects, and the basic steps you need to follow to complete a research project. Undoubtedly, your college has one or more libraries, and they are all organized in a similar fashion.

The Main Sections of a Library

Libraries are depositories of information and ideas that will help further your education and enhance your life. Librarians run libraries; their major duties are to select and organize new library materials and to assist you in finding the sources you need in your particular research area.

Libraries are typically divided into three sections. The *reference* section provides you with dictionaries, encyclopedias, and other volumes of brief, specific information that allow you to pursue your research on a particular subject. The *stacks* are where you find those books that you can check out. This is invariably the largest section of the library. And this is where you will spend much of your time in finding particular books on a topic you are studying. Finally, the third section of a library is the *periodical* area, where magazines, newspapers, and journals are found. Here you can locate specific articles on the topic you are interested in studying.

Types of Materials You Will Find in a Library

Libraries contain four types of reading material: books to borrow, periodicals, reference books, and pamphlets. Each type of reading material will advance your knowledge of a topic in particular ways.

Books to borrow are by far the most abundant type of material you will find in the library. These books are arranged on the shelves by subject matter; college libraries generally have more scholarly texts—that is, books that examine a particular topic with more detail and analysis. If you are researching material on the political leader Cesar Chavez, for example, in the stacks you will probably come across books on Chavez's political beliefs, his contributions to the status of the migrant farmer, his biography, and so on. A good college library has both earlier material on Cesar Chavez and recent studies.

Periodicals are newspapers, magazines, and journals that are usually published on a weekly, monthly, or quarterly basis. You will probably find titles of articles on your particular topic in the *Readers' Guide to Periodical Literature,* an index that is published each month and that will tell you what has been published in that time frame on your topic. You then need to determine whether your library has the particular periodical that contains the article. For newspaper articles, you can use the *New York Times Index* or *Los Angeles Times Index* to locate information on your subject. If you are researching a particular book, you can find out what reviewers of that book had to say through the *Book Review Digest.* If your topic is in the arts and humanities, you may want to look through the *Art Index* or the *Humanities Index.* Similarly, if your topic concerns the social sciences, there is also a *Social Science Index.* All of these indexes work like the *Readers' Guide,* telling you what journal or magazine has material on the topic you are studying.

At times you will find the article in question in the magazine or journal. At other times, the article is on *microfilm* or *microfiche,* which is a film that has reduced the article in size. You need to use a microfilm or microfiche reader in order to enlarge the material so it can be read.

In the reference section, you may find a host of encyclopedias and dictionaries. General encyclopedias like the *Encyclopedia Britannica* and the *Encyclopedia Americana* provide you with an introduction to the topic you are studying. The articles in these encyclopedia sets are arranged alphabetically by subject, but the index in the last volume is usually the best place to begin searching. The *Encyclopedia Britannica* is an often-used source for general information, while you may want to turn to the *Encyclopedia Americana* for information on issues concerning North America and scientific technological subjects. Finally, the *New Columbia Encyclopedia* is helpful if you want a short summary concerning the subject you are studying. Your library may have a host of other encyclopedias, particularly specialized encyclopedias on art, science, philosophy, and so on. Ask your college reference librarian for the types of encyclopedias your college provides.

You will find several dictionaries in your college library. *Webster's Third International Dictionary of the English Language* is a comprehensive American dictionary on the English language, providing definitions and pronunciations of the words you are interested in. The *Oxford English Dictionary* is another dictionary that you will probably come across in your library. This multivolume dictionary is unique in that it gives the history, or *etymology,* of each word in the English language, providing a chronological history of its use in literary and historical texts. And there are a number of briefer or collegiate dictionaries on the shelves in the reference section. You may also find specialized dictionaries on various fields like music, medicine, and law. Again, your reference librarian will provide you with information about the kinds of dictionaries available to you.

Most libraries also carry pamphlets in a special pamphlet file. These are often government or business publications that may provide useful information on a topic that you are interested in. The librarian can help you find any pamphlet on your topic.

How Library Books Are Classified

Library books are commonly organized under two classification systems: the *Dewey decimal* system and the *Library of Congress* system. It is important that you have a general understanding of how these two systems work.

The Dewey decimal system is the older of the two, classifying its books by subject. Each subject has a number that you will find on the outside of the book. The number is usually a whole number and a decimal. Here are the general numbers and their subject classifications:

000–099	General works, including bibliography
100–199	Philosophy and psychology
200–299	Religion
300–399	Social sciences
400–499	Language
500–599	Pure science
600–699	Technology, medicine, business
700–799	The arts
800–899	Literature
900–999	History and geography

Underneath the book's Dewey decimal number, you will find additional numbers and letters that serve as codes for the author and title. All of this is called the book's *call number,* which identifies where the book will be located. Here is an example of a Dewey decimal classification and an explanation of its abbreviations. The book in question is *The Gang as an American Experience* by Felix M. Padilla:

364.1 — Dewey decimal number for crime

P134g

    First word of title begins with "g."

    Number based on author's last name.

    Author's last name begins with a "P."

Figure 3-1   *Example of a Dewey decimal classification.*

A second system of classifying books in the stacks is the Library of Congress system. This system provides additional categories for classifying books. Here are the nineteen categories:

A	General works
B	Philosophy, psychology, religion
C–D	History and topography (except America)
E–F	History: North and South America
G	Geography and anthropology
H	Social sciences
J	Political science
K	Law
L	Education
M	Music
N	Fine arts
P	Language and literature
Q	Science
R	Medicine
S	Agriculture
T	Technology and engineering
U	Military science
V	Naval science
Z	Bibliography and library science

Often an additional letter next to the first further divides the topic. PL, for example, would refer to the language and literature of East Asia and Africa. Here is an example of a Library of Congress classification and what each abbreviation means:

BF——— Library of Congress letters and numbers for psychology of knowledge
311.

G59——— Letter and number based on author's last name

1990——— Year of publication

Figure 3-2   *Example of a Library of Congress classification.*

If you are looking for a magazine or journal article, you will probably be searching in one of the periodical indexes in the reference or periodical section of your library. These guides are generally organized alphabetically around subjects. The information given in each entry is sometimes difficult to understand because much of it is placed in a small amount of space. The following is an excerpt from the *Readers' Guide to Periodical Literature*—the most widely used text. Study all the bibliographical information, and note how the abbreviations are used to condense the information:

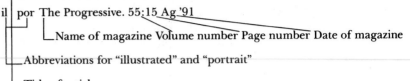

Homeless as Authors

Voice for the homeless. B. Marshall. — Author

il | por The Progressive. 55:15 Ag '91

Name of magazine Volume number Page number Date of magazine

Abbreviations for "illustrated" and "portrait"

Title of article

Figure 3-3   *Example of an entry in the* Readers' Guide to Periodical Literature.

Computers in Libraries

Many large college libraries, perhaps even your own, have computerized bibliographical information. These have replaced the traditional card catalogs, which are 3×5 cards listing the books and journals of the library, arranged alphabetically by subject, author, and book title, in rows of drawers. Computerized information is often referred to as an on-line catalog. You gain access to this information by using the keyboards and screens provided in the library. You find information on this terminal by searching for a subject, a title, or an author. Sometimes there is also a printer, which allows you to print the bibliographical information you may need.

What you will find is often the same information that you could find in a card catalog. In addition, however, the computer screen may tell you if the book has been checked out. The advantage to using the computer screen is that you have an up-to-date listing of all library material that has been checked out or purchased. Usually, as soon as a new publication is purchased or material is checked out, the information is automatically added to the on-line catalog. More and more libraries are now going to computer cataloging of their materials, so it is wise for you to learn how to operate the computer commands.

Your library may also have library sources on the computer known as *CD-ROM,* which is an abbreviation for "compact disc read-only memory." This material is different from the on-line computer material in that it is not continually updated. CD-ROM material is on compact discs, so you can read this information much as you would listen to music on a compact disc. CD-ROMs contain bibliographical information on various topics, particularly in the form of book, magazine, and journal titles. Here you will find more extensive listings of titles in the area you are researching.

CD-ROMs are also being used commercially to market encyclopedias that are on computer screens. Unlike the traditional encyclopedias, CD-ROM material can provide video and sound accompaniments to the topic you are researching. You can see, for example, film footage of a particular battle or hear a historical leader's speech as you read about the historical event. Your college library may or may not have this type of CD-ROM material, but you can be certain that CD-ROMs will play a key role in the library research materials of the future.

Moreover, some college libraries now allow you to use their computers to access titles of works in other neighboring libraries. This is known as *computer networking*. So with the library's computer system—online, CD-ROM, and computer networking to other libraries—you can determine just about all that has been written on the topic you are studying.

You will find that your college librarians are particularly helpful in answering any questions that you may have about the library. They frequently provide tours of the library and may even have developed a short-term course that will acquaint you with all aspects of the library, including their computers. Make use of these services before you begin doing any lengthy research.

Another computer source for research is the Internet. Sometimes called the "information highway," the Internet is a computer service that allows you to access information on nearly any topic. It is a network of information services from varied sources that is constantly being updated. Such information can be a magazine article, a scholarly essay, a speech, even encyclopedia material. By using the Internet effectively, you can locate a wealth of information on a topic in a short amount of time. College libraries often have several computers that are dedicated solely to Internet research. Once you find an appropriate piece of material for your research using the Internet, you can print it, or *download* it, directly from the computer printer. Learning to locate information on the Internet, or "surfing the net," takes practice, so you need to spend several hours familiarizing yourself with ways to access this information. Your research librarian or other library staff can help you to learn how to gather information on the net. They often even provide workshops for the purpose of teaching students to do research via this new information highway. You may have noticed that at the end of each chapter in this textbook, you are asked to do some Internet research to understand the chapter further and to become more familiar with ways to do research on the Internet.

The Research Project

Throughout your college education, you will find that your college library and neighboring libraries are invaluable when you are doing research projects. These assignments generally call for you to do research in books, magazines, journals, and other related types of material found in the library. Much of the information you have been introduced to in this chapter will help you conduct your research.

You may recall that in Chapter 2 you studied the time-management steps necessary to complete a research project on the Native Americans known as the Hopis. Let's assume that you have chosen this topic to research. There are five important steps to follow to complete a research paper on the Hopis or on any research topic of your choice. You need to: (1) select a topic, (2) locate materials, (3) take notes, (4) organize and evaluate the notes, and (5) draft the paper.

Select a Topic. The most important step in the research process is selecting a topic that you can adequately research. Often students begin by selecting a topic that is too general. A ten-page paper on the Hopis would not begin to cover all the important points concerning these people. A full-length book could easily be written on all aspects of the Hopi culture. You need then to ask yourself: What aspect of the Hopi civilization do I want to research: their religion, their migration patterns, their social organization? These examples of subtopics can be adequately covered in a ten-page paper.

Let's assume that you select the topic: The Hopi's Family Structure. You are now ready to share this topic with your instructor and your peers. Ask them whether the topic is still too general and whether they know of materials you can turn to to begin your research.

Before you begin your research, write out the topic you intend to examine—The Family Structure of Hopi Society—so that when you begin your research, you will have a more directed sense of the kinds of materials that will help your research, and you will be able to show your topic to librarians whom you ask for assistance.

Locate Materials.   With your topic in mind, you can begin locating your research materials. Start with your college library. Begin looking in encyclopedias treating the subject of the Hopi. Encyclopedias are excellent places to begin your research, for they can provide you with accurate general information.

Your next step is to begin looking in the various periodical indexes. If you have any questions, consult with the *reference librarian,* whose specialty is tracking down sources. Reference librarians are often very helpful, because they can direct you to areas where you will probably find material for your research, and, more important, they can tell you where *not* to look.

Also consider full-length books, whose titles you can find in the card or on-line catalog of your library, in computer networks that direct you to titles in other libraries, or on the Internet.

You may also choose to do some of your research on the Internet. You may even find relevant material on the Hopi. Be very careful, though, that the material you select is quality research. Unlike a book or journal in the library that has been purchased by a knowledgeable professional, material on the Internet can be placed by anyone. So be sure you use Internet sources that are named, especially respected sources of information like *The New York Times* newspaper or a professional publication like the *Journal of American Medicine.* All too often, students locate information on the Internet that sounds useful but is in fact incorrect or plagiarized.

Be creative in tracking down your sources. Think of other titles under which material on the Hopi can be found, such as Native Americans, Native Americans of the Southwest, Native American Social Structures, and so on.

By the end of your first search, you should have titles to at least ten sources that will allow you to begin your research.

Take Notes. It is best to take notes on 4 × 6 cards, because they are easy to organize when you begin writing your drafts. Summarize information on the Hopi, and copy down direct quotes that you might consider using in your paper. Each card should have all the necessary bibliographical information on the first and second lines so that, in the event that you must return the book, your source is fully identified. A note card on the Hopi could look like this:

> Serena Nanda Cultural Anthropology, 5th ed.
> Belmont: Wadsworth, 1994. 347-348.
> extended matrilineal families: "The Hopi
> revolves around a central and
> continuing core of women." (347)
> father's obligations economic.
> mother-daughter relation very close.
> sister relation very strong: children
> of sisters raised together.

As you continue taking notes, keep asking yourself: Is my topic adequate? Is it too general? Can I rephrase it somehow? As you complete your note taking, the key points that you want to make in your paper should begin to emerge.

Organize and Evaluate Your Notes. You should now be able to write out five or six of the most important points you intend to cover. At this time, these points should be used to support a particular argument that you have come upon: The Hopi women exert a strong force on their family, and it is seen in their relationships with their sisters, mothers, and brothers. A beginning list of issues that you may want to cover to support this argument could look like this:

Roles of Women in Hopi Society

— closeness of mothers and daughters
— closeness between sisters
— importance of mother's brother's role
— the economic role that men play

Share this working outline with your instructor and your peers. Take note of their questions, and revise your statements based upon their input. You may have noted that the original topic, "The Hopi's Family Structure," has evolved into the more specific concern of "The Roles of Women in Hopi Society." After you have thought through your revised outline, begin attaching sources to each subsection. You may even want to number all of your note cards and refer to each source by number. An excerpt of your outline could look something like this:

— closeness of mothers and daughters. See notes 7–12, 18–21.
— closeness between sisters. See notes 30–35, 47.

With this outline in hand, you can begin to draft your paper.

Draft the Paper.   Now is the time to begin writing. Since this is your first draft, do not fret over a perfect copy at this juncture. Write quickly, incorporating your summaries and relevant quotes. As you write, examine the outline you have set up. Feel free to revise it, rearranging the subtopics or even adding entirely new ones.

As you draft your essay, ask for feedback from your instructor and your peers. Let them read the parts you have completed, and incorporate their suggestions when their comments seem appropriate to you.

Each research project has different requirements, depending on the course you are taking and the conventions the particular discipline uses to do research. Yet what all research projects share is this five-step process: selecting a topic to research, finding appropriate materials, taking notes on these materials, organizing and evaluating the research, and writing the drafts. As you continue to do research, these steps will become habitual.

It is clear, then, that your college library is a significant resource for your education. But your college library and your neighborhood library are also places for you to read and browse for pleasure. During those moments when school and work are not too hectic, it is often very relaxing just to browse through the rows of books, the periodical section, or the Internet. As you continue your education, you will find that libraries are those special places that help make learning a life-long experience and pleasure.

Summary

The college library is the campus's central location for the information you need to gather as a student. You will find materials in various sections of the library: reference, stacks, and periodicals. The materials are organized either by the Dewey decimal system or the Library of Congress system. This information is often indexed in a card catalog or on-line computer catalog. CD-ROMs and the Internet can also provide you with sources of titles for your research that may not be in your college library.

Doing a research project involves five important and sequential steps: locating a topic, finding material, taking notes on the material, organizing and evaluating these notes, and drafting your paper.

Summary Box   *Using the Library*

What is the college library?	*Why do you use it?*
A central location for scholarly information Materials are located in specific sections: reference, stacks, and periodicals Books are organized according to either the Dewey decimal system or the Library of Congress system in a card catalog, on an on-line computer catalog, on CD-ROM, or on the Internet	To assist your education To provide resources for your college research To allow you to become a more independent learner To build backgrounds for life-long interests and pleasures

What is library research?	*Why do you do it?*
An organized search of the key studies on a particular topic	To learn about a topic by analyzing what researchers have discovered about this topic

Skills Practice

Exercise 3.1
Using the Library to
Locate Sources

Choose a topic that interests you, go to the library, and complete the following activities. You may want to work in groups of four or five and divide up these activities after you have agreed upon a topic:

1. State your topic:

   _____

2. Go to the catalog system (either card catalog, on-line computer, CD-ROM, or Internet) and locate five titles that would help you research this topic. Include author and title. Also, be sure you include the Dewey decimal or the Library of Congress call number for each book.

   a. _____

b. _____

c. _____

d. _____

e. _____

3. Go to the periodical indexes and locate five magazine, journal, or newspaper entries that you could use to research your topic. Include author (if listed), title, and name of periodical, as well as any other bibliographical information that you find in your search.

a. _____

b. _____

c. _____

d. _____

e. _____

4. Now go to your reference librarian with these titles. Ask her or him if there are any other library materials (such as pamphlets or audio-visual material) available to help you with your research topic. List these additional sources.

Score: Answers will vary.

Follow-up on Chapter 3

Now that you have studied this introduction and completed this exercise, it may be helpful to see how much you have learned about using the library and what you still need to learn about the library. You may want to go back over this introduction and the exercise in order to review what you have learned. Then answer the following questions either individually or in small groups.

On Using the Library

1. What areas of the library do you now feel confident using? What areas are still new to you?

2. How can computers now help you do library research?

3. Are the steps in the research project clear to you now? Do you now know how the library can assist you in completing a research project?

4. Which areas of your particular college library are you now familiar with? Which areas of your library do you still need to explore?

 **Internet Activity**

In groups of four or five, explore the following Web site to collect any additional information on how best to use the Internet in your research in college.

Access to Major English-Language Libraries On-Line

http://www.clark.net/pub/abaa-booknet/research/librar.html

Each of you may be assigned an Internet question to answer from the following three from this Web site. Then you can report back to your group with your information.

1. What three new facts did you learn about using college libraries by researching this Web site?
2. How can you locate and use a book or article that is not in your college library?
3. Describe the procedures you used to access information at this Web site.

Basic Reading, Listening, and Writing Skills

In this part of the book, you will learn skills that will help you read, listen, and write better. These are very important skills for you to acquire in order to succeed in college. So read each chapter introduction carefully, and do as many of the exercises as you can. When you finish Part Two, you will have some very useful study skills at your disposal.

CHAPTER 4

Locating the Main Idea

In this chapter, you will learn about:

- How to identify topics in writing and speech
- How to identify main ideas in writing and speech
- How to infer a main idea
- How to apply main ideas in your own writing

Determining main ideas in textbooks and lectures is perhaps the single most important study skill that you can learn. If you do not know what the main ideas are, you cannot follow a writer's or lecturer's train of thought. Details can become confusing and meaningless. On the other hand, if you have the main ideas in mind, a textbook chapter, lecture, or discussion will seem organized and informative. Furthermore, the main ideas will usually stay with you long after you have forgotten many of the details.

Understanding the Role of Main Ideas

Every well-planned lecture and textbook has a series of main ideas. But finding them is not always a simple matter. You often have to know what main ideas do and how they're used in order to find them.

In Relationship to the Topic.   The first step in locating any main idea is to determine the *topic* of your reading or lecture material. If you determine the topic early in your reading or listening, you will be on your way to identifying main ideas.

The topic is generally easy to find in a reading selection because it is the title of the material. Most titles clearly tell you what the selection is about. An article with the title "Pollution: Research in the Nineties" is almost sure to tell you what scientists have found out about pollution in this decade. "Pollution: A Hopeless Problem?" will no doubt try to explain why pollution is not yet under control and may never be controlled. It is best to lock the title in your mind before you start reading, to begin examining what the material will cover.

In some articles, the title may be more indirect. For instance, the writer may use a quotation as a title. In this case, you may understand the meaning of the title only while reading or after reading the selection.

Let's say an article on pollution uses a question from Henry David Thoreau as its title: "What Is the Use of a House If You Don't Have a Decent Planet to Put It On?" You may not at first understand what this question has to do with pollution. But as you read this article, you may find that the article is not about building houses but about the uselessness of technology if the earth is too polluted to use the technology. When you encounter indirect titles, you may want to begin by jotting down a few notes about what you think the title means.

Locating the topic of a lecture or discussion is usually quite easy, because most instructors list the subjects for class meetings in the syllabus, next to the class dates. For example, an environmental studies instructor might write "Monday, June 7—Water Pollution." Write this title on the first line of your page of lecture or discussion notes for that day. You should then try to figure out how this topic fits into what your instructor said in the previous meeting. Did she discuss air pollution on Friday, June 4? As you start seeing connections among lectures, you will derive more meaning from each one.

What if your instructor does not provide a syllabus or does not begin the lecture or discussion with a stated topic? Then you are responsible for determining the topic. Spend no more than five minutes listening to the lecture to determine the topic. Then write your own title on the first line of your lecture notes.

In Outlines.   With the topic in mind, you are now ready to read or listen for main ideas. Consider main ideas as umbrellas under which all significant details are included. Perhaps you can best see the main ideas as Roman numerals in an outline, where Roman numerals like "I" represent the main idea and capital letters like "A" and "B" represent the supporting details. If you are already familiar with the traditional outline form, you know that the main ideas, preceded by Roman numerals, are placed farthest to the left on your page of notes. You may also have learned that the farther to the right you go, the more details you add. A main idea, then, is more general than its details but more specific than the topic. See how a main idea is sandwiched between the topic and the details of support in the following outline of a lecture on air pollution:

Types of Pollution

I. Air pollution

    A. Types of pollution in the atmosphere
    B. Effects of air pollution on rivers, lakes, and oceans
    C. Effects of air pollution on vegetation

Notice that "I. Air Pollution" is one issue under the topic "Types of Pollution" and that A, B, and C call out specifics of that main idea.

Whether you are reading or listening, see the main idea as the level of information between the topic and the details. Keep this "I, A, B, and

C" organization in mind when you are locating main ideas in writing, lectures, or discussions. When you are comfortable with the traditional outline structure, you will be able to identify main ideas effortlessly.

Seeing and Hearing Main Ideas

Almost every paragraph or group of paragraphs and list of statements in a lecture should contain one main idea and one or more details. Here are some hints for finding main ideas.

At the Beginning.   In many of the paragraphs you read, you will find the main idea in the first sentence. In the sentences that follow the first sentence, you will usually read details that support this main idea. Study the following paragraph on air pollution to see how the first sentence expresses the main idea and the sentences that follow present details:

> Most air pollution is made up of a combination of gaseous substances. Some of the air pollution is caused by automobile exhaust fumes in the form of carbon monoxide. Other types of air pollution, often found in smog, are made up of chemical oxides. The two most common oxides found in air pollution are nitrogen oxide and sulfur oxide.

Did you notice that the first sentence is the most general, the umbrella under which the other three sentences fall? Did you also notice that in each detail sentence specific types of air pollution are cited? In main-idea sentences you do not usually read a specific fact or figure. In this sense, main-idea sentences are more general. Thus in the main-idea sentence of the sample paragraph, gaseous substances are introduced, not specific gaseous substances.

Similarly, instructors usually present main-idea sentences at the beginning of their lectures or parts of lectures. So you need to listen carefully when they begin a presentation or when they introduce new ideas during the lecture or discussion. These introductory remarks will usually be the I, II, and III of your notes.

At the End.   Occasionally, the main idea of a paragraph is presented at the end. In these cases, the detail sentences are presented first. The process of presenting specific information that leads to a general statement is called *induction*. Information is collected, and from this a main idea emerges. Study this paragraph on the sources of air pollution:

> Forest fires occur throughout the world. Wherever there are insects, they disperse pollen. The wind erodes the soil, and it ends up in the atmosphere. Volcanoes erupt and spew their material into the air. All of these are examples of natural events that create air pollution.

Did you notice the specific details in the first four sentences? Did you also notice how these sentences lead to a main-idea sentence at the end?

This statement about natural air pollution, like an umbrella, covers all the information about volcanoes, wind, insects, and fires.

This same pattern sometimes occurs in lectures or discussions. The speaker presents several details at the beginning of the lecture, and the main idea, or induction, is presented last. In your outline, you need to leave the blank next to item I temporarily empty while you jot down the details (A, B, C) of the lecture or discussion. Then, when the speaker presents the main idea, you can go back to fill in the space next to I.

In Longer Selections.   You can also look for the main idea of an entire essay, lecture, or discussion. In these longer pieces, the main idea can usually be found in the first paragraph of an essay or the first section of a lecture or discussion, called the *introduction.* In these longer works, the main idea may be stated in more than one sentence.

In the paragraphs or sections that follow the introduction, which are often called the *body,* details are usually presented to support the main idea. The last paragraph or section—the *conclusion*—is usually as general as the introduction. It either summarizes the main idea of the essay or presents new conclusions that logically follow from the details. So when looking for the main idea in most essays, it is wise to read through the first and last paragraphs and then write out the main idea in your own words.

This outline should help you understand better the relationship between main idea and details in longer works:

I. Introduction: expresses main idea; introduces details

A. ⎫
B. ⎬ Body: explains the details more thoroughly in a series of
C. ⎭ paragraphs or sections

II. Conclusion: either summarizes the main idea or presents a new main idea that follows from the details in A, B, and C.

Through Signal Words.   Several *signal words* may introduce a main idea. You will find signal words most often in the introduction or conclusion of an essay, lecture, or discussion. Become familiar with these words and phrases: "in general," "generally," "above all," "of great importance," "the main idea is," "the main point is," "the main feature is," "the key feature is," "the truth is." Look at how the following paragraph incorporates signal words into its sentences:

> *Generally,* the most significant cause of pollution in big cities is the emissions that come from automobiles and factories. *The main feature* of pollutants from both these sources is that they do not easily decompose or decay on their own. *Of great importance* is how these pollutants return to the earth in the form of acid rain. It is acid rain that we need to study more carefully next.

Do you see how these signal words introduce the key points this author intends to cover?

The following words and phrases signal main ideas in conclusions: "in conclusion," "to conclude," "to summarize," "therefore," "thus," "consequently," "as a consequence," "as a result," "so," "it can be seen that," "it is suggested that," "it follows that," "from the above reasons," "it is safe to say." Let these words be signals for you to locate concluding main-idea sentences in your reading and in lectures and discussions. Authors frequently use these words and phrases to introduce a general statement that you may want to remember. Also, you need to use these signal words when writing conclusions of your own.

Inferring Main Ideas

The preceding suggestions about finding main ideas in first and last sentences cover most of what you will read and hear. In some material, though, you will not find a main idea explicitly stated. In these cases, you need to infer a main idea from the details. You will frequently find paragraphs with implied main ideas in descriptive writing, especially in short stories and novels, where the author is creating a mood or re-creating an experience. Descriptive writing, therefore, does not follow the "main-idea-followed-by-details" pattern.

Read the following description and infer a main idea:

> The leaves on the trees seemed to have been burned by a harmful chemical. The water in the pond was stagnant, and strangely, it did not seem to have any living things swimming in it—no fish, no algae, no insects teeming above the water. All I could see was the stifling, brown air that seemed to hover around everything—the trees, the pond, and me.

Nowhere does the author state that he is describing a dangerously polluted environment, but do you see that all the details lead you to infer that he is? The leaves on the trees are brown, the pond has no living organisms in it, and the air is brown and stifling. The author wants the reader to be disgusted by the details in order to come upon the main idea: how ugly and life-threatening a polluted environment can be.

Applying Main-Idea Rules to Writing

Learning to spot signal words and knowing how essays and lectures are organized will help you locate main ideas. They will also help you write organized essays. You will frequently be asked to write essays as a test of your understanding of reading and lecture material.

Consider these suggestions when beginning a writing assignment. First, use the traditional outline form to jot down notes before you begin writing. Second, use some signal words to introduce your main idea in introductions and conclusions. Finally, fortify your essays with several well-developed paragraphs: an introduction, paragraphs introducing and explaining details, and a conclusion summarizing or synthesizing what you have said. (You will learn more about the extended essay in Chapter 16.)

Are you beginning to see that reading, listening, and writing involve similar processes? The same organizational rules apply to all three activities. The major difference is that when you read and listen, you take in information and consider what it means; when you write, you write down more carefully what you think this new material means to you. Good readers and listeners are often good writers. You will learn more about this reading–listening–writing interconnection throughout this book.

Summary

Determining the main idea of a paragraph and locating the main ideas in a longer passage or in lectures are very important skills for students to learn. About half the main ideas that one reads or hears are found in the first sentence of a paragraph. In fewer cases, the main idea is in the last sentence. Implied main ideas are not stated at all but may be inferred from the details.

Whether the material is spoken or written, the relationship between a main idea and its supporting details is seen in the outline pattern:

I.

    A.
    B.
    C.

Dividing information into general and specific is a mental exercise you should constantly perform when you read, listen, or write. In Chapter 5 you will study the A, B, and C of the outline form—the details.

Summary Box   *Main Ideas*

What are they?	*Why do you need to use them?*
Key statements made in writing or lecturing, usually found at the beginning and end of material, and implied in most descriptions More specific than topics, less specific than details	To understand the important points in what you read, hear, or write To serve as umbrellas for the details that support them

Skills Practice Topic: Environmental Studies

All the exercises in this chapter deal with the issue of environmental pollution, a topic of concern to us all and one that you will examine carefully if you enroll in environmental studies courses in college.

Before you begin these exercises, answer the following questions either by yourself or in small groups to get a sense of what you already know about the environment. Recalling what you already know about a topic is very effective preparation for studying that topic.

1. What does the term *environment* mean?
2. What are the most common environmental problems that we face today?
3. How have human beings contributed to environmental problems?
4. How are environmental problems being dealt with in the world today?

Exercise 4.1 Determining Stated or Implied Main Ideas

The following paragraphs discuss the ways humans affected the planet in ancient times. The main idea may be found in the first sentence or the last sentence, or it may be implied. Locate the letter of the main-idea sentence, and place it next to the appropriate number in the answer box. If there is no main-idea sentence, write *imp* for "implied" next to the number in the answer box.

Ancient Hunters and Gatherers

(1) (a) For the vast majority of their time on earth, human beings have been hunters and gatherers. (b) They found that some wild plants could be eaten, so they began to gather them to share them with their family. (c) When they found that fish and game were edible, they became hunters. (d) The hunting was generally done by men, and the gathering was performed by women and children.

(2) (a) These early hunters and gatherers formed groups of approximately fifty members. (b) As a group, they worked together to hunt game and gather food in order to feed their people. (c) Once the group grew beyond fifty, it often split up and began forming a second group, which hunted and gathered food on its own. (d) These groups, known as tribes, seemed to be the fundamental social group for hunters and gatherers.

(3) (a) Often these tribes were forced to move from one place to another to find new game and edible plants. (b) The people in the tribes often could not tell how long their supply of game in a particular area would last, which was a source of frustration for them. (c) They also had a difficult time gauging when a particular type of edible plant would no longer be plentiful enough to feed the entire tribe. (d) As nomads, they were also subject to the changes of seasons and were forced to move when the weather proved intolerable.

(4) (a) These tribes soon learned much about coping with weather changes. (b) They also found reliable water sources, even in dry areas. (c) These people eventually became shrewd enough to know which plants were edible and which could serve as medicine. (d) Each tribe also learned to use sticks and stones in preparing its plant and animal foods.

(5) (a) Our current picture of these ancient hunting and gathering tribes calls our modern lifestyle into question. (b) In these tribes of fifty, women and children spent only fifteen hours per week gathering food. (c) The men tended to hunt only one week each month.

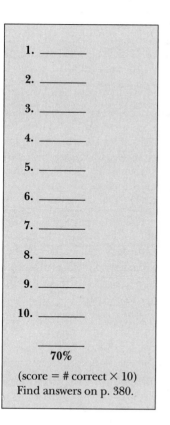

1. _____
2. _____
3. _____
4. _____
5. _____
6. _____
7. _____
8. _____
9. _____
10. _____

_____
70%

(score = # correct × 10)
Find answers on p. 380.

(d) Furthermore, our ancient ancestors ate a healthy and varied diet, and the notion of stress was foreign to them.

(6) (a) A negative aspect of the hunter–gatherer lifestyle was their high mortality rate. (b) Many infants died of infectious diseases. (c) For adults, the average life expectancy was about thirty years. (d) Because of this high death rate, the population increased slowly.

(7) (a) The impact of the hunter–gatherer lifestyle on the environment was very slight. (b) Because their population did not grow quickly, they did not deplete the resources in the environment. (c) Also, because these people were nomads, they did not exploit any one area. (d) Finally, these people relied on their own energy rather than on energy resources in the environment to get most of their work done.

(8) (a) About 12,000 years ago, hunters and gatherers began to change some of their behavior. (b) Most important, they improved their tools; cutting tools became sharper, and the bow and arrow were invented. (c) Also, hunters from various tribes began to work together to hunt herds of animals such as bison and mammoths. (d) These people also began to burn some of their inedible vegetation to give the edible vegetation room to grow.

(9) (a) As these hunters developed more advanced skills, some of the forested hunting areas began to turn to grassland. (b) As they became more proficient, these hunters were able to kill off a few more game. (c) The gatherers also changed some of the vegetation patterns by allowing more of the edible vegetation to grow. (d) All in all, though, both hunters and gatherers tended to live in harmony with their neighbors and with nature.

(10) (a) Today people living in industrial areas rarely consider where the piece of meat they eat for dinner comes from. (b) They also tend not to reflect on where or how the vegetables they buy for their salads are grown. (c) They also rarely ask what resources are needed to make the plastics and metal items they use each day. (d) Moreover, people in modern industrial cities often tend to consume more food and purchase more manufactured items than they really need.

Exercise 4.2
Determining Topics
and Main Ideas

The following exercise is a series of paragraphs on the history of agricultural societies, continuing the discussion on hunters and gatherers begun in Exercise 4.1. Read the following ten paragraphs carefully; you may choose to reread them. As you read each one, ask the following questions: What is the topic? What is the main idea? Remember that the topic—the subject of the paragraph, usually phrased in two or three words—tends to be more general. The main idea is the point of the paragraph, what all the sentences in the paragraph are about. Choose the correct letter of the topic and main idea for each paragraph and put it in the answer box next to the appropriate number.

Ancient Agricultural Societies

The use of agriculture began about 10,000 years ago. That is when people began to plant crops in one area and began to tame animals so they didn't have to migrate to hunt. What is interesting is that the use of agricultural methods occurred in several parts of the world at about the same time. These methods ultimately made hunting and nomadic living less attractive. Agriculture had some profound effects on how human beings lived.

1. The topic is

   a. the dangers of agriculture
   b. the birth of agriculture 10,000 years ago
   c. hunting and nomadic living
   d. where agriculture was first introduced

2. The main idea concerns

   a. the importance of taming animals
   b. the lack of interest in hunting
   c. the difficulty of introducing agriculture into tribal life
   d. the effect of agricultural methods on social behavior

It is believed that the first cultivation of plants occurred in the tropical areas of Burma, Thailand, and eastern India. The women of the tribes in these areas began to cultivate small vegetable gardens. Anthropologists believe these women realized that their staple food, yams, could be planted and harvested successfully in one area. These pioneering farmers realized that they could clear an area by cutting down the vegetation and then burning it. The ash from the burned vegetation provided rich fertilizer for the yams they planted on this cleared area of land. Food could now be grown and cared for in one area.

3. The topic is

   a. the invention of cultivation
   b. the use of yams in the diet
   c. the value of using rich fertilizer
   d. the ancient people of Burma, Thailand, and eastern India

4. The main idea concerns

   a. new farming methods
   b. the use of ash in cultivating yams
   c. how cultivation changed farming methods
   d. how cultivation kept farming methods the same

These pioneer women farmers invented the notion of *shifting cultivation*. That is, they realized that planting their crops in one area would yield rich harvests for no more than five years. Then they had to clear a new agricultural area. The old agricultural plot needed to remain unplanted, or fallow, for ten to thirty years. During this fallow time, the soil replenished itself; then it was ready for a new round of planting and harvesting. Shifting cultivation is still used by farmers throughout the world.

5. The topic is

   a. the invention of shifting cultivation
   b. rich harvests
   c. keeping land fallow
   d. where shifting cultivation is used today

6. The main idea concerns

   a. the difficulty of shifting cultivation
   b. ways of clearing new agricultural areas
   c. the value of shifting cultivation
   d. how soil replenishes itself

Where the climate was less warm and humid, farmers devised different agricultural techniques. In such areas as East Africa and China, farmers had to clear forested areas; chopping down trees was often quite difficult. Once the area was cleared, the women often planted grains like rice or wheat instead of yams. The farmers in these temperate climates learned the same thing as those in tropical climates: that the area they cleared could yield a successful harvest for only a certain number of years. Shifting cultivation was the most profitable way to get consistently rich harvests.

7. The topic is

   a. temperate climates
   b. the farmers of East Africa and China
   c. the agricultural techniques of farmers in East Africa and China
   d. the planting of rice and grain

8. The main idea concerns

   a. the difficulty of clearing forested areas
   b. the similar agricultural techniques of farmers in tropical and temperate areas
   c. the success of harvesting in temperate climates
   d. the differences between the farmers of temperate and tropical areas

What pioneering farmers in both tropical and temperate climates learned was the value of *subsistence farming.* That is, they learned to harvest enough food to feed their tribe and no more. These farmers did not want to make a profit from any harvest that remained. Subsistence farming proved to be an environmentally sensible type of agriculture, because it used relatively small areas of land. Also, the people did not deplete their area's resources in an attempt to make the farms productive. They used their own strength to clear the farm areas, and they fertilized their farms with burning vegetation grown in the same area.

For these reasons and many more, subsistence farming had little negative impact on the environment.

9. The topic is

    a. the depletion of the environment
    b. the negative effect of subsistence farming on the environment
    c. the nature of subsistence farming
    d. burning vegetation as fertilizer

10. The main idea concerns

    a. the use of land in subsistence farming
    b. subsistence farming as environmentally wise
    c. the profit resulting from subsistence farming
    d. the difficulty of feeding family and tribe

To this day, farmers throughout the world continue to use shifting cultivation and subsistence farming techniques. In Latin America, Southeast Asia, and parts of Africa, up to 200 million people still use these agricultural procedures. Environmentalists call them very sound because they do not deplete the environment. With shifting cultivation, the soil is never wasted; with subsistence farming, no area's resources are ever overused. When these two techniques are not used effectively, the soil becomes depleted, which leads to erosion and sometimes permanent damage to the soil and the surrounding environment.

11. The topic is

    a. farming techniques in Latin America and Southeast Asia
    b. the use of subsistence farming today
    c. the use of subsistence farming and shifting cultivation today
    d. the cause of erosion

12. The main idea concerns

    a. the dangers of soil erosion
    b. the hazards of depleting the environment
    c. soil cultivation and subsistence farming as environmentally sensible today
    d. how poor people farm

Plows were invented about 5000 B.C. These early plows, made of metal, were pulled by tamed animals and steered by the farmer. With a plow, farmers could plant more crops and therefore harvest more food. The plow also allowed farmers to plant in areas that, before introduction of the plow, could not be cleared because the roots in the soil were too deep. Plows also allowed farmers to dig ditches and bring water to dry areas. By helping the farmer harvest more, the plow gave him more food than his family could eat, and he could then sell some of the excess to families with less food.

13. The topic is

    a. the invention of the plow
    b. the use of water in agriculture
    c. the profit resulting from farming
    d. how farmers fed their families

14. The main idea concerns

    a. the origin of the plow
    b. why the farmer dislikes the plow
    c. how plows clear roots that are deep in the soil
    d. how the plow changed farming in fundamental ways

Farmers' ability to save and sell their product had several effects on society. Because more food was harvested, more people could settle in an area. Because food products could now be bought, not everyone had to be a farmer. Some people began to work in other occupations and use their earnings to purchase food from farmers. After introduction of the plow, jobs began to be specialized. Finally, in part because of the plow, cities emerged, and farming towns grew on the outskirts of these cities. The plow, therefore, had a profound effect on the structure of society.

15. The topic is

    a. why farmers lost their power
    b. why farming became a popular occupation
    c. the emergence of cities
    d. the plow's effect on society

16. The main idea concerns

    a. the plow's important role in changing occupations and altering city and town life
    b. the plow's dangerous effect on society
    c. the importance of profit in society
    d. why farmers moved out of the city

The separation of cities from farm areas had additional effects on human society. Most important, wealth became a reality. That is, some people had more food and more manufactured products than others had. So there emerged a need for a class of people who could manage the city's wealth. Also, problems emerged between those who had more and those who had less—or the *haves* and the *have nots*. Conflict between these groups and wars between cities were some of the unwanted results of the development of wealth.

17. The topic is

    a. the development of city managers
    b. the problems caused by war

1. _____
2. _____
3. _____
4. _____
5. _____
6. _____
7. _____
8. _____
9. _____
10. _____
11. _____
12. _____
13. _____
14. _____
15. _____
16. _____
17. _____
18. _____
19. _____
20. _____

_____
75%

Ask instructor for answers.

    c. how wealth was given to the people

    d. how wealth came to be

18. The main idea concerns

    a. how wealth restructured society and caused conflict and war

    b. the greed of city managers

    c. why the farmers became wealthy

    d. the occasional need for wars

With increased and more intensive farming came environmental concerns that the hunters and gatherers had never known. City people were no longer living in harmony with the environment. When more land was cleared for larger harvests and bigger cities, certain plants and animals were forced out of their natural habitat. Some plants and animals even died out completely. Overuse of the land led to a depletion of the soil's riches. What was once fertile territory sometimes became a desert because of overfarming. Urban or city life generally had a negative effect on the environment.

19. The topic is

    a. urban life

    b. the death of certain plants and animals

    c. overuse of the land

    d. city life and its effect on the environment

20. The main idea concerns

    a. how cities create deserts

    b. how city dwellers moved the farmers out

    c. how the hunter–gatherer is similar to the city dweller

    d. how city dwellers did not live in harmony with their environment

Exercise 4.3
Determining More
Topics and Main
Ideas

The following ten paragraphs address the issue of industrialization and continue the discussion begun in the previous two exercises. After reading each paragraph, write a topic and a main idea for each. Remember that the topic is normally expressed in a phrase that can serve as the title of the passage. The main idea, often stated in the first or last sentence of the paragraph, expresses the passage's intent. For example, "industrialized countries" can serve as the topic of a paragraph with the main idea "the pollution caused by industrialized countries." Writing out your own topics and main ideas is a big part of what you do when you take lecture, discussion, and study notes.

How Industrialized Societies Developed

The next big change in human society occurred during the mid-1700s in England. It was called the Industrial Revolution. Industry seemed to take over because there were so many inventions in such a short time. These inventions included the steam engine (1765), the steamship (1807), and the steam locomotive (1829). They made England and most of Europe less farm-based and more urbanized, or city-centered.

1. *Topic:* _____

2. *Main idea:* _____

All of these new inventions had one thing in common: They were driven by natural resources. Coal was the first fuel used to run these machines. Then oil and natural gas were discovered as energy sources to replace human energy. The results were far-reaching, extending the plow's effects on society thousands of years before. Fewer people were needed to do most work, because machines replaced them. Farmers found themselves out of work, and they began to move from the outlying farms to the large cities to find jobs. They often found jobs in large factories.

3. *Topic:* _____

4. *Main idea:* _____

By World War I (1914–1918), machines were becoming more and more sophisticated. These machines helped society in several ways. Because products could be produced in larger quantities, they were often cheaper to buy. Also, the average wage of each working individual went up. Furthermore, farming was more productive, so food was more plentiful. Industrialization also improved practices in medicine, sanitation, and nutrition. Consequently, people tended to live longer. So along with its negative effects on the environment, industrialization had some positive effects on human beings.

5. *Topic:* _____

6. *Main idea:* _____

Industrialization had a negative effect on the environment. Industry tended to create pollutants. The quality of the air, water, and soil was damaged by the waste materials expelled from smokestacks and drainpipes. People soon found that air, water, and soil pollution affected not only their own city but also cities and countries beyond their border. Environmental pollution was no longer a local concern, but a *global* one. That is, people soon began to realize that the actions of a factory in London could affect the entire country and even the world.

7. *Topic:* _____

8. *Main idea:* _____

Industrialization has caused additional social problems. When farmers moved to the cities to find work, the population density of urban areas increased. If the migrants could not find work, the city government had to provide them with some sort of welfare. By increasing the city's population density, these migrants also made the transmission of diseases easier. Furthermore, unemployment and poverty made crime a more serious problem in large cities.

9. *Topic:* _____

10. *Main idea:* _____

How did industrialization affect the city's environment? Like developing cities throughout human history, industrialized cities destroyed topsoil and ate up forests and grasslands. Urban sprawl into the farmlands forced farmers to move farther out. Wildlife was either pushed out of the city or made extinct. What was a city's problem then became a global problem—one that affected all of nature.

11. *Topic:* _____

12. *Main idea:* _____

The Industrial Revolution also affected the economy of the city and the overall economy of the country. Solving each social and environmental problem required money. To cover increased welfare benefits, the city needed to collect taxes. Furthermore, taxpayers needed to address the pollution problems created by large factories. Cleaning up the air and the rivers and lakes took money. So, although the Industrial Revolution improved the average citizen's standard of living, it also made him pay for the social and environmental problems it caused.

13. *Topic:* _____

14. *Main idea:* _____

Today people in industrialized countries throughout the world are asking the same question. Is industrialization helping us or hurting us? Obviously, the Industrial Revolution has made humans more productive. It has increased our standard of living, lengthened human life, and made our life more comfortable. But the Industrial Revolution has also created an unhealthy environment. It has made much of our air unfit to breathe and our water unfit to drink. Environmental pollutants have also created many cancer-related diseases.

15. *Topic:* _____

16. *Main idea:* _____

The Industrial Revolution has also given us an attitude toward nature very different from that of our ancestors. In ancient times, human beings saw themselves as living in harmony with nature. They never took too much from nature and respected the power nature had over them. As human inventions came to the fore, we started seeing ourselves in a much more powerful role. Nature no longer controlled human beings; we controlled nature. Today we often see ourselves as *superior* to nature.

17. *Topic:* _____

18. *Main idea:* _____

It is this superior attitude toward nature that industrialized society needs to question. Yes, in many ways we can control parts of nature. We can build bridges and dams and send satellites outside of the earth's atmosphere. Yet nature still has some power over the organisms that live within it. Our challenge in the twenty-first century is to enjoy the benefits of industrialization but also to respect nature and live in harmony with it. We have to realize that our inventions can make life both better and worse.*

19. *Topic:* _____

20. *Main idea:* _____

70%
(score = # correct × 5)
Find answers on p. 380.

Exercise 4.4
Determining the
Main Idea in a
Longer Passage

To determine the main idea of a passage, you can apply the same rules that you used to determine the main idea of a paragraph. Read the following extended essay on nuclear war and pollution, a major concern of environmentalists, and follow these steps to determine the main ideas:

1. Read the introductory paragraph to determine the main idea of the entire passage.

2. See how the four paragraphs that follow (the body) give details to support this main idea. Locate the main-idea sentence for each of these paragraphs. In two of these paragraphs, the main idea is implied.

After you have taken these steps, answer the five questions that follow the essay. You may look back. Place all answers in the answer box.

Nuclear War and Pollution

(1) Environmentalists generally believe that the biggest threat to our world is a nuclear war. They believe this because of what they know

---

*Exercises 4.1–4.3 adapted from G. Tyler Miller, Jr., *Living in the Environment*, 5th ed. (Belmont, Calif.: Wadsworth, 1988), pp. 25–31.

about the atomic bombs that were dropped at the end of World War II and because they can accurately predict the amount of nuclear destruction countries today possess. Environmentalists have also conducted several studies concerning what would happen to the people and the environment if there were a nuclear war today.

(2) Two atomic bombs were dropped by Americans in August of 1945—one over Hiroshima and the other over Nagasaki in Japan. It is estimated that up to 140,000 people were killed immediately after the blast, and over 100,000 died later from exposure to radiation created by the atomic bomb. The radiation contaminated the dirt in the area of the explosion. This radioactive debris then entered the atmosphere and fell back to the earth as far away as thousands of kilometers from the original explosion.

(3) The threats to humans and to the environment caused by nuclear bombings is much worse than it was at the end of World War II. The damage that could happen today is 952,000 times as great as that to hit Hiroshima almost fifty years ago! One nuclear submarine today can carry enough nuclear warheads to equal 4,570 Hiroshima bombs. By the year 2000 it is predicted that sixty countries will either have nuclear warheads or will have the technology necessary to construct them.

(4) If a nuclear bomb were to explode today, as many as four billion people could die, as much as 80% of the human population. Within two years after the explosion, it is predicted that over 1 billion more people would die of starvation due to the reduced agricultural yields caused by the rdioactive fallout from the atomic explosion. Moreover, the average temperature would suddenly drop to typical fall and winter temperatures.

(5) An atomic explosion would also severely harm the already damaged ozone layer. Environmentalists predict that up to 70 percent of this layer could be destroyed, leading to what they characterize as an ultraviolet summer. This ozone layer reduction would reduce both crop yield and fish harvest. In humans, skin cancers would dramatically increase as well as eye cataracts. Further, those who are prone to infections could die of diseases their immune system would normally have protected them from.*

1. The main idea of paragraph 1 concerns

   a. how an atomic bomb explosion will negatively affect the environment and its people
   b. the effects of the atomic bombs exploded during World War II
   c. environmentalists' predictions
   d. Hiroshima and Nagasaki

2. The implied main idea of paragraph 2 concerns:

   a. The number of people killed in Hiroshima and Nagasaki

---

*Adapted from Miller, *Living in the Environment,* 7th ed., pp. 302–304.

b. the dirt that was made radioactive after the atomic bomb explosion

c. the negative effects on people and the environment of the Hiroshima–Nagasaki atomic bombings

d. the negative effects of an atomic explosion

3. The main idea of paragraph 3 concerns

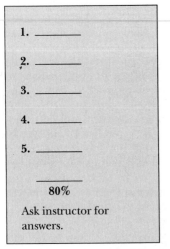

1. _____

2. _____

3. _____

4. _____

5. _____

_____
80%

Ask instructor for answers.

a. the severity of nuclear bombing

b. the severity of nuclear bombing today compared to nuclear bombings in World War II

c. how many weapons a nuclear submarine can carry

d. the number of countries that will have nuclear capability by the year 2000

4. The implied main idea of paragraph 4 concerns

a. the effects of a nuclear bomb

b. the negative effects of a nuclear explosion on people and the environment, if it were to occur today

c. the number of people who would starve because of a nuclear explosion

d. the drop in temperature due to a nuclear explosion

5. The main idea of paragraph 5 concerns:

a. crop yield and fish harvest

b. the reduction in crop yield and fish harvest after a nuclear explosion

c. the increase in skin cancer due to a nuclear explosion

d. the negative effects on the ozone layer if a nuclear explosion were to occur today

Exercise 4.5 Determining the Main Idea in a Second Longer Passage

To determine the main idea of a passage, you can apply the same rules that you used to determine the main idea of a paragraph. Read the following extended essay on the greenhouse effect, another important environmental issue caused by technology, and follow these steps to determine the main idea:

1. Read the introductory paragraph to determine the main idea of the entire passage.

2. See how the four paragraphs that follow (the body) give details to support the main idea. Locate a main-idea sentence for each of these paragraphs.

After you have taken these steps, answer the five questions that follow. You may look back. Place all answers in the answer box.

The Greenhouse Effect

(1) Of the sun's rays that reach earth, 70 percent are absorbed by the land, sea, and air; 30 percent are reflected back into the atmosphere.

When the earth's environment cools, the absorbed heat is released in the form of infrared rays, or heat. Some of the energy escapes into space, and some of it is absorbed by water vapor and carbon dioxide in the atmosphere. The carbon dioxide and water vapor then repeat the cycle, returning some of this energy into the atmosphere and giving some back to the earth. This returning to earth of heat originally absorbed by the carbon dioxide and water of the atmosphere is called the *greenhouse effect.* Because of the greenhouse effect, the earth's temperature has increased about 10 degrees centigrade, or 18 degrees Fahrenheit, from what it would be without water vapor and carbon dioxide in the atmosphere.

(2) This natural cycle is being altered by the burning of coal as a fuel. Coal burning increases the amount of carbon dioxide and water in the atmosphere. This increase then allows for more heat to be returned to the earth because of the greenhouse effect.

(3) What might happen if the greenhouse effect causes average temperatures to rise worldwide? Scientists speculate that an overall increase in temperature will cause rainfall patterns to shift and crop-growing patterns to change. For example, the wheat belt in the United States might shift upward to Canada, where the soil is not so rich. Ultimately, the greenhouse effect might be responsible for less food production.

(4) A second result of an increase in temperature would be melting of the polar ice caps. This melting would increase the water level in the oceans of the world. Scientists now speculate that the sea-level increase would be gradual, probably taking place over hundreds of years.

(5) Despite its potential to flood the land, the greenhouse effect seems to pose greater potential danger to the earth's food-producing capacity. If less food is produced in the next fifty years, the worldwide hunger problem might increase, because in the same fifty-year period the world's population is expected to double.*

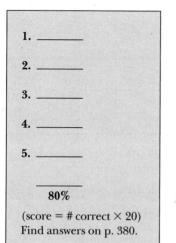

1. _____

2. _____

3. _____

4. _____

5. _____

80%

(score = # correct × 20)
Find answers on p. 380.

1. The main idea of paragraph 1 concerns

   a. how the sun reaches the earth
   b. how the earth cools
   c. how carbon dioxide is created
   d. how the greenhouse effect returns heat to the earth

2. The main idea of paragraph 2 concerns

   a. how coal burns
   b. the value of burning coal
   c. how coal burning increases the vapor and carbon dioxide level
   d. how coal burning decreases the vapor and carbon dioxide level

3. The main idea of paragraph 3 concerns

   a. the difficulty of producing food

---

*Adapted from Miller, *Living in the Environment*, 5th ed., pp. E20–24.

b. how the greenhouse effect might cause less food to be produced
c. where the wheat belt is in the United States
d. why wheat can be grown effectively in Canada

4. The main idea of paragraph 4 concerns

a. how ice caps are created
b. the greenhouse effect and its relationship to water level
c. how fast the polar ice caps are melting
d. how carbon dioxide affects polar ice caps

5. The main idea of paragraph 5 concerns

a. the greenhouse effect and food production
b. food production
c. world hunger
d. world hunger and the increase in population

Exercise 4.6
Writing Your Own
Paragraph from
Main Ideas

The excerpt on the greenhouse effect in Exercise 4.5 can easily be outlined in the following way:

I. Main Idea of the Passage (expressed in paragraph 1)

A.
B. Supporting details for the main idea of the passage (consisting
C. of the main ideas of paragraphs 2–5)
D.

If you are still unclear about what the main idea of each paragraph is, review the correct answers to questions 1–5 in Exercise 4.5.

Now use the following outline to state, in a phrase, the main idea of each of the five paragraphs in Exercise 4.5.

I. _____

A. _____

B. _____

C. _____

D. _____

_____
70%

Ask instructor for answers.

With this outline to guide you, answer the following essay question in a paragraph of five sentences (one main-idea sentence and four supporting sentences).

Essay question: In one paragraph, define the greenhouse effect and discuss its four possible effects on the environment.

*Exercise 4.7
Determining the
Main Ideas in a
Textbook Excerpt*

The following excerpt is from a textbook chapter on global warming. It adds more information to the previous excerpt you have read on the greenhouse effect. Read through it quickly to get a sense for the topic. Then go back and read it slowly.

When you finish reading, answer the following five questions. You may return to the excerpt in deciding on your answers. Two important terms are not defined in the excerpt: *developing country,* which refers to a country that has a fairly low level of industrialization and income per person, and CO_2, which is the chemical symbol of carbon dioxide.

Solutions: Dealing with the Threat of Global Warming

(1) **Should We Do More Research or Act Now?** There are three schools of thought concerning global warming. A *very small* group of scientists (many of them not experts in climate research and heavily funded by the oil and coal industries) contend that global warming is not a threat; some popular press commentators and writers even claim it is a hoax. Widespread reporting of this *no-problem* minority view (not regarded as plausible by most climate experts) in the media has clouded the issue, cooled public support for action, and slowed international climate negotiations.

(2) A second group of scientists and economists believe we should wait until we have more information about the global climate system, possible global warming, and its effects before we take any action. Proponents of this *waiting strategy* question whether we should spend hundreds of billions of dollars phasing out fossil fuels and replacing deforestation with reforestation (and in the process risk disrupting national and global economies) to help ward off something that might not happen. They call for more research before making such far-reaching decisions.

(3) A third group of scientists point out that greatly increased spending on research about the possibility and effects of global warming will not provide the certainty decision makers want because the global climate system is so incredibly complex. These scientists urge us to adopt a *precautionary strategy.* They believe that when dealing with risky and far-reaching environmental problems such as possible global warming, the safest course is to take informed action *before* there is overwhelming scientific knowledge to justify acting.

(4) Those favoring doing nothing or waiting before acting point out that there is a 50% chance that we may be *overestimating* the impact of rising greenhouse gases. However, those urging action now point out that there is also a 50% chance that we could be *underestimating* such effects.

(5) If global warming does occur as projected, it will take place gradually over many decades until it crosses thresholds and triggers obvious and serious effects. By then it will be too late to take corrective action. During the early stages of projected global warming it is easy for people to deny that anything serious is happening. Psychologist Robert Ornstein calls this denial the *boiled frog syndrome.* He describes it as like trying to alert a frog to danger as it sits in a pan of water very slowly being heated on the stove. If the frog could talk it would say, "I'm a little

warmer, but I'm doing fine." As the water gets hotter, we would warn the frog that it will die, but it might reply, "The temperature has been increasing for a long time, and I'm still alive."

(6) Eventually the frog dies because it has no evolutionary experience of the lethal effects of boiling water and thus cannot perceive its situation as dangerous. Like the frog, we also face a possible future without precedent, and our senses are unable to pick up warnings of impending danger.

(7) Suppose that the threat of global warming does not materialize. Should we take actions that will cost enormous amounts of money and create political turmoil based on a cloudy crystal ball? Some say that we should take the actions needed to slow global warming even if there were no threat, because of their important environmental and economic benefits. This so-called *no-regrets strategy* is an important part of the precautionary strategy. Others charge that environmentalists are exaggerating the threat of global warming in order to increase the urgency for reducing fossil-fuel use and deforestation.

(8) **How Can We Slow Possible Global Warming?** According to the 1994 IPCC report, stabilizing CO_2 levels at the current level of about 360 parts per million would require reducing current global CO_2 emissions by 66–83%—a highly unlikely and politically charged change. Instead of reductions, the International Energy Agency projects that CO_2 emissions will increase by nearly 50% between 1990 and 2010, with most of the increase coming from developing countries. According to climate models, even stabilizing CO_2 concentrations at 450 ppm requires cutting CO_2 emissions by more than half before the end of the next century.

(9) The quickest, cheapest, and most effective way to reduce emissions of CO_2 and other air pollutants over the next two to three decades is to use energy more efficiently.

(10) Some analysts call for increased use of nuclear power because it produces only about one-sixth as much CO_2 per unit of electricity as coal. Other analysts argue that the danger of large-scale releases of highly radioactive materials from nuclear power-plant accidents (and the very high cost of nuclear power) make it a much less desirable option than improving energy efficiency and relying more on renewable energy resources.

(11) Using natural gas could help make the 40- to 50-year transition to an age of energy efficiency and renewable energy. When burned, natural gas emits only half as much CO_2 per unit of energy as coal, and it emits far smaller amounts of most other air pollutants as well. Shifting from high-carbon fuels such as coal to low-carbon fuels such as natural gas could reduce CO_2 emissions by as much as 40%. However, without effective maintenance, more reliance on natural gas can increase inputs of methane (a potent greenhouse gas) from leaking tanks and pipelines—and thus increase global warming.

(12) One method for reducing CO_2 emissions would be to phase out government subsidies for fossil fuels over a decade and gradually phase in *carbon taxes* on fossil fuels (especially coal and gasoline) based on their emissions of CO_2 and other air pollutants. To be politically feasible, these consumption tax increases should be matched by declines

in taxes on income, labor, or capital. Ideally, such tax revenues would be used to improve the energy efficiency of dwellings and heating systems for the poor in developed countries and developing countries; to provide them with enough energy to offset higher fuel prices; and to subsidize the transition to improved energy efficiency and renewable energy resources. Economists argue that such a carbon tax is based on the *polluter pays* principle, which requires industries and consumers to pay directly for the full environmental costs of the fuels they use.

(13) Another approach is to agree to global and national limits on greenhouse gas emissions and allow industries and countries to sell and trade emission permits in the marketplace. Companies and nations exceeding their limits could reduce their emissions or buy emissions permits from other companies or countries that have reduced their emissions below their allowed limits. Some believe that this approach is more politically feasible than carbon taxes.

(14) Halting deforestation and switching to more sustainable agriculture would reduce CO_2 emissions and help preserve biodiversity. Slowing population growth is also crucial. If we cut per capita greenhouse gas emissions in half but world population doubles, we're back where we started. Some analysts argue that it is vital to global environmental security that developed countries transfer energy efficiency, renewable energy, pollution prevention, and waste reduction technologies to developing countries as soon as possible.

(15) It has also been suggested that we remove CO_2 from the exhaust gases of fossil-fuel-burning vehicles, furnaces, and industrial boilers. However, available methods can remove only about 30% of the CO_2, and using them would double the cost of electricity.

(16) Some call for a massive global reforestation program as a strategy for slowing global warming. However, to absorb the CO_2 we put into the atmosphere, each person in the world would need to plant and tend an average of 1,000 trees every year; the total planting would have to cover an area roughly equal to that of Australia. Moreover, once the planted trees grow to maturity their net uptake of CO_2 is greatly reduced, and when they die and decompose the CO_2 they removed from the atmosphere is returned by the respiration of decomposers.

(17) Studies suggest that a massive global reforestation program would offset only about three years of our current CO_2 emissions from burning fossil fuels. However, a global program for planting and tending trees would help restore deforested and degraded land and reduce soil erosion and loss of biodiversity.

(18) **Can Technofixes Save Us?** Some scientists have suggested various *technofixes* (technological solutions) for dealing with possible global warming. They include:

- Adding iron to the oceans to stimulate the growth of marine algae, which would remove more CO_2 through photosynthesis. Experiments done on small patches of ocean suggest that if this were done on a continuous basis by several hundred ships over an area of ocean the size of Asia, it might offset only about one-third of global CO_2 emissions, at an estimated cost of $10–110 billion per year.

- Unfurling gigantic foil-surfaced sun mirrors in space to reduce solar input. The mirrors would have to be replaced frequently at great cost because of collisions with space debris. They would also cast undesirable shadows (like eclipses) on parts of the earth's surface.

- Injecting sunlight-reflecting sulfate particulates into the stratosphere to mimic the cooling effects of giant volcanic eruptions. However, this would also increase harmful air pollution in the troposphere and would speed up destruction of ozone in the stratosphere.

(19) Many of these costly schemes might not work, and most will probably produce unpredictable short- and long-term harmful environmental effects. Moreover, once started, those that work could never be stopped without a renewed rise in CO_2 levels. Instead of spending huge sums of money on such schemes, many scientists believe it would be much more effective and cheaper to spend the money on improving energy efficiency and in shifting to renewable forms of energy that don't produce carbon dioxide.*

1. _____

2. _____

3. _____

4. _____

5. _____

1. The topic of this excerpt concerns:

   a. global warming
   b. research on global warming
   c. how carbon dioxide affects global warming
   d. ways to solve the global warming problem

2. The topic of paragraph 5 concerns:

   a. global warming
   b. ways that global warming affects animals
   c. the likely rate of global warming
   d. Robert Orenstein's contribution to global warming research

3. The main idea of paragraph 2 concerns:

   a. what those who follow the waiting strategy in global warming believe
   b. what a second group of scientists believes
   c. the danger of fossil fuels to global warming
   d. the research necessary to solve the global warming problem

4. The main idea of paragraph 10 treats:

   a. ways that nuclear power can improve global warming
   b. ways that nuclear power can improve global warming but pollute the environment
   c. how little carbon dioxide (CO_2) nuclear power produces
   d. how expensive nuclear power is

*Adapted from Miller, *Living in the Environment*, 10th ed., pp. 376–379.

5. The main idea of paragraph 16 concerns:

    a. a definition of reforestation
    b. the effect of each person planting 1,000 trees on global warming
    c. the positive results of reforestation on global warming
    d. the positive and negative results of reforestation on global warming

Now go back and reread the excerpt, concentrating on those paragraphs that are referred to in each question. Frame your answers in a phrase or sentence.

6. Reread paragraph 3, and explain what the precautionary strategy is. (1 point)

7. Reread paragraph 8, and list two of the difficulties in cutting down on the production of CO_2. (2 points)

8. Reread paragraph 19, and list two practical ways to reduce the emission of CO_2. (2 points)

70%

Ask instructor for answers.

Follow-up on Chapter 4

Now that you have studied this introduction and completed the exercises, it may be helpful to see how your reading of this topic has changed your ideas about the environment and improved your abilities to use main ideas. You may want to go back to the exercises and reread them just for their content, or for what they have to say about the environment, and you may want to review the introduction. Then answer the following questions either individually or in small groups.

On the Topic of Environmental Studies

1. How would you now define the terms *environment* and *environmental studies?*

2. In history, how have human beings contributed to the environmental problem? How have they helped solve some of the problems in the environment?

3. What one environmental problem that you read about in these exercises is of most concern to you? Why?

4. What other issues related to the environment do you now want to study further?

On Locating the Main Ideas

5. Are you now able to locate main ideas better? When is it still difficult for you to locate main ideas?

6. Can you locate main ideas easily in textbook material? When do you have difficulty locating main ideas in textbooks?

7. Are you able to write main ideas easily? Are you able to differentiate a topic from a main idea in your writing?

8. What areas about locating or writing main ideas do you still want to develop?

Internet Activity

In groups of four or five, use the Internet to research the following questions on the environmental issue of the ozone layer. When you have done your research, check back with your group to see what information each member has gathered.

1. What is the ozone layer?
2. How fast is it being depleted?
3. What can be done to help stop ozone depletion?
4. Which Internet sources provided information on the ozone layer?

CHAPTER 5

Locating Major
and Minor Details

In this chapter, you will learn about:

- Major details such as examples, steps, causes, and effects
- Minor details
- The signal words introducing major details and minor details

Now that you have practiced locating and writing main-idea sentences, you are ready to learn about detail sentences in reading, lecture, and discussion materials. You can also use them in your own writing. Details may be either major or minor.

Major Details

Major details are the A, B, C, and so on of the outline format I., A., B., C. They support the main idea, giving examples, steps, characteristics, causes, or effects. Major details often answer the who, what, where, when, why, which one(s), or what kind(s) of a sentence or passage. Also, remember that major details are usually found in the body of a paragraph, essay, lecture, or discussion.

Major Details That Give Examples. Main-idea sentences often express a point of view, as in the following: "America is experiencing a series of economic problems." In the major-detail sentences supporting this point of view, you would be looking for examples. The examples should answer the question "What kinds of economic problems?" And your answers would be sentences discussing unemployment, inflation, poverty, and so on.

Look at how a writer uses examples in the following paragraph:

ex Business is a study that involves how organizations produce and sell goods and services at a profit. In studying this field, one can analyze many organizations, both large and small. A business analyst can examine how a small organization like a family bakery is operating to make a profit. This same analyst can study how a huge bakery corporation makes its profit. In both studies, the analyst considers the same issues: production, sales, and profit.

Do you see how the business concerns of a small bakery and those of a large bakery corporation become the examples that support the main idea—that business is the study of how organizations produce and sell at a profit?

When you come across the names of persons, places, and things, you probably have found details. The details become the support that you will need when defending a point of view. Start using the abbreviation *ex* in the margins to remind yourself that you are reading or listening to examples. Did you notice that this abbreviation was used in the margin of the previous paragraph to signal the two examples?

Major Details That Give Steps.   Details are sometimes laid out in sequence. For example, your instructor may be discussing the steps involved in reading a graph in an economics textbook, or you may be reading about the steps the federal government took to close down a savings and loan that was going bankrupt. The main-idea sentence that comes before the steps usually alerts you to the number of steps involved. Steps are details that often answer the question "Which ones?"

Consider this main-idea sentence: "There are three steps to remember in reading a graph in business." The details that follow this sentence should include these three steps. Be alert to the following signal words when you read or listen for steps: *first, second, third, and so on, last,* and *finally.*

Look at how the details in the following excerpt provide steps on how to read a graph in business:

steps   There are four basic steps to follow in reading a business graph. *First,* look to see what the horizontal axis represents. *Second,* see what the vertical axis measures. *Third,* study how these two variables relate to each other. *Finally,* study what the graph shows about this relationship.

In this paragraph, the main-idea sentence introduces the number of steps necessary in reading a graph in business. This sentence is general but is followed by specific directions for reading a graph. Did you notice the signal words *first, second, third,* and *finally,* which led you through the four steps? Like examples, steps provide specific information. Unlike examples, steps are more closely interrelated. A writer cannot present step two before step one. A writer presenting examples is usually not concerned with correctly sequencing them. You will learn more about steps as details in Chapter 6, "Identifying Organizational Patterns."

Finally, did you note how the marginal note *steps* in the previous paragraph reminds you of the steps in the excerpt? Marginal notes such as *steps* and *ex* help direct your reading or listening.

Major Details That Present Characteristics.   Some major details are neither examples nor steps. Rather they are descriptive. Major details of characteristics frequently include adjectives or adverbs. Such details may be used to draw a character sketch, be the key points in a film or book review, or be used to define a word. Look at how the following main-idea sentences require characteristics to support their points of view: "Hershey Foods Corporation's recycling activities are interesting ones to study," or "Lee Iacocca is known as an innovative American businessman." Saying that Hershey Foods recycles many of its waste products would not describe the characteristics of Hershey's recycling activities, nor would mentioning that Lee Iacocca brought Chrysler out of its economic hard times necessarily describe the kind of businessman he is. Each of these main-idea statements needs details expressing qualities or feelings that answer the "why" of the main-idea statement.

Look at how the following paragraph on the kind of study business is effectively uses characteristics:

reasons why   Business is a peculiar study in several ways. It is not a pure science like physics, because it studies how people behave in business matters. Yet some of business work is *mathematical* and *formulaic* in that it studies business trends and predicts profits and losses. On the one hand, business is *descriptive* of how people act in business matters; on the other, it is *prescriptive*, in that it tries to show how businesses will respond in certain economic situations.

In this paragraph, do you see that the author does not refer to specific business studies or works? This passage, rather, emphasizes the qualities that make business a unique study. See how the author uses the adjectives *mathematical, formulaic, descriptive,* and *prescriptive* to describe what business is. By placing the comment *reasons why* in the margin, you remind yourself that you are emphasizing the characteristics of business as a discipline.

Major Details That Present Causes and Effects.   A great number of major-detail sentences are closely related to the main-idea sentence. They do not give examples or qualities to support the main idea, nor do they list steps that follow from the main-idea sentence. These sentences of cause or effect are either the reasons for or causes of what the main idea suggests, or they are the results or effects of what the main idea suggests. These sentences usually answer the "what" questions suggested in the main-idea sentence. Words that signal causes include *cause, reason, factor, source,* and *influence*; those suggesting effect are *effect, consequence, result,* and *outcome*.

Read the following paragraph and note how all major-detail sentences provide some suggested causes of poverty:

causes   Some business analysts believe that bankruptcy is *caused* more by economic legislation than by the individual. They contend that a major *source* of bankruptcy is federal and state legislation that influences how a company will survive. They often show that some economic legislation makes it difficult for small companies to make a profit. They contend that a major *reason* for bankruptcy is little or no federal or state contact with the business community concerning the laws it passes.

Do you see how the words *caused, source,* and *reason* signal causes? Do you note as well that these major-detail sentences provide specific information to support the main-idea's point of view that business legislation, not the individual, is the cause of bankruptcy? Finally, note how the word *causes* in the margin reminds you of the kind of information found in this paragraph.

Now look at this paragraph, which deals with the effects of bankruptcy:

effects   Bankruptcy has numerous negative *results* for the individual and society. An individual who files for bankruptcy will have a poor credit rating for several years. *Consequently,* she cannot engage in those business transactions involving bank loans. This in turn *results* in less potential profit for the individual and less taxable income for society. The *outcome* is often a much less confident and secure business person who then shares this insecurity with the larger business community.

Do you see how the signal words, *results, consequently,* and *outcome* suggest a paragraph of effect? Again, note how in the major-detail sentences, you are given specific information concerning the results of bankruptcy. And the word *effects* in the margin becomes your signal that this paragraph is addressing bankruptcy's results.

Major-detail sentences of cause and effect often provide important information. Like steps and examples, they are specific; but unlike examples, causes and effects require you to see relationships in time—how one occurrence may lead to another. You will learn much more about how cause-and-effect details are used in lectures and textbooks in Chapter 6, "Identifying Organizational Patterns."

Remember that in your lecture, discussion, and reading notes, you should mark major details as examples, steps, characteristics, causes, or effects, as you have done in the previous paragraphs used as illustrations. Actively identifying details gives direction to your reading or listening and to organizing and connecting information. By identifying details, you will also be able to review this study material for exams.

Signal Words in Major-Detail Sentences.   A number of words and phrases can be used to introduce any type of major detail. Once you become familiar with these words, you will have another way of locating major details in reading materials or lectures.

for example	furthermore	again	last
for instance	moreover	another	of course
in addition	besides	specifically	
also	next	finally	

You should also begin using these words and phrases when you write essays. By using these signal words, you alert your reader to details that you consider important.

You may now want to complete Exercise 5.2 on page 84.

Minor Details

By now, you should be able to recognize the four types of major details. So it should be easier for you to locate minor details. You will find minor-detail sentences right after major-detail sentences; minor details provide you with more information about the major detail. When you come upon a minor detail, ask yourself whether you want to include it in your notes. Often, all you need to learn are the main ideas and the major details.

However, you will need to use minor details when you write paragraphs or essays. Adding a minor detail on an essay exam, for example, shows your instructor that you are well prepared. Often a minor-detail sentence picks up a word or phrase that was used in the preceding major-detail sentence.

Look at the following paragraph on inflation, and note that the last sentence further explains the preceding sentences. It is therefore a minor-detail sentence.

> Inflation is defined as a general rise in prices for a long period of time, usually for at least a year. Inflation generally means that what you buy costs more each month, yet your salary does not seem to increase to pay for these higher prices. Therefore, your money does not go as far. *That is, you cannot buy as many items or at the same quality as you did in the previous year.*

Do you see how this last sentence further explains how inflation influences your purchasing power?

You can see more clearly what minor-detail sentences are by studying an outline of the previous paragraph. You will note that the minor detail is the material farthest to the right in the following outline—point 1 under B.

I. Inflation—A General Rise in Prices

   A. Items cost more each month
   B. Money does not stretch as far as it once did

      1. You buy fewer items, or they are not as good quality as they once were

Remember that it is the I (main idea) and the A and B (major details) that you often need to write as lecture or discussion notes and remember on exams. You may use the 1 (minor detail) more effectively in your essays.

Signal Words for Minor Details.   The following words and phrases are frequently used to introduce minor-detail sentences. You should use these words when you introduce minor details in your essays, and you should look for these words to introduce minor details in lectures, discussions, and textbooks.

a minor point to be made	another way of saying
incidentally	restated
that is to say	namely
in other words	as an aside
of less importance	related to this issue
this is further clarified by	a corollary to this issue
as further clarification	subordinate to this issue

You may now want to complete Exercises 5.1 and 5.3 on pages 81 and 86.

Summary

Major details provide the information necessary to support main ideas. Major details may be examples, steps, characteristics, causes, or effects. They answer the questions "who," "what," "where," "when," "why," "which one(s)," or "what kind(s)." When you can identify the types of major details that are in your reading or listening, you tend to understand the material better. A minor-detail sentence further explains a major-detail sentence that comes before it. Minor details are not often necessary in your reading, lecture, and discussion notes, but you should use them in essays.

The following summary box should help you see how main ideas, major details, and minor details interrelate.

Summary Box   *Main Ideas, Major Details, and Minor Details*

What are they?	Why do you use them?
Main ideas (1): general statements in a paragraph or longer passage	To read and listen more effectively for major and minor details
Major details (A, B, C): support for the main ideas, presented as examples, steps, characteristics, causes, or effects.	To understand the main idea better. To see whether the main idea is based on sound evidence.
Minor details (1, 2, 3): further support for the major-detail sentence that comes before it.	To further explain a major detail. Used in essays, but often not necessary in reading, lecture, or discussion notes.

Skills Practice Topic: Business

All the exercises in this chapter deal with the issue of business, a topic you may study in college and one you face every day as you make purchases.

Before you begin these exercises, answer the following questions either individually or in small groups to get some sense of what you already know about business matters. Remember that recalling what you know is effective preparation for learning new material:

1. What do you think is studied in an introductory college business course?
2. What are the most common problems facing small and large businesses today?
3. What do you think makes a successful small business?
4. What do you think makes a successful large business or corporation?

Exercise 5.1
Locating Major
Details

Under each of the following ten main-idea sentences are five sentences, three of which support the main-idea sentence. The other two sentences are either minor details or main-idea sentences that would themselves introduce a new topic. Place the letters of the three major-detail sentences in the answer box.

All the sentences in these exercises address the issue of the unincorporated American business, an important introductory concept for students studying business. *Unincorporated* simply means a business that is not legally separate from its owners.

The Unincorporated American Business

1. *Main-idea sentence:* A business owned by one person is called a *sole proprietorship.*

   a. This is the oldest form of business.
   b. It is also the most common type of business, with 73 percent of all businesses in the United States being sole proprietorships.
   c. That is, almost three out of four businesses in the United States are sole proprietorships.
   d. There are many advantages to the sole proprietorship business.
   e. Yet sole proprietorships contribute only 6 percent of the total business revenues in the United States.

2. *Main-idea sentence:* There are five basic categories in which sole proprietorships operate.

   a. The largest is the service category, or a business that serves others.
   b. The second largest category includes wholesale and retail trade.

    c. An example of a small service business would be a neighborhood barbershop.

    d. The last three categories, in order of size, and manufacturing, construction, and insurance.

    e. Sole proprietorships are relatively inexpensive to create.

3. *Main-idea sentence:* Sole proprietorships are advantageous because they are easy to operate.

    a. Once a businessperson has decided on what product to sell or what service to perform, she is ready to start.

    b. There are also very few legal restrictions attached to sole proprietorships.

    c. Finally, as sole owner, the sole proprietor can claim all the profits.

    d. That is, the better the business, the more money the sole proprietor makes.

    e. Yet there are some disadvantages to being a sole proprietor.

4. *Main-idea sentence:* The major disadvantage to being a sole proprietor is that she is liable for anything that may go wrong in the business.

    a. If the business goes into debt, for instance, the sole proprietor must pay what she owes from her own personal savings.

    b. One restaurant owner's business did poorly, and the bank repossessed her car.

    c. Further, the sole proprietor may have limited funds to expand her business.

    d. A sole proprietorship is different from a partnership.

    e. The sole proprietorship may also have limited business and management skills needed to steer her business in the right direction.

5. *Main-idea sentence:* A partnership is another major form of small business where two or more people co-own a business for profit.

    a. In the best of circumstances, each partner brings a different ability to the business.

    b. There are several advantages to a partnership business.

    c. In a partnership, there is often more money to draw from than in a sole proprietorship.

    d. A partnership allows for the members to discuss a business decision before making it.

    e. Incidentally, making the right decision can make or break a small business.

6. *Main-idea sentence:* As with any form of business, there are disadvantages to a partnership form of small business.

    a. As with a sole proprietorship, each partner is liable for the debts the business may accrue.

    b. A partnership may dissolve if one of its members chooses to back out.

c. Moreover, there is often the possibility that partners may begin as friends and then find that they are continually disagreeing.

d. The two types of partnerships are the *general* and the *limited*.

e. A joint venture is a special type of partnership.

7. *Main-idea sentence:* A joint venture is a special type of partnership where two or more people agree to complete a specific project.

   a. Once this project is completed, the joint venture dissolves.

   b. For a general partnership to be dissolved, each partner must agree.

   c. A limited partnership has a limited start-up cost.

   d. During the joint venture, the partners are responsible for all the debts the venture may accrue, as with a sole proprietorship.

   e. One finds joint ventures often in the real estate business.

8. *Main-idea sentence:* Joint ventures are popular in the real estate business for three important reasons.

   a. First, each person contributes to the money needed to purchase a property.

   b. Second, these members of the joint venture can buy a large piece of property, one they could probably not afford by themselves.

   c. Joint ventures are exciting for anyone who wants to enter the business field quickly.

   d. Finally, these members of the joint venture can develop, divide, or resell this large piece of property.

   e. Any profit derived from a small business is considered income, according to the Internal Revenue Service.

9. *Main-idea sentence:* It is one thing to form a partnership, another to make this partnership successful.

   a. Cooperation is the key to any successful business partnership.

   b. By cooperation, I mean identifying areas of agreement over how the business should be run.

   c. Another way to help a partnership be successful is to establish clear goals for the business.

   d. Psychologists have also shown that partners who work well together have a positive attitude toward the success of their partnership.

   e. That is, each partner needs to focus on the strengths of the other members of the partnership.

10. *Main-idea sentence:* Not all joint ventures involve individuals with limited capital.

    a. Completing short-term projects is the main function of joint ventures.

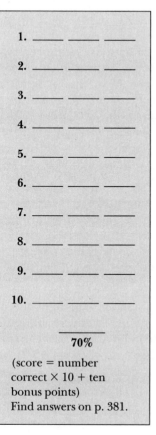

1. ___ ___ ___
2. ___ ___ ___
3. ___ ___ ___
4. ___ ___ ___
5. ___ ___ ___
6. ___ ___ ___
7. ___ ___ ___
8. ___ ___ ___
9. ___ ___ ___
10. ___ ___ ___

_____
70%

(score = number correct × 10 + ten bonus points)
Find answers on p. 381.

    b. The tissue manufacturer Kimberly-Clark formed a joint venture with a large German tissue manufacturer.

    c. Hewlett-Packard and a large Swedish company worked on a joint venture concerning a computer network program.

    d. Finally, the beer company Anheuser-Busch teamed up with Kirin, a Japanese beer company, to boost their sales.

    e. For this venture to get off the ground, Anheuser-Busch provided $80 million.*

Exercise 5.2
Identifying Types of
Major Details

The following paragraphs present different kinds of details to support the main-idea sentences. Your job is to read each paragraph and identify the kind of detail that is used. Write in the answer box *EX* if the details are examples, *ST* if the details are steps, *CH* if the details are characteristics, *CS* if the details are causes, and *EF* if the details are effects. The signal words used in some of the paragraphs should help you recognize the kinds of details that are used.

All of the paragraphs deal with the business concept of a corporation, which is different from the unincorporated businesses you studied in the previous exercise.

The Business Corporation

1. A *corporation* is defined as a legal form of a business authorized by a government and considered separate from its owners. One can characterize a corporation in the following ways. Most important, it is a separate entity not in partnership with its owners, who are called *shareholders* or *stockholders*. It is humanlike in that it can be sued or can sue as an independent citizen. In a sense, it is stronger than its owners because it does not cease to exist when its owners have passed away.

2. How does one form a corporation? The process first involves applying to the appropriate state official for a form titled a Certificate of Incorporation. Once this certificate has been approved by the state, the corporation has an official charter that describes the corporation's type of business and its purpose. Any change in its purpose or business dealings requires the members of the corporation to file a separate form, called a *charter amendment*, with the state.

3. There are three common types of corporations. The first type of corporation, called a *domestic* corporation, does business within the state that approved its application. A second type is a *foreign* corporation, which does business in the other forty-nine states of the

---

*Adapted from Joseph T. Straub and Raymond F. Attner, *Introduction to Business*, 5th ed. (Belmont, Calif.: Wadsworth, 1994), pp. 71–87.

United States. Finally, a corporation doing business outside of the United States is known as an *alien* corporation.

4. How would one describe a *closed* corporation, that is, one that does not sell its stock to the general public? It is more secretive because it can conceal information about its finances. A closed corporation is less burdened with *red tape,* or state papers that must be completed by an open or public corporation. Also, the managers of a closed corporation may be more focused on the well-being of their company because they are not required to make formal reports and hold regular meetings with their stockholders.

5. Some closed corporations decide to go public—become *open* corporations. What are some of the possible results? First, if the economy is good, the stock sold to new shareholders could bring a quick increase in revenues to the corporation. But if the economy is depressed, the stock may yield much less income than the original owners had anticipated. And as an open corporation, the once-closed corporation may also be forced to reveal many of its trade secrets.

6. What are some of the events scheduled on the yearly calendar for a public corporation? First, management must report to its stockholders in an annual or semiannual report, which discloses the financial condition of the corporation. Afterwards, the public corporation is required to schedule an annual stockholders' meeting whose date each year must be in the corporation's by-laws. Here, the stockholders can question any of the decisions made by the company during that fiscal year.

7. What influences corporations to join with others, as many do each year in the United States and abroad? Some corporations merge with other corporations to increase their profits. Still others point to a need for greater efficiency as their major reason for merging. Finally, most corporations that merge contend that their desire to be more competitive is their primary motivation.

8. A corporate merger occurs when two or more companies become a single company. Major mergers have occurred several times in American history, and they often involve billions of dollars. Powerful companies like United States Steel, DuPont, and Standard Oil are examples of mergers that occurred at the turn of this century. Recently, a part of the telecommunications giant ITT merged with a French corporation for $3.6 billion. In this same year (1992), 2,578 mergers were announced.

9. How would one describe a nonprofit corporation? They are often concerned with educational, religious, charitable, or cultural issues. They cannot make a profit, as their name suggests, but can have a cash surplus, which must be used to improve the corpora-

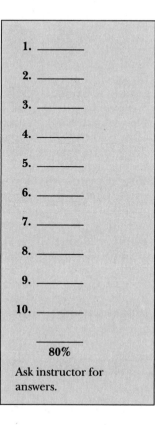

1. _____

2. _____

3. _____

4. _____

5. _____

6. _____

7. _____

8. _____

9. _____

10. _____

_____
80%

Ask instructor for answers.

tion in some way, such as its facilities, services, or personnel. Some of the most successful nonprofit corporations are truly philanthropic, helping those people who cannot help themselves or be helped by government assistance.

10. What are some of the most widely known nonprofit corporations in the United States today? The single largest type of nonprofit organization in the country is private colleges and universities, whose profits must be reinvested in some aspect of the institution. The American Cancer Society, one of the largest cancer research institutions, is also nonprofit. Even the American Automobile Association is a nonprofit organization.*

Exercise 5.3
Identifying Main
Ideas, Major Details,
and Minor Details

The following paragraphs contain main-idea sentences, major-detail sentences, and minor-detail sentences. Read each paragraph carefully. Then, next to the appropriate number in the answer box, write *MN* for main-idea sentence, *MA* for major-detail sentence, and *MI* for minor-detail sentence. Look for transition words that signal the kind of sentence each one is.

The ten paragraphs define the key business terms involving payments. You will learn how concepts like rent, interest, wages, and profit are related.

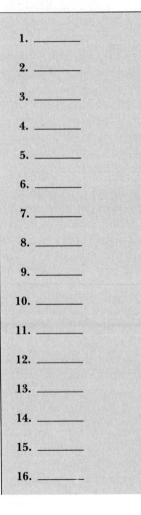

1. _____
2. _____
3. _____
4. _____
5. _____
6. _____
7. _____
8. _____
9. _____
10. _____
11. _____
12. _____
13. _____
14. _____
15. _____
16. _____

Payments and Related Issues

(1) Payments are made to owners of property or business for a variety of reasons. (2) Landowners receive rent. (3) This rent is often paid monthly but may be paid weekly. (4) Owners of businesses receive payments in the form of interest on their investments.

(5) Rent is defined in business as the money one pays for the use of land. (6) Rent is determined by how profitable the land is to the owner and how much the renter is willing to pay. (7) Clearly, owners want to make a profit on their property. (8) Equally clearly, renters want the rent to be less than what the property earns or what they make as wages.

(9) In a business sense, wages are similar to rent. (10) In this case, employers buy the labor of their employees. (11) Employers want to know that their employees are making a profit for the business. (12) That is to say, owners want what the workers do for the company to bring in more money than the cost of their salaries.

(13) But wages do not always work out so neatly. (14) Some people earn more than they are really worth, and others earn less. (15) Some people criticize movie stars' and athletes' high salaries, arguing that they would gladly work for less if others in their field earned less as well. (16) A corollary to this issue is that some athletes earn several million dollars a year.

(17) Some people are blocked from advancing to another job because of racial discrimination. (18) Others are kept in the same unsatis-

*Adapted from Straub and Attner, *Introduction to Business*, pp. 92–115.

17. _____

18. _____

19. _____

20. _____

21. _____

22. _____

23. _____

24. _____

25. _____

26. _____

27. _____

28. _____

29. _____

30. _____

31. _____

32. _____

33. _____

34. _____

35. _____

36. _____

37. _____

38. _____

39. _____

40. _____

75%

(score = # correct × 2.5)
Find answers on p. 381.

fying position because of their age. (19) Still others do not have the extra money to be trained in a field they are particularly interested in pursuing. (20) All of these job factors are known in economics as *barriers to entry.*

(21) A term related to wages is *capital.* (22) Capital includes products such as tools, equipment, and buildings. (23) Tools and equipment, incidentally, include items used by workers in their particular jobs. (24) A word processor would thus be part of the equipment used by a secretary.

(25) What constitutes the capital of fishermen in a primitive tribe? (26) The nets used to catch the fish would, of course, be part of their capital. (27) The value of a fishnet in business terms is how much profit it can create. (28) That is to say, if a fishnet can allow the fisherman to catch more fish than before, then it is capital that provides for profit.

(29) Profit is different for an independent businessperson than it is for a wage earner. (30) If your concession stand can make you $500 a week, but you can earn $510 a week working for a larger fast-food business, then your stand is not making you a profit. (31) To make a profit in your own business, you must be able to earn more than what you would earn as a wage earner. (32) Analysts believe that independent businesspeople should earn more than wage earners because they are taking greater risks.

(33) How much profit is considered good enough for an independent businessperson? (34) There is no fixed percentage. (35) That is, there is no number that will tell a businessperson that the business is profitable. (36) Psychological factors are involved, such as how much you value working for yourself.

(37) Clearly, rent, wages, profit, and capital are closely related. (38) When people consider the profit of a particular investment, they must factor in issues like rent and wages. (39) They must also determine how much capital they must purchase initially and must replace in time. (40) As an aside, note that it is often the initial cost of capital investments that discourages businesspeople from going into a particular venture.*

*Adapted from Philip C. Starr, *Economics: Principles in Action,* 5th ed. (Belmont, Calif.: Wadsworth, 1988), pp. 22–24.

Exercise 5.4
Writing Effective
Topic Sentences

In composition textbooks, main-idea sentences are often called topic sentences. *Topic sentences* are general statements usually found at the beginning of a paragraph. Like main-idea statements, topic sentences direct the reader to what the paragraph will say.

Effective topic sentences are neither too specific nor too general. They should steer the reader to the details of support and not become details of support themselves.

Look at the following ineffective topic sentences and their revisions:

1. A sole proprietorship is a business. (too general)
   A sole proprietorship is a business owned by one person. (acceptable)

Note that the first sentence does not mention the kind of business a sole proprietorship is. Effective topic sentences clearly identify the "what" of an issue.

2. Being a business partner may be disadvantageous. (too general)
   Being a business partner may be disadvantageous because one or more of the partners may not agree on important issues. (acceptable)

Note how the revised sentence introduces a reason why a partnership may not succeed. In this case, the revised sentence clarifies the "why" of the general topic sentence.

3. The business partners were taught to take time out when they began to argue. (too specific)
   The psychologist provided the partners with a helpful time-out strategy they could use to help resolve their differences. (acceptable)

Do you see that the example of the partners taking time out when they argue would be better used as a supporting detail after the topic sentence introducing the psychologist's strategy?

Your task is to determine whether the following ten topic sentences are too general or too specific. Write in the answer box "general" or "specific." Then revise the topic sentences, making them more effective. These sentences have been taken from the material you have studied in Exercises 5.1–5.3. Review these exercises before or while you complete this assignment to gather information for your responses. You may choose to work in groups of four or five to complete this exercise.

1. Three out of four businesses in the United States are sole proprietorships.

   Revision: _____

2. A joint venture is a type of partnership.

   Revision: _____

3. A corporation does not cease to exist when its owners have passed away.

Revision: _____

4. One type of corporation is a closed corporation.

Revision: _____

5. Public corporations must schedule certain events.

Revision: _____

6. In 1992, a part of ITT merged with a French corporation for $3.6 billion.

Revision: _____

7. Another type of organization is a nonprofit corporation.

Revision: _____

8. A word processor is an example of equipment a secretary uses.

Revision: _____

9. In business, rent is defined in a certain way.

Revision: _____

10. Profit is another important business term.

Revision: _____

1. _____

2. _____

3. _____

4. _____

5. _____

6. _____

7. _____

8. _____

9. _____

10. _____

_____
80%

Ask instructor for answers.

Exercise 5.5
Locating Major and
Minor Details in a
Longer Passage

In this exercise, you will be reading a longer passage that briefly traces the history of American business. It should help you understand how large and small American businesses have changed over the centuries.

Your job is to read for the main idea, major details, and minor details. After you have read the passage, answer the ten questions. You may return to the passage as you answer the questions. Place the answers to the first five questions in the answer box.

A Short History of American Business

(1) American business has changed drastically over the past 200 years. Much of this change has come about because of the technology,

wealth, and power that large American corporations have amassed over these years.

(2) Before 1800, American business was largely structured upon the production and sales of agriculture. American farmers and businessmen did much of their business with England. The Americans often exported precious metals and agricultural products to England in exchange for finished goods like furniture and machines. Most of American industry was based on the cottage system, where goods were made at home.

(3) The Industrial Revolution, which began around 1750, changed the way Americans produced their goods. Large machines were now used, and workers moved from their homes to factories to work. These workers made products in great quantities, a working system known as mass production. Moreover, the reaper on the farms in the Midwest allowed for more grain to be planted and harvested, while the telegraph and the railroad allowed products to be sold and transported more quickly than before.

(4) Between 1850 and 1930, the United States became a modern industrial giant. All types of production were now available within American boundaries, so the United States did not need to rely on Europe to produce its machinery. That is, the United States became more independent industrially. Also, American money was in greater supply because of better banking systems and the development of a national treasury.

(5) Since the end of World War II, the United States has become the leading industrial power in the world. American industry has many strengths. First, it has a sophisticated technology, which allows the United States to produce advanced technical products. It is also a wealthy country so it can produce these products in large quantities and frequently conduct ongoing research to develop new products and improve old ones. Finally, the United States has managerial talent so that its administrators can oversee what is produced and provide for a more efficient business operation.

(6) What recent business developments have suggested to analysts in the United States is that to stay successful, American business must be very sensitive to changes in the market and must be prepared to change quickly to respond to the market's demands. When a business does not respond rapidly to change, it may very soon go out of business. Three American industries that are vitally connected to change are telecommunications, transportation, and computers. That is, in each of these fields, the technology is changing at such a staggering rate that sophisticated technology and accurate marketing research are essential.*

1. The topic of this passage is

   a. change in American history
   b. the power of technology in America

---

*Adapted from Straub and Attner, *Introduction to Business*, pp. 20–22.

c. the historical role of technology, wealth, and power in American business practices

d. the power of American corporations in the past century

2. The main idea of paragraph 2 concerns

a. the agricultural emphasis of American business before 1800

b. agriculture and American business

c. how Americans exported precious metals to England before 1800

d. how Americans imported machinery from England before 1800

3. Which is *not* a major detail in paragraph 3?

a. Large machines replaced small ones during the Industrial Revolution.

b. The Industrial Revolution changed the ways Americans produced their goods.

c. Mass production became a popular form of labor during the Industrial Revolution.

d. The reaper revolutionized the way grain was harvested.

4. A minor detail presented in paragraph 4 is

a. The United States became an industrial giant between 1850 and 1930.

b. American money was in greater supply between 1850 and 1930 than in previous years.

c. Americans were able to construct their own machinery between 1850 and 1930.

d. The United States developed industrial independence between 1850 and 1930.

5. The first sentence in paragraph 5 is a

a. major-detail sentence

b. minor-detail sentence

c. main-idea sentence

d. topic for the entire excerpt

6. List one major detail in paragraph 2. _____

_____

7. What is the main idea of paragraph 3? _____

_____

8. List one major detail in paragraph 3. _____

_____

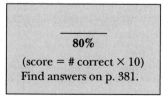

1. _____

2. _____

3. _____

4. _____

5. _____

_____
80%
(score = # correct × 10)
Find answers on p. 381.

9. What is the main idea of paragraph 6? _____

_____

10. What type of detail is presented in the last sentence of paragraph 6? What is the signal word or phrase that suggests the kind of detail

it is? _____

_____

Exercise 5.6
Locating Major and
Minor Details in a
Second Longer
Passage

In this exercise, you will be reading a longer passage that explains the three major economic systems in our world. It should help explain further how economic terms like *capital, wages,* and *profit* are used in studying a country's economic system.

Your job is to read for main ideas, major details, and minor details. After you have read the passage, answer the ten questions. If necessary, you may return to the passage while you answer the questions. Write your answers to the first five questions in the answer box.

Socialism, Communism, and Capitalism

(1) Today the world seems to be divided into three types of economies: socialism, communism, and capitalism. Communism and socialism seem to be more closely related to each other than they are to capitalism. But careful study reveals that even socialism and communism have important differences.

(2) What are the major features of socialism? In socialism, the government plays an important role, controlling all of the major industries. There are many different kinds of socialism. For example, in France and Italy the government controls many of the major industries. In the People's Republic of China, the government owns and operates much of the country's industry.

(3) One must keep in mind that socialism is not dictatorship. That is, in most socialist countries the people can still vote in free elections. In many socialist countries, the government is trying to control some or many industries in order to provide more jobs for its people and prevent serious economic declines.

(4) Communism can be seen as an extreme form of socialism. In theory, communists believe that the people, not the government, run the country. All of its people work together and take from the country only what they need. Theoretically, no one would want to earn a huge salary. No country has as yet reached this communist ideal. Countries like the People's Republic of China, which is seen by others as a communist country, exert a tremendous amount of government control over their people.

(5) Like communism, capitalism is also an economic system in theory only. In a capitalistic society, people, not government, own property. Also, people are free to choose their own occupation and earn the

amount of money they want. That is, capitalism emphasizes self-interest. Competition is encouraged, not discouraged as it would be in communism.

(6) No capitalistic country follows these ideals to the letter. In capitalistic countries like the United States, the government does control some industries, like transportation and utilities, and wholesale competition is sometimes discouraged if people or industries are treating other people unfairly. Some economists have called this more realistic type of capitalism *mixed capitalism.**

1. The topic of the passage is

    a. a definition of socialism
    b. a description of communism
    c. a definition of capitalism
    d. all of these

2. The main idea of paragraph 2 concerns

    a. socialism in France and Italy
    b. how socialism as an economic system differs from country to country
    c. reasons why the People's Republic of China controls much of its industry
    d. how socialism differs from communism

3. A major detail presented in paragraph 3 is

    a. most citizens in socialist countries can vote
    b. socialism is not dictatorship
    c. socialism provides fewer jobs to its people than dictatorships do
    d. there are never economic declines in socialist countries

4. The major details in paragraph 4 include all *but*

    a. communists believe that the people run the country
    b. the citizens from a communist country take only what they need
    c. in theory, there would be no rich people in a communist country
    d. the People's Republic of China comes closest to being a true communist state

5. The last sentence in paragraph 5 is a

    a. major-detail sentence
    b. minor-detail sentence
    c. main-idea sentence
    d. topic sentence

6. What is the main idea of paragraph 3? _____

_____

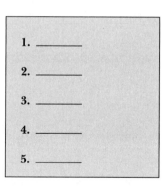

1. _____
2. _____
3. _____
4. _____
5. _____

*Adapted from Starr, *Economics*, pp. 29–30.

7. What is the main idea of paragraph 4? _____

_____

8. List one major detail from paragraph 5. _____

_____

9. What is the main idea of paragraph 6? _____

_____

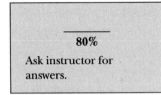

80%

Ask instructor for answers.

10. List a major detail from paragraph 6. _____

_____

Exercise 5.7
Writing Your Own
Paragraph from
Main Ideas, Major
Details, and Minor
Details

Now go back to the passage on economic systems in Exercise 5.6 and locate its main idea (found in paragraph 1); the four major details (found in paragraphs 2, 4, 5, and 6); and the minor detail (found in paragraph 3). Jot down this information in the following outline:

I. _____

    A. _____

       1. _____

    B. _____

    C. _____

    D. _____

From this outline, answer the following essay question. Use only the outline to answer this question.

Essay question: Identify the three major economic systems in the world today, and briefly describe each.

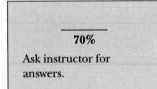

70%

Ask instructor for answers.

Exercise 5.8
Determining Main
Ideas and Major
Details in a Text
Excerpt

The following is an excerpt from a textbook chapter on the small business. It adds more information to the first exercise on the unincorporated business, focusing on ways that small businesses can be financed. Read through this excerpt quickly to get a sense of the topic. Then go back and read it slowly.

When you finish rereading, answer the following five questions. You may return to the excerpt in deciding on your answers. Place the answers to the first five questions in the answer box.

Sources of Financing

(1) In Chapters 3 and 4 we introduced some fundamental points on the financing of sole proprietorships, partnerships, and corporations, and in Chapter 16 we will discuss the topic of finance at length. For now, however, it is necessary to explore specific sources of financing for small businesses.

Personal Savings

(2) Personal savings is the source of financing used most often. Many observers advise small business owners to avoid excessive borrowing. Firms that start off under the heavy weight of creditors' claims may take years to struggle out of debt, while their owners have to put up with the nervous questions and suggestions of the creditors. Still, under the right circumstances, a firm can profit impressively using the leverage of borrowed money. Thus the question of how much debt a firm should carry in relation to the owner's investment has no simple answer.

Credit from Suppliers

(3) Businesspeople, especially retailers, buy inventory on trade credit or open-book accounts with suppliers. Under this arrangement, which will be discussed in Chapter 16, payment is not due for a credit period such as thirty, sixty, or ninety days, giving the buyer time to sell the goods before the bill is due.

(4) A credit pyramid of sorts may arise within at least one of the distribution chains (discussed in Chapter 14). Assume that a manufacturer gives a wholesaler ninety days' credit and the wholesaler in turn decides to give its retail customers a sixty-day credit period. Under that relationship, the retailer could conceivably sell the goods to final consumers and pay the wholesaler, and that party could in turn pay the manufacturer so that each bill is paid within its respective credit period.

Manufacturer Financing of Equipment

(5) Manufacturers (and sometimes distributors) of equipment and fixtures may be willing to finance purchases made by financially sound customers or help them to arrange financing through a commercial bank. Even if suppliers do not get involved directly, a supportive phone call from a well-established manufacturer to a bank lending officer might make it considerably easier for a customer firm to get a loan. An equipment manufacturer could also cosign for a loan along with the buyer or be a reference for that buyer at a bank where the manufacturer obtains financing.

Commercial Banks

(6) A commercial bank may make a term loan that the small business can pay off within several years. In addition, commercial banks give qualified small businesses short-term loans. Naturally the business owner will have to provide financial statements listing personal and company assets and debts. Unfortunately, banks are often reluctant to lend money to new companies because of their failure rates unless the loan also is secured by the Small Business Administration.

The Small Business Administration

(7) The federal government defines a small business as a profit-making concern with less than $9 million in assets, a net worth under $4.5 million, and profits below $450,000 for the last two years of operation. The SBA, however, uses different yardsticks to determine smallness among firms in different industries. A nearby SBA field office can provide you with specific standards for a business in a particular industry.

(8) Under its guaranteed loan program, the SBA may secure up to 90 percent or $750,000 of a bank loan, whichever is less. If the bank declines to be involved in that arrangement, the SBA may lend up to $150,000 directly to the business.

(9) Entrepreneurs who start a new firm instead of buying a functioning business are expected to contribute approximately half of the required funds before qualifying for SBA assistance. They must also present **pro forma financial statements,** which are *financial statements that forecast expected sales, expenses, profits, and other financial data for a future accounting period.* These statements are evidence that the owner can make payments on SBA loans and any other long-term debts incurred to finance the business. The SBA is prohibited from lending to a company that can borrow money from another source, so applicants must first attempt to borrow from such private lenders as commercial banks.

(10) The steps in the SBA lending process are:

1. Describe the kind of business to be started.
2. List the owner's experience and management capabilities.
3. Estimate the amount the owner is prepared to invest and the amount he or she will need to borrow.
4. Prepare a personal financial statement listing the owner's assets and debts.
5. Develop pro forma statements of the business's sales, expenses, and profits for the first two years.
6. List the owner's collateral (security) for the loan, at current market value.
7. Ask a commercial bank for a letter stating the amount of the loan the owner requested, the interest rate, the payment terms, and the reason for rejecting the application.
8. If the bank agrees to be involved in the SBA's guarantee or participation plans (in which the bank joins with the SBA to make the loan), the banker will contact the SBA to negotiate the terms.
9. If the bank declines to be involved, contact the SBA for a direct loan.

Selling Stock

(11) Some small businesses raise money by issuing and selling stock. Only corporations can sell stock, and open corporations, those whose stock is traded publicly, must comply with extensive state and federal regulations on stock sales. The founder of a company must also be concerned about surrendering control if a majority of the shares are sold to other persons. The firm could remain a closed corporation if the owner raises capital from a select and restricted group of investors. In Chapter 16 we'll discuss the kinds of stock a corporation can sell and the characteristics of each kind.

pro forma financial statements Financial statements that forecast expected sales, expenses, profits, and other financial data for a future accounting period.

Venture Capital Firms

venture capital firm A company that buys stock in new firms that make products or offer services with strong profit potential.

(12) A **venture capital firm** is *a company that buys stock in new firms that make products or offer services with strong profit potential.* Venture capitalists take greater risks than such lenders as the SBA or commercial banks. Venture capital firms often are owned by successful entrepreneurs who have come up the hard way themselves. These companies shop for soundly managed firms with unique products or services in growing markets. Many specialize in specific industries (such as high technology, consumer products, or manufacturing companies). Recently companies with ideas for new minicomputers, electronic medical instruments, or communications equipment have been looked on favorably by venture capital firms.

(13) Although venture capitalists are willing to take large risks, they also want large rewards. Typically they may want 50 percent or more of the fledgling corporation's stock in exchange for an infusion of cash and will require that their own people be seated on the small company's board of directors.

(14) A really sound venture capitalist should provide far more than just capital, however. The small business owner should deal with a firm that can help arrange short-term financing through a network of sympathetic commercial banking contacts. A venture capital firm should also be able to place the company in touch with potential customers for its products and help negotiate favorable contracts with suppliers. Companies such as Atari, Apple Computer, Compaq Computer, and Lotus Development Corporation (a producer of popular microcomputer software) all got assistance from venture capital firms during their infancy.

Sources of Continuing Help

(15) Most small business owners find they need advice after their business opens its doors. Among sources that can provide this ongoing assistance after the firm is on its feet are the SBA, SCORE, the National Family Business Council, business students, educators and consultants, trade associations, and wholesalers.

The SBA

(16) The Small Business Administration has more than 300 free or inexpensive booklets with information on everything from procedures for incorporation to personnel selection. Approximately eighty field offices provide management advice and offer management training for owners with the assistance of nearby colleges and business schools. In addition, SBA assistance loans help companies that have been damaged by natural disaster or by the economic changes brought on by urban renewal or other government-funded construction programs. There are even loans to help small companies meet federal air and water pollution standards.

Service Corps of Retired Executives (SCORE) A volunteer organization of over 13,000 active and retired higher managers who advise small business owners in conjunction with the Small Business Administration.

Score

(17) The **Service Corps of Retired Executives (SCORE)** is *a volunteer organization of over 13,000 active and retired higher managers who advise small business owners in conjunction with the Small Business Administration.*

Business owners can request the assistance of a SCORE adviser whether or not they have received an SBA loan. They need only apply at an SBA field office. An adviser whose expertise fits the nature of the problem (finance, personnel, marketing) will meet with the owner to analyze the problem and develop a solution. A team of volunteers may be called on to attack problems with a broad scope. The advice is free, but the company will be expected to pay the SCORE volunteer's out-of-pocket expenses.

(18) In addition to its free business counseling, SCORE members also conduct workshops on various specialized subjects at more than 750 locations nationwide. Attendees must pay a modest fee, which might be considered a bargain, considering that the average SCORE counselor has thirty-five years of business experience.

The National Family Business Council

(19) The National Family Business Council (NFBC) consists of employees of family-owned companies who work in managerial or trainee positions and are related to the owners by birth or marriage. Any company that hires relatives of the owners—a common situation in closely held corporations—may benefit from joining this organization, which focuses attention on the unique interpersonal management problems found in family-operated businesses. In addition to its various chapters and management education programs, the NFBC publishes a newsletter and stages cooperative educational programs with leading universities and private management development firms.

Business Students

(20) Many business professors include a small business assistance project among the requirements for their graduate courses. Students may be called on to answer a business owner's request for help, analyze problems (possibly as part of a team or task force), and design and implement plans that will help a small firm back onto its feet. This type of program, which may be available through the business school at a nearby university, offers an inexpensive and reliable introduction to many of the latest concepts in the study of business operations.

Local Educators and Consultants

(21) In his famous lecture "Acres of Diamonds," noted nineteenth-century clergyman and educator Russell Conwell dramatized how easy it is to overlook riches in one's own backyard. Business owners who live in a moderately or heavily populated area with colleges and universities nearby will find abundant management advice available from local business professors, authors of books on management, and consultants. Some recommendations of specific people to contact may be obtained from the local chamber of commerce.

Trade Associations

(22) There is at least one trade association for practically every line of business, from funeral parlors to massage parlors. Some confine themselves to highly specialized fields, such as the Power Crane and Shovel Manufacturers Association and the Fir and Hemlock Door Asso-

ciation. Others, such as the National Association of Manufacturers and the National Retail Merchants Association, cover more ground. Trade associations can give advice on financing, inventory management, personnel management, accounting procedures, physical layout, marketing research, supplier relations, site selection, and advertising for their specific lines of business. They exist to help member firms prosper by communicating proven management practices and information.

Wholesalers

(23) Well-equipped wholesalers can boost a small retailer's success in merchandise promotion by:

- Pooling orders from many customers, buying in large quantities, and receiving lower prices, thus allowing independent firms to offer prices that compete with those of chains and larger independents
- Selling certain items at cost, thus encouraging retailers to buy others later at regular prices
- Providing an inventory rotation plan to ensure fresh merchandise and ideal stock levels
- Distributing manufacturers' point-of-purchase displays to help retailers sell merchandise more effectively.

(24) They can make market information available by:

- Assessing market trends by monitoring trends in sales
- Distributing market information in newsletters and bulletins
- Forewarning customers of trends and changes in demand
- Providing information on competitors' prices and marketing practices
- Staying abreast of changing conditions that influence the supply of staple items
- Notifying customers of new products, improved store fixtures, and innovative equipment
- Advising on efficient store layouts, effective marketing practices, and productive floor displays

(25) Wholesalers can give small retailers financial help, too, by selling merchandise on open-book accounts and by delaying billings for seasonal merchandise until the selling season arrives and sales improve. They can also provide accounting forms and booklets that help customer firms establish and maintain good recordkeeping habits, and offer accounting services through an umbrella contract with a local accounting firm.*

1. The topic of this excerpt concerns:

   a. the failures of small businesses
   b. sources for financing small businesses
   c. where to set up a small businesses
   d. the most successful small businesses

---

*Adapted from Straub and Attner, *Introduction to Business*, pp. 131–138.

2. The main idea sentence of paragraph 5 is:

    a. found in the third sentence
    b. found in the second sentence
    c. found in the first sentence
    d. implied

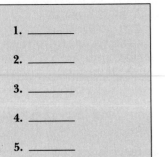

1. _____

2. _____

3. _____

4. _____

5. _____

3. A major detail *not* mentioned in paragraph 6 is:

    a. Commercial banks almost always grant small businesses loans.
    b. Commercial banks can also provide small businesses short-term loans.
    c. Small businesses are required to provide commercial banks with financial statements.
    d. Commercial banks require small businesses to secure loans from the Small Business Administration.

4. A major detail *not* mentioned in paragraph 14 is:

    a. Venture capitalists do not need to provide small business owners with information on short-term financing.
    b. Venture capitalists should help the small business owner find customers.
    c. Atari is a company that benefited from a venture capitalist.
    d. Venture capitalists should also help small business owners negotiate contracts.

5. A major detail mentioned in paragraph 17 is:

    a. It is necessary to have secured a loan before a small business owner can ask for SCORE advice.
    b. Volunteer teams are rarely called on to solve small business problems.
    c. SCORE only provides marketing advisers to small business owners.
    d. A small fee is required for SCORE advice.

    Answer these three questions by carefully reading the paragraphs mentioned in each question. Your answers should be in a short phrase or sentence.

6. Reread paragraph 20. How are business students used to assist small business owners? (1 point)

7. Reread paragraph 22. What are trade associations, and how can they help the small business owner? (2 points)

8. Reread paragraph 23 on wholesalers. What are the first two ways that a wholesaler can increase the profit of a small business owner? (2 points)

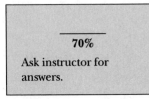

_____
70%

Ask instructor for answers.

Follow-up on Chapter 5

Now that you have studied this introduction and completed these exercises, it may be helpful to see how your reading of this topic has changed some of your ideas about business and improved your abilities in using major and minor details. You may go back to reread these exercises just for their content, or for what they have to say about the business field, and you may want to review the introduction before you answer the following questions. Answer these questions either individually or in small groups:

On the Topic of Business

1. How would you now define the term *business studies*?

2. Discuss as thoroughly as you can three business issues that you were introduced to in these exercises.

3. What type of American business would you prefer being a part of? Why?

4. What issues in business would you now like to study more?

On Locating Major and Minor Details

5. Are you now able to identify major and minor details in what you read and hear? What is still difficult for you about identifying major and minor details?

6. Do you see how major and minor details differ from main ideas and topics? Can you identify these four types of information when you read textbooks?

7. Are you able to write paragraphs that effectively use major and minor details? When you write, can you separate out the major details from the minor details?

8. What other aspects of major and minor details do you want to learn more about?

 **Internet Activity**

In groups of four or five, answer the following questions about college and university business majors by doing research on the Internet. You may want to locate the Web sites of various colleges and universities to gather your information. When you have completed your research, get back to your group and share your information.

1. What does a college business major prepare students to do?
2. List three or four colleges or universities in your state that offer a business major.
3. Select one business program in a college or university out of your state, and list five of the courses it offers.
4. Which Internet sources were you able to locate to find information on business majors?

CHAPTER 6

Identifying Organizational Patterns

In this chapter, you will learn about:

- The organizational patterns of cause–effect, problem–solution, definition, sequence of events, spatial–geographic, thesis–support, comparison–contrast, and description
- The signal words introducing the various organizaional patterns

Information is frequently organized in one of a few standard patterns: cause–effect, problem–solution, definition, sequence of events, spatial–geographic, thesis–support, comparison–contrast, and description. If you know what those standard organizational patterns are, you can look for one as you read or listen to lectures and discussions and thereby have one more insight into the writer's or speaker's meaning. Then you will understand the material better. Main ideas and important details will also be clearer if you understand which organizational pattern is being used.

The Cause–Effect Pattern

Cause–effect is perhaps the most common organizational pattern that you will come across. You will find it in almost every subject that you study, but it is most evident in the sciences and social sciences. You learned something about cause and effect in Chapter 5, which discussed major details. You will now study cause and effect as a pattern that can organize an entire chapter, lecture, or discussion. Cause–effect sentences, paragraphs, and essays have two parts: the cause, or the source of the change, and the effect, or the result of the change.

In addition, cause–effect relationships can be either direct or indirect. If cause–effect statements are *direct*, they are always true. Look at the following cause–effect statement from chemistry: "When water is lowered to 32 degrees Fahrenheit, it freezes." Do you see that lowering the water's temperature to 32 degrees is the cause and that the water freezing at this temperature is the effect? This relationship is direct because water always freezes at this temperature (at least under normal physical conditions). In your notes, you can show this relationship by using an arrow. "Lowering temperature of water to 32 degrees F. → water freezing."

An *indirect* cause–effect relationship is one whose effect is caused by several factors. Indirect causes are also called *contributory* causes. Indirect cause–effect relationships are often found in the social sciences and the humanities. Consider the following statement from sociology: "Criminal behavior seems to be caused by a deprived social environment." The term of qualification *seems* suggests that this relationship is indirect. A deprived social environment may be one of several influences on criminal behavior. One frequently finds contributory causes in relationships dealing with people and events, and often these relationships are worded with qualifying terms.

The following terms of qualification are often associated with indirect cause–effect relationships:

it appears	perhaps	one can safely say
it seems	probably	one can say with reservation
apparently	likely	there seems to be a link
one can assume	contributing to	there seems to be a relationship

For a more thorough list of terms of qualification, see the lists in Chapter 8 titled "Words and Phrases That Express a Little Doubt" and "Words and Phrases That Express Some Doubt," p. 163. Certain transitional phrases also suggest results, like *consequently, therefore, so, as a result,* and *as a consequence.*

How should you note cause–effect relationships? If you find them in your reading, you may want to separate cause from effect in the margin. For the previous example dealing with crime, you could write:

cause: crime   Criminal behavior seems to be caused by a deprived social environment.
effect: bad environment

You should also note whether the cause is direct or indirect. You can write the same kinds of comments when you take or review your lecture or discussion notes.

The Problem–Solution Pattern

In a sense, the problem–solution pattern is a special type of cause–effect relationship, because the solution is the result of the problem. In this pattern, the writer presents a problem needing solution. Early on in their presentation, successful writers of problem–solution material present the problem as clearly and completely as they can, and they are equally clear and specific about the ways they intend to solve the problem. This pattern is commonly used in business and political material because a large part of the work businesspeople and politicians do is finding ways to solve problems: balancing a budget, making a more effective product, developing a product that conforms to environmental and consumer legislation.

Signal words that suggest a problem–solution pattern include:

problem	answer	findings	plan
question	explanation	suggestion	proposal
issue	interpretation	compromise	intent
solution	decision		

Look at how the sociological issue of crime prevention is addressed by a politician in the following problem–solution paragraph:

Teenage crime is rampant; thirteen-year-olds are killing each other with guns and knives, sixth graders are on LSD and cocaine, and teenage car theft is startlingly high. The crime issue will not go away unless we present some concrete proposals. I suggest that we begin discussing crime and its dangerous effects in schools, from kindergarten through high school. We should have police going to the schools and talking about the effects of being picked up for drunk driving or drug possession. Children need to know that these early violations may adversely affect their chances of finding employment later on. Finally, we need to provide federal, state, and private money for counseling families where there is teenage crime.

Do you see how the problem is presented early on, with details of killings, drug use, and car thefts? And do you also see that the solutions are explicitly listed—school programs, police programs, and counseling services? Also note that signal words like *issue, proposals,* and *suggest* alert you to the problem–solution pattern.

The Definition Pattern

You will find definitions in the lecture, discussion, and textbook material of every course you take. Definitions make up a large part of what you will be asked on examination questions, so you should listen and read carefully when you come upon a definition. Definitions are often expressed concisely, so you should also write down every word of a definition.

In your lecture, discusison, and reading notes, use the abbreviation *def* as your signal that a definition follows. Look at the following example from sociology:

def: social class   A social class is a particular category of a social system. Working, lower, middle, and upper are the most common classes.

Another successful technique to use when you are learning definitions is to list the general category of the term first and then to give examples or features of the term. See how the preceding definition of *social class* can be effectively divided into these categories:

Term	General Category	Specific Features
social class	social system	divided into working, lower, middle, and upper

This method of categorizing is similar to classifying information into main ideas and details. Also, the chart helps you visualize each part of the definition.

When you come upon a definition, you should listen or read more actively. At first you may have trouble remembering all the parts of a definition, because each part tends to be written concisely. But learn to remember definitions, because they are the foundations for any course that you take. They are especially important in your understanding of introductory courses. More will be said about how to remember definitions in Chapter 14, "The SQ3R Study System," and Chapters 15 and 16, which are about examination strategies.

You may now want to complete Exercise 6.3 on page 114.

The Sequence-of-Events Pattern

You will find the sequence-of-events pattern in all subjects, but you will often see it in historical material in which dates are presented chronologically. You will also find the sequence-of-events pattern in vocational material in which you must follow procedures to make or repair an object or to work a machine like a computer. You were introduced to this pattern in the previous chapter, where it was presented as a type of major detail. Now you will see it as a structure that can organize a textbook chapter, lecture, or discussion.

The following signal words often introduce a sequence-of-events pattern: *first, second, third,* and so on; *last, now, later, before, often, soon, finally, next.*

When you listen to or read material arranged in a sequence-of-events pattern, you should number the events or steps. Make the number stand out so that, in reviewing your notes, you can picture the sequence in your mind. Look at how information is sequenced in the list that follows this paragraph on a juvenile offender:

> James's history follows a particular pattern that many juvenile offenders seem to fall into. First, he was born to a single parent, a mother who did not work. Second, he did most of his own child rearing, feeding and clothing himself from the age of four. Third, when he began school, he returned home to an empty house. Finally, as a teenager he found himself spending more time on the streets with dropouts than at home.

James's Childhood History

1. Born to a single mother who did not work
2. Began caring for himself at age four
3. Returned from school to an unattended home
4. When he was a teenager, his friends were dropouts

By arranging the sequence of events vertically, you get a clearer picture of the significant moments in James's life.

You may now want to complete Exercise 6.2 on page 112.

The Spatial–Geographic Pattern

The spatial–geographic pattern is frequently used in biology and geography courses. In this pattern, you must visualize the various parts of an organism or the relative location of countries, states, or cities on a map.

In biology courses, the following signal words are used to direct you to various parts of an organism:

above	between	inward	anterior	distal
below	upper	external	posterior	
next to	lower	dorsal	medial	
behind	outward	ventral	lateral	

In a biology lecture or discussion, your instructor will use these terms along with a slide or diagram. Start associating these terms with what you see. If you can sketch, make a rough picture of the organism during the lecture or discussion. In biology textbooks, organs and organ parts are often mentioned in conjunction with a diagram. As you read, refer to the diagram. After you have read the material and studied the diagram, close your book and draw the organ or organism from memory. Your biology instructor may well ask you to label an organism on an exam. On such exams, your spatial–geographic skills will assist you.

The same skills are necessary in geography courses. Your geography instructor may present maps in a lecture or discussion and ask you to remember the correct location of various parts. If you can, copy any maps that you see in lectures or discussions and important maps that you find in your reading. If you cannot draw well, be sure to use accurate signal words as you take notes. Here are some signal words found in geography readings, lectures, and discussions:

north	bordering	up
south	adjacent	down
east	next to	opposite to
west		

Let signal words like these help you visualize parts of a city, state, country, or continent. "Southwestern," for example, should be the key word that you hear in the statement "The southwestern border of the city is the area with the most affluent homeowners—the city's upper class."

The Thesis–Support Pattern

The thesis–support pattern is used in all disciplines; its organization is similar to that of the multiple-paragraph essay, which is discussed in Chapter 16. A *thesis* is a point of view expressed by a speaker or writer. Usually the thesis is in the first paragraph of an essay or at the beginning of a lecture.

When you locate a statement that seems to be the thesis, write *thesis* in the margin; then summarize it. For example, if your sociology instructor begins a lecture with a statement like "Power is a fundamental drive that seems to organize all types of society," you could write something like this:

Thesis: power—a basic drive organizing societies

Underline the term "thesis" so that, in reviewing your notes, you will remember to reread this statement. On exams, you are expected to know well the thesis of a lecture, a discussion, or an article.

Be sure that you can distinguish between a thesis and a fact. Like a main idea, a thesis expresses an opinion that needs support. Like a detail, a *fact* may support a thesis. Unlike a thesis, a fact does not ask you to question it. Which of the following two statements is the thesis and which is the fact that supports it? (1) "Power is expressed in the amount of money and capital an individual possesses." (2) "Members of the upper class always possess more money than the classes below them do." Do you see that in the second statement the writer is not presenting an argument, merely a fact? But in the first statement, you may question whether money is the only indicator of power.

Once you have located the thesis, you need to analyze its details. Remember that a thesis is only as good as its details. Some details are well chosen; others are not. Start training yourself to look for the well-chosen detail. Make marginal comments in your textbook or when taking lecture or discussion notes, stating whether the details support the thesis well. If a sociology instructor said that social power is expressed in several ways, you would be correct in wanting to know what is meant by "several." Are there three ways or thirteen? In your notes, you should identify important details with the abbreviation *det.*

Here are some signal words that introduce a thesis–support pattern:

the thesis is	for example	especially
it is theorized that	for instance	one example is
the hypothesis is	specifically	the idea is supported by
it is my belief that	in particular	proof is found in

You can use these same signal words in writing your own thesis–support essay.

The details used to support a thesis may be causes, effects, spatial or geographic words, or descriptions. The thesis–support pattern is the most general of the seven and may include other organizational patterns.

You may now want to complete Exercise 6.1 on page 111.

The Comparison–Contrast Pattern

The comparison–contrast pattern is used in all disciplines. Like the thesis–support pattern, it may be made up of several paragraphs, and it may include other organizational patterns. The comparison–contrast pattern asks you to find similarities and differences in what you read or hear.

Here are some of the most common signal words for the comparison–contrast pattern:

Contrast

but	on the one hand	although	opposed
however	on the other hand	while	opposing
yet	contrary	different from	conversely
nevertheless	on the contrary	differently	whereas
at variance	in contrast	oppositely	
otherwise	rather	opposite	

Comparison

and	similar	as	parallel to	exactly like
also	similarly	just as	much the same	analogous
like	as if	resembling	comparable	analogously

Use these signal words not only to recognize comparison–contrast patterns but also to write essays that show comparison or contrast. Use them to highlight the similarities and differences that you present in your writing.

When you take reading, lecture, or discussion notes that show comparison or contrast, you can best show these similarities or differences in a chart like this one:

Similarity or Difference

Topic		*Topic*
1.		1.
2.		2.
3.		3.

In this chart, you can neatly place similarities and differences side by side and thus more easily see how the various pieces of information relate. As you listen to a lecture or discussion or read textbook material, be sure that you can identify the topic or topics that explore particular similarities or differences. You studied ways to locate and express topics in Chapter 4. It is only with an accurate topic in mind or with appropriate categories of comparison and contrast that you can create a useful comparison–contrast chart.

Look at the following information taken from a sociology lecture; then see how a chart can be used to explain the material.

Capitalism and socialism begin with different ideologies. While capitalism implies private ownership, socialism assumes state ownership of certain property. Capitalism allows people to pursue economic gain; socialism controls the economic gains of people.

Differences

Capitalism	*Socialism*
1. Private ownership of property	1. State ownership of most property
2. Economic freedom for people	2. Economic control of people

Do you see how this chart highlights the differences between socialism and capitalism?

A speaker or a textbook author may present similarities and differences by using such a chart. If you come upon comparison–contrast patterns and the information is presented in paragraph form, you may want to create your own chart. Sometimes you will read or hear material that presents both similarities and differences. Here you can create two charts next to each other, showing similarities in one and differences in the other. These charts often allow you to remember compare–contrast information more easily. More will be said about comparison–contrast charts in Chapters 15 and 16 on preparing for objective and essay exams.

You may now want to complete Exercise 6.4 on page 116.

The Descriptive Pattern

The descriptive pattern is different from the other organizational patterns. You will find it most often in literature: short stories, novels, poems, plays. Descriptive patterns re-create experiences through the suggestiveness of language and often use characteristics as details. Your job is to see how description awakens your senses. In your notes, comment on how well the description re-creates an experience.

Read this excerpt about a young man fleeing from the law, from John Edgar Wideman's *Brothers and Keepers*:

visual images

Johnny-Boy wasn't from Pittsburgh. *Small, dark, greasy,* he was an outsider who knew he didn't fit, ill at ease in a middle-class house, the meandering conversations that had nothing to do with anyplace he'd been, anything he understood or cared to learn. Johnny-Boy had trouble talking, trouble staying awake. When he spoke at all, he *stuttered* riffs of barely comprehensible ghetto slang. When the rest of us were talking, he'd *nod off.* I didn't like the way his *heavy-lidded, bubble eyes* blinked open and searched the room when he thought no one was watching him.

Do you see how the descriptions *small, dark, greasy* and *heavy-lidded, bubble eyes* present a clear picture of this young fugitive? Also, *stuttering* and *nodding off* are vivid actions that describe him. If you were reading this novel, a marginal comment like *vivid picture* would be helpful as you reread the work.

In any literature course you take, you will come upon the descriptive pattern. Your literature instructor will probably give you reading suggestions to use in analyzing descriptions. When you read any descriptive passage, remember to study the words and what they suggest rather than analyzing the thesis and details of support.

You may now want to complete Exercises 6.5 and 6.6 on pages 119–123.

Summary

Organizational patterns are used by speakers and writers to present their ideas more clearly and to show the structure of their arguments. Recognizing which organizational pattern is being used and knowing how that pattern works will help you understand the material better. Organizational patterns often overlap; that is, several structures may be used by a speaker or writer. Don't expect each paragraph you read or each lecture or discussion you hear to use only one organizational pattern. The eight most common organizational patterns are cause–effect, problem–solution, definition, sequence of events, spatial–geographic, thesis–support, comparison–contrast, and descriptive. Each organizational pattern has its own logic and signal words that show you how the material is organized. Being familiar with these eight organizational patterns will make your reading, lecture, and discussion notes clearer and will improve your writing.

Summary Box   *Organizational Patterns*

What are they?	*Why are they used?*
Structures used in writing and speaking to explain ideas, describe experiences, or show the logic of an argument Eight common patterns: cause–effect, problem–solution, definition, sequence of events, spatial–geographic, thesis–support, comparison–contrast, descriptive	To help a reader or listener understand an argument better and take better reading and lecture notes To help a writer compose logical and organized essays

Skills Practice Topic: Sociology

All the exercises in this chapter deal with some issue from sociology, a subject you will probably study sometime during your college career.

Before you begin these exercises, answer the following questions either individually or in small groups to get some sense of what you already know about sociology:

1. What do you think sociology covers?
2. What are some of the problems that you currently see in society?
3. How do you think these problems should be addressed?

4. Why do people in society act the way they do? Are they born to act in a certain way? Or does society teach them?

Exercise 6.1
Identifying Thesis
Statements

Some of the following ten statements express a point of view and would qualify as thesis statements; others are statements of fact. All of the statements discuss what sociology is, so they should provide you with an introduction to this discipline. In the answer box, write "thesis" or "fact" on the appropriate lines. You may choose to work in groups to complete this exercise.

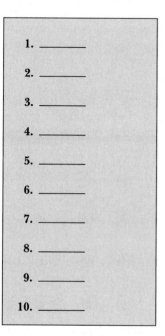

1. _____
2. _____
3. _____
4. _____
5. _____
6. _____
7. _____
8. _____
9. _____
10. _____

Some Introductory Statements About Sociology

1. Sociology is the study of how people make agreements and how they organize, teach, break, and change them.
2. Sociology is a less difficult discipline than psychology.
3. Sociology also studies how people come to disagree.
4. People who study sociology usually become dissatisfied with society.
5. Sociology is a scientific study of how people agree and disagree.
6. Sociology tests what it knows by carefully measuring and analyzing how people behave.
7. Sociology is the most intelligent discipline to have emerged in the past fifty years.
8. Sociology focuses on action, or on what people do.
9. People tend to accomplish goals more by acting than by speaking.
10. Actions are shaped by what has come before, or previous actions.

The following five paragraphs on social activities each have only one thesis statement. Write in the answer box the letter of the sentence that is the thesis statement.

Social Activities

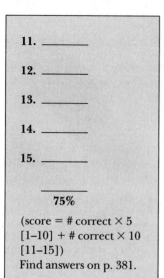

11. _____
12. _____
13. _____
14. _____
15. _____

_____
75%

(score = # correct × 5
[1–10] + # correct × 10
[11–15])
Find answers on p. 381.

11. (a) A conversation is one of the most amazing examples of human social activity. (b) People meet, and they exchange glances. (c) They shake hands. (d) And they proceed to get to know one another by sharing experiences in their lives.

12. (a) A fistfight is an example of social interaction. (b) A mugging is also a type of social activity. (c) The mugger points a gun at you and demands your money. (d) Some social interactions are painfully inharmonious.

13. (a) Sociologists study many interesting aspects of social interaction. (b) They may focus on spoken communication. (c) They may specialize in aggressive behavior. (d) Still others may specialize in aggressive behavior manifested in speech.

14. (a) When two people interact, they establish a system of roles. (b) These roles may be learned before the interaction or as the interaction occurs. (c) During the interaction, the particular roles a

person plays may even be challenged. (d) These roles form the basis of human relationships, which are the fundamental ways people express meaning to one another.

15. (a) In the roles people play, status relationships are set up. (b) One person may feel more important than another and act accordingly. (c) One's status in a relationship determines the respect or lack of respect received from the other partner. (d) Status has proven to be a very important way of wielding power over others.

Exercise 6.2
Locating Steps in
an Argument

Read the following paragraphs on how sociologists conduct their research. Then reread them and list in correct sequence the steps presented in each paragraph.

Research Methods in Sociology

1. Some sociologists use deductive reasoning in their research. A deduction starts with a general idea—for example, "All people will eventually die." Then the deduction moves to a particular case: "John is a person." It then applies the general premise to the particular case and comes upon a new idea: "John will eventually die."

   Three Steps in a Deduction

   1.

   2.

   3.

2. Sociologists more often use inductive reasoning in their research. It involves three basic steps. The sociologist observes a particular human action. She then begins to record those actions that seem to follow a particular pattern. From a study of these observations, known as *data,* the sociologist comes upon a general statement or idea. Inductions move from the specific observation to the general conclusion, but deductions start at the general level and move to the specific conclusion.

   Three Steps in an Induction

   1.

   2.

   3.

3. The general ideas developed from inductions are also called *hypotheses.* To determine whether a hypothesis is accurate or valid, sociologists do what is called *hypothesis testing.* The first step in this procedure

is to state the hypothesis clearly. Then the researcher studies the data she has collected and sees if they follow a pattern. She usually sets up graphs to see what kind of pattern the data show. Finally she studies the graph to see if the hypothesis is supported by what the graph shows.

Steps in Hypothesis Testing

1.

2.

3.

4. Sociologists often study what large groups of people do. The first question they ask is which population they are studying. Once they have answered the "which" and have observed this group, they put their observations into categories. Finally, once the data have been put into categories, they are analyzed, and researchers then draw conclusions about the group in question.

Steps in Studying Large Groups

1.

2.

3.

Now read the following four paragraphs, and look for the proper sequence of events in each. Before you list the steps, write an appropriate title.

5. Random sampling is sociologists' way of determining what a large group of people will do, even though they study a small number of individuals. In studying attitudes toward abortion, for example, sociologists often select telephone area codes at random and numbers from all over the area they are focusing on. They then check to see if these numbers are random by testing them with mathematical equations. Finally, they publish their conclusions, usually in the form of percentages and graphs, to report how most people in that area feel about abortion.

6. Some sociologists engage in field research. In field research, they both observe a particular action in society and participate in this activity in some way. During this activity, sociologists gather data. They use

the data to write a report—which is often a *case study,* or an in-depth report on a particular social event.

7. Sociologists also conduct surveys to try to answer a particular sociological question—for example, "Are schoolteachers satisfied with their jobs?" Once the overall question has been formulated, researchers devise more specific survey questions. The people they question are asked to respond either over the telephone or in writing.

8. Most sociological studies, then, follow a set sequence. The researcher begins with an interest in a particular social activity—crime, for example. This interest then leads to an unsupported idea or intuition: "Society creates criminals." Finally, this intuition is tested and made into a theory: the social theory of criminal behavior.*

80%

Ask instructor for answers.

---

*Exercise 6.3
Understanding
Definitions*

The following ten statements define sociological terms that you have read about in Exercises 6.1 and 6.2. After reading each statement, separate the definition into a general category and an example. Be brief. Place all of your information in the columns that follow the statements. Use the following definition of *survey research* as a model: "A sociological research method is one using questionnaires that people answer, either on their own or with the help of an interviewer. Asking a large number of people about their attitudes on tax increases is an example of a survey question."

Term	*General Category*	*Examples*
survey research	determining a group of people's attitude on a topic	tax increases

Key Sociological Terms

1. Conflict theory is the aspect of sociology that studies why people disagree; sociologists who study crime often use conflict theory.

---

*Adapted from Thomas R. Dye, *Power and Society,* 5th ed. (Belmont, Calif.: Wadsworth, 1990), pp. 23–30.

2. A deduction (as used in sociology) is a logical process that moves from a general idea to a theory about a specific person or group. A sociologist who contends that women are discriminated against on the job might deduce that female executives receive a smaller salary than male executives.

3. Demography is a careful sociological look at population—what it is and why it acts the way it does. A study of the movement of Mexicans into California in the 1990s would be a demographic study.

4. An empirical study involves gathering data from what the researcher observes. A sociologist observing how American males greet each other would collect empirical, or observational, data.

5. In sociology, field research requires going into the natural setting to observe a particular activity. Carefully observing political rallies would qualify as field research in sociology.

6. A hypothesis in sociology is a conclusion that a researcher draws through either observation or intuition. Assuming that criminals are victims of society is a hypothesis.

7. An induction in sociology is a conclusion that a researcher draws based on the careful study of data, or observations. A sociologist who concludes after studying a statewide survey that New Yorkers are not in favor of increased state taxes is using inductive logic.

8. In sociology, a population is a group or category of people that merits careful study. Students in community colleges nationwide are an example of a sociological population.

9. Random selection is a sociological research tool designed to ensure that a large group of people are selected for a study by chance and not through a particular researcher's bias. Random selection can be achieved by asking a computer to select a group of people through the use of random numbering.

10. Social interaction is defined as the way one person directs the responses of another person or persons. A conversation is an excellent example of social interaction.*

Term	*General Category*	*Examples*
1.		
2.		
3.		

---

*Adapted from Earl R. Babbie, *Sociology: An Introduction,* 2nd ed. (Belmont, Calif.: Wadsworth, 1980), pp. 574–584.

4.

5.

6.

7.

8.

9.

10.

<hr/>

____

80%

(score = # correct × 5)
Find answers on
pp. 381–382.

*Exercise 6.4
Identifying
Comparisons and
Contrasts*

The following ten statements compare various disciplines to sociology or compare pairs of terms used in sociology. In a one-sentence explanation of each statement, identify the issue that is compared or contrasted. Be sure that you use the word "compare" or "contrast" in your explanation. Here's an example:

> Although inductions and deductions are both ways by which sociologists explain their data, they begin with very different ways of looking at the data.
>
> *Explanation:* This statement contrasts inductions and deductions as ways sociologists interpret their data.

You may choose to work in small groups to complete this exercise.

1. Sociology and psychology are different in that psychology generally studies what an individual does and sociology analyzes what occurs between people.

   Explanation: _____

2. The major difference between sociology and anthropology is that until recently anthropology studied preliterate peoples, those unable to read and write, and sociology generally studied literate people. The distinctions between these two studies have recently been blurred.

   Explanation: _____

3. Economics and sociology share a focus on how people relate and interact. Economics specifically focuses on financial interaction.

   Explanation: _____

4. Political science differs from sociology in that it specifically addresses how people use power. In sociology, power is just one of many areas that is studied.

   Explanation: _____

5. Social welfare and sociology are very similar disciplines, except that social welfare focuses on how to help people and sociology considers ways to study them.

   Explanation: _____

6. Socialism is not sociology. Socialism is an economic system in which most industry is controlled by the government; sociology studies how humans interact. Socialism could, therefore, be a topic studied in sociology.

   Explanation: _____

7. Furthermore, sociology is not synonymous with social reform. Social reformists want to make the world better; that is not the goal of sociology, which merely studies social behavior.

   Explanation: _____

8. Sociology differs from history in that history records, narrates, and interprets human experience. Sociology focuses exclusively on interpreting human interaction.

   Explanation: _____

9. Racial inequality and sexual inequality can be considered similar in that both express how a group of people—a race or women—have been treated unfairly by the ruling class.

   Explanation: _____

10. Urban life is characterized by large numbers of people living in a concentrated area, whereas rural life is characterized by fewer people and more space between groups of people.

    Explanation: _____

The following five paragraphs present either comparisons or contrasts of terms used in sociology. Read over the paragraphs carefully. Then complete the comparison and contrast chart that follows each paragraph. In paragraphs 13–15, you need to provide the topics as well.

11. There are several similarities between the upper-class population and the middle-class population. For one, both are future-oriented;

that is, they are constantly making plans for a better life. Both groups are self-confident, believing that they have reasonable control over the experiences in their lives. Finally, both are also willing to make financial investments that will improve their future financial status.

Similar Beliefs

Upper Class	Middle Class
1.	1.
2.	2.
3.	3.

12. The differences between the working class and the lower class are minor. The working class generally works to pay the bills for themselves and their family; the lower class often does not work, and when they do they often move from one job to another. Working-class families are often married couples, but lower-class families are more often run by single women. Finally, a working-class person often belongs to and regularly attends church; the lower-class individual attends church infrequently.

Differences

Working Class	Lower Class
1.	1.
2.	2.
3.	3.

13. An issue that continues to surface in sociological studies is the difference between *nature* and *nurture*. Believers in the influence of nature contend that heredity, or one's genetic makeup, determines one's actions. Proponents of the influence of nurture assume that social forces—family, friends, environment—determine how one acts. Nurture theorists would say that one's mother is a dominant force in one's behavior. Nature theorists would say that some of a mother's genetic makeup is given to her child and that is why the child behaves in a particular fashion. In studying twins that were separated at birth, a nature proponent would be looking for evidence of similar behavior. A nurture theorist, in contrast, would be looking for proof that their behavior is different because it is shaped by a different environment.

How Their Ideas Differ

1.   1.

2.   2.

3.   3.

14. There are three differences between the liberal and the conservative positions in the United States today. Whereas liberals favor federal aid for education, health, and Social Security, conservatives work toward cutting funds in these areas. Conservatives believe in spending more on defense; liberals see military spending as too high and want to cut it. Finally, conservatives often favor aid to foreign countries; in contrast, liberals frequently fear that aid to foreign countries will lessen the amount spent on the needs of the American people.

Different Beliefs

1.   1.

2.   2.

3.   3.

15. Are urban and suburban lifestyles and environments different? Suburbs tend to be less densely populated than their urban counterparts. Homes in the suburbs tend to be built on larger parcels of land than urban dwellings, which are often built on smaller pieces of land and are several stories high. Violence is also an important factor for those who decide to move from a large city to a suburb. Suburban violence tends to be less common than that experienced in large cities.*

Differences in Lifestyle and Environment

1.   1.

2.   2.

3.   3.

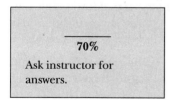

———
70%
Ask instructor for answers.

Exercise 6.5
Identifying
Organizational
Patterns

The following ten paragraphs discuss the sociological issues of heredity versus environment and the sense of self, expanding on the issue of

———

*Adapted from Dye, *Power and Society*, pp. 5–9, 76–77.

nature and nurture that you read about in Exercise 6.4. Each paragraph is structured according to one of the organizational patterns described earlier. Read each paragraph; then identify the organizational pattern that describes it. Some paragraphs use more than one organizational pattern. In this case, choose the one that seems to dominate the paragraph. Place the appropriate code in the answer box: *C-E* = cause–effect, *DEF* = definition, *C-C* = comparison–contrast, and *SEQ* = sequence of events.

Heredity, Environment, and the Self

1. What is the nature–nurture controversy? Some sociologists believe that we are the product of our genes, or nature, and that our sex, our race, and our physical characteristics are qualities we inherit at birth. Others believe that nurture, or our upbringing, is more important. Our ability to use language and our attitudes toward politics and religion, they argue, are shaped by our environment.

2. Identical twins have been studied carefully for answers to the nature–nurture question. Some studies have asked what causes intelligence. Identical twins, even if they are raised apart, seem to show very similar intelligence quotients (IQs). This result would suggest that heredity greatly influences intelligence.

3. What are the social forces that a typical child faces in the first seven years of life? During the first weeks, months, and sometimes years, a child is cared for by her mother. In our present society, this child is then often cared for by baby-sitters or day care workers. Then, at the age of three, she is often enrolled in preschool, where she experiences the influence of teachers and a large group of peers. Finally, at five she moves to a formal schooling experience, interacting with a teacher and a large group of peers in a self-contained classroom.

4. Two studies have offered different views of how intelligence is shaped. One study, using evidence from identical twins who have been raised apart, suggests that intelligence is transmitted genetically. Another study of foster children suggests that environment plays a key role in intelligence. This study shows that foster children, who are not related biologically to their parents, have an IQ similar to that of their foster parents.

5. Related to this issue of nature–nurture is the sense of self, which seems to develop in identifiable stages. A newborn has no sense of self apart from his attachment to his mother. Before the child begins to speak, at about the age of one, he begins to see himself as separate, often pointing to himself in the mirror. By the age of three, the child often is able to use language to explain who he is in relationship to others in his family.

6. What is the sociological meaning of the self? The self is one's sense of being, apart from one's occupation or social position. It is the

continuous sense of who one is, in private, at work, and in social interaction. Some sociologists are finding that this continuous sense of oneself cannot be separated from the society feeding this self.

c/e T

7. How does socialization affect the sense of self? As children mature, they learn to wear various masks—one at school, one at church, and so on. As they interact more with society, they learn that each occasion calls for a different side of themselves. Their notion of who they are thus becomes more and more complex.

8. Socialization, then, is a process in which the individual learns to use a variety of social selves. It is also a process by which these social selves become integrated with one another. Socialization thus gives to each individual both a personal and a social identity.

9. Sigmund Freud did much to help us understand the concept of self. He was interested in the effect of childhood experiences on adult behavior. He believed that people held many of their painful childhood experiences in what he called the *unconscious*. These unconscious memories often caused individuals to express themselves in strange, unexplained ways. These strange behavior patterns often led troubled individuals to seek help from psychoanalysts like Freud.

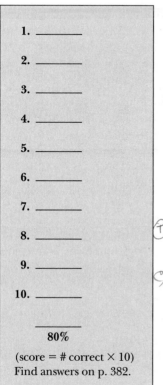

1. _____

2. _____

3. _____

4. _____

5. _____

6. _____

7. _____

8. _____

9. _____

10. _____

_____
80%

(score = # correct × 10)
Find answers on p. 382.

T

10. Both Sigmund Freud and Erik Erikson were psychologists interested in the development of the self, what they both termed the *ego*. Freud and Erikson differed slightly in their concept of how the ego developed. Freud believed that the ego resulted from a constant battle between the unconscious (the *id*) and the *superego* (society's values). In slight contrast, Erikson believed that the ego developed as a result of the individual's sense of sameness, or continuity, from one experience to the other. When there is a sharp contrast between who the individual thinks she is and who society thinks she is, the ego faces a crisis.*

c/c

**Exercise 6.6
Identifying More
Organizational
Patterns**

The following ten paragraphs concern the sociological issue of groups—what they are and how they operate. This discussion ties in with the previous discussion of the self. Again, these paragraphs are structured around various organizational patterns. Your job is to identify the organizational pattern that best describes each paragraph. If more than one pattern seems to apply, choose the pattern that seems to dominate the paragraph. Place the appropriate code in the answer box: *S-G* = spatial–geographic, *T-S* = thesis–support, *DES* = descriptive, and *C-E* = cause–effect.

_____

*Adapted from Babbie, Sociology, pp. 127–132.

A Sociological Look at Groups

1. In general speech, the term *group* has several meanings. A teacher can refer to a group gathered outside the classroom door. A spokesperson for the manufacturer of a sports car can refer to a group that consistently buys that car. And a rock star can mention the "groupies" who follow her from concert to concert.

2. What is key to understanding groups in sociology is how each group fits into a particular category. Brown-eyed Americans constitute a category. So do college professors. And so do people who buy the same sports car. What is common among all these groups is that, although the people in them belong to a particular category, they do not necessarily know or interact with one another.

3. How do groups influence behavior? Sociologists would argue that your membership in a group determines to a large degree your sense of self, or who you think you are. The friends you had in school determine how you see yourself as a student. Whether you thought you were part of the "in-group" or the "out-group" also determines how successful a student you see yourself to be.

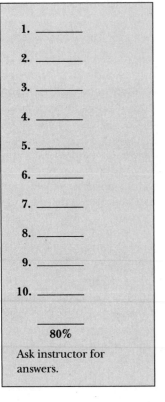

1. _____

2. _____

3. _____

4. _____

5. _____

6. _____

7. _____

8. _____

9. _____

10. _____

80%

Ask instructor for answers.

4. To be part of an in-group is meaningful only if you see that another group—an out-group—is not as successful as the group you identify with. The in-group often refers to the others in the group as "we" and to those in the out-group as "them." In schools, students are often categorized as athletes (the "jocks") and academic types (the "nerds"). Each one of these groups sees itself as part of a "we" that is unlike, and in conflict with, the "them."

5. What do in-groups provide people? By being in an in-group, you develop a sense of being wanted. Your group members support you and are loyal to you. Being part of an in-group gives you a sense of stability and, as Erik Erikson would argue, this stability lets your ego develop without conflict.

6. A *reference group*, or the group that one looks up to as a standard, gives individuals ways to improve. If you are a "B" student in sociology and your close and respected friend consistently receives "A" grades, she may provide you with a reference point for how well you are doing and for how much better you may want to become. Her "A" may very well prod you to study more for the next sociology examination. Reference groups are important because people need to see themselves in a better light if they are ever to develop their abilities.

7. But comparing yourself to others can also lead to what sociologists call *relative deprivation*—or doing poorly because others are doing better. Instead of looking up to a successful person or group, an individual may develop feelings of inadequacy whenever she compares herself to the more successful peer or acquaintance. This feeling of inadequacy may prevent the individual from trying her

hardest. In extreme circumstances, relative deprivation can lead to feelings of apathy or even depression.

8. In-groups and reference groups can be visualized as two or more floating platforms, with individuals on each. The people below can look up at the other individuals above them. They see them as happy and somehow more comfortable. In contrast, the people above—the in-group—can look down and feel better because the out-group seems to be more crowded and uncomfortable, wishing in vain that they could join the in-group. But if the in-group looks up from where they are, they will invariably see still another group—even less crowded and more comfortable, enjoying life even more than they do.

9. One sociology student described herself this way in a journal entry: "In college, I usually have not felt part of an in-group. I've always looked to others and envied who they were. I envied them for their grades and for how well they could speak up in class and get the teacher to listen. I see myself as a shy student who still has a long way to go before I can feel comfortable expressing myself in class and with other students outside of class. I want to be like these more successful students. They are becoming my models."

10. Another student had this to say about his first day in college: "I was born in Taiwan and went to school there until I was thirteen. This college is big. The buildings are large, and there is much land between buildings. I still have not gotten used to how much of everything there is here. There are three cafeterias in this school and five libraries. The parking lots are as large as the land that my elementary school was on in Taiwan. I still feel a little strange when I compare my college to the schools back home."*

Exercise 6.7 Recognizing Organizational Patterns in a Longer Passage

Read the following passage on *stratification* (a sociological term that treats a person's relative ranking in society). The discussion of stratification is a further elaboration of the discussion of in-groups and out-groups in the previous exercise. Make marginal comments on the major organizational patterns that you come across. Then answer the questions that follow the passage. You may go back to review it as you answer the questions. Place the first five answers in the answer box; then answer the rest of the questions in the spaces provided.

Various Views on Stratification

(1) Sociologists refer to inequalities in society with the term *social stratification*. Each stratum in society is made up of a group of people who have a similar social rank. Sociologists have found that social rank

---

*Adapted from Babbie, *Sociology,* pp. 201–204.

depends on factors that vary from one culture to another. Some of the most common criteria for assigning social rank are status within the family, possessions, occupation, education, and religion.

(2) In most cultures, newborns achieve a particular status because of the family they are born into. If a child is born into a rich family, that child is automatically part of the rich stratum of society. A child who is born into a royal family automatically becomes part of a royal stratum at birth. Some families are considered morally upright, and a child born into such a family will have high social standing as long as he continues to practice the values of his family and the community continues to share these respected values.

(3) In the United States, money seems to give an individual the greatest social status. Many types of wealth define a rich American: a high salary, expensive possessions, a lot of property. Alongside these physical manifestations of wealth are the people of equal wealth whom a rich American knows. High status is assured if the rich American belongs to exclusive clubs or is selected to be a member of an exclusive organization. The number of wealthy contacts one has in a society that values possessions automatically increases one's status as a wealthy person.

(4) One's occupation also plays an important role in status. Interestingly enough, the amount of money one makes is not always the only criterion for assigning rank. Some of the most prestigious occupations are Supreme Court justice, doctor, scientist, governor, and college professor. Although doctors and governors often earn a high salary, scientists and college professors sometimes do not. So clearly, in some cases, factors other than salary are often involved in assigning status to an individual's occupation.

(5) In many cultures, particularly developed ones, education is a consistently important way to improve one's social status. People in most cultures seem to assign value to an educated individual, even if that individual does not earn a lot of money. Something about education confers instant respect on an individual. And this has been true throughout history. In most cultures, the wise person has been awarded a special place in the community.

(6) The same value seems to be given to people who choose a religious vocation, like priests. Although religious people tend not to earn a big salary, and some even live in poverty, society consistently seems to rank religious vocations high on their list of respected occupations. Society seems to believe that both educated and religious people possess valuable knowledge. In a sense, spiritual or intellectual possessions are as important as the physical possessions of the wealthy.

(7) The issue of social stratification is a difficult one to understand, because it seems that many factors are involved. Material wealth, education, religious knowledge—all seem to give certain individuals a privileged position in society. The reasons for assigning social status, like so many expressions of group behavior, are mysterious and the result of many different motivations.*

---

*Adapted from Dye, *Power and Society*, pp. 66–69.

1. The bulk of the sentences in paragraph 1 fit into the organizational pattern of

   a. sequence of events
   b. description
   c. cause–effect
   d. definition

2. The last sentence in paragraph 1 is a

   a. topic sentence
   b. main-idea sentence
   c. minor-detail sentence
   d. major-detail sentence

3. The major organizational pattern of paragraph 2 is

   a. description
   b. sequence of events
   c. definition
   d. thesis–support

4. Paragraph 2 presents three

   a. topic sentences
   b. minor-detail sentences
   c. major-detail sentences
   d. none of these

5. The main idea of paragraph 3 concerns

   a. the value of knowing rich people in the United States
   b. the value of belonging to exclusive clubs in the United States
   c. the value of wealth in achieving social status in the United States
   d. the number of wealthy people one knows

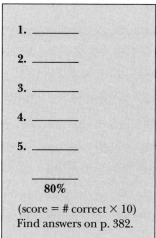

1. _____

2. _____

3. _____

4. _____

5. _____

_____

80%

(score = # correct × 10)
Find answers on p. 382.

Answer each of the following five questions in a short phrase or sentence.

6. What is the main idea of paragraph 4?

7. Find a major detail in paragraph 4.

8. What organizational pattern does paragraph 4 seem to fit into?

9. What is the main idea of paragraph 6?

10. What organizational pattern does the entire excerpt seem to fit into?

**Exercise 6.8
Writing an Effective
Paragraph Using
Organizational
Patterns**

Now that you have read the selection on stratification in Exercise 6.7, go back and reread it. As you do, complete the following outline:

I. Main Idea of the Excerpt:

II. Factors That Influence Social Status

A. Family:

B. Wealth:

C. Occupation:

D. Religion and education:

70%

Ask instructor for
answers.

Refer only to this outline in answering the following:

> *Essay question:* In an organized paragraph, define *social stratification.* Then show how it applies to one's family and one's occupation.

*Exercise 6.9
Determining Main
Ideas, Major Details,
and Organizational
Patterns in a Text
Excerpt*

The following is an excerpt on deviant behavior from a sociology text-book. This material further explains the previous exercise on heredity, environment, and the self.

Read through the excerpt quickly to get a sense of its organization. Then go back and reread it slowly. When you finish, answer the five questions that follow. You may refer to the excerpt in deciding on your answers. Place your answers to the first five questions in the answer box.

Control Theories

(1) To formulate a more comprehensive sociological theory of deviance, the famous French sociologist Émile Durkheim (1858–1917) proposed, in effect, that we dismiss the question, Why do they do it? and ask instead, Why *don't* they do it? Since Durkheim's time, his advice has been heeded by many leading sociological and criminological theorists; this approach to deviance is known as **control theory.**

(2) The initial assumption all control theories make is that life is a vast cafeteria of temptation. By themselves, *deviant acts tend to be attractive, providing rewards to those who engage in them.* To some, theft produces desired goods, and alcohol and drugs supply enjoyment. Indeed, control theorists argue that norms arise to prohibit various kinds of behavior because without these norms such behavior would be frequent.

(3) Put another way, when we consider what things people should not be allowed to do, we don't bother to prohibit behavior that people find unpleasant or unappealing. We assume that people won't do these things anyway. So we concern ourselves with things that people find rewarding and therefore might be tempted to do.

(4) Thus, control theorists take deviance for granted and concentrate instead on explaining why people conform. Their answer is that people vary greatly in the degree of control their groups have over them. In any group, some people are rewarded more for conformity and punished more for deviance than other people are. Control theorists argue that conformity occurs only when people have more to gain by it than they have to gain by deviance.

(5) In a classic paper, Jackson Toby (1957) described teenagers as differing in terms of their **stake in conformity.** This phrase refers to *what a person risks losing* by being detected in deviant behavior. Toby suggested that all of us are tempted but that we resist to the extent that we feel we have much to lose by deviant behavior; for instance, a boy with a low stake in conformity has little "incentive to resist the temptation to do what he wants when he wants to do it."

(6) Therefore, like strain theorists, control theorists accept that access to desired rewards is unequal among members of any society: Some people succeed; some get left out. But while strain theory argues that inequality pushes the have-nots to deviate, control theory stresses how the have-nots are free to deviate. In the words of the song, "Freedom's just another word for nothing left to lose." Some people are free to deviate because they risk very little if their deviate behavior is detected. But for others the costs of detection far exceed the rewards of deviance.

(7) For control theory, the causes of conformity are the **social bonds** between an individual and the group. When these bonds are strong, the individual conforms; when these bonds are weak, the individual deviates. Because the strength of these bonds can fluctuate over time, control theory can explain shifts from deviance to conformity (and vice versa) over a person's lifetime. Because many bonds are not related to social class, control theory can explain both the conformity of the poor and the deviance of the wealthy. But what are these bonds? There are four kinds between the individual and the group: *attachments, investments, involvements,* and *beliefs* (Hirschi, 1969; Stark and Bainbridge, 1997).

Attachments

(8) In accordance with Homans' law of liking, the more often people interact, the more they will come to like one another—they will become attached. Here group solidarity enters the picture. The degree to which an individual is attached to a group (has a social bond) is a function of the number and closeness of her or his **attachments**—how much that individual cares about others and is cared about in return. When we are embedded in an intense local network, we are under intense pressure to live up to the standards and expectations of the group. In accordance with Homans' law of conformity, it is necessary for us to live up to group norms in order to retain the affection and respect of our intimates—we risk isolation from our primary group(s) if we are detected in serious norm violations. We shall explore this more extensively in the next chapter.

(9) When we are alone, we often break norms—we pick our noses, belch, and otherwise act grossly. We usually do not break these norms so freely in company. Moreoover, if we knew for certain that our friends would never find out, we might even commit serious norm violations. Those who lack significant attachments are, in effect, *always alone,* and their friends never know about the norms they break. They do not put relationships with others at risk because they have none to risk. For them, the costs of deviance are low.

(10) By focusing on bonds of attachment, control theory is able to deal with a great many research findings about deviant behavior. The more that young people care about others—parents, friends, and teachers—the less likely they are to commit acts of delinquency (Hirschi,

1969; Liska, 1987). Conversely, delinquents are very weakly attached, even to their delinquent friends (Hirschi, 1969; Kornhauser, 1978).

(11) As Gove noted, sociological theories have trouble explaining why deviance declines with age. Delinquency rates rise rapidly from age 12 through about age 16 and then begin to fall rapidly. Gove's theory of physical fitness would not apply here. In addition, deviant behavior is much higher in the late teens and early twenties than it is after age 30. This is the phenomenon Gove addressed. But Gove's theory does not address the fact that all forms of deviance, not just those requiring physical prowess, decline with age. Gove's theory is pertinent because it may tell us what causes some deviance rates to fall so rapidly with age. But we also must know why "sit down" crimes such as embezzlement also decline with age—albeit not so dramatically. Control theory fills this gap. With the onset of the teens, deviance rates rise rapidly not only because people become stronger but also because attachments weaken for many. Adolescence is a time when parent-child relations often become stressful, and teenagers often feel alienated from other family members. As this occurs, they have reduced stakes in conformity.

(12) Then, in their later teens many young people form strong new attachments, often to persons of the opposite sex. Hence their stakes in conformity rise. Young adults are frequently very deficient in attachments. Often they leave family and childhood friends behind and go out on their own, relatively unattached. With marriage, the birth of children, and steady employment, they form new attachments; thus, the tendency to commit even sedentary crimes lessens as people get older.

(13) Perhaps the most powerful aspect of control theory is its ability to account for weak or missing correlations between social class and most forms of deviance. Close attachments are not confined to the middle and upper classes. Most poor kids love their parents too, and most poor adults love their families and friends. Thus, most poor people have a strong stake in conformity. By the same token, some middle- and upper-class kids don't love their parents, and not all privileged people love their families and friends. Thus, their stake in conformity is low.

(14) Durkheim answered the question, Why don't they do it? on the basis of attachments. As he put it, "We are moral beings to the extent that we are social beings."

(15) The family serves as the primary source of the strong attachments that most effectively make us "social beings." Table 7-11 shows the

Table 7-11 *Current Marital Status and Arrest Among American Males and Females (not including widowed)*

	Married	Single	Divorced and Separated
Percent who have been "picked up" by the police			
Males	17	32	32
Females	5	9	10

Source: Prepared by the author from the General Social Surveys, 1982 and 1984.

impact of marital attachments on the percentage of American adults who have been picked up by the police. Among both men and women, those who were currently married were much less likely to have been picked up by the police than were persons who have never married or persons who were currently divorced or separated. When they are detected in deviant behavior, married people have more to lose: their families.

Investments

(16) The idea of **investments** is simple. We are tied to conformity not only through our attachments to others but also through the stakes we have built up in life—the costs we have expended in constructing a satisfactory life and the rewards we expect. The more we have expended in getting an education, building a career, and acquiring possessions, the greater the risks of deviance. That is, we could lose our investments if we were detected in deviant behavior. An unemployed derelict may have very little to lose if caught sticking up a liquor store and a considerable amount to gain if he or she gets away with it. But it would be crazy for a successful lawyer to risk so much for so little, and most people rarely make really irrational decisions. When successful lawyers and bankers fail to resist the temptation to steal, they usually steal huge sums that seem to them to make the risks worthwhile. But the underlying processes of choice are the same for rich and poor.

(17) Variations in investments also help account for the tendency of delinquents to reform as they reach adulthood. At age 14, most people have little investment at stake when they deviate. However, after people have begun to build normal adult lives, their investments mount rapidly.

Involvements

(18) The **involvement** aspect of control theory takes into account that time and energy are limited. The more time a person spends on activities that conform to the norms, the less time and energy that person has to devote to deviant activities.

(19) To a considerable extent, involvements are a consequence of investments and attachments. People who have families, or play football after school, or are engrossed in hobbies, or are busy with careers have much less time and energy left for violating norms than do people with few attachments and investments. Popular wisdom has it that "idle hands are the devil's workshop." Many studies have reported that the more time young people spend "hanging around" or riding in cars, the more likely they are to commit delinquent acts (Hirschi, 1969). And the more time they spend doing schoolwork or even talking with friends, the less likely they are to get into trouble. That is, people neglect to do all sorts of things for lack of time. College couples even delay breaking up until between terms or until the summer holiday, when they have more time (Hill, Rubin, and Peplau, 1976). People also tend not to do deviant things when they are pressed for time.

Beliefs

(20) Control theory stresses human rationality: Whether people tend to deviate or to conform depends on their calculations of the costs

Table 7-12   *Church Attendance and Arrest Among American Adults*

	Attend Church			
	Weekly	*Monthly*	*Yearly*	*Less Than Yearly*
Percent who have been "picked up" by the police	5	13	15	22

Source: Prepared by the author from the General Social Surveys, 1982 and 1984.

and benefits of deviance or conformity. But control theorists also recognize that through socialization we form **beliefs** about how the world works and how it *ought* to work. That is, we develop beliefs about how people, including ourselves, should behave. Sociologists often describe this as the **internalization of norms,** instead of using the word *conscience.*

(21) We accept norms not only because our friends expect us to but also because we risk our self-respect if we deviate. The phrase "I'm not that kind of person" indicates that we hold certain beliefs about proper behavior. When a friend suggests a deviant act and assures us that nobody will know, we display internalized norms if we respond, "Yes, but *I* will know."

(22) By themselves, our beliefs may or may not cause us to conform. As we saw in Chapter 4, individual religious beliefs will prevent delinquent behavior only when the person is part of a community in which the majority belong to religious organizations. However, because most Americans live in such a community, a national sample of adults ought to display a negative correlation between attending church and having been picked up by the police. The data in Table 7-12 conform this hypothesis: People who attend church less than once a year are more than four times as likely as weekly attenders to have been picked up by the police.

(23) Put another way, religion gains the power to alter behavior when it is supported by attachments to others who accept the authority of the moral beliefs that religion teaches. This fact helps us to recognize that all four elements of control theory are interconnected. Attachments are also investments—much time and energy go into building close relations with others. Attachments and investments both act as involvements: Time spent with friends or at work is time not available for deviance. In addition, our beliefs will also determine with whom we choose to become attached and what investments we decide to make.

(24) As with other explanations of criminal and deviant behavior, control theory also cannot stand alone. It seeks to explain conformity to the norms of a social group, but it doesn't identify which group or note that conformity to the norms of one group may represent deviance from the norms of another group. In combination with subcultural theory, we have a more complete explanation of deviance. And control theory clearly implies and therefore requires elements of differential associa-

tion–social learning theory to specify mechanisms by which attachments generate conformity.*

1. The main idea of the entire excerpt seems to be about

   a. how people naturally want to control others
   b. how doing right is a natural human behavior
   c. how men tend to break the law more than women
   d. how it is natural for people to want to break the law

2. The main idea of paragraph 5 concerns

   a. how breaking the law is influenced by what the individual stands to lose
   b. teenagers breaking the law
   c. deviant behavior
   d. why teenagers demonstrate a high stake in conformity

3. The major organizational pattern of paragraph 8 seems to be

   a. definition
   b. cause–effect
   c. sequence of events
   d. description

4. The major organizational pattern of paragraph 15 seems to be

   a. thesis–support
   b. definition
   c. spatial–geographic
   d. sequence of events

5. The organizational patterns that seems to structure paragraphs 18 and 19 are:

   a. description and cause–effect
   b. compare–contrast and cause–effect
   c. definition and cause–effect
   d. definition and description

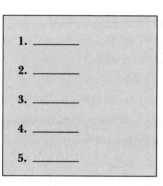

1. _____

2. _____

3. _____

4. _____

5. _____

   Read the following three questions. Then go back and reread the excerpt. Answer these questions in a phrase or sentence without looking back.

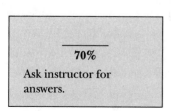

70%

Ask instructor for answers.

6. How does the question "Why don't they do it?" relate to Durkheim's control theory? (2 points)

7. According to control theorists, what happens to individual behavior when social bonds are strong? (2 points)

*Adapted from Rodney Stark, *Sociology*, 5th ed. (Belmont, Calif.: Wadsworth, 1998), pp. 186–191.

8. How would control theorists explain the fact that a married man is less likely to have a police record than a single man? (1 point)

Follow-up on Chapter 6

Now that you have studied this introduction and completed the exercises, it may be helpful to see how your reading of this topic has changed some of your ideas about social issues and improved your abilities in identifying organizational patterns. You may want to go back to the exercises to reread them just for their content, or for what they have to say about sociology, and you may want to review the introduction. Then answer the following questions either individually or in small groups.

On the Topic of Sociology

1. How would you now define *sociology*?

2. What sociological issue that you read about interests you the most? Why?

3. Where do you stand on the issue of nature–nurture?

4. What area of sociology do you now want to study further?

On Identifying Organizational Patterns

5. Are you now better able to identify organizational patterns?

6. Are you able to locate organizational patterns in longer material such as textbook chapters?

7. Are you starting to use various organizational patterns in your writing? Are you starting to use transitions for particular organizational patterns in your writing?

8. Which organizational patterns are still difficult for you to identify and use? Why do you think this is so?

 Internet Activity

In groups of four or five students, research on the Internet the following questions related to criminal behavior. If you have access to InfoTrac, locate information from that source. When you have completed your research, share your responses with your group.

1. Has the crime rate in the United States gone down or has it gone up in the past year?
2. Which crimes have shown the highest decrease?
3. Which crimes have shown the highest increase?
4. Which Internet sources on crime were you able to locate?

CHAPTER 7

Summarizing and Paraphrasing

In this chapter, you will learn about:

- How to summarize material you read or hear
- How to paraphrase material you read or hear

Being able to summarize information from textbooks, lectures, discussions, and lecture and discussion notes are some of the most important skills to master. Organized summaries will provide helpful study sheets for exams. A *summary* is an accurate restatement of material, presented in condensed form. The key terms to remember are *accurate* and *condensed*. Inaccurate summaries are useless, while lengthy summaries are much like the original.

Summarizing, like note taking and critical reading, is a complex activity that improves with practice. So do not expect to be an expert summarizer right away. Knowing how to summarize well will prepare you for Part Three on note taking, which relies heavily on summarizing.

How to Summarize

To be able to summarize efficiently, you need to identify main ideas and major details, both in lectures and in reading textbooks. As your summaries improve, you will be choosing the significant major details. In summaries, you rarely include minor details.

For now, follow these steps when you summarize textbook, lecture, and discussion material. Most of these hints apply to summarizing written material. In Part Three you will learn more about how to summarize while listening to lectures and discussions.

1. In each paragraph of text or on each page of lecture notes, locate the main idea, which is often the first sentence. You must include these main ideas in your summary. Underline the main idea twice or use a curved line. And underline the important parts of the sentence. Look at this example:

   Anthropology is a study that compares human societies and cultures, attempting to analyze, describe, and explain different ways of life in different parts of the world.

2. Sometimes main ideas are implied, and often in textbooks two or three shorter paragraphs work like one big paragraph. If you read

several paragraphs and cannot locate a main-idea sentence, write your own in the margin.

3. Underline one or two major details in each paragraph of text or section of lecture notes. Do not underline the entire sentence, just the important words. Underline these details once to differentiate them from main ideas. See how the major detail is highlighted in this sentence:

> <u>Cultural anthropology</u> focuses mainly on <u>human behavior that is learned</u> rather than behavior that is transmitted genetically and <u>considers what is typical</u> in a particular <u>group or society</u>

Which details should you include? This choice may be difficult at first; just keep asking yourself: Which are the important details? Which most directly support the main idea? The layout of the textbook should help you. Main ideas and certain major details are often in boldface print or in italics. In lectures and discussions, listen for such comments as "I want you to remember this," "It is important to remember," or "I repeat." Also, note what the instructor writes on the blackboard; these are his clues that he is presenting key points.

4. When you have finished five or six paragraphs of textbook material and have underlined main ideas and major details, stop reading. Also, when you have marked a page or two of lecture and discussion notes, put your pen down. Then, write a summary of five or six sentences or phrases, either in outline form or in a short paragraph. It is often better to put your summaries in outline form because you can separate main ideas from major details.

Put this summary in your own words. By putting the information in your own words, you make it easier to learn. When you are copying from a textbook or from your lecture and discussion notes, you are not actively thinking, and you will probably not remember what you have copied. Only when you read or hear a definition should you copy. Here, the exact wording is necessary for you to understand the term. Learning research consistently shows that when you make material your own by using the words familiar to you, you have a much greater chance of remembering it. You will learn more about summarizing text material in Chapter 14 on the SQ3R study system.

Read the following five-paragraph excerpt on the study of anthropology. See if you can locate the main ideas and significant major details by effective underlining. Then place your summary in the outline skeleton that follows the excerpt. Use your own words wherever possible.

(1) Who were the Nacirema? How did they live? What accounted for their extreme ideology of remaking the natural environment? Why did they disappear? What can we learn from a study of their culture?

(2) Anthropology, the comparative study of human societies and cultures, provides some answers to questions like these. The aim of

anthropology is to describe, analyze, and explain the different ways of life, or cultures, through which human groups, or societies, have adapted to their environments. Anthropology is comparative in that it attempts to understand both similarities and differences among human societies, in both the past and the present. Only by the study of humanity in its total variety can we understand the origins and development of our species.

(3) Anthropologists study our species from its beginnings several million years ago right up to the present. We study human beings as they live in every corner of the earth, in all kinds of physical environments. Some anthropologists are now trying to project how human beings will live in outer space. It is this interest in humankind throughout time and in all parts of the world that distinguishes anthropology as a scientific and humanistic discipline. In other academic disciplines, human behavior is studied primarily from the point of view of Western society. "Human nature" is thought to be the same as the behavior of people as they exist in the modern industrial nations of Europe and the United States.

(4) Human beings everywhere consider their own behavior not only right, but natural. For example, both "common sense" and Western economic theory see human beings as "naturally" individualistic and competitive. But in some societies, human beings are not competitive, and the group is more important than the individual. Anthropologists see the Western idea of "economic man"—the individual motivated by profit and rational self-interest—as the result of the particular socio-economic and political system we live in. It is not an explanation of the behavior of the Arapesh hunter in New Guinea, who makes sure he is not always the first to sight and claim the game, so that others will not leave him to hunt alone (Mead 1963:38). In anthropology, more than any other discipline, concepts of human nature and theories of human behavior are based on studies of human groups whose goals, values, views of reality, and environmental adaptations are very different from those of modern, industrial Western societies.

(5) In their attempts to explain human variation, anthropologists combine the study of both human biology and the learned and shared patterns of human behavior we call culture. Other academic disciplines focus on one factor—biology, psychology, physiology, or society—as the explanation of human behavior. Anthropology seeks to understand human beings as whole organisms who adapt to their environments through a complex interaction of biology and culture.*

I. Anthropology

A. Definition: _____

B. Three basic aims: _____

*Serena Nanda, *Cultural Anthropology*, 4th ed. (Belmont, Calif.: Wadsworth, 1991), p. 5.

C. How anthropology is different from other disciplines:

_____

D. Two studies anthropology combines: _____

_____

Compare your underlining and summary with that on pp. 382–384.

Now that you have completed your underlining and summary and checked it with the answer key, read the following comments about the excerpt.

1. Paragraph 1 is basically meant to catch your attention; your note taking should begin with paragraph 2.

2. In paragraph 2, did you notice that the first sentence defines anthropology and the next sentences address the specific concerns of anthropology?

3. Paragraphs 3 and 4 focus on the differences between anthropology and other disciplines.

4. Paragraph 5 emphasizes those studies anthropology relies on to conduct its research.

This excerpt has a fairly straightforward organization—general information usually comes before the details. Even when the organization is difficult to follow—when the main idea is implied—you are still following the same procedure as you summarize. You look for the general statement made by a paragraph or paragraphs; then you locate the specific information that supports it.

As you continue working through this book, you will be completing several summaries. As you complete each summary, your abilities will improve.

You may now want to complete Exercises 7.1, 7.2, and 7.3 on pages 140–146.

How to Paraphrase

Sometimes as you summarize, you may come upon a difficult sentence. Often you cannot understand this sentence because either it is long or the vocabulary is difficult. When you paraphrase, you try to make sense of a difficult sentence. A *paraphrase* is a simply worded, accurate restatement of a phrase, a sentence, or sentences. Unlike a summary, a paraphrase may be longer than the original statement.

Here are some steps that you need to follow when you paraphrase. Most of these suggestions apply to what you read.

1. Read each difficult sentence carefully. Reread the sentence that comes before it and after it. You do this to place the difficult sentence in its proper context.

2. If the sentence has difficult words, look them up in the dictionary or in the glossary of the textbook. Often your confusion abates when you understand the terminology. But don't simply find synonyms for words you do not know and plug them into your paraphrase. Let your understanding of any difficult words help you take a fresh look at the entire sentence. You may want to reread the sentence you are paraphrasing once you have looked up and understood a difficult word.

3. Divide long sentences into phrases or clauses. Phrases and clauses are often set off by commas, semicolons, colons, or dashes. If you hear a particularly long sentence in a lecture or discussion, listen for the pauses.

4. Determine the subject and verb of the sentence. The subject and verb should give you the core meaning of the sentence.

5. If the statement is written, reread the phrases and clauses. Even read these parts aloud if you have to.

6. Be sure your paraphrase is complete and that no part of the sentence has been omitted.

7. As much as possible, write your paraphrase in your own words, as you do with your summaries. By using your own words in your paraphrase, you have a better chance of understanding the difficult sentence because you will not be tied to the voice and style of the original sentence.

8. Write your paraphrase in the textbook margins or on the left-hand side of your notes.

Look at the following italicized sentence, and use these eight steps to paraphrase it correctly. It's the fourth sentence in paragraph 4 from the excerpt in anthropology that you just summarized. You are also given the preceding sentence and the one that follows:

But in some societies, human beings are not competitive, and the group is more important than the individual. *Anthropologists see the Western idea of "economic man"—the individual motivated by profit and rational self-interest—as the result of the particular socioeconomic and political system we live in.* It is not an explanation of the behavior of the Arapesh hunter in New Guinea, who makes sure he is not always the first to sight and claim the game, so that others will not leave him to hunt alone.

Write your paraphrase here: _____

_____

After writing your paraphrase, see whether you used some of the following practices:

1. You notice that the sentence before refers to societies in which competition is unimportant, and the sentence after describes the behavior of the New Guinea hunter. Your sentence concerns the notion of the economic man in the Western world.

2. You may have looked up the word *rational* to find that it means logical or reasoned and *Western* to refer to European and American history and civilizations.

3. You note that the sentence is broken up by dashes, with a description of economic man between the dashes. Without this parenthetical material, the sentence is quite clear.

4. You note that the subject of the sentence is *anthropologists* and the verb is *see.* You then ask: What do anthropologists see? Your answer is that anthropologists see something about economic man in the West.

5. It is the object of this sentence—what anthropologists see—that is confusing, mainly because this part of the sentence is long and written in a complicated syntax. After rereading this part of the sentence, you realize that economic man has the following characteristics: he focuses on himself in a desire to make money and this desire is shaped by his culture.

Once you have completed these steps, you are ready to write your paraphrase, which should say something like: "Anthropologists see economic man to be reasoned and self-centered in his desire to make money, and he is like this because of the particular environment that influences all Western people."

Paraphrasing may seem tedious, but as you continue to paraphrase, you will find that your critical reading practices will improve. Most students who cannot paraphrase simply ignore difficult passages and thus have poorer comprehension of the material, often incorrectly summarizing the material they read. As your paraphrasing abilities improve, you will be able to determine whether your difficulty in comprehension is due to difficult words or to long and involved sentences. In this way, you will begin to analyze the author's style. In some cases, you will find that your paraphrase is a simple statement after all—that in the original passage, the author used big words and many words to express a simple idea. In others, your paraphrase will allow you to uncover an essential and difficult concept in your reading. Finally, you will discover that as you learn more in a particular subject, it will be easier for you to paraphrase difficult sentences in that field.

You may now want to complete Exercises 7.4 and 7.5 on pages 146–151.

Summary

Summarizing and paraphrasing are necessary practices in reading textbooks, in listening to lectures and discussions, and in reviewing your notes. Both are sophisticated, critical activities. In summarizing, you locate main ideas and important details. It is an active process of sorting out the important from the less important and the unimportant. When you paraphrase, you attempt to understand a difficult sentence or sentences. Paraphrasing involves seeing a sentence in its context, looking up new words, and dividing the sentence into phrases and clauses. Finally, when you summarize and paraphrase, you are putting information into your own words and thus have a better chance of remembering it.

Did the summary of this introduction separate the significant from the less significant? Was it worded differently? Do you think it was a successful summary?

You are now ready to practice these two activities in the following exercises, which also deal with anthropology, and in Part Three on note taking.

Summary Box   *Summarizing and Paraphrasing*

What are they?	How do you use them?	Why do you use them?
Summarizing: accurate restatement of material in fewer words.	Locating ideas and significant details and put this information in your own words.	To remember more easily large chunks of information.
Paraphrasing: accurate restatement of difficult material to put it more simply.	Read sentence in its context; look up new words; divide sentences into smaller chunks.	To understand difficult sentences that you would otherwise skip over.

Skills Practice Topic: Anthropology

All the exercises in this chapter focus on anthropology, a subject you may study in your college career.

Before you begin these exercises, answer the following questions either individually or in small groups to get some sense of what you already know about anthropology.

1. How would you define the study of anthropology?
2. What is meant by the term *culture*?
3. Are there any topics in anthropology that you have already studied?
4. How do you think an anthropologist would study religion?

Exercise 7.1
Summarizing a
Longer Passage

The following excerpt is from an anthropology textbook, and it explains how anthropologists study religion. Your job is to underline main ideas and major details. Then, based on your underlinings, complete the five questions that follow. Remember not to underline entire sentences, just the important parts.

The Functions of Religion

The Search for Order and Meaning

(1) One of the most important functions of religion is to give meaning to and explain those aspects of the physical and social environment that are important in the lives of individuals and societies. Religion deals with the nature of life and death, the creation of the universe, the origin of society and groups within the society, the relationship of individuals and groups to one another, and the relation of humankind to nature. Anthropologists call this whole cognitive system a cosmology, or world view. Human societies create images of reality, often in symbolic ways, that serve as a framework for interpreting events and experiences, particularly those that are out of the ordinary. These "different realities" emerge as a way of imposing order and meaning on the world within which humans live and of giving humans the feeling that they have some measure of control over that world.

(2) Science and religion, which are often opposed in Western thought, are similar in that both involve "the quest for unity underlying apparent diversity; for simplicity underlying apparent complexity; for order underlying apparent disorder; for regularity underlying apparent anomaly" (Horton and Finnegan 1973). But where science provides explanations that are open to new data and explicitly acknowledges a possibility of various alternatives, religious systems tend not to be open to empirical testing.

(3) The separation between religion and science in our own society corresponds to our sharp separation of the supernatural and the natural. In other societies, these two concepts are less sharply separated. The supernatural can be seen as part of the natural and as intervening in all aspects of life. Thus, the kin group includes both living relatives and dead ancestors; power and leadership are often believed to have divine origins; rules of behavior are given divine sanction; and breaches are punished by the gods. The success of even ordinary undertakings in the physical world is ensured by enlisting the help of supernatural powers. Natural disasters, illness, and misfortune are believed to be caused by extrahuman or supernatural spirits. Natural and supernatural, human and natural, past, present, and future may be perceived as a unity in a way that violates the logic of Western thought. This makes it difficult for us to understand many non-Western religions and accounts for our ethnocentric labeling of them as "irrational," "contradictory," or the products of faulty thinking.

(4) **Reducing Anxiety and Increasing Control** Many religious practices are aimed at ensuring success in carrying out a wide variety of human activities. Prayers and offerings are made to supernatural beings in the hope that they will aid a particular individual or community. Rituals are performed to call on supernatural beings and to control forces that appear to be unpredictable, such as those in the natural

environment upon which humans depend for survival. One of the widespread practices used to control supernatural forces is magic. Although magical practices exist in many societies, magic seems to be more prominent in those in which there is less predictability in the outcome of events and thus less feeling of being in control of the social and physical environment. In the Trobriand Islands, for example, magic is not used for ordinary canoe trips within the lagoons, but only when the Islanders undertake the long-distance and dangerous canoe trips to other islands in their kula trade. Magic is also prevalent in sports and games of chance.

(5) Even if magic cannot "work" from the standpoint of Western science, it may be effective in achieving results indirectly, mainly by reducing the anxiety of the individuals and groups that practice it. This reduced anxiety allows them to proceed with more confidence, and the confidence may lead to greater success. Where technological advance and science are able to increase predictability and control over events and human relations, magic tends to become less important.

(6) **Maintaining the Social Order**   Religion has a number of important functions that either directly or indirectly help maintain the social order and the survival of a society. To begin with, religious beliefs about good and evil are reinforced by supernatural means of social control. Thus, religion is a powerful force for conformity in a society. Furthermore, through myth and ritual, social values are given sacred authority and provide a reason for the present social order. Religious ritual also intensifies solidarity by creating an atmosphere in which people experience their common identity in emotionally moving ways. Religion is also an important educational institution. Initiation rites, for example, almost always include the transmission of information about cultural practices and tradition.

(7) By supporting the present social order and defining the place of the individual in society and in the universe, religion also provides people with a sense of personal identity and belonging. When individuals have lost a positive identity, or when life has no meaning because of the disintegration of a traditional culture, religion can supply a new and more positive identity and become the basis for a new adaptation. Religion can also provide an escape from reality; in the religious beliefs of an afterlife or the coming of a Messiah, powerless people who live in harsh and deprived circumstances can create an illusion of power through the manipulation of religious symbols. Religion in these circumstances is an outlet for frustration, resentment, and anger and is a way of draining off energy that might otherwise be turned against the social system. In this way, religion indirectly contributes to maintaining the social order.

(8) In summary, religion has both instrumental and expressive functions. The instrumental aspect of religion has to do with actions performed in the belief that, if people do certain things, they can influence the course of natural or social events to their advantage. The expressive aspect of ritual refers to the ways in which religious symbolism is used to express ideas about the relation of humans to nature, self to society, or group to group. In its expressive aspect, religion is an important force for social integration.*

---

*Nanda, *Cultural Anthropology*, pp. 361–363.

1. The main idea of paragraph 1 is:

   a. Anthropology can effectively study religion.
   b. Cosmology is a world view.
   c. Religion serves to give meaning to and explain what is important in a particular society.
   d. Religion serves to give its members control of their world.

2. Paragraph 2 serves to:

   a. define science
   b. introduce the similarities and differences between religion and science
   c. show how religion tends to organize that which is disorganized in life
   d. show how religion is not scientific

3. The main idea of paragraph 3 concerns:

   a. the separation of the natural and supernatural in our society and their connection in other societies
   b. the power that the dead exert in other cultures
   c. how common practices rely on the supernatural for their success
   d. the irrational side of non-Western religions

4. The last sentence in paragraph 6 is a:

   a. main-idea sentence
   b. major-detail sentence
   c. minor-detail sentence
   d. none of these

5. Which of the following is *not* a main idea of this excerpt?

   a. Religion serves to ensure the success of a culture's activities.
   b. Magic tends to create anxiety among the peoples who practice it.
   c. Religion helps maintain the social order.
   d. Religion helps people derive a sense of belonging.

1. _____

2. _____

3. _____

4. _____

5. _____

_____

(score = # correct × 20)
Find answers on p. 384.

Exercise 7.2
Summarizing a
Second Passage

The following is a second excerpt from an anthropology textbook, focusing on how a New Guinea tribe uses religion to satisfy several of its needs. As in the previous exercise, underline the main ideas and significant details in each paragraph. Underline only key sentence parts. From your underlinings, finish the partially completed outline that follows.

Religious Ritual and Adaptation

(1) Recent research has shown that religious belief and ritual not only indirectly contribute to the survival of a society but may also directly affect the relationship between a social group and its physical environment. A study by Roy Rappaport (1967) of the Tsembaga of New Guinea shows how religious belief and ritual may produce "a practical result on the external world."

(2) The Tsembaga, who live in the valleys of a mountain range in New Guinea, are swidden cultivators who also raise pigs. Small numbers of pigs are easy to keep, as they eat anything and help keep residential areas free from garbage. Although pigs can ruin gardens in the early stages of planting, after the trees are well established, pigs are allowed to root in the gardens, where they actually help cultivation by eating seeds and tubers (sweet potatoes). If pig herds grow very large, however, feeding them becomes a problem, and it becomes necessary for extra food to be harvested just to feed the pigs. Furthermore, when pig herds become too large, they are more likely to invade gardens and require more supervision. The Tsembaga kill pigs only on ritual occasions—either at pig feasts or in times of misfortune such as illness, death, or warfare.

(3) The Tsembaga have a ritual cycle that they perform, they say, in order to rearrange their relationships with the supernatural world. This cycle can be viewed as beginning with the rituals performed during warfare. In Tsembaga warfare, opponents generally occupy territories next to each other. After hostilities have broken out, each side performs certain rituals that formally designate the other group as the enemy. Fighting may continue on and off for weeks, sometimes ending with one group's being routed. In this case, the survivors go to live with their kinsmen, and the victors destroy the losers' gardens, slaughter their pigs, and burn their houses. The victors do not occupy their land, however, as this is believed to be guarded by the ancestors of the defeated group.

(4) Most Tsembaga warfare ends in truce, however, with both groups remaining on their territory. When a truce is declared, each group performs a ritual called "planting the rumbin." The rumbin is dedicated to the ancestors, who are thanked for helping in the fight. At this ritual planting, there is a wholesale slaughter of adult pigs. Some of the meat is eaten by the local group itself, and the rest is distributed to other groups that have helped it fight. After this feast, there is a period in which the fighting groups are still considered to be in debt to their allies and their ancestors. This period will not end until the rumbin plant is uprooted. This ritual also requires a pig feast and occurs when there are sufficient pigs.

(5) The question is: How many pigs are sufficient? It is when pig herds reach over four per woman caretaker that they become too troublesome to manage and begin to compete with humans for food. Thus, it is the wives of the owners of large numbers of pigs who begin agitating for the ritual to uproot the rumbin. This ritual, which is followed by a pig festival lasting about a year, involves much entertaining among villages. Food is exchanged, and hosts and guests spend the nights dancing. At this time, future alliances may be set up between hosts and guests. At this time, also, much trade takes place, involving such items as axes, bird plumes, and shell ornaments. For one festival, Rappaport observed that between 4,500 and 6,000 pounds of pig meat were distributed over 163 occasions to between 2,000 and 3,000 people in seventeen local groups. The pig festival ends with another pig slaughter and the public presentation of a salted pig belly to one's allies. This concludes the ritual cycle. A local group would now consider itself free to attack its neighbors, knowing that assistance from both human allies and

ancestors would be forthcoming because their obligations to feed them pork has been fulfilled.

(6) This ritual cycle among the Tsembaga shows a number of functions of religion. It adjusts the man-land ratio, as survivors in a defeated group seek refuge in other local groups. It also facilitates trade through the markets and exchanges that take place during the year of the pig festival. Most directly in terms of survival, however, it ensures the distribution of local surpluses of pig meat, which is a source of high-quality protein, throughout the whole Tsembaga region. The ritual cycle also helps to maintain an undegraded environment, as pigs are killed when there get to be too many of them and when they threaten the source of human food.*

I. Tsembaga's use of pigs

> Answers will vary. Ask instructor for sample underlinings and outline.

   A.

   B.

   C.

II. The Tsembaga ritual cycle

   A.

   B.

   C.

III. Description of "planting the rumbin" _____

IV. Description of pig festival _____

V. Functions of ritual cycle

   A.

   B.

   C.

   D.

_____

*Nanda, *Cultural Anthropology,* pp. 364–365.

Exercise 7.3
Summarizing a
Third Passage

This third excerpt deals with the anthropological examination of various kinds of beliefs. In this excerpt, several important terms related to belief are introduced and explained. As with the previous two exercises, underline main ideas and significant details. Then complete an outline—this time without any help—summarizing the main ideas and major details.

Kinds of Beliefs: Animism and Animatism

(1) A basic distinction in types of religious beliefs is that between animism and animatism. **Animism** is the belief that not only living creatures but also inanimate objects have life and personality; these supernatural persons are referred to as spirits, ghosts, or gods. Such beings are believed to behave as people do: They are conscious, they have will, and they feel the same emotions as human beings feel. Such spirits may reside in features of the physical environment, such as trees or stones, or they may reside in animals. In hunting societies—for example, the Lele of Africa and the Inuit—the spirits of animals are worshipped because it is believed that a hunt will be successful only if an animal allows itself to be killed. Souls, which may also reside in human bodies, are believed to be able to leave the body at will, temporarily during sleep or permanently as in death. Spirits or souls that leave the body at death turn into ghosts, which come in a variety of forms and relate in various ways to the living in different cultures.

(2) The distinction between a spirit and a god is mostly one of scale. A god is a supernatural being of great importance and power; a spirit is a lesser being. **Polytheism** is the term used for a religion with many gods, and **monotheism** refers to a religion with only one god. Whether a religion is polytheistic or monotheistic is not so clear-cut in real cultures, however. In so-called polytheistic religions, the many gods may be just so many aspects of the one god. In India, for example, it is said that there are literally millions of gods; yet even an uneducated Indian will understand that in some way (which does not confuse him or her, though it may confuse us), these are all aspects of one divine essence.

(3) The Nuer are another culture in which the distinction between the Great Spirit and lesser spirits is fuzzy to the outsider. The Nuer, of course, have no difficulty in understanding the different contexts in which different aspects of the Great Spirit are invoked. E. E. Evans-Pritchard (1968) describes a ceremony held to end a blood feud. All the speakers, representing both clans and including the Leopard Skin chief, addressed the various gods: Great Spirit, spirit of the sky, spirit of our community, spirit of the flesh (this refers to the divine power of the Leopard Skin chief), and spirit of our fathers. Each clan representative appealed to God not only as God but also as God in relation to the group he represented. The Leopard Skin chief referred to God in his special relation to his religious role as mediator, as well as to the priestly lineage he belonged to.

(4) Just as in polytheistic religions, in which all gods and spirits may be reflections of one god, so in monotheistic religions, the one god may have several aspects. In the Roman Catholic religion, for example, there is God the Father, the Son, and the Holy Ghost, in addition to a number of lesser supernatural spirits such as the saints, ghosts, the devil, and the

souls of people in heaven, hell, and purgatory, as well as the souls of those living on earth.

(5) **Animatism** is the belief in an impersonal supernatural power. *Mana* is perhaps the most widely known term for this power. **Mana**, or supernatural power, may be inherent in the universe but may also be concentrated in individuals or in objects. We have seen earlier that Polynesian chiefs had a much higher degree of mana than ordinary people did. Mana is the key to success, but it can also be dangerous. That is why the belief in mana is so frequently associated with an elaborate system of taboos, or prohibitions. Mana is like electricity; it is a powerful force, but it can be dangerous when not approached with the proper caution.

(6) A cross-cultural approach seems to indicate that mana, or power, is often found in those areas (spatial, temporal, verbal, or physical) that are the boundaries between clear-cut categories. Hair, for example, is believed to contain supernatural power in many different cultures (remember the Old Testament story of Samson and Delilah). Hair is a symbol of the boundary between the self and the not-self. It is both part of a person and can be separated from the person. Hence its ambiguity and its power. Doorways and gates are also familiar symbols of supernatural power. They separate the inside from the outside and can thus serve as a symbol of moral categories such as good and evil, pure and impure. Because these symbols of boundaries contain supernatural power, they are frequently part of religious ritual and are surrounded by religious taboos.*

Write your outline of this passage here.

Answers will vary. Check your underlinings and outline with the sample underlinings and outline on pp. 386–388.

Exercise 7.4
Paraphrasing
Sentences in
Paragraphs

Four paragraphs on practices and rituals follow, and you will be able to apply what you have learned so far about religion and anthropology to the concepts of ritual and prayer. In these paragraphs, you will be asked to paraphrase five sentences. Before you answer these questions, read through the excerpt to get a general understanding of it. Then apply the rules for paraphrasing to these sentences. Read through the four paraphrasing choices and select the paraphrase that is most like yours. Place all of your answers in the answer box.

Nanda, Cultural Anthropology, pp. 367–369.

Practices and Rituals

(1)   [1]A religious ritual is a patterned act that involves the manipulation of religious symbols.   [2]Most religious rituals use a combination of the following practices to contact and control supernatural spirits and powers: prayer, offerings and sacrifices, manipulation of objects, telling or acting out myths, altering the physiological state of the individual (as in trance and ecstatic experiences or through drugs), music, dance, and drama (Wallace 1966).

Prayers and Offerings

(2)   [3]Prayer is any conversation held with spirits and gods. [4]Prayer can involve a request or a pleading; it can be in the form of a bargain or consist of merely praising the deity.   [5]In many religions, it is common to make a vow in which the individual promises to carry out a certain kind of behavior, such as going on a pilgrimage or building a temple, if the gods will grant a particular wish.   [6]Other forms of prayer are less familiar to the Westerner. In some cultures, gods can be lied to, commanded, or ridiculed.   [7]Among the many Northwest Coast tribes of North America, the insulting tone used to one's political rivals was also used to the gods.   [8]In these ranked societies, the greatest insult was to call a man a slave; when calamities fell or their prayers were not answered, people would vent their anger against the gods by saying, "You are a great slave" (Benedict 1961:221).

(3)   [9]Making offerings and sacrifices to supernatural beings is also a widespread religious practice.   [10]Sometimes these offerings consist of the first fruits of a harvest—grain, fish, or game.   [11]Sometimes the offering of food is in the form of a meal for the gods; among the Hindus, the gods are given food that they eat behind a curtain.   [12]After the gods have eaten, this food is distributed among the worshippers.

(4)   [13]In some societies, animals or humans may be sacrificed as an offering to the gods.   [14]Among cattle pastoralists of East Africa, such as the Nuer and the Pokot, cattle sacrifices are an important part of religious practices.   [15]The essence of the East African "cattle complex" is that cattle are killed and eaten only in a ritual and religious context, which seems to be an inefficient use of resources.   [16]This ritual use of cattle in sacrifice has always been of interest to anthropologists, and at one time it was given as a common example of how religious practices interfere with rational exploitation of the environment.   [17]More recent research has shown, however, that the sacrifice of cattle in a ritual context may be quite adaptive.   [18]Cattle sacrifices are offered in community feasts that occur on a fairly regular schedule, averaging once a week in any particular neighborhood.   [19]The feasts are thus an important source of meat in the diet.   [20]Furthermore, the religious taboo that an individual who eats ritually slaughtered meat may not take milk on the same day has the effect of making milk more available to those who have no meat, or conserving milk, which can be consumed as sour milk on the following day.   [21]In addition, the Pokot prefer fresh meat, which is also healthier than meat that is not fresh.   [22]Because one family could not consume a whole steer by itself, the problem of how to utilize beef most efficiently without refrigeration techniques is solved by offering it

to the community in a ceremonial setting.   [23]In this way, meat can be shared without fighting over the supply, because the portions are distributed according to age and sex by a rigid formula (Schneider 1973).*

1. An effective paraphrase for sentence 8 is:

   a. These tribes disliked the term *slave.*
   b. In anger, these tribes would insult the gods by accusing them of being slaves.
   c. For these tribes the term *slave* was insulting, and during bad times even the gods were accused of being slaves.
   d. The greatest slave was often considered to be the one who defied the gods somehow.

2. An effective paraphrase for sentence 15 is:

   a. In this case, cattle is only eaten when a religious service is practiced.
   b. This East African practice requires that cattle be killed and eaten during a religious experience, but this seems to be a wasteful practice.
   c. Cattle are eaten in a ritualized context, which makes use of the resources.
   d. The basis of cattle killing for these tribes must be ritualized and religious.

3. An effective paraphrase for sentence 16 is:

   a. The use of cattle in a ritualized sacrifice is of interest to anthropologists because it was evidence that religion was in conflict with a reasoned use of the environment.
   b. Destroying the environment is often not in agreement with the practices of ritual.
   c. Anthropologists see that religion interferes with the correct use of the environment.
   d. Sacrificing cattle is an interesting phenomenon for anthropologists studying the respectful uses of the environment.

4. An effective paraphrase for sentence 22 is:

   a. Eating an entire cow is difficult, even for a tribe.
   b. How to keep meat cold was a problem in keeping the beef from spoiling.
   c. Since one family could not eat all of the cow, offering the cow as a sacrifice to the rest of the tribe solved the problem of the meat keeping.
   d. The consumption of an entire cow was indeed a problem, especially since refrigeration was unknown to this tribe.

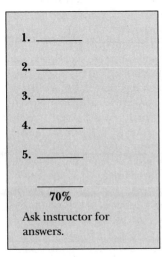

1. _____

2. _____

3. _____

4. _____

5. _____

_____
70%

Ask instructor for answers.

---

*Nanda, *Cultural Anthropology,* p. 369.

5. An effective paraphrase for sentence 23 is:

a. Distributing the meat was logically solved by the tribe.

b. The young as well as the old got an equal portion of the meat, so fighting was avoided.

c. Thus, meat can be eaten harmoniously because a mathematical system is established.

d. Thus, meat is divided up without conflict because a clear system has been established that takes into consideration the age and sex of the community members.

Exercise 7.5
More Paraphrasing
of Sentences in
Paragraphs

The following paragraphs continue the discussion of practices and rituals, this time focusing on human sacrifices. Read through the paragraphs carefully; then, using your paraphrasing skills, write appropriate paraphrases for the numbered sentences that come after the paragraphs. If you did not complete the previous exercise, read it through to get a sense of where this excerpt begins.

Human Sacrifices

(1)   [1]Human sacrifice has also been a widespread practice, although it was often stamped out by European colonial governments. [2]The Aztecs of Mexico, for example, had a religion in which human sacrifice was an important element, as we saw in the opening passage of this chapter.   [3]The Aztec gods, such as the jaguar and the serpent, were bloodthirsty and fierce and required human victims to appease their appetites.   [4]The victims, most of whom were captured in war, were ritually killed at the top of a pyramid built for this purpose.   [5]Although Aztec cannibalism was limited to the ruler, nobles, and those who had captured victims in a war, it was practiced on a rather grand scale, perhaps totaling about 20,000 victims a year.

(2)   [6]A wide-ranging debate has occurred in anthropology over the meanings and purposes of Aztec cannibalism.   [7]Michael Harner (1977) proposes an ecological interpretation of Aztec sacrifice and cannibalism.   [8]He holds that human sacrifice was a response to certain diet deficiencies in the population.   [9]In the Aztec environment, wild game was getting scarce, and the population was growing.   [10]Although the maize-beans combination of food that was the basis of the diet was usually adequate, these crops were subject to seasonal failure.   [11]Famine was frequent in the absence of edible domesticated animals.   [12]To meet essential protein requirements, cannibalism was the only solution. [13]Although only the upper classes were allowed to consume human flesh, a commoner who distinguished himself in a war could also have the privilege of giving a cannibalistic feast.   [14]Thus, although it was the upper strata who benefited most from ritual cannibalism, members of the commoner class could also benefit.   [15]Furthermore, as Harner explains, the social mobility and cannibalistic privileges available to the commoners through warfare provided a strong motivation for the "aggressive war machine" that was such a prominent feature of the Aztec state.

(3)   [16]A more symbolic approach to understanding Aztec cannibalism has been suggested by Marshall Sahlins (1978) and Peggy Sanday (1986).   [17]According to Sahlins, materialist anthropologists such as Harner have focused too much on Aztec cannibalism and have not paid enough attention to the context of human sacrifice.   [18]For the Aztecs, the consumption of human flesh was less emphasized than the sacred character of the sacrificial rite, the aim of which was to bring humans into communion with the gods.   [19]Without the proper nourishment of human hearts and human blood, the gods could not work on behalf of humans.   [20]The gods depended on human sacrifice for energy, without which the sun would not come up, the sky would fall down, and the universe would return to its original state of chaos.   [21]The sustenance given to the gods in the sacrificial offering and to humans in their houses ensured the regeneration of every individual and of Aztec society.

(4)   [22]Sanday's cross-cultural study, appropriately named Divine Hunger, emphasizes the ritual context of Aztec and other forms of cannibalism, viewing it "as a system of symbols and ritual acts through which human beings explore their relationship to the world, to other beings, and to being itself" (1986:31).   [23]Thus she, like Sahlins, sees Aztec cannibalism as making a statement about the sources of life and death and how these sources can be controlled by human beings.   [24]While both Sanday and Sahlins agree that the practice of cannibalism involved political and economic factors, as well as relations of the Aztec state with its enemies, both see Harner's materialist approach as too simplistic and partly as a projection of the American cost-benefit ideology.

(5)   [25]Other criticisms of the materialist approach have also been offered.   [26]To begin with, some anthropologists question whether the Aztecs even practiced ritual cannibalism, and there is no agreement about the extent of this practice.   [27]Harner, for example, bases his arguments on the evidence from early Spanish chroniclers such as Cortez, who wrote journals and letters describing Mexican customs.   [28]But as one critic (Ortiz de Montellano 1978) points out, the Spanish conquistadors did not necessarily write straightforward accounts of what they saw; they slanted their descriptions to make the Aztecs seem like barbarians in order to convince the king of Spain to support the conquest and undertake a large conversion effort by the Roman Catholic church.   [29]Ortiz de Montellano further argues that Aztec cannibalism can be fully explained by religious ideology and the desire to achieve status.   [30]He holds that neither the need for a dietary supplement nor the significance of the dietary contribution of human flesh has been convincingly demonstrated by Harner.   [31]The point here is not to prove one side of the argument or the other but to indicate some of the ways in which anthropologists have tried to "make sense" out of (to us) seemingly bizarre religious practices, by relating them to the sociocultural systems of which they are a part.*

---

*Nanda, *Cultural Anthropology*, pp. 370–372.

Paraphrase the following numbered sentences:

15. _____

18. _____

21. _____

24. _____

31. _____

70%

(score = # correct × 20)
Find answers on p. 388.

Exercise 7.6
Using Summarizing
and Paraphrasing
Skills in a Longer
Passage

The following excerpt contains several paragraphs on magic and sorcery from an anthropologist's perspective. The sentences in italics will require paraphrasing on a separate sheet of paper or in the margins. When you have completed your reading, answer the five questions that follow. In answering the questions, you may refer to the passage. Place answers 1–5 in the answer box.

Magic and Sorcery

(1) Magic and sorcery play major roles in the religious practices and rituals of many cultures throughout the world. Magic and sorcery are slightly different practices—magic more concerned with supernatural forces, sorcery with the harming of a specific individual.

(2) It is worthwhile to do a careful study of magic in order to understand how it differs from sorcery. Magic is defined as the attempt to control supernatural forces. By practicing magic, the magician is suggesting that he or she can control the supernatural world. *In this sense, magic is different from prayer because the magician is not asking a higher power to intervene.*

(3) There are two kinds of magic—imitative and contagious. In imitative magic, the magician copies the action she wants to happen: drawing a picture of a captured animal before a hunt or reciting lines like "Water is cold. Snow is cold." to stop one's pain caused by a burn. Contagious magic differs because it uses a part of an object that the magician wants to influence. For example, if a magician wants to cure an individual, she may use the individual's fingernail to cure the entire person.

(4) Magic is common practice in many countries. The Asoro society in New Guinea buries a new-born infant's umbilical cord so that the sorcerer cannot harm the infant. In courting his first girl, the young boy is taught to use love magic, which may cause the girl to see him as another boy to whom she is attracted. In this same society, pigs are supposedly tamed by blowing smoke into their ears. In this way, the magician tries to cool down the pig's hot temper.

(5) In many cultures in the East and the West, divination is practiced. Divination is defined as the method of deriving information from a supernatural figure. The Naskapi tribe on the Labrador Peninsula

scorch the shoulder blade of an animal's skeleton. The magician then reads the information on this scorched bone to determine where the tribe can hunt by seeing the lines on the charred bone as a map. In Western society, the flipping of a coin is an example of divination because a higher power is invoked in determining "heads or tails."

(6) Sorcery—the magical practice used to harm an individual—is performed in tribes of Melanesia. The sorcerer throws a stick in the direction of the person he intends to hurt. He performs this act in a tone of anger and passion.

(7) There are several documented cases where sorcery seems to be successful. *Anthropologists attribute the success of a sorcerer's magic to the susceptibility of the victim.* If the victim believes that sorcery is powerful, she may succumb to it. Some common symptoms of a victim giving in to sorcery include general sadness, loss of appetite, and even starvation.

(8) *Sorcery and magic are becoming more popular supernatural practices in the United States because it seems Americans feel more vulnerable and they often have fallen away from the consolation that traditional religion used to provide them.* A witch cult in San Francisco has been studied by an anthropologist. This cult provides its members with curses which they can use on their enemies. In this particular cult, the recipient of the curse may also have his name written on lamb skin by the cult leader. This high priest then burns the name at the altar while he chants dangerous threats against the victim. As with victims of sorcery in Melanesia, if the victim is made aware that he is a target of sorcery, he may develop symptoms of illness.*

1. An effective summary of paragraph 2 is:

   a. Magic is different from prayer.
   b. Magic attempts to control the supernatural and, unlike prayer, is not asking a higher power for assistance.
   c. The magician can control the supernatural and has greater powers than those who pray.
   d. Magic and sorcery are entirely different forms of supernatural power.

2. The best summary of paragraph 3 is:

   a. Imitative magic mimics in action what the magician wants to happen.
   b. Contagious magic uses a part for the whole in making its magic happen.
   c. The two forms of magic are imitative and contagious—imitative copies the desired action; contagious uses a part of an object to achieve its result.
   d. Fingernails are often the materials used by magicians performing contagious magic while pictures are used by those performing imitative magic.

---

*Adapted from Nanda, *Cultural Anthropology*, pp. 372–374.

3. A major detail in paragraph 4 is:

   a. In New Guinea, pigs are tamed by blowing smoke into their ears.
   b. Magic is commonly practiced in many countries.
   c. The Asoro tribe is found in New Guinea.
   d. All of these.

4. The main idea of paragraph 5 is:

   a. Divination is practiced in many cultures.
   b. The Naskapi tribe practices divination on dead animals.
   c. Divination is the method of getting information from a supernatural figure.
   d. The flipping of a coin is a kind of divination.

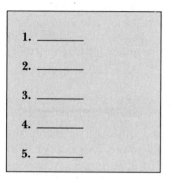

1. _____
2. _____
3. _____
4. _____
5. _____

5. The best summary for paragraph 6 is:

   a. Sorcery is performed in Melanesia.
   b. Sorcery is magic used to harm a person.
   c. Sorcery is magic with the intent of hurting an individual, an example being a sorcerer throwing a stick at a person he wants to harm.
   d. By throwing a stick at a person, a sorcerer is able to harm an individual that he is practicing sorcery on.

Answer the following five questions in a short phrase or sentence.

6. Reread paragraph 1. List the two points that this excerpt intends to cover.

7. Reread paragraphs 7 and 8. What are the reasons given for the sorcerer's supposed success?

8. Paraphrase the italicized sentence in paragraph 2.

9. Paraphrase the italicized sentence in paragraph 7.

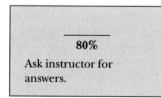

80%
Ask instructor for answers.

10. Paraphrase the italicized sentence in paragraph 8.

Exercise 7.7
Writing a Paragraph
Using Summarizing
and Paraphrasing
Skills

Your job is to go back to the excerpt on magic and sorcery and to find the information to answer the following questions. Much of this information is to be found in your paraphrases and your answers to the summary questions. From your responses to these questions, answer the essay question that follows. Write as much as you can in your own words.

1. Define magic and sorcery.

2. Provide two examples of magic.

3. Provide two examples of sorcery.

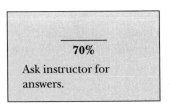

70%

Ask instructor for answers.

Essay question: In one paragraph, define magic and sorcery as these terms are used in anthropology. Then provide an example of each, preferably one from the West and another from a non-Western culture.

Exercise 7.8
Using Summarizing
and Paraphrasing
Skills on a Textbook
Excerpt

The following is an anthropologist's explanation of how religious leaders function in various cultures. Read through the excerpt quickly to get a sense of its organization. Then go back and read it slowly, paying particular attention to longer sentences that you may want to paraphrase. You also may want to underline the main ideas and major details in various paragraphs that you come across. When you finish, answer the five questions that follow and place your answers in the answer box. You may refer to the excerpt in deciding on your answers.

Religious Practitioners

(1) Like other human behavior, religious behavior is patterned and organized. A useful way of examining religious organization is in terms of the degree of specialization of religious **clerics,** who conduct ceremonies and perform rituals. This generally reflects the social organization of the society in which the practitioners are found.

Shamans

(2) **Shamans** are people who are able to achieve direct contact with the spirit world. They may use prayer, meditation, song, dance, pain, drugs, or any combination of techniques to achieve a trance state in which they understand themselves (and are understood by their followers) as able to enter into the real world of the supernatural. They may use such contact to bring guidance to themselves or their group, heal sick people, or divine the future. Although learning to be a shaman may involve arduous training, people become shamans because they have direct experiences of the supernatural. In effect, they are chosen by the spirit world. Almost all societies have some shamans, but they are likely to be the only clerics in band and tribal societies. In most cases, shamans are part-time clerics. In many respects, they are average members of the community and must hunt, gather, or garden like anyone else. Their shamanic activities are reserved for specific ceremonies, times of illness, or crisis.

Vision Quest

(3) In some cultures, almost every adult may be expected to achieve direct contact with the real world of the supernatural. The vision quest common among many Native American groups was an example of this. In these cultures, a person was expected to develop a special relationship with a particular spirit that would give the person power and knowledge of specific kinds. The spirit acted as a personal protector or guardian. The vision seeker was under a strong emotional impulse and by various means, such as fasting, isolation in a lonely spot, or self-mutilation intensified his or her emotional state.

(4) The Thompson Indians of western Canada had a vision quest that included most of the traits typical of this pattern. When a boy became old enough (usually between the ages of 12 and 16) to dream of an arrow, a canoe, or a woman, he began his search for a guardian spirit. Before the quest itself, the boy had to run, with bow and arrow in his hands, until he was exhausted. Then he was made to plunge into cold water. He did this four times a day for four days. His face was painted red and he put on a headband of cedar bark and tied ornaments made of deer hoof to his knees and ankles. He also wore a skin apron decorated with symbols of the life occupation for which he sought the spirit's assistance. The nights before the quest were spent in dancing, singing, and praying around a fire on a nearby mountain peak.

(5) The boy then went on lonely pilgrimages into the mountains, eating nothing for several days on end. He intensified his physical suffering by sweating himself with heated rocks over which he threw water and by whipping his body with nettles. During all this time, he also threw rocks and ran for miles to avoid disease, laziness, and bad luck. This strenuous regimen continued until the boy had a dream of some animal or bird and received the inspiration for a spirit song that he would then always use to call his protector. He also prepared a medicine bag of the skin of the spirit animal and filled it with a variety of objects that had taken on symbolic significance for him during his quest. These became the symbols of his power (Pettitt 1972).

(6) Although the vision quest was an intensely individual experience, it was nevertheless shaped by culture in a number of ways. Among the Crow Indians, for example, several informants related the same vision and interpretation to the anthropologist Robert Lowie (1963). They told of how on their lonely vigil they saw a spirit or several spirits riding along and how the rocks and trees in the neighborhood turned into enemies who attacked the horsemen but were unable to inflict any harm. They interpreted this to mean that the spirits were making the visionary invulnerable. This motif is part of Crow mythology and is unconsciously worked into their experience by the vision seekers. Another cultural influence is that most Crow Indians obtained their spiritual blessing on the fourth night of their seclusion, and four is considered a mystical number among the Crow.

(7) In other societies, shamanism is more rare and a community may have only one or two shamans who act to connect the community and the supernatural world. The shaman makes contact with (and often travels to) the real world of the supernatural in order to perform a variety of activities on behalf of his or her group. These may include

curing, divination, sorcery, and reading fortunes. Among Inuit coastal communities, the shaman's most important service is to make a yearly spiritual trip to the bottom of the sea to persuade the sea goddess (Sedna), who is the keeper of the sea animals, to release the game so that the Inuit can live through one more year.

Shamanic Curing

(8) Among the Inuit as well as other groups, shamans are often called on to cure illness; this is done by discovering which supernatural being has been offended by a broken taboo. Often, the illness is treated by extracting a confession from the victim and, through a ritual procedure, the possessing spirit is then exorcised.

(9) In shamanic curing, the shaman, usually in a trance, travels into the supernatural world to discover the source of illness and what might be done to cure it. This may consist of combat, pitting the shaman, in his or her supernatural state, against the spirits that are responsible for the illness, as in this description of a Netsilik Inuit curing performance described by Asen Balikci:

> The shaman, adorned with his paraphernalia, crouched in a corner of the igloo . . . and covered himself with a caribou skin. The lamps were extinguished. A protective spirit called by the shaman entered his body and, through his mouth, started to speak very rapidly, using the shaman's secret vocabulary. While the shaman was in trance, the tupiliq (an evil spirit believed to be round in shape and filled with blood) left the patient's body and hid outside the igloo. The shaman then dispatched his protective spirits after the tupiliqs; they, assisted usually by the benevolent ghost of some deceased shaman, drove the tupiliqs back into the igloo through the entrance; the audience encouraged the evil spirits, shouting: "Come in, come in, somebody is here waiting for you." No sooner had the tupiliqs entered the igloo than the shaman, with his snow knife, attacked them and killed as many as he could; his successful fight was evidenced by the evil spirits' blood on his hands. (1963:385)

(10) If the patient died, it was said that the tupiliqs were too numerous for the shaman to kill or that after the seance evil spirits again attacked the patient.

(11) Shamanistic activity has important therapeutic effects for individual clients, who are often relieved of illness through the cathartic effects of the ritual. Like all other religions, shamanism also has important integrating functions for the society. Through a wide variety of symbolic acts, shamanistic performances bring together various beliefs and religious practices in a way that dramatically expresses and reinforces the values of a culture and the solidarity of a society. Such performances often involve participation by the audience, whose members may experience various degrees of ecstasy themselves. These performances are cathartic in the sense that they release the anxiety caused by various disturbing events. The natural and supernatural forces, which have the power to do evil in a society, are brought under control, seemingly inexplicable misfortunes are given meaning within the traditional cultural pattern, and the community is better able to carry out its normal activities.

Priests

(12) In most state level societies, religion is bureaucratized; that is, it is an establishment consisting of a series of ranked offices that exist independently of the people who fill them. Anthropologists use the term **priest** to refer to a person who is formally elected or appointed to a full-time religious office. Priests are responsible for performing certain rituals on behalf of individuals, groups, or the entire community. Members of the community are supposed to have access to supernatural power only through these intermediaries.

(13) Priests are most often associated with gods who are believed to have great power; they may be members of a religion that worships several such high gods, as in the religions of the ancient Greeks, Egyptians, and Romans, or just one high god, as in the Judeo–Christian– Islamic tradition. Where priests exist, there is a division betwen the lay and priestly roles. Lay people participate in ritual largely as passive respondents or audience rather than as managers or performers.

(14) People become priests through training and apprenticeship. For example, to become a cleric in any mainstream American religion, you would enter the training program (usually a seminary) of the appropriate religion. If you were successful, at graduation you would be certified by the religious body (or church) as a cleric and generally given an assignment. Your authority in that assignment would derive from your certification by the religion you represent.

(15) In most mainstream religions in the United States, it is generally not considered necessary for priests to have ecstatic religious experiences. However, this is not the case in all priestly religions. Although ultimately the priest's authority derives from position, such status may give a person the right to seek ecstatic experience. For example, in ancient Maya states priests were members of a ranked bureaucracy. In many cases they werre also political leaders; kings and members of the nobility exercised not only secular political authority but priestly authority as well. Their religious position gave them the right to use ecstatic techniques to travel in the spiritual world. At the dedication of buildings consecrated to the royal lineage, priests, including the king and other nobles, would let blood by perforating their penises and other body parts with special lancets and take hallucinogenic drugs. These methods created an ecstatic state in which the priest/kings would travel to the supernatural underworld to inform their ancestors of the new building and invite the souls of these former rulers to inhabit the building. A Mayan ritual might have appeared like this:

> Against a backdrop of terraced architecture, elaborately costumed dancers, musicians, warriors, and nobles entered the courts in long processions. Dancers whirled across the plaza floors and terrace platforms to music made on rattles, whistles, wooden trumpets and drums of all sizes. A crowd of participants wearing bloodletting paper or cloth tied in triple knots sat on platforms and terraces around the plaza. According to Bishop Landa [an early Spanish writer], these people would have prepared themselves with days of fasting, abstinence and ritual steam baths. Well into the ceremony, the ruler and his wife would emerge from within a build-

ing high above the court, and in full public view, he would lacerate his penis, she her tongue. Ropes drawn through their wounds carried the flowing blood to paper strips. The saturated paper—perhaps along with other offerings, such as rubber (the chicle resin from which chewing gum is made)—were placed in large plates, then carried to braziers and burned, creating columns of black smoke. The participants, already dazed through deprivation, public hysteria and massive blood loss, were culturally conditioned to expect a hallucinatory experience. (Schele and Miller 1986:178)

(16) As among the Maya, priests in state societies may pursue ecstatic religious experience, but states generally attempt to suppress independent shamans as a source of power competing with that of the state.*

1. An appropriate summary of paragraph 3 is:

    a. Native American cultures encouraged their people to experience the supernatural through the vision quest.
    b. In the vision quest, the individual has a strong relationship with the spirit but has to experience pain to achieve this relationship.
    c. The spirit was the key figure in the vision quest.
    d. The world of the supernatural is experienced in many cultures.

2. The main idea of paragraph 8 concerns:

    a. the practices of the Inuit
    b. the curing of illnesses
    c. how the ill are forced to confess
    d. how the Inuit rely on the shaman to cure illness

3. An appropriate summary of paragraph 11 is:

    a. Shamans have are very effective in curing the ill.
    b. Shamans can both cure the ill and help keep the society united.
    c. Shamans help relieve the anxiety of their sick patients, thus making them well.
    d. Shamans help to destroy the evil in society and thus bring their people into a state of extreme emotion.

4. A major detail in paragraph 12 is:

    a. Religion is a bureaucracy.
    b. A priest is one who performs religious activities.
    c. Community members have supernatural powers.
    d. Priests perform certain rituals for one or several members of the community.

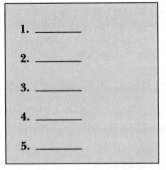

1. _____
2. _____
3. _____
4. _____
5. _____

*Adapted from Serena Nanda and Richard L. Warms, *Cultural Anthropology,* 6th ed. (Belmont, Calif.: Wadsworth, 1998), pp. 289–292.

5. An appropriate summary of paragraph 14 is:

    a. Priests need much training.

    b. Religious groups must certify their priests through successful graduations from their seminaries.

    c. Not all priests are given assignments immediately.

    d. Priests both must be trained in a seminary and serve as apprenticeship.

      Read the following questions; then go back and reread the excerpt. After you have reread the excerpt, answer the following questions without looking back.

6. Paraphrase this sentence from paragraph 11: "The natural and supernatural forces, which have the power to do evil in a society, are brought under control, seemingly inexplicable misfortunes are given meaning within the traditional cultural pattern, and the community is better able to carry out its normal activities." (2 points)

7. Paraphrase this sentence from paragraph 16: "As among the Maya, priests in state societies may pursue ecstatic religous experience, but states generally attempt to suppress independent shamans as a source of power competing with that of the state." (2 points)

8. Why is the vision quest a necessary part of the religious expeirence in some cultures? (1 point)

> **70%**
> Ask instructor for answers.

Follow-up on Chapter 7

Now that you have completed these exercises, it may be helpful to see how your reading of this topic has changed some of your ideas about what anthropology as a study is, and whether it has improved your abilities to summarize and to paraphrase. You may want to go back to these exercises and reread them just for their content, or for how they introduce the various ways anthropologists study religion, and you may want to review the introduction. Then answer the following questions either individually or in small groups.

On the Topic of Anthropology

1. How would you now define *anthropology*?

2. From an anthropologist's perspective, what are the major functions of religion?

3. In what ways are religious practices in non-Western cultures different from those in the West?

4. What issue or issues in anthropology do you now want to study further?

On the Topic of Summarizing and Paraphrasing

5. Are you now able to summarize and paraphrase better?

6. Can you easily summarize textbook material? Can you easily paraphrase difficult sentences in reading selections and textbooks?
7. What part of summarizing do you still need to develop?
8. What part of paraphrasing do you still need to develop?

Internet Activity

In groups of four or five, you may want to do Internet research on the following cultures mentioned in the exercises in this chapter: the Tsembaga, the Thompson Indians, and the Crow Indians. You may want to break up this assignment into specific tasks. If you have access to Info-Trac, locate information from this source.

Come back to your group with answers to the following questions:

1. What new information on these cultures did your Internet research uncover?
2. What were some of the ways that you accessed this information on the Internet?

CHAPTER 8

Reading and Listening for Inferences

In this chapter, you will learn about how to infer meaning from:

- Terms of qualification
- Word choice
- Figurative language
- The evidence you read or hear

Now that you have begun to identify various organizational patterns in writing and speech and you are summarizing and paraphrasing what you read and hear, you are on your way to reading and listening more critically. But sometimes knowing the main idea, the detail, and the organizational pattern is not enough. Books, lectures, and discussions often leave much unsaid, and you must "read between the lines." Making judgments and drawing conclusions about what is suggested is called *making inferences*. The successful student is an efficient inference maker, gleaning important points from what is suggested. It is the correct inference that instructors are looking for on exams and essays. You can make inferences about most material by looking for: (1) the terms of qualification in a sentence, (2) the author's or speaker's word choice, (3) the figurative language used by the author or speaker, and (4) the kinds of evidence used by a writer or speaker.

Terms of Qualification

A single word or phrase can change the message of a sentence. Terms of qualification can give strong support for a statement, or they can add doubt. A *term of qualification* is a word or phrase that limits the truth of a statement. In most cases, the speaker or writer will not tell you the degree of certainty intended in a statement. You need to infer this certainty from the term of qualification.

Terms of qualification can be divided into four categories: (1) terms expressing no doubt, (2) terms expressing much doubt, (3) terms expressing some doubt, and (4) terms expressing much doubt. Study the terms under each category.

Words and Phrases That Express No Doubt

all	surely	assuredly	there is no doubt
none	conclusively	undoubtedly	without reservation
never	clearly	absolutely	without hesitation
always	unequivocally	constantly	it is a proven fact
certainly	precisely	undeniably	it is undeniable
definitely	plainly	without a doubt	without question

Let these words and phrases become signals to you that what you are reading or listening to carries certainty. You can also use them when you write particularly strong statements.

See how the use of the word *absolutely* adds conviction to the following statement: "Mozart is absolutely the most brilliant musician ever to write classical music." The writer here evidently has positive feelings for Mozart and uses *absolutely* to establish these positive feelings. Sometimes, when you find such strong terms of qualification, you may want to underline them and make a marginal comment such as "strong statement."

Now consider some terms that express a small degree of doubt:

Words and Phrases That Express a Little Doubt

most	seldom	there is little doubt	it is believed
mostly	rarely	almost never	almost always
usually	slightly	with little reservation	
consistently	one can safely say	the consistent pattern	

When you find such words and phrases in your reading and listening, you should ask yourself what the exceptions to the statement might be. These exceptions are often not discussed by the author. By failing to notice the term of qualification, you might wrongly conclude that the statement has no exceptions.

Consider how in the following statement the word *usually* plants a question in your mind: "College students usually find Mozart's opera *The Marriage of Figaro* to be the most exciting work they study in the course." If the author does not discuss the exceptions, it would be wise for you to underline the term of qualification and write in the margin something like "When do students not enjoy this opera?" Also begin using these terms in your own writing when you want to show a little doubt.

Now look at this list of terms expressing some doubt. If these terms are used, you need to consider the exceptions, which often may not be fully explained by the writer.

Words and Phrases That Express Some Doubt

many	ostensibly	it seems
frequently	apparently	one can infer
often	somewhat	one can say with some
may	likely	reservation
might	this might mean	the hypothesis is
perhaps	this could mean	the theory is
one would assume	the results imply	it is possible that
the assumption is	possibly	it is probable that
one would infer	at times	
it is suggested that	it appears	
seemingly		
generally		

Let's look at the following sentence, which uses the term of qualification *it appears*. How does this term alter the meaning of the statement? "It appears that rock music will continue to be the important musical experience for teenagers." Because the writer includes *it appears* in this statement, you cannot conclude that rock music will always be the teenagers' preferred form of music. In a marginal comment, you might ask: "What are the author's reservations?" You can also start using these terms in your own writing when your statements are not definite.

Finally, consider the following words, which suggest much doubt. When you see or hear these words, you should question the truth of these statements.

Words and Phrases That Suggest Much Doubt

supposedly	it is suspected that
it is guessed that	it is rumored that
it is conjectured that	

Look how *it is rumored that* makes the following statement questionable: "It is rumored that the federal government is trying to ban rock concerts that sell over 10,000 tickets for one show." Because this statement is rumor, you cannot include it in any serious discussion of rock concerts. Many irresponsible speakers and publications use rumor as the basis for their arguments. You should never cite these speakers or publications as sources in a serious essay or speech.

You may now want to complete Exercise 8.2 on page 169.

Word Choice

You can make many inferences through the kinds of words a speaker or author uses. *Connotations* are the suggested meanings of words, telling you whether an author or speaker has a positive, neutral, or negative attitude toward the topic. Authors or speakers often do not directly tell you their attitude toward their topic, because they do not want to be accused of being biased. But you can infer these attitudes from the connotations of their words.

Look at the following sentence on Duke Ellington. See if you can locate the word with a strong positive connotation: "Duke Ellington continues to be one of the most revered figures in the history of American jazz." Do you see that *revered* is a positive word, suggesting that Ellington still commands a great deal of respect among jazz historians? To be revered is to be greatly respected, almost worshipped. In a marginal note about this sentence, you could include a comment: "'Revered' suggests great respect, almost worship."

Look at the use of *destructive* to see how it gives negative associations to the following sentence about heavy metal music: "Heavy metal music clearly has a destructive effect on the behavior of young people, particularly at concerts." Do you see that *destructive* has antisocial and violent associations? Though the author does not directly state that young people lose their sense of right and wrong, it is suggested in the connotations of *destructive*. With a marginal comment noting the connotations of this word, you would understand better the author's intent.

Note how this third statement uses a neutral language: "The swing era in jazz lasted for about fifteen years—from 1935 to 1950." Do you see that the author uses no words that suggest that the swing era was either a positive or negative musical event? Here the author purposely may be using neutral language so as not to express an opinion about swing.

The total effect that an author's choice of words has on a particular passage is called its *mood,* or the feeling that a reader gets from the words used in a passage. A passage's mood can thus leave the reader with positive, negative, or neutral feelings. After you read a work, ask yourself what overall feeling the work gives you. Then try to see what type of language in the work makes you feel that way.

You may now want to complete Exercise 8.3 on page 171.

Figurative Language

Like the connotations of words, figurative language is also suggestive and requires you to make inferences. Figurative language is often expressed as a metaphor or simile. A *metaphor* is a comparison between two objects or ideas that do not at first seem related. A *simile* is the same sort of comparison, but it makes the comparison more explicit by using the word "like" or "as."

Consider the following metaphor and simile about rap music:

Rap music is the knife that cuts open the pain of city life.

Rap music is like the knife that cuts open the pain of city life.

All metaphors have two parts: the *subject* and the *image.* The subject is the topic, in this case rap music. The image is what the subject is compared to, or the knife in our example.

In making inferences about any metaphor, you need to place the subject next to the image. Next, list all of the associations you may have for the image. Finally, study your list to see how it sheds new light on your subject.

Look at how the knife metaphor is analyzed:

Subject	*Image*
rap music	knife: cuts, hurts, kills, exposes, cleans, defends, is sharp, is strong

As you consider these associations, you probably realize that the knife metaphor shows the power of rap music in exposing the pain of city life in America. This pain may be difficult for people to hear; but in hearing this pain, listeners may begin to correct or "clean up" the problems that exist in American cities.

Are you beginning to understand how much you can infer from studying metaphors and similes? Powerful metaphors leave much unsaid. By pulling out these associations, you can make responsible inferences regarding what the speaker or writer is saying about his topic.

You may now want to complete Exercise 8.4 on page 173.

Drawing Conclusions from Details You Read or Hear

When you read a longer passage or hear a lecture, you can infer the writer's or speaker's overall attitude toward her subject. To *draw a conclusion* is to make an appropriate inference from the details you read (or hear) about a writer's (or speaker's) overall purpose. You can draw a conclusion about an individual, for example, by considering the language that the writer or speaker uses to describe him. You should be alert to terms of qualification, to the connotations of the words used in the description, and even to the figurative language that may be used. These are topics that you have just learned about in this introduction.

Consider the following description of Motown Records. As you read, draw a conclusion about the writer's attitude toward Motown. Consider how she uses language.

> It is clear that Motown Records is the most famous and successful rhythm and blues company in America. Its founder is Berry Gordy, a man with a vision. He began this musical empire with only $700 of borrowed money. Through Motown, such now renowned artists as Diana Ross, Smokey Robinson, and Stevie Wonder became popular with both African American and white listening audiences. Gordy's company was clearly a gold mine when he sold it to MCA, Inc., for $61 million in 1988. (Adapted from Charles R. Hoffer, *The Understanding of Music*, 6th ed. [Belmont, Calif.: Wadsworth, 1989], pp. 518–519.)

Did you note the positive connotation of *vision* in reference to Berry Gordy, and the positive association of the word *renowned* in reference to the Motown celebrities? Also, did you note the figurative language associated with Motown: *empire* and *gold mine*? Both metaphors suggest immense wealth and power. By analyzing the language in this excerpt, you can conclude that the writer's attitude toward Motown and Berry Gordy is strongly favorable.

At times, you can draw a conclusion about a writer's or speaker's attitude toward her subject by studying the actions that are narrated. As with the language in descriptions, you can conclude that the writer has a favorable, neutral, or unfavorable attitude toward her subject by studying the actions that are presented. Consider the actions of George Frederic Handel in the following excerpt to see what conclusions you can draw.

> When Handel began composing *Messiah* in 1741, he was facing financial difficulties. Instead of brooding over his financial losses, he immersed himself into the *Messiah* project. He worked at this project feverishly, working day and night. It is reported that Handel did not even bother to eat the food left by his servant at his door. When he finally finished *Messiah,* his servent found him in tears, exclaiming that he had seen God himself! (Adapted from Hoffer, *The Understanding of Music,* p. 168.)

Did you note that all of Handel's actions are portrayed as heroic because he sacrifices himself for the completion of his project? Instead of complaining about his financial losses, he begins work. He doesn't sleep or eat for long stretches of time during its composition. And he is so overwhelmed by the completion of *Messiah* that he feels closer to God. The conclusion that you can draw from these actions is that Handel sacrificed his well-being for his music and expressed a remarkable passion for his composing of *Messiah.*

In relating these actions, the writer does not directly express his attitude toward Handel and his musical work. It is only from his relating of these heroic actions that you can infer his positive attitude toward Handel's composing of *Messiah.*

You may now want to complete Exercise 8.5 on page 173.

In longer written passages or in longer lectures and discussions, you can also infer something about the competence of the author or speaker by the details that are presented. If the details are presented logically, you can conclude that the speaker or author is in command of the material. But if the details are disorganized, you can conclude that the speaker or author is poorly prepared. You also can infer something about the speaker or writer by studying the sources used in the work. If known publications or experts are cited, you will be more likely to value the argument. If the speaker or author does not mention sources, you would be justified in questioning the thesis. Again, the author or speaker will probably not comment on the nature of the details. It is up to you to determine the value of the work from the nature of the details. Look at the following paragraph on the Beatles. What do the details say about the competence of the writer?

> The Beatles were a very famous rock group several years ago. There were four of them, and they acted and dressed strangely. This made people like them even more. They made their first appearance in America in the early sixties on a popular television show.

Even if you agree with the thesis of the excerpt, the evidence is vague. The author does not name who these Beatles were, nor does she mention how they acted and dressed. The author also does not name the American TV show they appeared on. Because these details are vague, you can infer that the writer, though logical, is not well prepared and therefore not convincing.

Study the details of this second passage on the Beatles, and infer something about the author:

> The Beatles were decidedly the most famous rock group to emerge from England in the sixties. There were four of them: John, Paul, George, and Ringo. Fans in America and Europe loved them for their long hair and their often irreverent sense of humor. They gained great notoriety in America in 1964 when they appeared on *The Ed Sullivan Show*—the most popular variety show on television at the time.

Note that the author of this excerpt has researched the subject. She knows the names of each member, how they acted and looked, and the name of the show that made them famous in America. You will likely read this writer carefully, because the material is both logical and detailed.

When you write your own critical essays, be sure to cite your sources and present accurate details. If you do, your reader will read your work more carefully. You will learn more about effective essay writing in Chapter 16.

You may now want to complete Exercise 8.1 on page 168.

Summary

An inference is an insight that a reader gains that is not stated directly in the text. By making correct inferences, you better understand your material. You make inferences by considering: (1) terms of qualification, (2) word choice, (3) figurative language, and (4) the kind of details used by the speaker or writer. You should make marginal comments on your inferences.

The more you read and listen, the more sophisticated your inferences will become. You will begin comparing past knowledge with what you are currently learning. And your learning will be that much more rewarding.

Summary Box   *Inferences*

What are they?	How do you make them?	Why do you need them?
Insights or deductions made by a reader or listener but not directly stated in the text.	By studying terms of qualification, word choice, figurative language, and details.	To give more meaning to your reading and listening. To become more questioning of what you read and hear.

Skills Practice Topic: Music History

All the exercises in this chapter deal with the issue of music history, a course that you might one day take in college. Before you begin these exercises, answer the following questions either individually or in small groups to get some sense of what you already know about music history.

1. How would you define *music history*?
2. What do you know about classical music? Who are some of the great classical composers?
3. Are rock music and jazz in any way like classical music?
4. What is your favorite type of music? Why?

*Exercise 8.1
Making Inferences
from Details*

You can make inferences from the examples an author uses. If the examples are accurate, you can infer that the author is credible; if the examples are inaccurate, you can infer that the writer is unprepared.

Read the following paragraphs carefully, and determine whether the author is being detailed or vague. All of the paragraphs describe musical instruments. Write *D* in the answer box if the paragraph is detailed and *V* if the paragraph is vague.

You may want to complete this assignment in small groups.

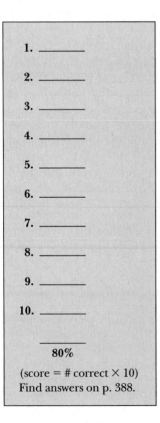

1. _____
2. _____
3. _____
4. _____
5. _____
6. _____
7. _____
8. _____
9. _____
10. _____

80%

(score = # correct × 10)
Find answers on p. 388.

The Instruments of the Orchestra

(1) The string instruments are very important to an orchestra: They make up about half of all of the instruments. They include the violin, viola, cello, and double bass. What makes these instruments different is their relative size. Their differing sizes produce different pitches or sounds.

(2) How does a string instrument make sound? Part of the instrument is hollow. Another part transmits the sound to the body. Then the body changes the sound. This change in sound makes each instrument different.

(3) Woodwinds are another type of orchestral instrument. As their name suggests, these instruments rely on wind to make their sound, and each one is made of wood. Examples of woodwind instruments are the flute, piccolo, oboe, English horn, clarinet, and bassoon. Each of these instruments has a hollow body and holes along the length that let air in and out.

(4) The flute is a peculiar instrument. In recent times the material it is made of has changed. The flute and piccolo produce a particular sound. This sound is made by air moving and colliding with other air. The flute also has a particular sound range.

(5) The oboe is another interesting orchestral instrument. The wood that oboes are made of is specially treated. The reeds used in oboes are an important part of the instrument's sound. The range of sound that the oboe produces is not very wide.

(6) The saxophone is sometimes included in an orchestra. It is considered part of the woodwind family, even though its body is made of

metal. What makes it like other woodwind instruments is the reed that it uses to produce its distinctive sound. Although it is only an occasional member of the orchestra, the saxophone is always part of concert and jazz bands.

(7) Brass instruments make up another musical family. They are unlike woodwinds. The unique sound of a brass instrument is its buzzing. Brass instruments come in various sizes, and the size of each instrument can be changed.

(8) What types of brass instruments does the orchestra use? In most orchestras, three trumpets, four French horns, two tenor trombones, one brass trombone, and one tuba are included. Of these instruments, the trumpet has the highest pitch. Its pitch is altered by changing the length of its tubing. There are three piston valves in a trumpet that alter its size and therefore its range.

(9) Another instrument in the brass family is the cornet, which is similar to the trumpet. The cornet's tube is shaped like a cone. It produces a mellow sound. Finally, a cornet is also equipped with a mute, which softens its tone even more.

(10) The trombone has a different sound from the trumpet. It is also shaped differently from the trumpet. Also, the trombone's sound is powerful. Its sound is unique but very difficult to describe.*

Exercise 8.2 Locating and Analyzing Terms of Qualification

The following paragraphs discuss Johann Sebastian Bach (1685–1750), one of the great classical composers. In these paragraphs are five terms of qualification, which are underlined. In the spaces provided, explain how each term of qualification alters the meaning of the sentence. Comment on whether the term makes the statement stronger or casts doubt on it. You may want to refer to the lists of terms of qualification on pp. 162–163.

Example: Almost every student of music knows Bach's work and is impressed by it.

Explanation: This is a strong statement about Bach's abilities, but the use of "almost" suggests that not all students of music find him to be great.

Johann Sebastian Bach

(1) Most students of music would say that Johann Sebastian Bach is one of the greatest composers of all time. Bach's life was uneventful. The most important biographical detail is that he was part of an extremely talented musical family that spanned six generations.

(2) What is Bach's appeal? Why is he an undeniably dominant figure in music history? Scholars of music constantly refer to his skill in writing counterpoint. The way that he ordered musical relationships, it seems, has a pleasing effect on the listener's mind.

---

*Adapted from Hoffer, *The Understanding of Music*, pp. 52–57.

(3) The *fugue* is Bach's greatest musical contribution. In a fugue, lines of music imitate each other in carefully organized ways. Scholars generally agree that the fugue evolved over several generations and with several composers.

(4) Analyzing a Bach fugue shows how fugues are frequently structured. Bach's Fugue in C Minor begins with a melody divided into four parts. This main melody is called the subject, and this subject is expressed by various imitations called voices, which constantly reinterpret the subject.*

1. *Term:* _____

    Explanation: _____

2. *Term:* _____

    Explanation: _____

3. *Term:* _____

    Explanation: _____

4. *Term:* _____

    Explanation: _____

5. *Term:* _____

    Explanation: _____

Now read the following series of paragraphs, continuing the discussion on Bach. In these paragraphs are five additional terms of qualification. This time they are not underlined. Locate them and determine their effect on the sentence. Place each term and explanation on the lines provided at the end of the excerpt.

(5) The fugue is certainly not the only form of music that Bach wrote for the organ, although perhaps it can be seen as the most important. Two others known as the *chorale variation* and the *chorale prelude* also use the fugue format, but these two musical forms vary the main musical theme each time it is introduced into the composition.

(6) Another type of music Bach wrote for the organ is called the *passacaglia.* This musical form continues one musical theme throughout but adds variations over it. The passacaglia is usually seen as a fascinating,

---

*Adapted from Hoffer, *Understanding of Music*, pp. 185–188.

demanding listening experience. Without question, one of Bach's finest works is the Passacaglia in C Minor.

(7) There is no doubt that anyone interested in seriously studying European music will spend time experiencing this amazing composer— J. S. Bach.*

6. *Term:* _____

Explanation: _____

7. *Term:* _____

Explanation: _____

8. *Term:* _____

Explanation: _____

9. *Term:* _____

Explanation: _____

10. *Term:* _____

Explanation: _____

80%
Ask instructor for answers.

Exercise 8.3
Commenting on Word
Choice in Sentences

The following paragraphs describe the life and music of Wolfgang Amadeus Mozart (1756–1791), a German composer who came after Bach. The writer of these paragraphs has a definite attitude toward Mozart. Read these paragraphs carefully to determine what he is saying about Mozart and what his attitude toward him is; then go back and reread the underlined words to see how they alter the meaning of the sentence in which they appear. As you complete this exercise you may want to consult a dictionary or thesaurus to determine the meanings of the underlined words. Place your explanations on the lines provided at the end of the excerpt. You may want to complete this assignment with a partner.

Example: Mozart was one of the <u>dazzling</u> composers of the eighteenth century.

Explanation: To dazzle is to overpower by intense light. The author is suggesting that Mozart was clearly an overpowering and brilliant composer of his time.

---

*Adapted from Hoffer, *Understanding of Music*, pp. 185–188.

Mozart's Music and Life

(1) Wolfgang Amadeus Mozart is nothing less than a musical mira-cle. His compositions are consistently clear, delicate, and simple, yet they defy a simple musical analysis.

(2) Mozart was a child prodigy, composing his first pieces at the astonishing age of five. He was performing at six, and by the age of thirteen, he had written concertos, symphonies, and an opera.

(3) Mozart had a phenomenal musical memory. He was able to do the seemingly impossible task: compose entire musical pieces in his mind. He has been quoted as saying that when he committed a musical piece to paper, he had worked it all out in his mind beforehand.

(4) Although Mozart possessed an unfathomable musical gift, his personal life was disastrous. He was naive when it came to his finances and consistently found himself in debt. At thirty-five he died of uremic poisoning, and he did not have the money for a respectable funeral. This musical giant died a pauper.

(5) His short life notwithstanding, Mozart completed a remarkable number of musical compositions. He explored many musical genres: operas, symphonies, concertos, and string quartets. With each type of music he composed, Mozart left an indelible musical style. His works consistently reveal different aspects of his musical genius, so he contin-ues to be studied by musical scholars, performers, and musical compos-ers today for what he has to say about classical music.*

1. *Explanation:* _____

2. *Explanation:* _____

3. *Explanation:* _____

4. *Explanation:* _____

5. *Explanation:* _____

6. *Explanation:* _____

7. *Explanation:* _____

8. *Explanation:* _____

9. *Explanation:* _____

10. *Explanation:* _____

70%

(score = # correct × 10)
Find answers on p. 389.

---

*Adapted from Hoffer, *Understanding of Music*, pp. 210–212.

Now go back and reread the passage. What do you think is the overall mood of this passage? What words suggest this mood?

_____

_____

**Exercise 8.4
Making Inferences
from Figurative
Language**

Here is an excerpt on rap music. In it are three underlined statements using a metaphor and similes. Answer the questions about these images. You may want to complete this assignment with a partner.

Why Is Rap Music So Popular?

Rap music is here to stay. It is born out of the energy and violence of the urban world. Rap music speaks of decaying inner cities, which are (1) like cancers that do not stop spreading.

Rap is energetic music. Some have said that it is (2) like foreign food that provides tastes of worlds unknown to those who are wealthy and live in suburban enclaves. It is also a constantly changing music, forever listening to (3) the pulse and heart of the American streets.

Many listeners are offended by the profanity and painful, often cruel topics that rap music can portray. Yet few will argue that rap has given a voice to so many young urban men and women who have been silenced for so long.

1. Identify the subject and image of the first simile. What associations can you make with the image that the writer chooses? How do these associations help you understand the subject better?

2. Identify the subject and image of the second simile. List three or four associations that come to mind from the image the writer has chosen. How do these associations help you understand the subject better?

3. Identify the subject and image of the third metaphor. What associations does this image call to mind? How do they help you understand the subject?

4. Together, how do these two similes and metaphor help you understand the writer's attitude toward rap music and its environment?

75%

Ask instructor for answers.

**Exercise 8.5
Drawing Conclusions
from Excerpts of
Description and
Action**

Here are three excerpts on various European composers. These excerpts either describe the composer or relate various incidents in his life to his music career. Read each excerpt carefully. Then draw an appropriate conclusion about the composer. Write your conclusion in a sentence in the space provided. You may want to complete this assignment with a partner.

1. Starting from the age of 28 to the end of his life, Ludwig van Beethoven (1770–1827) began losing his hearing. As he aged, Beethoven's

hearing became progressively worse until he was completely deaf. For a composer to be unable to hear is like a basketball pitcher losing the use of his legs, yet he still is able to play. Amazingly, Beethoven continued to compose. He wrote his last compositions in his head, recreating what each note would sound like. We also know that Beethoven sketched out themes for many possible musical compositions before he became deaf. As a deaf composer, Beethoven turned to these sketchbooks for musical material to revise. Beethoven completed his most successful symphony—the Ninth—when he was deaf. When it was first performed, Beethoven was unable to hear the audience's applause when the symphony came to an end. (Adapted from Hoffer, *The Understanding of Music,* pp. 258–259.)

What can you conclude about Beethoven the composer when he was deaf?

_____

2. Felix Mendelsohn (1809–47) lived in an environment rich with musical experiences. There were many instruments available to him at his home. Mendelsohn was provided with a fine music education, and he used it well to become successful at playing piano, composing music, conducting music, and organizing concerts. Mendelsohn made his orchestra in Leipzig, Germany, one of the finest in the country, and he became one of the first conductors to conduct in front of the orchestra. In conducting many concerts of Bach's music, Mendelsohn also revived Germany's interest in this great composer. (Adapted from Hoffer, *The Understanding of Music,* pp. 292–293.)

What conclusion can you infer from this excerpt on Mendelsohn's music career?

_____

3. Frederic Chopin (1810–49) developed his early music education in Warsaw, Poland. Yet by twenty, Chopin had the desire to travel in Europe, since there were political problems in Poland. He finally settled in Paris, where he quickly made friends and close connections with many renowned artists from several fields: painters like Delacroix, composers like Lizst, and novelists like Hugo and Balzac. Yet of these artistic relationships, the most significant for Chopin was his friendship and eventual love for the female novelist George Sand, whom he lived with for nine years. Sand attracted Chopin because of her great writing talent and strong personality.

66%

(Score = # correct × 33)

What conclusion can you draw from these events in Chopin's life?

_____

Exercise 8.6
Making Inferences in
a Longer Passage

In the following passage on rock music, you will be asked to make inferences based on details, word choice, and terms of qualification. Read the passage carefully, marking the text for main ideas and major details as well as commenting on any word choice that seems particularly interesting to you. Then answer the questions that follow. You may refer to the passage when answering the questions. Place all answers in the answer box.

Rock Music in the Fifties and Sixties

(1) It seems that rock music got its start in 1955 when Bill Haley and the Comets sang "Rock Around the Clock" in the movie *Blackboard Jungle*. This film was about a group of rowdy teenagers in an urban high school. The simple blues-like music of the Haley song, coupled with the feelings of discontent among teenagers, seem to have laid the foundation for rock music, a kind of music that seems to speak to almost all teenagers today.

(2) Elvis Presley soon followed on the heels of Bill Haley. His striking good looks and sexually suggestive movements as he performed added more excitement to his singing. Songs like his "You Ain't Nothing but a Hound Dog" continued the simple yet catchy beat of "Rock Around the Clock." Presley was undeniably the most significant contributor to rock music in the fifties. Although he has been dead for over fourteen years, his legacy lives on in both the now middle-aged fans who remember him and the teenagers who know him today through his music.

(3) Rock music in the sixties became a more complex, more thoughtful type of music. There seemed to be a singing style for everyone in this decade: Motown, the Beatles, the Rolling Stones, as well as the folk music of balladeers like Bob Dylan and Joni Mitchell. By the sixties, some rock music had developed a keen social conscience. Good looks and physical movement would no longer always sell a lyric. Singers and songwriters like Bob Dylan and the Beatles began to introduce social questions into their lyrics. Many antiwar rock songs emerged as a response to the war in Vietnam, which began to escalate in the sixties and create violence and discontent in the entire nation.

(4) What defined rock music in both the fifties and the sixties was a clear beat and an often refreshing experimentation with musical form. Moreover, the musical instruments that rock employed were decidedly different from those used before the fifties. The saxophones and trumpets of the forties gave way to electronic instruments, especially guitars and organs. Rock music also often used music technology in interesting ways, amplifying the sound and playing with it through the engineer's skillful use of mixing and multiple tracks.

(5) What seemed to separate rock music of the fifties from that of the sixties was the electrifying popularity of the group in the sixties over the solo performer. The advantage of the group was that it was able to play several instruments—particularly electric guitar, electric organ, and drums—as it sang. Fans could now select their favorite group member among the several who performed in concert and on television.

(6) Thanks to the contributions of performers in the fifties and sixties, rock music seems to be here to stay. Its variety today seems to

have provided for a larger listening audience—from teenagers, its original audience, to young adults and middle-aged adults who grew up and in a sense were nourished on rock.*

1. What terms of qualification are used in paragraph 1?

    a. *seems* and *got*
    b. *seems* and *almost all*
    c. *almost* and *kind*
    d. *simple* and *this*

2. Which word from the following sentence in paragraph 2 has positive connotations? "His striking good looks and sexually suggestive movements as he performed added more excitement to his singing."

    a. looks
    b. movements
    c. performed
    d. striking

3. What term of qualification is used in the following sentence in paragraph 2? "Presley was undeniably the most significant contributor to rock music in the fifties."

    a. significant
    b. contributor
    c. undeniably
    d. fifties

4. Which word or words from this sentence in paragraph 3 have positive connotations? "Rock music in the sixties became a more complex, more thoughtful type of music."

    a. complex
    b. thoughtful
    c. both a and b
    d. neither a nor b

5. Which word or words in the last sentence of paragraph 3 has negative connotations?

    a. emerged
    b. discontent
    c. response
    d. nation

1. _____

2. _____

3. _____

4. _____

5. _____

    Now answer the following five questions with a short phrase or sentence.

---

*Adapted from Hoffer, *Understanding of Music,* pp. 511–516.

6. What do you think the writer means in paragraph 4 by the phrase "an often refreshing experimentation with musical form"?

7. Locate a word in the last sentence of paragraph 4 that positively describes the music engineer.

8. What do you think the writer means in paragraph 5 by the phrase "electrifying popularity of the group"?

9. What term of qualification is used in the first sentence of paragraph 6? How does it alter the meaning of this sentence?

10. What do you think is this author's overall attitude toward rock music in the fifties and sixties? Which words or statements help suggest this attitude?

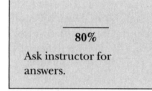

Exercise 8.7
Writing Your Own
Paragraph Using
Main Ideas and
Major Details

Your job in this exercise is to go back to the passage on rock music in Exercise 8.6 and determine the major characteristics of rock music in the fifties and sixties. As you locate this information, jot it down in the following outline. From the information in the completed outline, answer the essay question in one paragraph.

I. Characteristics of Early Rock Music

A. In the fifties: _____

_____

B. In the sixties: _____

_____

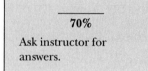

Essay question: Rock music developed in interesting ways in its first two decades. What were the characteristics of rock music in the fifties and sixties? In what ways was the music in these two periods similar? How was it different?

Exercise 8.8
Determining Main
Ideas and Major
Details and Making
Inferences from a
Textbook Excerpt

The following is an excerpt from a textbook on jazz, an American musical movement that came before rock. Read through the excerpt quickly to get a sense of its organization. Then go back and read it slowly, paying particular attention to the way jazz is described. You will not need to know the various technical terms to answer the questions that follow. You may refer to the excerpt in deciding on your answers.

Jazz

(1) Various types of popular music, especially jazz and rock, are among America's most recognized contributions to the world of music.

Travelers to other countries—Japan, Thailand, France, Greece, and so on—hear American popular music (often with the lyrics still in English). Each type of popular music has its promoters and detractors, and most of the styles have developed under a cloud of doubt about their musical quality. Regardless of their artistic merits, or lack of them, no presentation of American music can be complete without some discussion of jazz and other popular music.

Traditional Jazz

(2) The roots of jazz reach back to black Americans' African heritage. But other elements have also influenced jazz: minstrel show music, work songs, field hollers, funeral marching bands, blues, French-Creole and Spanish-American music, and, more recently, West Indian music. Jazz did not develop until about the beginning of the twentieth century. Basin Street in New Orleans is traditionally considered its birthplace, although clearly jazz did not just pop into being in one spot and at a fixed historical moment. It was brought to public attention by the funeral procession. On the way back from the cemetery the band played tunes in a way quite different from the somber sounds that accompanied the march to the gravesite. The players shifted the emphasis from the strong to the weak beat and launched into a decorated version of the melody. When Storyville, the New Orleans red-light district, was closed down in 1917, many jazz musicians lost their jobs and sought work in other cities. Jazz moved up the Mississippi River through Memphis and St. Louis to Chicago and the rest of the United States.

(3) Two types of Afro-American folk music existed before and during the early years of jazz and later merged with it. One of these was **ragtime**. It featured the piano, occasionally in combination with other instruments. The music sounds like a polished, syncopated march with a decorated right-hand part. Early musicians associated with ragtime are Scott Joplin in Sedalia, Missouri, and Ben Harvey, who published his *Ragtime Instructor* in 1897.

(4) The other type of music involved with early jazz was the folk **blues**. Its musical characteristics will be discussed shortly. Some of the most famous names associated with blues are Leadbelly, whose real name was Huddie Ledbetter; W. C. Handy, who was known for his "Memphis Blues" and "St. Louis Blues"; and Ferdinand "Jelly Roll" Morton, whose first published blues appeared in 1905—the "Jelly Roll Blues."

(5) Like folk music, jazz was created by generally untutored musicians who could not have written down what they played or sang, even if they had wanted to. Jazz is different from most folk music in two respects, however. It has sprung from the cities rather than the fields and forests; it is an urban form of music. And for most people, it is a spectator experience. Usually only a few people perform, although listeners may contribute a little hand clapping and foot stomping.

(6) **Musical Elements of Jazz**   What is traditional jazz? It has several elements.

(7) *Melody*   The most significant feature of jazz melodies is the **blue note**. These notes are derived from an altered version of the major scale. The blues scale merely lowers the third, fifth, and/or seventh steps.

Many times the performer shifts between the regular note and its lower alternative as if searching for a sound, which in a sense is what is happening. The blue-note interval is an approximation of a microtone, roughly half of a half step in this case. African music is the influence behind its use in jazz. Blue notes are a source of subtle color. Their effect in jazz is further enhanced by the fact that the chord in the harmony usually contains the particular note at its expected pitch while the lowered blue note is sounded in the melody. This combination creates an interesting and characteristic dissonance.

(8) ***Harmony***   Traditional jazz harmony is as conservative as any church hymn. The typical chords are the same three that form the backbone of traditional tonal harmony: tonic (I), dominant (V), and subdominant (IV). More recently, sophisticated types of jazz have employed the advanced harmonic idioms of Debussy, Bartók, and Stravinsky. The appeal of jazz, however, does not lie in its harmony.

(9) ***Rhythm***   Rhythm is one of the most important features of jazz. Although its meter is nearly always two beats per measure, with irregular meters occurring only rarely, the jazz musician employs an endless variety of syncopated patterns and rhythmic figures over this regular pulse. Syncopation—the redistribution of accents so that the rhythmic patterns do not occur as the listener expects—is the lifeblood of jazz.

(10) Jazz rhythms do not fit well into the usual divisions of time into sixteenths, eighths, and quarters. Jazz musicians perform rhythm with small deviations of timing and accent that cannot be rendered in notation. Players even make slight alterations of the patterns of conventional notation when reading them. These deviations in rhythm are one reason why traditionally trained musicians often cannot achieve an authentic jazz sound.

(11) ***Timbre***   The basic timbre sought by jazz instrumentalists is perhaps an unconscious imitation of the black singing voice: a bit breathy with a little vibrato (rapid and slight variance of pitch on a single tone). Certain instruments, therefore, have become associated with this idiom. The saxophone was intended to be a concert instrument, but it was taken up by jazz musicians because it can produce the desired quality. Mutes—metal or fiber devices inserted in or over the bell of brass instruments to change the tone quality—are often used, and their names are as distinctive as the sounds they produce: *cup, wahwah,* and *plunger* (like the end of a rubber sink plunger). Many jazz trumpeters use a particular type of mouthpiece that helps them produce a more shrill sound and makes high notes easier to play. In jazz style the clarinet is played in a manner that produces a tone quality like that of the saxophone. The timbres of other instruments also vary according to whether they are playing orchestral music or jazz.

(12) Some jazz timbres, like the bongo and conga drums and the Cuban cowbell, are from Afro-Cuban sources, while others, such as the Chinese woodblock, cymbals, and vibraphone, have an Oriental flavor.

(13) ***Repetition of Material***   Jazz has no form that is true for all its styles. Generally it is a series of stanzas based on the chords to a popular tune. The form of the blues is more definite. A line is sung and immediately repeated; then a third line concludes the stanza. Sometimes the

singer does not sing all the way through a section, and an instrumentalist fills in with a short solo called a *break*.

(14) **Text** The metrical scheme of the text is often one of the standard poetic meters. It is not uncommon to find iambic pentameter in verses of the blues. The texts seldom have literary value, but some are quite moving.

(15) **Improvisation** Improvisation is a fundamental component of jazz. Traditionally jazz is not written down because it is made up on the spot. This extemporaneous creativity is what gives jazz its ever-fresh quality. Sometimes people confuse a sexy or "hot" popular song with jazz. Jazz does not exist unless someone improvises on a tune.

(16) What happens is this: The musicians agree that they will play a certain song in a certain key. They also agree generally on the order of each player's featured section. Then the first player, while keeping in mind the harmonies and melody of the song, improvises a part that reflects the rhythmic and melodic characteristics of jazz. This procedure is followed as each player takes a turn. In the final chorus, all play together in simultaneous, semi-accidental counterpoint. It is like an improvised musical conversation. Throughout the number, no player knows exactly what the others will do, but each plays according to musical instinct so that every part fits in with the others. Nor are the individual players entirely certain what they themselves will do, because a player taking a "ride" on a number plays it somewhat differently each time.

(17) Sometimes there seems to be so much improvisation that the melody is no longer identifiable. Why does that happen? Because the player improvises on the basic harmony as well as the melody. For example, if the song starts on the tonic chord, as it often does, and if the piece is in the key of C, then the notes of the tonic chord are C E G. The improviser may play any or all of these three notes plus tones that are nonharmonic in relation to that chord. In other words, other pitches can be woven around the notes of the chord, which may rather obscure the tune.

(18) The particular song may get lost for another reason. Most popular songs have simple chord patterns and there is little difference between the chords of one popular song and another. When the melody is being improvised upon, the harmony is often not distinguishable from that of other songs. The rhapsodic nature of jazz improvisation also leads to a sameness of mood that makes it more difficult to distinguish the basic song.

(19) **Types of Jazz** The 1920s saw the real emergence of jazz, which was given impetus in 1918 by Joe "King" Oliver's famous Creole Jazz Band in Chicago. Other musicians soon became prominent: Bix Beiderbecke, who started "white" jazz with his cornet and a band called the "Wolverines"; Paul Whiteman, whose band presented the first jazz concert in 1924, featuring the premiere of George Gershwin's *Rhapsody in Blue*; Bessie Smith, the famous blues singer; Fletcher Henderson and his band; and the notable Louis Armstrong. Through his trumpet playing and vocal renditions, Armstrong had much influence on the basic sound and style of jazz

(20) **Dixieland** The prevailing style in the 1920s was dixieland. It is characterized by a strong upbeat, a meter of two beats to the measure,

and certain tonal and stylistic qualities that are impossible to notate. It has a "busy" sound because there is simultaneous improvisation by perhaps four to seven players. The result is a type of "accidental" counterpoint that is held together only by the song's basic harmony and the musical instincts of the players. The presence of simultaneous improvisation in both African music and jazz can hardly be a coincidence. Dixieland style is often described as "hot"; it is rather fast and usually loud.

(21) **Boogie-Woogie**   During the depression of the 1930s the hiring of bands became prohibitively expensive. So pianists enjoyed increasing popularity, especially as they developed a jazz piano style called boogie-woogie. It features a persistently repeated melodic figure—an ostinato—in the bass. Usually the boogie-woogie ostinato consists of eight notes per measure, which explains why this type of music is sometimes called "eight to the bar." Over the continuous bass the pianist plays trills, octave tremolos (the rapid alternation of pitches an octave apart), and other melodic figures.

(22) **Swing**   The swing era in jazz lasted from 1935 to about 1950. It featured intricate arrangements and big bands of about seventeen players under the leadership of such musicians as Benny Goodman, Count Basie, and Duke Ellington. It was also the era of the featured soloist—Gene Krupa, Fats Waller, and Tommy Dorsey, to name a few. Other notable figures from the period include Artie Shaw, Harry James, Glenn Miller, Coleman Hawkins, and Fletcher Henderson. Musically, swing has four beats to the measure and rhythm with a "bounce." The swing era was one in which the audience danced. Its "concert halls" were such places as the Roseland Ballroom in New York and the Hollywood Palladium.

(23) There were many great bands and arrangers during the swing era. The most enduring, and the one probably still heard today more than the others, is Duke Ellington and his orchestra. Ellington's group spanned nearly five decades and produced varied and interesting music. "Take the 'A' Train" was one of Ellington's more popular works, and it demonstrates well the style of the bands in the swing era. The melody is taken in four rather fast beats per measure. There is a contrasting phrase to the eight bars in the example. The remainder is the same sixteen measures repeated with new improvised solo material or played in a different key. The chord symbols in the example indicate the chords on which the soloists improvise.

(24) **Bop**   Following World War II there emerged a style called bebop, or more commonly, bop. It was developed chiefly by Charlie "Bird" Parker (see pages 508–9) and Dizzy Gillespie, who once defined the term by saying that in bop you go *Ba*-oo *Ba*-oo *Ba*-oo instead of *Oo*-ba *Oo*-ba *Oo*-ba. What he was describing was the nearly continuous syncopation that occurs in bop. It also features dissonant chords and freely developed melodies. Often the performers play in unison at the octave instead of presenting the traditional improvised counterpoint. In bop the fifth step of the scale is lowered, which is a carry-over of the blue notes discussed earlier. The bass drum does not sound all the time—a change from earlier styles. Instead, the double bass is given the responsibility for keeping the beat. Bop bands were much smaller than the bands of the swing era.

(25) ***Progressive and Free Form Jazz***   Stan Kenton was the leader of progressive jazz, which is characterized by big bands and highly dissonant chords. In a sense, the progressive style is an updated, intellectual version of the swing style that prevailed about fifteen years earlier. With Miles Davis, the Modern Jazz Quartet, and Dave Brubeck, jazz turned toward a "cool" style, still intellectual and well ordered, but performed by much smaller groups. Charlie Mingus, Ornette Coleman, and John Coltrane led a movement toward free form jazz, in which all restraints were removed. No longer was improvisation held together by the harmony.

(26) Over the years jazz has become more of a listener's type of music, in contrast to its early history. Gone is much of jazz's image as a "music of the people." It has matured in the sense that it is not always played just for fun, at least not by many jazz musicians. It is now serious business, performed by musicians who have studied Stravinsky and Bartók. One need only listen to works by jazz composers such as Miles Davis, Dave Brubeck, Herbie Hancock, and Chuck Mangione to hear how far jazz has progressed from what its "founding fathers" started.

(27) Jazz represents the rediscovery of the art of improvising, which was largely neglected after the time of Bach and Mozart. Perhaps it was a better counterbalance to the deadly seriousness of nineteenth-century music than were the arty, chic attempts at ridicule by Satie and his followers.*

Place the answers to the first five questions in the answer box.

1. The second paragraph

    a. discusses jazz's roots
    b. focuses on the influence of the African-American culture on jazz
    c. discusses the types of jazz
    d. both a and b

2. In the first sentence of paragraph 5, what term of qualification is used?

    a. jazz
    b. untutored
    c. generally
    d. not

3. What word in the last sentence in paragraph 7 has a positive connotation?

    a. combination
    b. dissonance
    c. interesting
    d. creates

----

*Hoffer, *Understanding of Music*, pp. 501–510.

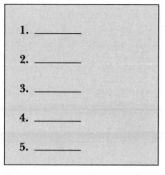

1. _____

2. _____

3. _____

4. _____

5. _____

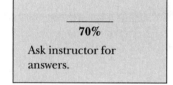

70%

Ask instructor for answers.

Follow-up on Chapter 8

4. The main idea of paragraph 8 is

a. jazz has a conservative harmony
b. jazz's attraction is not based on the type of harmony it uses
c. jazz has used some of the music styles of Debussy and Stravinsky
d. both a and c

5. The last sentence in paragraph 9 uses a word with a positive connotation. The word is

a. lifeblood
b. listener
c. rhythmic
d. accents

Read the following questions, then go back and reread the excerpt. Finally, without looking back, answer the following questions in phrases or short sentences.

6. Describe three of the seven most important characteristics of jazz. (3 points)

7. Briefly describe two types of jazz. (2 points)

Now that you have completed the exercises, it may be helpful to see how your reading of this topic has changed some of your ideas about music history and improved your abilities in reading and listening for inferences. You may want to go back to the exercises and reread them just for content, or for what they have to say about music history, and you may want to review the introduction. Then answer the following questions either individually or in small groups.

On the Topic of Music History

1. How would you now define *music history*?
2. What do you now know about Bach and Mozart?
3. What do you now know about rock and jazz? How are they similar? different?
4. What area in music history would you now want to pursue further?

On the Topic of Reading and Listening for Inferences

5. Are you now able to understand how terms of qualification change the meaning of a sentence?
6. Are you now able to analyze the connotations of words in sentences and longer selections?
7. Can you draw appropriate conclusions from descriptions and narrations in what you read or listen to?
8. What aspects of reading and listening for inferences do you still need to develop?

Internet Activity

You may want to break up into groups of four or five and research on the Internet the following musical topic or one of the composers that were mentioned in this chapter: rap music, Mendelsohn, or Chopin. If you have access to InfoTrac, locate information from this source. You may choose to divide up this research into specific tasks.

As you do your research, answer some or all of the following questions. Then return to your group to share your responses.

1. What new information did you learn about the composer you selected?
2. What new information did you learn about rap music?
3. Describe the steps you used to access this information on the Internet.

CHAPTER 9

Reading Graphs, Charts, and Tables

In this chapter, you will learn about ways to read:

- Circle, bar, and line graphs
- Charts
- Tables

Reading graphs, charts, and tables is a necessary college reading skill. A graph and a chart are visual representations of information. A table presents information compactly. If you learn more easily visually, graphs and charts should help you learn.

Circle Graphs

Circle graphs show how the whole is broken up into recognizable parts. The entire circle equals 100 percent, and the divided sections represents the parts. When you study circle graphs, you must first determine the subject. Then you should see how the various parts relate to this subject and then how the various parts relate to each other.

Look at the graph in Figure 9-1 on how the earth's land is classified. Answer the following questions as you study this graph:

1. What does the whole circle represent?
2. How are the parts organized? smallest percentage to largest? largest percentage to smallest? variuos uses of the land?
3. Can you remember the percentage of land that is not usable? the percentage that is usable?

Having studied this circle graph, you should have noted that the entire circle represents the various ways the earth's land is classified, or its six basic classifications. You should have then noticed that the bulk of the earth's land is not usable (51%) and that only 21% of the earth is in use (11% cultivated and 10% grazed). If on an ecology exam, for example, you had to remember the various uses of the earth's land and their percentages, this circle graph would have helped you greatly.

Bar Graphs

Bar graphs are usually a series of rectanges comparing a group of quantities, like production of various foods or populations. Each rectangle

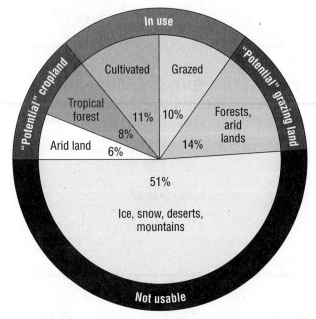

Figure 9-1   *Earth's land. (Source: G. Tyler Miller, Jr.,* Living in the Environment, *10th ed. [Belmont, Calif.: Wadsworth, 1998], p. 609.)*

represents a particular quantity, usually expressed in numbers. There are frequently several bars in a bar graph, starting with the largest bar or number and moving progressively to the smallest. You should ask the same questions that you would when studying a circle graph:

1. What is the subject?
2. How do the parts relate to this subject?
3. How do the parts relate to each other?

Look at the bar graph in Figure 9-2 on the hazards to life. Determine the subject, what each bar represents, and how these bars relate to each other.

Having studied this material, you should have determined that this graph represents the average amount of time a person in the United States would lose from his life if he werre exposed to a particular hazard. Each bar represents a particular life hazard and the amount of time taken from a person's life when exposed to this hazard. Did you determine the three most dangerous hazards—poverty, being male, and smoking—and the three least dangerous hazards—living near a nuclear plant, hurricanes and tornadoes, and flying?

Bar graphs are effective study aids when you need to remember much information and how each part of this information relates to the other parts.

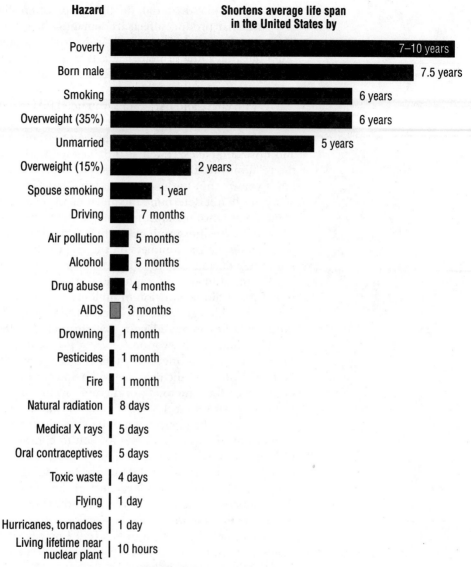

Hazard	Shortens average life span in the United States by
Poverty	7–10 years
Born male	7.5 years
Smoking	6 years
Overweight (35%)	6 years
Unmarried	5 years
Overweight (15%)	2 years
Spouse smoking	1 year
Driving	7 months
Air pollution	5 months
Alcohol	5 months
Drug abuse	4 months
AIDS	3 months
Drowning	1 month
Pesticides	1 month
Fire	1 month
Natural radiation	8 days
Medical X rays	5 days
Oral contraceptives	5 days
Toxic waste	4 days
Flying	1 day
Hurricanes, tornadoes	1 day
Living lifetime near nuclear plant	10 hours

Figure 9-2   *Hazards to life. (Source: G. Tyler Miller, Jr.,* Living in the Environment, *10th ed. [Belmont, Calif.: Wadsworth, 1998], p. 277.)*

Line Graphs

With line graphs, you may have a more difficult time than with circle or bar graphs. Line graphs are made up of three important parts: (1) the vertical axis, or the line going up and down; (2) the horizontal axis, or the line going from side to side; and (3) the diagonal line, or the line either going up or down or parallel to the horizontal axis. Line graphs always illustrate relationships, usually cause–effect relationships. In business or economics material, the line graph often shows how the supply of a particular product affects its demand—how, for example, lowering the supply increase the demand. In biological material, the line graph often illustrates how a biological activity is affected by a particular variable or change—how, for instance, temperature (a variable) affects cell movement (a biological activity).

As with circle and bar graphs, you need first to determine the subject of the graph and what the numbers on the vertical and horizontal axes mean. Unlike circle and bar graphs, you then need to study the vertical and horizontal axes as well as the diagonal to determine the nature of the relationship. Determining this relationship is crucial, because without it you will not understand what the details of the line graph mean, and you will not determine the meaning of the diagonal's movement in going up or down or staying parallel to the horizontal axis.

Look at the line graph in Figure 9-3 on world grain production. First, determine what the numbers on the vertical and horizontal axes represent. Then decide what the diagonal's upward movement suggests.

Having studied this graph, did you determine that the vertical axis represents grain production in millions of tons and the horizontal line the year in which grain was produced? Did you also determine that grain production has increased from 1950 through the 1990s?

With line graphs, you may have a problem in correctly estimating where the diagonal meets each axis. Using a six-inch ruler to locate a particular point on the diagonal will help your calculation. With the aid of the ruler, find the total world grain production for 1970. Did it help you to calculate about 1,000 million, or 1 billion, tons of grain?

Sometimes line graphs get more complicated because there are two or more diagnoals or variables for you to consider. And at times these diagonals intersect. No matter how complicated the line graph, though, your approach should be the same as in reading a line graph with one diagonal: (1) determine the subject of the graph, (2) determine what the numbers on each axis represent, and (3) determine how the diagonals relate to each other.

Look at the line graph in Figure 9-4 on sex partners in the United States. Determine the subject, what the numbers on each axis mean, and how the three lines relate to each other.

Having studied this more complex line graph, you should have determined that it is comparing the age of the adult (18–59) to the percentage of this population that has had no, one, or two or more sexual partners during a twelve-month period. The vertical axis measures the percentage of the population; the horizontal axis lists the age of the adults. The three lines in the graph represent no partner, one partner, and two or more partners. After studying this more complicated line graph, you can conclude that age plays a major role in the number of sex partners an American adults has. Those adults in the 55–59 category are the least likely to have two or more partners (about 3%) and the most likely to have no partner (about 30%). Only the 18–24-year-

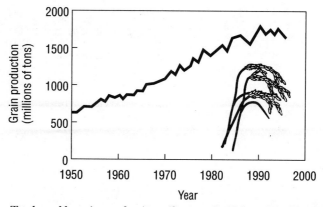

Figure 9-3 *Total world grain production. (Source: G. Tyler Miller, Jr.,* Living in the Environment, *10th ed. [Belmont, Calif.: Wadsworth, 1998], p. 601.)*

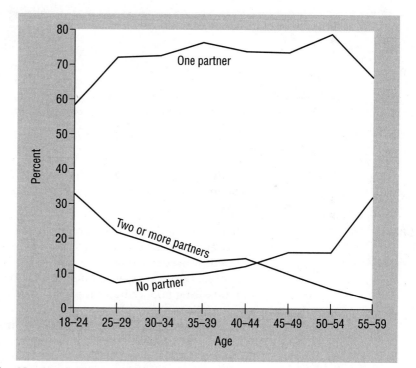

Figure 9-4 *Number of sex partners in the last 12 months for U.S. adults. (Source: James W. Kalat,* Introduction to Psychology, *4th ed. [Pacific Grove, Calif.: Brooks/Cole, 1996], p. 488.)*

olds have a slightly lower percentage of one-partner experiences than the adults of ages 55–59 (approximately 58% as opposed to approximately 63%).

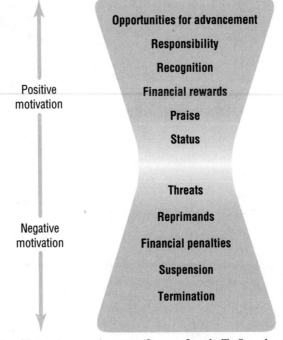

Figure 9-5   *Motivation continuum. (Source: Joseph T. Straub and Raymond F. Attner,* Introduction to Business, *5th ed. [Belmont, Calif.: Wadsworth, 1994], p. 283.)*

By carefully reading a line graph such as this one with two or more diagonals, you can appreciate the wealth of information presented.

Charts

Charts are another way to present information visually and compactly. They are often used in the business field to categorize information and present procedural sequences and in the history field to show time sequences. Business analysts often use charts in their oral presentations, summarizing important information, making it more understandable to their audience.

Look at the figure on motivation (Figure 9-5) to see how various elements of positive and negative motivation are represented in these two connected four-sided shapes, with the arrows indicating the degree of positive and negative motivation. Such a chart can be effectively used at the end of an oral presentation on motivation as a memory and summarizing device. As you study charts like this, ask yourself the following questions: (1) How do the shapes relate to the material? Do larger shapes represent greater relative importance? smaller shapes lesser importance? (2) How is the material positioned? Does the positioning suggest relative importance? Do you see how the chart on motivation is set up so the more important terms are in the larger parts of the shape, while the farther up or down you go as you follow the arrows, the more important the material?

Flowcharts have become particularly popular in the business and computer fields to show the sequences of various procedures. Note how the steps in purchasing a product are graphically presented in Figure 9-6. The first step is at the top and the last is at the bottom, with the steps being connected by curved arrows. Flowcharts can also be used to indicate more complicated procedures, meaning you need to follow the arrows carefully to see where they end. In Figure 9-7—on marketing a product—you see how, after a product is created, it branches out into three steps (distribution, pricing, and promotion), all of which lead to after-sales service. Then note how after-sales service requires collection of feedback and analysis of needs, so the chart loops back to the second step.

With flowcharts, be sure you follow the arrows very carefully so that you are familiar with the sequence presented, and study particularly thoroughly those more complicated flowcharts that loop back into a previous step or procedure.

In history material, charts known as time lines present the sequence of historical events in chronological order, usually in a left-to-right de-

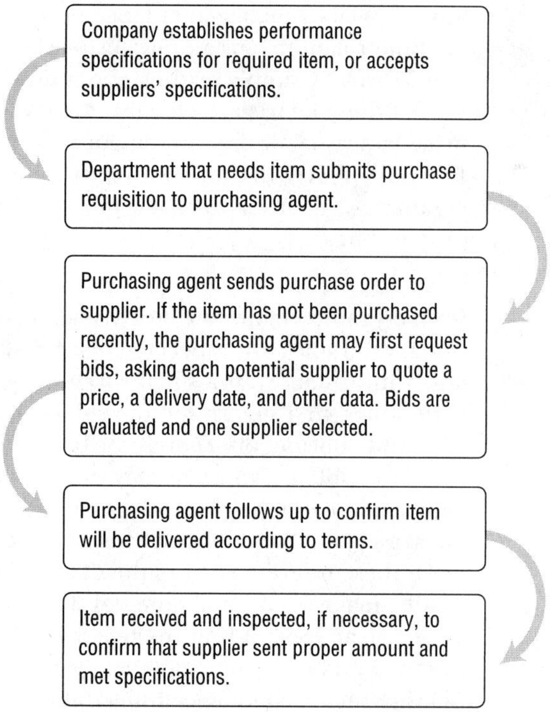

Company establishes performance specifications for required item, or accepts suppliers' specifications.

Department that needs item submits purchase requisition to purchasing agent.

Purchasing agent sends purchase order to supplier. If the item has not been purchased recently, the purchasing agent may first request bids, asking each potential supplier to quote a price, a delivery date, and other data. Bids are evaluated and one supplier selected.

Purchasing agent follows up to confirm item will be delivered according to terms.

Item received and inspected, if necessary, to confirm that supplier sent proper amount and met specifications.

Figure 9-6   *A typical purchasing procedure. (Source: Joseph T. Straub and Raymond F. Attner,* Introduction to Business, *5th ed. [Belmont, Calif.: Wadsworth, 1994], p. 355.)*

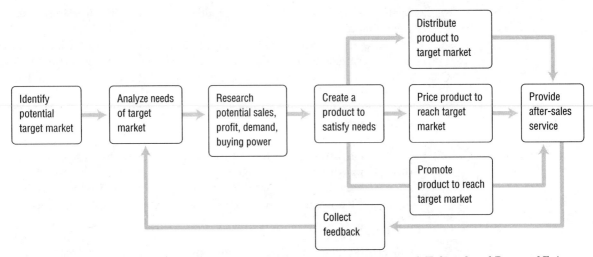

Figure 9-7   *The process of marketing a product. (Source: Joseph T. Straub and Raymond F. Attner,*
Introduction to Business, *5th ed. [Belmont, Calif.: Wadsworth, 1994], p. 355.)*

sign, with the material on the right being the most recent and that on
the left the earliest. Note how the time line works in Figure 9-8 on the
history of labor management. See how the time line gives you a sense of
the time relationships among historical events that you may not appreciate as well by simply reading about these events.

All these charts are effective ways to organize material and provide
successful visual designs to remember what you are studying. In Chapter
11, you will create your own charts, known as study maps or advance
organizers, in order to make more comprehensible the material you
read and hear.

Tables

Unlike graphs, tables are not visual. They simply present information
concisely. Tables are especially helpful study aids because they present
much information in a small space. As you did with graphs, when you
read tables, first determine the subject. Then establish what each category and subcategory represent. If you do not know what a particular
part of a table means, you may not be able to use the table efficiently.
Unlike a line graph, whose diagonal shows a trend (up, down, or staying
the same), a table does not spell out such trends for you. You need to
make these inferences from the data in the table. If you note a trend in
a table, make a marginal note stating what that trend seems to be.

Look at Table 9-1 on the major types of pesticides. Note the categories of the table: type, examples, persistence (how long they last), and
whether they are biologically magnified (whether their volume increases
the longer they remain in the environment). What inferences can you
draw from the data? What conclusions do you come to?

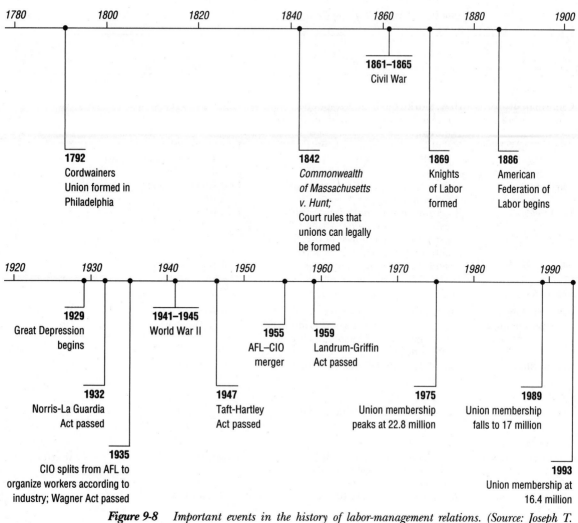

Figure 9-8   *Important events in the history of labor-management relations. (Source: Joseph T. Straub and Raymond F. Attner,* Introduction to Business, *5th ed. [Belmont, Calif.: Wadsworth, 1994], pp. 302–303.)*

Table 9-1 presents several types of pesticides: insecticides, herbicides, fungicides, and fumigants. These pesticides are not ordered from most dangerous to least dangerous. Insecticides like DDT seem to be the most dangerous because they stay in the environment from 2 to 15 years, and they are biologically magnified. Fumigants are found at the end of the table, and they are almost as dangerous as insecticides because they have a mostly high persistence and are often biologically magnified. The least dangerous pesticide seems to be soil sterilants, which persist in the environment for days instead of years and are not biologically magnified.

Do you see how densely packed with information this table is? Most tables that you will come across are equally informative. As you continue

Table 9-1   *Major Types of Pesticides*

Type	Examples	Persistence	Biologically Magnified?
Insecticides			
Chlorinated hydrocarbons	DDT, aldrin, dieldrin, toxaphene, lindane, chlordane, methoxychlor, mirex	High (2–15 years)	Yes
Organophosphates	Malathion, parathion, diazinon, TEPP, DDVP, mevingphos	Low to moderate (1–12 weeks), but some can last several years	No
Carbamates	Aldicarb, carbaryl (Sevin), propoxur, maneb, zineb	Low (days to weeks)	No
Botanicals	Rotenone, pyrethrum, and camphor extracted from plants, synthetic pyrethroids (variations of pyrethrum) and rotenoids (variations of rotenone)	Low (days to weeks)	No
Microbotanicals	Various bacteria, fungi, protozoa	Low (days to weeks)	No
Herbicides			
Contact chemicals	Atrazine, simazine, paraquat	Low (days to weeks)	No
Systemic chemicals	2,4-D, 2,4,5-T, Silvex, diruon, daminozide (Alar), alachlor (Lasso), glyphosate (Roundup)	Mostly low (days to weeks)	No
Soil sterilants	Trifualin, diphenamid, dalapon, butylate	Low (days)	No
Fungicides			
Various chemicals	Captan, pentachlorphenol, zeneb, methyl bromide, carbon bisulfide	Mostly low (days)	No
Fumigants			
Various chemicals	Carbon tetrachloride, ethylene dibromide, methyl bromide	Mostly high	Yes (for most)

Source: G. Tyler Miller, Jr., *Living in the Environment,* 10th ed. (Belmont, Calif.: Wadsworth, 1998), p. 622.

to read tables, you will be able to make more subtle inferences and conclusions and determine more patterns that are suggested in the data. You will also find yourself relying on tables more for study purposes, particularly for tests and final examinations.

Summary

Graphs are visual, concise means of presenting information. There are three kinds of graphs: circle, bar, and line. Line graphs show relationships among two or more variables and are sometimes difficult to understand. Charts are visual ways of presenting material in order to show relatinships, particularly procedures and time sequences. Tables are not visual; rather, they present information in categories. In reading a table, you need to make inferences and draw conclusions regarding the patterns that emerge from the data.

Graphs, charts, and tables are often effective study aids because much information is presented in a small amount of space. You may choose to create your own graphs, charts, and tables for study purposes when you want to condense the material that you are studying.

Summary Box   *Graphs, Charts, and Tables*

What are they?	*Why use them?*

Graph: a visual way to present information either in circles, bars, or lines.
Chart: a visual way of representing relationships, especially procedures and time sequences
Table: a concise way to relate information by setting up categories and subcategories
	Graph: to present information visually and to help you learn material more easily
	Chart:
	    to condense information into a visual, easy-to-remember form
	    to create your own in studying and remembering lecture, discussion, and textbook material
	Table:
	    to present information concisely
	    to show relationships among facts and figures
	    to gain insights about the material you are studying
	    to help you remember information for exams

Skills Practice

Exercise 9.1
Reading Graphs,
Charts, and Tables

Use the reading skills you have just learned to answer the following questions concerning graphs, tables, and charts on topics that are familiar from the exercises you have completed in previous chapters. Place all answers in the answer box.

1. Table 9-2 concerns:

   a. what women want
   b. what men like about women
   c. harassment against women
   d. whether women prefer to work or to stay at home

2. The country that seems to have the most traditional attitude toward women and work is:

   a. Denmark
   b. Canada

Table 9-2 *"A Job Is Alright, But What Most Women Really Want Is a Home and Children."*

	Percent Who Agree		
Nation	Total Population	Men	Women
Lithuania	97	96	97
India	94	91	96
Czech Republic	93	92	95
Slovak Republic	92	93	92
Bulgaria	90	92	88
Latvia	90	93	89
Russia	90	91	89
Nigeria	88	90	85
Turkey	88	89	87
Estonia	85	87	84
Romania	82	84	80
Japan	81	84	78
Belarus	81	83	78
China	78	81	75
Chile	77	79	76
Slovenia	77	80	73
Hungary	76	81	72
Argentina	73	79	69
Brazil	72	76	69
Iceland	71	75	67
South Korea	70	66	73
France	68	70	67
Italy	65	65	65
Austria	62	64	60
Portugal	62	60	63
Belgium	61	61	60
Mexico	**61**	**64**	**57**
Ireland	59	62	55
Spain	56	58	55
United States	**56**	**58**	**55**
Norway	51	53	48
Germany	50	52	49
Great Britain	45	48	43
Canada	**43**	**45**	**42**
Finland	42	53	32
Netherlands	39	44	36
Denmark	25	25	25

Source: Rodney Stark, *Sociology,* 7th ed. (Belmont, Calif.: Wadsworth, 1998), p. 319.

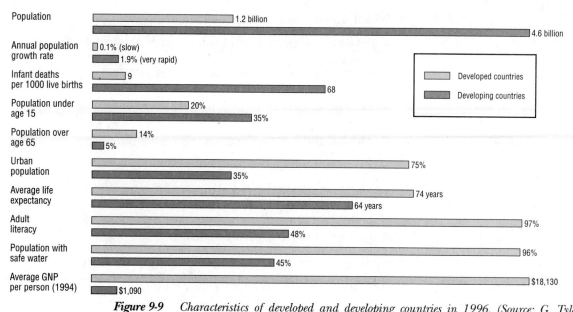

Population
Annual population growth rate
Infant deaths per 1000 live births
Population under age 15
Population over age 65
Urban population
Average life expectancy
Adult literacy
Population with safe water
Average GNP per person (1994)

Figure 9-9   *Characteristics of developed and developing countries in 1996. (Source: G. Tyler Miller, Jr., Living in the Environment, 10th ed. [Belmont, Calif.: Wadsworth, 1998], p. 9.)*

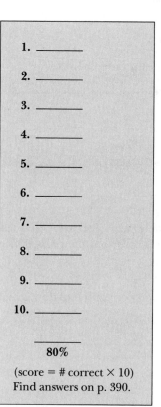

1. _____
2. _____
3. _____
4. _____
5. _____
6. _____
7. _____
8. _____
9. _____
10. _____

_____
80%
(score = # correct × 10)
Find answers on p. 390.

   c. Lithuania
   d. Mexico

3. The country that seems to favor women in the workforce the most is:

   a. the Netherlands
   b. Denmark
   c. the United States
   d. Belgium

4. The subject of the bar graph in Figure 9-9 is:

   a. characteristics of developed countries
   b. characteristics of developed and developing countries
   c. adult literacy in developed and developing countries
   d. urban population growth in developed countries

5. What does the bar graph say about infant deaths?

   a. There are more infant deaths in developed countries than in developing countries.
   b. There are five times as many infant deaths in developing countries as in developed countries.
   c. There are six times as many infant deaths in developing countries as in developed countries.
   d. There are over seven times as many infant deaths in developing countries as in developed countries.

6. Which countries have the greater population?

    a. developed countries: almost four times as great as developing countries

    b. developing countries: almost four times as great as developed countries

    c. Both developed and developing countries have about the same population.

    d. The bar graph does not say.

7. What conclusion(s) can you draw from this bar graph?

    a. People in developing nations seem to live a harder life.

    b. The problems in developing nations will likely only get worse.

    c. both a and b

    d. neither a nor b

8. In the flowchart in Figure 9-10, where should an employee go first?

    a. to the employee's supervisor

    b. to the union steward

    c. to the chief steward

    d. to the industrial relations manager

9. You can conclude that as the grievance progresses,

    a. Fewer personnel are involved.

    b. More personnel are involved.

    c. The same number of personnel are involved.

    d. The employee filing the grievance must represent herself.

10. At what step would a grievance be sent to the president of a company?

    a. Step 2

    b. Step 3

    c. Step 4

    d. Step 5

Exercise 9.2
Reading More
Graphs and Tables

Here are two more graphs and another table, each followed by questions. Some of the topics you have studied in previous chapters. Place your answers in the answer box.

1. From Figure 9-11, determine the combined population of developed nations for 1950:

    a. less than 1 billion

    b. 1 billion

    c. more than 1 billion

    d. 2 billion

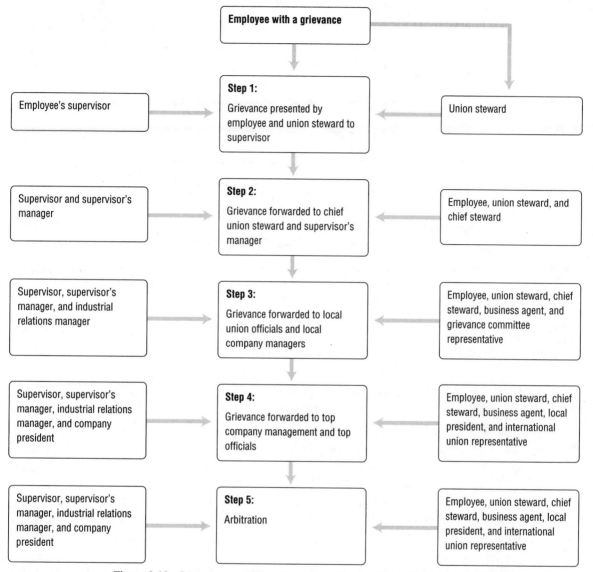

Figure 9-10 *Steps in a grievance procedure. (Source: Joseph T. Straub and Raymond F. Attner,* Introduction to Business, *5th ed. [Belmont, Calif.: Wadsworth, 1994], p. 318.)*

2. What can you conclude about the population growth in developed nations?

   a. It is decreasing at a rapid rate.
   b. It is decreasing.
   c. It is increasing.
   d. It has increased slowly.

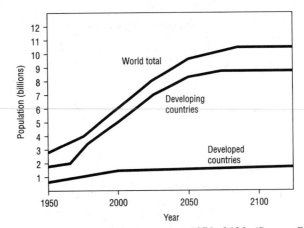

Figure 9-11   *Past and projected population size, 1950–2120. (Source: G. Tyler Miller, Jr.,* Living in the Environment, *10th ed. [Belmont, Calif.: Wadsworth, 1998], p. 9.)*

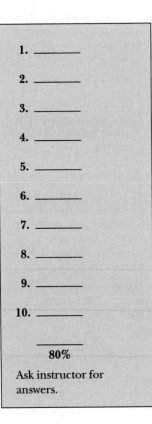

1. _____

2. _____

3. _____

4. _____

5. _____

6. _____

7. _____

8. _____

9. _____

10. _____

_____
80%

Ask instructor for answers.

3. In the year 2050, what is the projected population for developing countries?

a. over 6 billion
b. over 7 billion
c. over 8 billion
d. 9 billion

4. Between the year 2000 and the year 2050, world population is projected to increase by about how many billion?

a. 3 billion
b. 2 billion
c. 1 billion
d. one-half billion

5. What does the dark shaded area in Figure 9-12 on the graying of America show?

a. a 90-year representation of the numbers and percentages of older Americans
b. a 50-year representation of the numbers and percentages of older Americans
c. the increase in the percentage of older Americans over a 75-year period
d. the decrease in the percentage of older Americans over a 90-year span

6. A conclusion you can draw regarding older Americans between 1900 and 1990 is that their percentage has:

a. doubled
b. tripled
c. quadrupled
d. increased by five

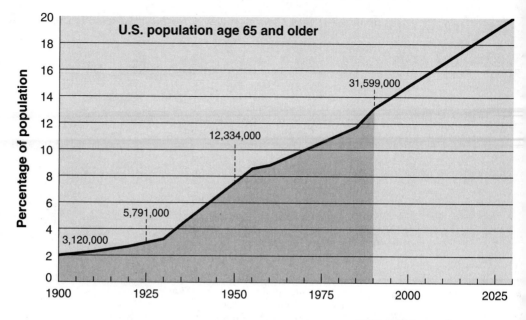

(1990-2030 figures are projected)

Figure 9-12   *The graying of America (1990–2030 figures projected). (Source: Thomas Dye,* Power and Society, *5th ed. [Pacific Grove, Calif.: Brooks/Cole, 1990], p. 265. Data from U.S. Bureau of the Census,* Statistical Abstract of the United States 1988 *[Washington, D.C.: U.S. Government Printing Office, 1988], p. 15.)*

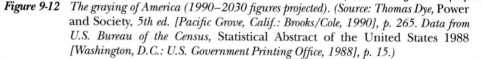

7. The projections for the years 2000–2025 suggest that:

   a. The number of older Americans will decrease.

   b. The number of older Americans will increase, but their percentages will decrease.

   c. Older Americans will increase to about 32 million.

   d. The percentage and numbers of older Americans will continue to increase.

8. Table 9-3 analyzes:

   a. the most popular religions in the United States

   b. the least popular religions in the United States

   c. the religions in America that are growing in numbers

   d. the religions in America that are both growing and losing in numbers

9. Which church has doubled its membership over the 30-year span from 1960 to 1990?

   a. Assemblies of God

   b. Jehovah's Witnesses

   c. United Pentecostal Church

   d. Church of the Nazarene

Table 9-3   *Some Growing and Some Declining American Denominations*

Denomination	Members per 1,000 U.S. Population		Percent Change
	1960	*1990*	
Christian Church (Disciples)	10.0	4.1	−59
Unitarian-Universalist	1.0	0.5	−50
United Church of Christ	12.4	6.4	−48
Episcopal Church	18.1	9.8	−46
United Methodist Church	58.9	35.8	−39
Presbyterian Church (U.S.A.)	23.0	15.2	−34
Evangelical Lutheran Church in America	29.3	21.1	−28
Roman Catholic	233.0	235.5	+1
Southern Baptist Convention	53.8	60.5	+12
Church of the Nazarene	1.7	2.3	+36
Seventh-day Adventist	1.8	2.9	+60
United Pentecostal Church	1.0	2.0	+100
Church of Jesus Christ of Latter-day Saints (Mormons)	8.2	17.1	+109
Jehovah's Witnesses	1.4	3.5	+150
Church of God (Cleveland, TN)	0.9	2.5	+177
Assemblies of God	2.8	8.8	+214
Church of God in Christ	2.2	22.1	+905

Source: Rodney Stark, *Sociology,* 7th ed. (Belmont, Calif.: Wadsworth, 1998), p. 397.

10. Which religion seems to have had the least growth between 1960 and 1990?

   a. Roman Catholic
   b. Church of the Nazarene
   c. Evangelical Lutheran Church in America
   d. Southern Baptist Convention

Exercise 9.3
Writing a Paragraph
with a Main Idea
and Supporting
Details from
Information in a
Graph

In this writing exercise, you are to use only the information presented in the circle graphs and bar graphs in Figure 9-13 to answer the following essay question. This material concerns the Hispanic population in America and comes from a sociology textbook.

Use the following outline to jot down notes you will use in your paragraph.

I. Basic Information on Hispanics in the United States

   A. Where Hispanics generally come from: _____

   B. Where they live: _____

   C. Income: _____

   D. Education: _____

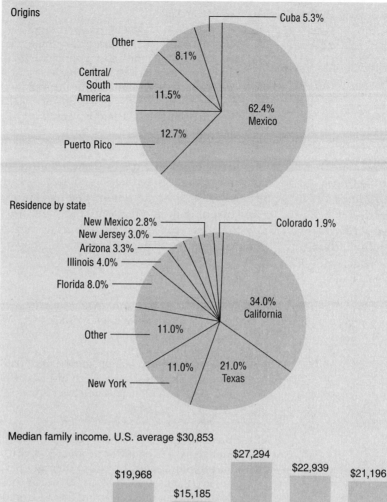

Origins

Other —— 8.1%

Cuba 5.3%

Central/ South America —— 11.5%

62.4% Mexico

12.7%

Puerto Rico ——

Residence by state

New Mexico 2.8% ——
New Jersey 3.0% ——
Arizona 3.3% ——
Illinois 4.0% ——

Colorado 1.9%

Florida 8.0% ——

34.0% California

Other —— 11.0%

11.0%

21.0% Texas

New York ——

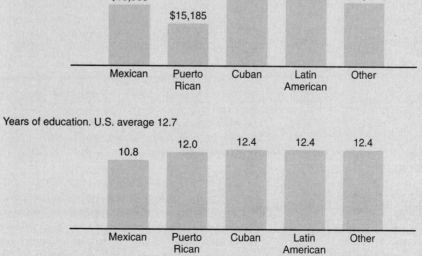

Median family income. U.S. average $30,853

Mexican	Puerto Rican	Cuban	Latin American	Other
$19,968	$15,185	$27,294	$22,939	$21,196

Years of education. U.S. average 12.7

Mexican	Puerto Rican	Cuban	Latin American	Other
10.8	12.0	12.4	12.4	12.4

Figure 9-13 *Hispanic Americans. (Source: Thomas Dye,* Power and Society, *5th ed. [Pacific Grove, Calif.: Brooks/Cole, 1990], p. 241. Data from U.S. Bureau of the Census,* Statistical Abstract of the United States 1988 *[Washington, D.C.: U.S. Government Printing Office, 1988].)*

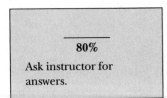

Essay question: In an organized paragraph, discuss where most Hispanics have come from, the most populated Hispanic areas in the United States, the Hispanics with the highest and lowest incomes, and their educational levels compared to the U.S. average. Where appropriate, provide specific figures. Start with a topic sentence discussing where Hispanics generally live and how their lifestyle compares to the average American's.

Exercise 9.4
Determining Main Ideas and Major Details and Interpreting Charts and Tables in a Text Excerpt

The following is an excerpt from a college business text on the ways consumer products are distributed. Read through the excerpt quickly to get a sense of its organization. Then go back and read it slowly, paying particular attention to the four charts and two tables and their relationship to the excerpt. When you finish, answer the following five questions. You may refer to the excerpt in deciding on your answers.

Distribution Strategy

(1) Distribution strategy and pricing strategy are the third and fourth ingredients in a company's marketing mix. When these elements are "blended" with product and promotional strategy, the organization has created its marketing strategy to reach the selected target market. In this chapter we will examine the importance, objectives, and components of distribution strategy. We will also investigate pricing: its objectives, methods of determination, and potential strategies.

The Importance of Distribution Strategy

(2) Distribution strategy encompasses physical distribution systems and the channels used to place the product in the customer's hands. It is responsible for getting the product to the right place at the right time. A firm can have the best products in the world (product strategy) and people can know about them and want them (promotional strategy), but all this will be useless if people cannot get the products when and where they want them.

(3) Distribution involves (1) the routes goods take and the people involved in that process and (2) the activities involved in getting the goods to the consumer—a physical distribution system. Element 1 deals with the channels, choices of channels, and channel members. Element 2 deals with the actual components of a physical distribution system—transportation, warehousing, order processing, materials handling, and inventory control.

Channels of Distribution

channel of distribution *or* marketing channel A route that goods follow on their journey from manufacturers to consumers.
wholesalers Those who sell products to other sellers of goods.
retailers Those who sell products to the ultimate consumer.

(4) A channel of distribution, or marketing channel is *a route that goods follow on their journey from manufacturers to consumers.* Distribution channels are composed of organizations or people known as channel members, middlemen, or intermediaries: **wholesalers**—*those who sell products to other sellers of goods*—and **retailers**—*those who sell products to the ultimate consumer.* The channels and the organizations that comprise them serve as pipelines by which the manufacturer moves goods to the final customer—either an individual consumer or industrial buyer.

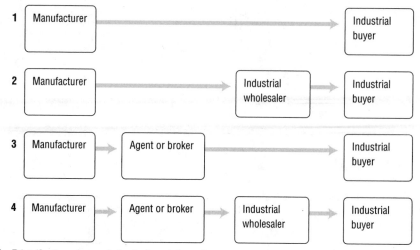

Figure 9-14 *Distribution channels for industrial goods.*

(5) Based on these two types of customers, there are two major distribution channel categories by market: the industrial goods market and the consumer goods market.

Channels for Industrial Goods

(6) Industrial goods channels tend to be more direct than consumer goods channels—many industrial goods are designed solely for the end user. For example, Otis Die and Casting Company designs and manufactures tool dies for Cummings Tool. But in other instances—accessory equipment, supplies—longer channels are required. Figure 9-14 illustrates the four main distribution channels that producers can use to reach the industrial goods market. Let's discuss each of them:

(7) 1. *Manufacturer to industrial buyer.* The shortest and sometimes most practical way for a manufacturer to distribute industrial goods is to sell them directly to industrial customers. Direct distribution is used if goods are awkward to handle, the market segment is small, the seller must train the buyer's employees to operate the product, or, as previously noted, the product is specifically designed for the end user. Computers, textile manufacturing equipment, and iron ore often are distributed in this way.

(8) 2. *Manufacturer to industrial wholesaler to industrial buyer.* Industrial goods with a broad market, such as welding rods, printing paper, and construction materials, need wider distribution. They utilize a distribution channel featuring wholesalers known as *industrial distributors.* These distributors resell to the industrial buyer.

(9) 3. *Manufacturer to agent or broker to industrial buyer.* In some instances the product being sold does not require the intermediate warehousing service provided by a wholesaler but still needs some intermediary to sell the products. An agent or broker can serve as the contact point

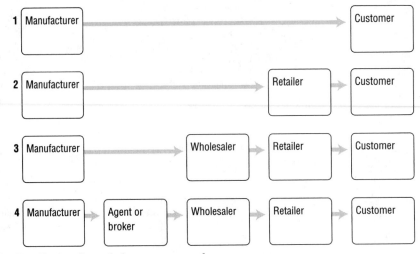

Figure 9-15 *Distribution channels for consumer goods.*

for the manufacturer without taking possession of or title to the goods and can provide the necessary sales support.

(10) 4. *Manufacturer to agent or broker to industrial wholesaler to industrial buyer.* Small manufacturers often need to contract with an agent or broker to represent products to wholesalers. This agent serves the purpose of bringing the wholesaler and manufacturer together but does not take title to the goods.

(11) **Channels for Consumer Goods**   Consumer goods channels tend to be longer and more complex than industrial channels. Because a large number of consumer goods are low-priced convenience goods, by necessity more middlemen need to be involved. Chewing gum, razor blades, and paper plates cannot be effectively marketed directly from the manufacturer to the consumer. Figure 9-15 shows the four distribution channels that manufacturers of consumer goods can use. Let's examine each:

(12) 1. *Manufacturer to consumer.* Although the direct channel is favored for reaching industrial users, only approximately 5 percent of consumer goods are moved in this way. Such products as plants at nurseries, vegetables at farmers' markets, and arts and crafts items at fairs are often sold directly to consumers. Firms such as L. L. Bean, Omaha Steaks, Wolverman's (muffins, bagels, crumpets) sell direct through their mail-order catalogs.

(13) 2. *Manufacturer to retailer to consumer.* Some manufacturers choose to select their own retail outlets to represent them. Automobiles and large household appliances are products that traditionally are distributed directly to retailers without the need for wholesalers.

(14) 3. *Manufacturer to wholesaler to retailer to consumer.* Some products—magazines, combs, lipstick, hair spray—need a broad channel of distribution. This is provided by incorporating a wholesale and retail link in the channel. The wholesaler aids in allocating the product to the

retailers in order to have the product available when and where needed by the consumer. The success of consumer product manufacturers such as Gillette and Schick is related directly to the distribution networks the firms have developed. As convenience goods, the products are placed in supermarkets, convenience stores, drug stores, and discount stores across the country.

(15) 4. *Manufacturer to agent or broker to wholesaler to retailer to consumer.* When goods are produced by a large number of small companies—canning, frozen-food packing, meat packing—an agent or broker brings the buyers and sellers together. In some cases the agent or broker contacts the wholesalers, who in turn buy from the producers. In other instances the wholesaler may be seeking a source of supply.

(16) **Selection of a Distribution Channel**   Which of these distribution channels should a manufacturer use? The decision is based on a number of variables, such as:

(17) • *The market segment.* As we have seen, a major factor in the decision is whether the product is intended for the consumer or industrial market. Industrial purchases normally deal directly with the manufacturer, while consumers make most purchases at retail stores.

(18) • *The size and geographic location of the market segment.* A market that is large and geographically dispersed, as in the case of many consumer goods, requires the use of marketing intermediaries. On the other hand, a direct channel is more effective when the manufacturer's potential market is small and geographically concentrated.

(19) • *The type of product.* Product type also dictates channel selection. Convenience goods require broad distribution to have them available where the consumer wants them—therefore a long channel with multiple intermediaries. Specialty goods are distributed directly to retail stores.

(20) • *The ability to perform the marketing functions.* A critical factor is whether the manufacturer can perform the required marketing functions (selling, transporting, storing, financing, risk bearing) or has the need for others—intermediaries—to do so. If a company has adequate resources—managerial, financial, marketing—it feels less pressure to use intermediaries.

(21) • *The competitor's distribution strategy.* Sometimes it is necessary to respond to a competitor's distribution strategy. Dell Computers, by bypassing retail outlets and going directly to the consumer, revolutionized computer sales and forced similar actions by IBM.

(22) • *The degree of market coverage.* Adequate market coverage—the number of dealers or outlets where the good can be purchased—for some products could mean one store for 70,000 people, while for another it may mean one store for 200,000. As seen in Figure 9-16, there are three degrees of market coverage: intensive distribution, selective distribution, and exclusive distribution. A firm that markets convenience products will want **intensive distribution**, *widespread market coverage that utilizes a large number of wholesalers and retailers.* Another manufacturer that markets shopping goods may wish to emphasize image and a good sales volume through **selective distribution**, *utilizing a moderate number of retailers and wholesalers.* Finally, for a specialty good, a manufacturer

intensive distribution Widespread market coverage that utilizes a large number of wholesalers and retailers.

selective distribution Utilizing a moderate number of retailers and wholesalers.

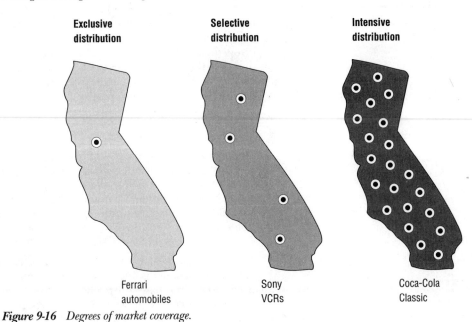

Exclusive distribution   **Selective distribution**   **Intensive distribution**

Ferrari automobiles   Sony VCRs   Coca-Cola Classic

Figure 9-16   *Degrees of market coverage.*

exclusive distribution Limiting distribution to one retailer or wholesaler in a geographic area.

may use **exclusive distribution**: *limiting distribution to one retailer or wholesaler in a geographic area.*

(23) With these factors in mind, let's examine the roles of the two major channel members.

Channel Members

(24) As mentioned earlier in the chapter, the various channels of distribution we have examined are composed of organizations or people known as *channel members, middlemen,* or *intermediaries.* These intermediaries perform the marketing functions of buying, selling, storing, transporting, risk taking, and collecting marketing information for the manufacturer. In addition, marketing intermediaries are vitally important in creating time, place, and possession utilities. The intermediaries ensure that products are available when and where they are needed.

(25) Two types of middlemen operate between the manufacturer and consumer or industrial user: wholesalers and retailers. In the next sections we will discuss each.

(26) **Wholesaling Middlemen**   Wholesalers are middlemen who sell goods to retailers, to other wholesalers, and to industrial users, but who do not sell in significant amounts to the final consumer. As shown in Figure 9-17, if wholesalers did not exist, retailers would have to spend a great deal of time dealing with many different manufacturers, attempting to coordinate numerous product orders and shipments, and acquiring and maintaining huge stock inventories.

(27) Not all wholesalers are the same. Some take title to the goods (merchant wholesalers); others do not (agents and brokers). Some provide a full range of services. As shown in Table 9-4, full-service merchant wholesalers

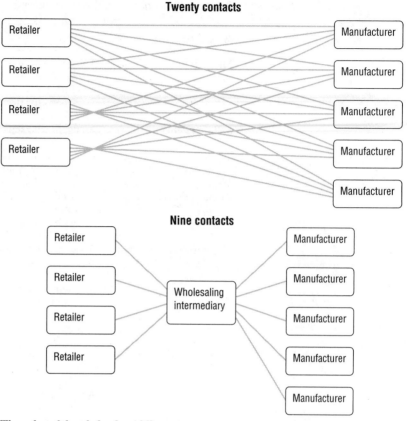

Figure 9-17   *The value of the wholesale middleman.*

Table 9-4   *Typical Services Provided by Full-service Wholesalers*

Services to Manufacturers	*Services to Retailers*
Relay market information from retailers	Advise retailer on layout, promotional activities, bookkeeping practices, inventory planning, and sources of credit
Employ sales force to sell products	
Save manufacturers work by extending credit to retailers	Tell of new products that manufacturers are bringing to market
Store products before resale and deliver them when sold	Deliver merchandise faster and in smaller quantities than producers are willing to do
Bear risk of market changes that may reduce demand for the product	Simplify retailers' recordkeeping and inventory-handling activities by gathering many manufacturers' products into a single delivery and billing

Table 9-5   *Types of Wholesalers and Their Characteristics*

Wholesaler	Characteristics	Takes Title
Manufacturers' agent*	An agent who sells products made by several manufacturers Has little authority to approve customer requests for price concessions, expedited delivery, or credit	No
Selling agent*	An agent who sells a producer's entire output Usually has broad authority to approve customer requests for price concessions, expedited delivery, or credit	No
Auction house*	Brings buyers and sellers together in one location Allows buyers to inspect products before purchase	No
Commission merchant*	An agent who represents producers Sells products for the best price possible; takes possession of goods Sells agricultural products	No
Broker	An agent who represents either buyer or seller for a commission on sales or purchases made Arranges for products shipped directly to the purchaser Distributes such products as coal, grain, and produce	No
Rack jobber	A type of consumer-goods wholesaler Sets up manufacturers' point-of-purchase displays in stores and restocks them as needed Distributes such products as magazines, panty hose, and candy	Yes
Drop shipper	An intermediary who does not take physical possession of goods Provides selling and credit Does not provide advertising or merchandising support Distributes primarily raw materials	Yes
Truck wholesaler	An intermediary who sells and delivers goods at the same time on a regular sales route Provides merchandising and promotion support Distributes potato chips, bakery, and dairy products	Yes

*Manufacturers' agent, selling agent, auction house, and commission merchant are all categorized as *agent* channels of distribution.

provide credit, store and deliver, and provide sales and promotional assistance. On the other hand, limited-service merchant wholesalers simply resell goods and provide little or no service. Table 9-5 provides a sampling of the various types of wholesalers and their characteristics.

(28) **Retailing Middlemen**   Retailers are the last stage in the channel of distribution: they perform the business activities involved in the sale of goods and services to the ultimate consumer for personal use. The activities may include buying and selling of products, transportation or delivery, storage of inventory, financing, and risk bearing. Retailers can be classified by type of ownership and where business is conducted.*

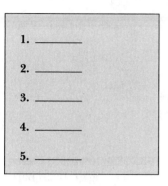

1. _____

2. _____

3. _____

4. _____

5. _____

1. The main idea of paragraph 2 suggests that:

   a. Distribution strategies are often inefficient.
   b. Distribution strategies must focus on delivering goods on time at the right location.
   c. Product strategy and promotional strategy are extremely important in understanding distribution.
   d. Distribution strategies have often been incompletely studied by business analysts.

2. The main idea of paragraph 11 is that consumer goods channels:

   a. move items like chewing gum and razor blades
   b. move inexpensive items
   c. generally have four types of distribution
   d. are more complicated and time consuming than industrial channels

3. Which is *not* a major detail in paragraph 14?

   a. Lipstick is one product that needs a broad distribution.
   b. Gillette and Schick have successfully implemented a broad distribution strategy.
   c. Some products require a broad distribution.
   d. Products like magazines are distributed to supermarkets, drugstores, and discount stores across the country.

4. The second flowchart (Figure 9-15) suggests that:

   a. Some products go directly from the manufacturer to the consumer.
   b. Other products need a retailer.
   c. The most complicated distribution pattern requires three channels before it gets to the consumer.
   d. all of these

5. What can you conclude from the chart showing degrees of market coverage (Figure 9-16)?

   a. Exclusive distribution requires many distribution sites.
   b. Intensive distribution seems to market popular, inexpensive products.

---

*Joseph T. Straub and Raymond F. Attner, *Introduction to Business,* 5th ed. (Belmont, Calif.: Wadsworth, 1994), pp. 438–445.

c. Sony VCRs require exclusive distribution.

d. Selective distribution often markets extremely expensive items.

Now reread various sections of this text excerpt and then answer the following questions in a phrase or sentence.

6. Reread paragraphs 24–28. What is the difference between a wholesaling middleman and a retailing middleman? (1 point)

7. Study the table that lists the typical services provided by full-service wholesalers (Table 9-4). Without looking back at the table, list two services full-service wholesalers provide manufacturers and two services they provide retailers. (2 points)

8. Study the table that lists the types of wholesalers and their characteristics (Table 9-5). Without looking back at the table, list the characteristics of two of these wholesalers. (2 points)

70%

Ask instructor for answers.

Follow-up on Chapter 9

Now that you have studied this introduction and completed the exercises, it may be helpful to see how your abilities in reading graphs, charts, and tables have improved. You may want to go back to reread the introduction and review the exercises. Then answer the following questions either individually or in small groups.

On Reading Graphs, Charts, and Tables

1. Of the three—graphs, charts, and tables—which are the easiest for you to read? Which are the most difficult?
2. Are graphs, charts, and tables helpful when you read textbook material incorporating such visual material?
3. What about reading graphs, charts, and tables do you still need to work on?

Internet Activity

Work in groups of four or five to conduct some research on the Internet. Download two graphs, charts, or tables from your research on one of the following topics. Bring them back to your group and explain them.

1. the projections of the number of people to be infected with the human immunodeficiency virus (HIV) over the next ten years
2. the changes in the average American income over the past five years
3. the number of bachelor degrees granted in the United States over the past five years

When you present your research to your group, also describe the ways in which you found this material on the Internet.

PART THREE

Taking Lecture, Discussion, and Study Notes

In this part, you will learn several note-taking skills that you can successfully use in listening to lectures and in study reading. You will find that when you take effective notes, you are using several of the reading and listening skills that you acquired in Part Two. When you can effectively use these note-taking techniques, studying for exams will become both organized and worthwhile.

CHAPTER 10

Characteristics of Lectures and Discussions

In this chapter, you will learn about:

- The speaker in a lecture or discussion
- The subject of a lecture or discussion
- Your obligations as a participant in a lecture or discussion

Lectures and discussions are special kinds of communication. Lectures and discussions are dialogues between you and the speaker or speakers. Your response to the lecturer or to the speaker in a discussion often takes the form of notes rather than oral comments. Accurate notes are important, for they are your only record of what was said during a lecture or discussion. In this part of the text, you will learn how to write useful notes. Consider the following parts of a lecture or discussion: (1) the speaker at a lecture, (2) the speaker or speakers in a discussion, (3) the subject of the lecture or discussion, and (4) your obligations as a listener to the lecture and discussion.

The Speaker at a Lecture

A lecturer's speaking style is as varied as a writer's. It is up to you to adjust your listening practices to the speaker's style. Some lecturers speak loudly, others softly. The average lecturer speaks at the rate of 125 words per minute (the average reading rate is 250 words per minute). But some lecturers speak quickly, others slowly. With a lecturer who speaks quickly, you may have a difficult time getting down all of the information. With a lecturer who speaks slowly, your mind may wander and you may become bored. With whatever style the lecturer uses, you need to focus on the main ideas and the major details of the materials.

If a lecturer presents too much information too quickly, you can consult with classmates who may have written down some of the information you did not get. With lecturers who speak slowly and present too little information, you need to concentrate on the important points of the lecture.

Also, you should realize that most instructors are not professional speakers. Their delivery will usually not be polished or humorous. Lecturers are not entertainers; they are trained to impart information, not to be comedians. Some students have even commented that the entertaining lecturers are generally not the most informative.

Most instructors present organized lectures, so your focus must be on the instructor's organization, which often centers on general and specific bits of information. Instructors often use the same signal words in their lectures that you have found in written material. In fact, good lecturers use these signal words to direct you to important information. Good lecturers also realize that students can reread what is in writing, but that "relistening" without a tape recorder is impossible. Successful lecturers also understand that lectures are not as formal as written discourse, so they repeat themselves and make obvious comments like "This is important" or "Write this down."

Along with repeating themselves and using signal words, lecturers use vocal and visual signals to punctuate their speaking. A lecturer's most effective visual aid is the chalkboard or whiteboard. When an instructor writes a term on the board or draws a chart or map, be sure to write this material down. A lecturer may also list important steps on the board or say something like: "There are three steps to remember." Jot these steps down. Third, a lecturer's tone of voice or rate of speech may change when an important point is made. If lecturers speak rapidly, their rate will probably slow down when they say something important. And lecturers who normally speak softly may present a key point in a louder tone. Get acquainted with each lecturer's speaking style, and look for their verbal signals. Finally, lecturers may sometimes read directly from the textbook. You should write down the page number of these passages, because they are probably important points.

A few lecturers are disorganized in their presentations, making your note taking a difficult chore. They may not consistently present main ideas and major details in proper proportion, and they may digress often so that main ideas lose their focus. Unfortunately, you will need to overcompensate for this lack of organization by noting what information is missing. You will then need to rely more on your textbooks and on library material. You may also need to consult with classmates who may have understood more of the lecture.

You may now want to complete Exercise 10.1 on page 219.

The Speaker or Speakers in a Discussion

Some instructors today rely more on the discussion format to teach their courses. In discussion, instructors often focus on carefully considered questions that encourage student response. Discussion is often more effective in small classes of 20 students or fewer, where everyone has the opportunity to respond during class. Students may answer the instructor's questions to the class at large, or in small groups of four or five when the instructor has posed certain questions that she wants the group to consider.

Much of what you do when you listen to class discussion is similar to what you do when you listen to a lecture. You attend carefully to main ideas and supporting details, and you make accommodations for the fast or slow speaker and for the disorganized discussion. In contrast to listening to a lecture, in discussion you must accurately write down the questions the instructor asks. You must attempt to determine the logic and organization of the questions that the instructor presents. Furthermore, you must listen just as intently to the students' responses. Their answers and questions can help you make sense out of the material. Instructors in a discussion want students to understand the material as the class unfolds. They see learning as a *process* of give and take between the questioning teacher and questioning and responding students, not merely information that students have to memorize. Often teachers who rely on discussion do see their course as a body of knowledge that cannot easily be explained and learned in lecture format.

Along with writing down the questions in class discussion, you should jot down the responses of the students in the class. You should also feel free to respond to the classroom conversation, because this give and take between members of the class is the best way to understand the material. You should not assume that everything that is said is correct. Soon after class, look over your notes to determine which responses seem to agree with how you are understanding the material. Go back to the instructor's questions, because in the questions she asks you can see how the instructor is attempting to present the material. If you are unclear about a question your instructor has posed, ask classmates for their interpretation of the question. In discussion classes, do not assume that all your questions will have been answered by the time the class ends for that day.

You may now want to complete Exercise 10.2 on page 221.

The Subject of the Lecture or Discussion

All of the skills that you have learned so far in this text should be used when you take notes. Lecturers and speakers in discussion will organize their material around main ideas, major details, and minor details as well as the seven patterns of organization. You should listen for the words that signal a particular organizational pattern. You will also use your paraphrasing skills when the instructor or student speaks in difficult sentences, and you will need to make appropriate inferences when a speaker is being indirect.

Though you will be using all of these skills when you listen to a lecture or discussion, you also need to know how lectures and discussions are different from writing. Speakers are often repetitive, whereas writing is not. Consider repetition in lecture and discussion as a kind of rereading. What a speaker repeats is often important and may be difficult to understand the first time.

A speaker may also *digress,* or get off the main point. She may occasionally relate a humorous anecdote that is associated with the lecture or discussion. Such digressions might not make sense if you were to read them. Because writing is often concise, digressions in writing are seen as flaws. When you hear digressions in a lecture or discussion, you should both see how they apply to the topic and enjoy them. Consider digressions as unique to speaking, a feature that makes speech more intimate than writing.

The subject matter of the lecture or discussion also dictates the kinds of notes you will take. You will often take notes using main ideas and major details in the arts and humanities, the social sciences, and in some biological sciences. In a history lecture or discussion, for example, you will often group your information around main ideas and details of support. On the other hand, in physical science and math courses, you will need to copy down solutions to problems and ignore the traditional note-taking format. The successful note taker in a math or science course accurately writes down the steps in a problem. Finally, in a foreign language course you will be responding orally, so your notes will be brief— a grammatical rule or a new vocabulary word. With each course, you need to be flexible and devise a note-taking style that fits the subject matter best.

Student Obligations

The key to successful listening to lectures and discussions finally rests on you. You must see listening to a lecture or discussion as a concentrated activity. You must anticipate the instructor's comments and determine the structure of the lecture or discussion.

Here is a list of hints that should help you to become a more effective note taker. Some of these points have already been discussed in this chapter, but it will help if you see them put together.

1. Listen attentively for the topic, main idea, and details of support. Train your listening to hear both general and detailed statements. Keep asking yourself: Is this the topic? the main point? What details relate to this main idea?

2. Listen for signal words that introduce a particular organizational pattern. Once you identify the pertinent organizational pattern, you will understand the logic of the lecture or discussion better.

3. Listen for auditory cues and look for visual cues—what the instructor puts on the board, when and why the speaker's tone of voice changes. These cues often suggest important points.

4. Familiarize yourself with the topic before you begin listening to the lecture or discussion. If an instructor assigns a chapter before he talks about it, read the material even if you do not understand all of it. The more exposure students have to a topic, the less difficult they tend to find the material. Going to a lecture or discussion without having done the assigned reading is not wise.

5. Listen attentively during class discussions. Do not assume that because a student is speaking, you do not need to listen. What students ask or say often are the same questions and answers that you have. Student comments are worthy of being placed in your notes, espe-

cially if the class is centered on class discussion. Also, listen to the instructor's response to student comments. You will learn a lot about your instructor by listening to his responses to students' ideas. You may find that a particular instructor likes original thinking, while another is looking for the conventional answer. These inferences can help you in studying for exams in these courses.

6. Try to see the lecture or discussion material from the instructor's point of view. You have every right to disagree with the instructor, but only after you have listened to what the instructor has said. Many times students tune instructors out when they do not agree with their point of view. By not listening to the several points of view on each topic, they are being unfair both to the material and to the instructor.

Mastering these hints may take some time. But once these suggestions become habit for you, you will be able to anticipate the direction of the lecture or discussion—knowing beforehand when the speaker will introduce a new topic or main idea or what organizational pattern the instructor intends to use. When you are able to anticipate information and structure, you will find that listening to lectures and discussions becomes both interesting and challenging.

Your other obligation is to assess the value that is assigned to lecture and discussion material in each of your courses. By the second or third week of the semester, you should have determined the value of notes in each of your courses. You should have understood whether the lectures and discussions are like or unlike the textbooks. And after the first examination, you should have determined how much of the exam came from your notes. You will find that some instructors rely on the textbook when making up an exam, others rely on their lecture notes, and some formulate many of their questions from class discussion. Most instructors divide up their exam questions evenly between textbook, lecture, and discussion material. It is you who must resolve all of these issues, and you should do so early in the semester.

Some students think that attending lectures and discussions is a waste of their time, that they can learn everything from the textbook and from the notes of others. Except for the very bright student, not attending lectures and discussions is a bad idea. Even if most of the instructor's lectures or discussions follow the textbook, by attending class you will develop an appreciation for the subject that you cannot get from your textbook. You will also get to know your instructors from their lectures and discussions—both their personality and their attitude toward the material. If your instructor loves the subject, some of this enthusiasm will rub off on you. From the very best lectures and discussions, you will learn details and hear anecdotes that you cannot find in textbooks. And it may be in a particularly exciting lecture or discussion that you will decide to major in that subject, a decision that can affect the rest of your life.

You may now want to complete Exercise 10.3 on page 222.

Summary

Lectures and discussions are dialogues between the instructor and you. When you attend lectures or discussions, you must remember that speech is different from writing. Instructors repeat themselves in lectures and discussions, and they may digress. You should use all of the reading skills that you have learned in order to listen effectively to lectures and discussions. Each course that you take demands a different listening and note-taking style, and you must determine that early in the semester.

Attending lectures and discussions gives you an appreciation for a particular course that reading will not give you. If you listen carefully to lectures and discussions, you will have another important educational tool at your disposal.

Summary Box   *Lecture and Discussion Material*

What is it?	Why do you need it?
An oral means of transferring information from the speaker to you A dialogue between the speaker and you Information that is usually organized around main ideas and major details Information that is not as concise as writing and that requires active listening	To gather information in a particular area To record the speaker's attitude toward a subject To appreciate a subject—something you cannot acquire just by reading your textbook

Skills Practice

Exercise 10.1
Inventorying a
Lecture

Choose an instructor whose lectures are difficult for you. Then complete the following inventory on one of his or her lectures. This inventory may help you understand why you are having difficulty taking notes on the lecture material.

1. Name of instructor: _____

2. Name of course: _____

3. Place a check mark next to those qualities that describe your instructor's lecture style:

_____ a. speaks rapidly

_____ b. speaks slowly

_____ c. speaks loudly

_____ d. speaks softly

_____ e. does not use the chalkboard

_____ f. is disorganized

_____ g. makes statements you do not agree with

_____ h. other: _____

The following are some suggestions for dealing with the characteristics that you checked off in item 3, lettered to correspond to the list of problems.

a. If the instructor speaks too fast, you must try to keep up with the pace. Don't get upset if you cannot write down all of the important points. Just keep listening for main ideas and supporting details. Check classmates' notes to see what you may have missed.

b. If the instructor speaks too slowly, you may get bored and your mind may wander. Keep listening for the lecture's focus: main ideas and details of support.

c. Notice when the instructor's voice becomes softer or louder. A change in loudness may signal that an important point is going to be made.

d. If the instructor speaks softly, you need to listen more actively; try to find a desk nearer to the instructor. Notice when his or her voice changes volume and see whether this change signals important information.

e. If your instructor doesn't use the chalkboard to highlight important points, see whether he or she uses any other cues. Does your instructor repeat key words and phrases or use hand gestures that signal important material?

f. If your instructor is disorganized, you will need to listen more carefully, jotting down those questions that your instructor leaves unanswered. In this case, you will need to rely more on your textbook, library material, and your classmates.

g. If your instructor makes remarks you disagree with, try to follow his or her train of thought. You are free to disagree with your instructor, but you need to follow his or her line of argument first.

h. Bring any other problems that you may have to your study skills instructor. You may even choose to present your complaint to the instructor who is giving you difficulty. State what your criticism is and
what you would like to see changed. Some instructors will take your
criticisms seriously and try to adjust their lecture style.

Exercise 10.2
Inventorying a
Discussion

Choose a course in which the instructor focuses on discussions to conduct the class. Answer the following questions regarding this course.

1. Name of course: _____

2. Circle yes or no in answer to the following questions:

  a. yes no In class discussions, do you often write down the questions the instructor poses?

  b. yes no Do you often understand the questions the instructor is
aasking?

  c. yes no Do you often participate in the discussions themselves?

  d. yes no Do you sometimes write down students' responses to the
instructor's questions?

  e. yes no After class, do you go over your discussion notes?

  f. yes no Do you often talk to other students who are in the class
about the discussion?

  If you answered *no* to any of these questions, you may want to read
the following suggestions, lettered to correspond to the list of questions.

a. Begin jotting down the questions the instructor asks. As you continue
to write down the questions your instructor asks, you will understand
better how your instructor structures the course and what material he
considers important to learn.

b. Understanding the questions your instructor is asking is crucial to
your getting the most out of the discussions. If a particular question
is unclear to you, ask your instructor to rephrase it.

c. Participation is one of the most effective ways to learn material taught
in discussion format. If you are generally a quiet, unassuming student,
force yourself to begin responding to what the instructor is asking
and what other students are saying. Through your responses, your
instructor will be able to understand better how you are learning the
material.

d. Sometimes a student's response helps clarify what the instructor is
trying to teach; other times, the response shows how you disagree
with the student. When you write these student responses down, you

can understand better how your learning of the material may be different or similar to the other students'.

e. It is always helpful to review your notes—lecture or discussion. By reviewing your discussion notes, you understand better the questions and comments made by your instructor. You can also begin to determine the logic behind the questions your instructor posed. Furthermore, you can see how your understanding of the material compares to that of other students in the class.

f. Whenever you are having difficulty with discussion material, it is wise to ask how other members of the class understood the discussion. You may even want to become part of a study group that regularly goes over the discussion notes of the members in the study group.

Exercise 10.3
Inventorying Your
Notes

Choose one course whose notes you are not entirely satisfied with. Then complete the following inventory.

1. Name of course: _____

2. Place a check mark next to those qualities that describe your note-taking style:

_____ a. too brief

_____ b. too wordy

_____ c. disorganized

_____ d. inaccurate

_____ e. messy

_____ f. any other problem: _____

The following are some suggestions for dealing with the problems that you checked in item 2, lettered to correspond to the list.

a. If your notes are too brief, you need to listen for supporting details. You are probably concentrating too much on main ideas. Remember, you also need to recall supporting details. Keep in mind that supporting details may be examples, characteristics, steps, causes, or effects. So listen carefully for names, places, and numbers. However, remember that brief notes are acceptable in a foreign language course.

b. If your notes are wordy, you are probably trying to write down everything. Remember that minor details usually do not need to be part of your notes. Wordy notes obscure main ideas and supporting details. Before writing, ask yourself: Is this statement significant? Will it give support to the main idea? Is this statement a restatement of something I've already written? Does this statement elaborate further on a previous detail? Approximately two to three written pages of notes in an hour's lecture is usually adequate.

c. If your lecture notes are disorganized, you probably cannot differentiate well between main ideas and supporting details. You will learn more about this issue in the next chapter. For now, remember that separating general from specific information is a key to learning and remembering. You may want to review Chapters 4 and 5, which treat main ideas and supporting details.

d. If your notes are inaccurate, you must start listening more carefully. Inaccurate notes are often caused by a daydreaming note taker. Inaccuracy is especially problematic in a math or science course, where the right number or correct sequence is essential to a correct solution. Leave your personal life outside of class so that you can listen to the lecture material with full concentration. Anyone can listen more attentively; it just takes discipline.

e. If your notes are messy, go over them soon after class is over and rewrite any words that are hard to read. If your handwriting is poor, you may need to write more slowly, even if you write less. Notes with less information are better than those that you cannot read.

f. If you have any other problems with your notes, speak with your study skills instructor.

Follow-up on Chapter 10

Now that you have studied this introduction and completed the exercises, see how your knowledge of lectures and discussions has improved. You may want to reread the introduction and review the exercises. Then answer the following questions either individually or in small groups.

On Characteristics of Lectures and Discussions

1. How effective are your abilities to listen to a lecture or discussion? What do you still need to work on when listening to a lecture or discussion?

2. How effective a note taker are you now? What aspects of note taking do you need to develop further?

3. How much do you rely on your lecture and discussion notes when studying for tests and completing assignments?

 **Internet Activity**

Here is an opportunity to do some additional research on the Internet on the subject of lectures and discussions. This assignment is best completed in groups of four or five. Access the following Web site to see what it says about lectures and discussions. Then answer the following questions.

Dartmouth Study Skills Guide
http://www.dartmouth.edu/admin/acskills/index.html#study

If you cannot access this Web site, then research the Internet to find information on lectures and discussions to answer these questions:

1. What new information did you gather about lectures and discussions?
2. What other topics does this Web site explore?
3. How did you access this material? Did you have any difficulties accessing this Web site?

Return to your group with answers to these questions.

CHAPTER 11

Commonly Used Note-taking Techniques: Numeral–Letter, Indenting, and Cornell

In this chapter, you will learn about:

- The numeral–letter format of note taking
- The indenting format of note taking
- The Cornell note-taking system
- Note taking in math and math-related courses
- Condensing information when note taking
- Using abbreviations when note taking

Now that you have made an inventory of your strengths and weaknesses as a note taker, you are ready to study the note-taking tips and techniques that have helped many students. The three most common techniques are the numeral–letter format, the indenting format, and the Cornell system. All find ways to present verbal material efficiently. You will discover that taking notes in math and science courses requires different note-taking practices. With all these techniques, you can condense information and use abbreviations to save time writing. You can apply these suggestions to your lecture and discussion notes as well as to the notes you take as you study.

Numeral–Letter Format

The numeral–letter format is a commonly used note-taking system. You have already studied it in the beginning chapters on main ideas and major details. In this format, you identify main ideas with Roman numerals (I, II, III) and place them farthest to the left of your margin. You identify major details with capital letters (A, B, C) and indent them to the right of the Roman numerals. Look at the following example:

I. Two major sources for advertising

    A. Television
    B. Newspapers and magazines

In some cases you may want to include a minor detail. You represent minor details with Arabic numerals and place them to the right of your major details. Study the following example:

I. Two major sources for advertising

    A. Television

        1. Particularly prime-time television ads

There are many rules that go along with the numeral–letter format. In taking lecture or discussion notes, you do not need to know all of them. If you try to follow all of the rules, you may get confused. The main rule you should follow is that main ideas should be placed to the left of your paper, major details to the right. By now, you should realize that main ideas and major details organize so much of what you read and hear. Main ideas must be attached to major details; both bits of information are meaningless unless you place them in a general and specific context. Knowing that the business department offers a series of college courses is meaningless unless you know that business includes many disciplines, like consumer behavior, finance, and accounting. On the other hand, knowing that consumer behavior is a course of study does not make sense unless you connect this detail to the more general statement that it is part of the larger study of business.

You need to adhere to two minor procedures when you use the numeral–letter format. First, be sure to place a period after the numeral or letter (I. or A.) By using a period, you separate the number or letter from the words you write. The period thus shows that the numbers and letters are divisions and not part of your comments. Second, skip a line between Roman numerals (the main ideas). By separating main ideas, you give more emphasis to them, and you will be able to locate them more easily when you study your notes. Look at the following example:

I. Fields related to the study of consumer behavior

    A. Psychology
    B. Sociology
    C. Anthropology

II. Psychology and consumer behavior

    A. Focus on the psychology of motivation
    B. Focus on learning theory

By creating a space between I. and II., you make "Fields related to the study of consumer behavior" a different chunk of information from "Psychology and consumer behavior."

Don't expect to write all of the major details that you hear. As with summarizing, write down only the significant details, or those that most directly support the main idea. If for some reason you miss a few major details in a lecture or discussion, ask to see a classmate's notes.

Indenting Format

The indenting system, another popular format, does away with letters and numbers entirely. You simply place main ideas to the left, major details to the right, and minor details to the right of major details. You separate general from specific statements by their positioning on the page. Here is an example:

Topics in the study of mass culture
   Investigations of subcultures
      Example of elderly subculture

As you can see, the information becomes more specific as you move to the right. Many students prefer this format to the numeral–letter format because they do not have to remember the correct sequence of numerals and letters. They do not need to go back to their notes to see if their previous main idea, for example, was a II. or a III. Some students also complain that the numerals and letters clutter their notes.

Remember that both formats rely on the same idea: The farther to the right you put information, the more specific this information is. Try both techniques to see which one fits your listening and writing style.

The Cornell Note-taking System

A system developed at Cornell University incorporates several of the practices used in the numeral–letter and indenting formats and includes a successful recall technique. To use this system correctly, follow these ten steps:

1. When taking notes, use spiral-bound notebook paper and place all of your lecture and discussion notes in chronological order in a loose-leaf notebook. By using these two items, you can include material without destroying the sequence of the lectures or discussions. Also, title and date each lecture or discussion on the top line.

2. Draw a vertical line 2½ inches from the left edge of the page. You will have the remaining 6 inches of paper to write down your lecture or discussion notes.

3. During a lecture or discussion, take notes in any format you prefer— numeral–letter, indenting, or even short paragraphs.

4. Concentrate on writing only main ideas and significant details during a lecture or discussion.

5. Skip lines between main ideas, and use only one side of the paper.

6. Read through your notes after class, filling in any incomplete information and rewriting any illegible words.

7. As you review your notes, underline or box all main ideas.

8. After you have reviewed your notes once, jot down in the 2½-inch margin key phrases that summarize what you have learned. In this left-hand section, you may also want to formulate questions on this material that you believe may be on an exam.

9. Cover up the 6-inch side of your notes to see whether you can recall the important parts of the lecture or discussion using only the key phrases and questions on the left side of your notes as clues.

10. Continue this procedure until you can easily recall the important parts of the lecture or discussion.*

Look at the following notes on a lecture dealing with advertising. This student has correctly employed the Cornell system:

← 2½ inches →	← 6 inches →
	Major Characteristics of Ads
def of ad	Def: "Persuasive message intended to sell a product."

2 forms	Found in:
	    print: newspapers and magazines
	    broadcast: radio television

What are 3 goals of ads?	Used to:
	    create awareness of product
	    establish new product
	    immediately buy product

In this excerpt the student first used the indenting format; then she applied the Cornell system, as seen in the marginal comments. In reviewing her notes, this student was able to identify the definition, forms, and goals of advertising. In this way, she was able to organize this lecture material further. In some ways, the Cornell system is a refinement of the numeral–letter and indenting formats. Once you can easily work through the steps of the Cornell system, you will be able to organize and retain large amounts of study material in an efficient and intelligent manner. You will be asked to use this Cornell system in many of the exercises that follow.

Taking Notes in Mathematics and Math-Related Courses

In math and science courses, you will often find that the numeral–letter, indenting, and Cornell formats are inappropriate note-taking forms. Math and science instructors often present solutions to problems on the

---

*Adapted from Walter Pauk, *How to Study in College*, 6th ed. (Boston: Houghton Mifflin, 1997), pp. 204–209.

board, writing each step in sequence. With these solutions, you cannot separate main ideas from major details. In a sense, every step to the solution is a main idea.

Consider the following hints for taking notes in math and science courses.

1. Listen carefully when your instructor presents laws, axioms, theorems, or properties. When possible, write these statements down word for word, as you would a definition. In the margin, identify the particular statement as a law, axiom, theorem, or property. Look at the following example:

associative $a + b = b + a$ $5 + 3 = 3 + 5$
property $a \times b = b \times a$ $5 \times 3 = 3 \times 5$

Numbers may be added or multiplied in any sequence.

2. When an instructor solves a problem on the board, copy it down step by step. The problems an instructor writes on the board are probably important ones. These solutions will often be like homework problems and problems on exams. Number each step, and make comments after any step that is unclear to you. Put question marks next to those steps that you cannot follow. Try to answer these questions before you come to the next class. Look at this example:

Problem 3: $2(5x + 5) + 4x = 90 - 2x$. Solve for x.

Do operations in   (1) $10x + 10 + 4x = 90 - 2x$
parentheses first.   (2) $14x + 10 \qquad\ = 90 - 2x$
                              (3) $16x = 80$
+ 2x balances   (4) $x = 5$
both sides of the
equation.

3. Leave spaces next to the problems you did not complete. When you review your notes, try to complete them.

4. Leave extra spaces between problems or draw a line across your page of notes to show where one problem ends and another begins.

5. Reread your notes after every lecture and discussion. Math and science are disciplines that build upon information you have previously learned. If you are unclear about Monday's solutions, Wednesday's will be even more confusing.

6. Use the numeral–letter and indenting formats whenever the instructor presents material not requiring problem solving.

Note-taking Tips

Now that you have studied the numeral–letter, indenting, Cornell, and math–science outlining formats, you are ready for the following note-taking tips that apply to all the note-taking systems you have learned so far.

1. The notes you take for each course should be written in a separate, bound notebook or in a three-ring notebook with dividers for each class. Three-ring notebooks are especially useful because you can add supplementary material to your notes, you can take out material when you want, and you can insert notes for a lecture that you may have missed. Also, you can keep all of your lecture notes in chronological order. You may think that all of this organization is a waste of time, but you will find that such preparation will pay off when you have to study for an exam. You do not want to be one of those students who has difficulty studying for the exam because lecture notes are missing or disorganized. Divide your notebook into two sections—one for your lecture and discussion notes and another for your study reading notes. More will be said about preparing reading notes in Chapter 14 on the SQ3R study system.

2. Put the title of each day's lecture or discussion at the center of the top line of a clean sheet of paper. Put the date at the top right-hand corner of the same page. Look at the following title:

Consumer Behavior Terminology　　　　*11/24/98*

3. Use a ball point, fountain, or felt-tip pen when you take notes in courses that use traditional outlining formats. For math and science courses, which require figuring and refiguring, use pencil or an erasable pen.

4. Write on only one side of the page. As you review your notes, you may need the back side to write additional information.

5. In addition to posing key questions and summarizing your notes, you can also use the left-hand margin during a lecture or discussion to remind yourself of important dates: when a project is due, an examination date, and so on. By placing this information where you normally place important points of summary, you will be less likely to forget these dates. Look at how a test date is incorporated into the following lecture excerpt on purchasing:

What are 3 stages?

First test 3/18

The Purchasing Process

I.　Three major stages

　A.　Intentional
　B.　Buying
　C.　Post purchasing

6. Identify the kinds of details that you include in your notes, either during or after the lecture or discussion. The abbreviations that you will most commonly use are: *def* for definition, *ex* for example, *eff* for effect, and *char* for characteristic. *Cause* and *step* have no abbreviations. As you identify the details, you will understand better the lecture's or discussion's organization. See how the abbreviation *ex* is used in the following lecture excerpt on buyer satisfaction:

Buyer Satisfaction

Ex: | Buyer is so pleased with his new car, he tells his neighbor why she should buy the same model.

7. Do not recopy your notes. Recopying does not require much thinking, and it takes time that is better spent doing other assignments. Merely rewrite any words or phrases that are hard to read. You must edit your notes, though. After class or within twenty-four hours, reread your notes, summarizing and answering key questions, as you learned in the Cornell system. Reviewing information right after it has been introduced helps you to remember it.

8. Write legibly, even if you write less; students lose time trying to decipher their handwriting.

Condensing Information

Learning to condense information will help you write down more information in a shorter period of time. You can condense information when you use any of the note-taking systems you have been introduced to so far. When you summarize, you locate main ideas and major details from long passages; when you *condense*, you write the key elements in a sentence and delete unnecessary words and phrases. What you usually write down are the subject, verb, and object of a sentence. Often you reduce a complete sentence to a phrase. Look at the following sentence, and see how it is condensed: "In an important sense, consumers respond to ongoing signals in their environment" is condensed to "Consumers respond to signals." In condensing, you are often left with the *who* or *what* and the *what was done* of the sentence. In this sentence, the *who* are the consumers and the *what was done* is their response to signals. In a lecture or discussion, then, listen for names and for what these names accomplished.

Sometimes it is preferable to copy information exactly as it is stated. You have already seen the importance of copying down a mathematical or scientific law or theorem or the steps in a solution. When you hear a definition, try to write it exactly as you hear it. Definitions are the tools for understanding a subject, so it's best to write down their exact meanings, as in the following example:

I. Market

    A. *Def:* A group of potential customers with the authority and ability to purchase a particular product*

With the exception of definitions and mathematical solutions and laws, you will often not be copying information exactly as you hear it. So condensing is a key skill to learn, as important as summarizing. You cannot write down everything the instructor says unless you know shorthand. By condensing each sentence into the *who* or *what* and the *what was done,* you uncover the significant elements of the lecture or discussion. You will have several opportunities to condense lecture, discussion, and textbook material in the exercises in this chapter and in those that follow.

You may now want to complete Exercises 11.1 and 11.2 on pages 236–238.

Using Abbreviations

Now that you have learned various note-taking systems and have been introduced to the essentials of condensing, you are ready to use abbreviations to save even more time when you take notes. You can use these abbreviations for lecture, discussion, and study notes. Like condensing, abbreviations reduce words to their essential letters.

Abbreviation Symbols Here is a list of commonly used symbols that students use when taking notes; commit them to memory.

Symbol	Meaning	Symbol	Meaning
=	equals	<	less than
= ly	equally	+ or &	and or more
≠	does not equal	–	less or minus
" "	when you repeat the same information	.·.	therefore
⟶	causes	⊃	imply or suggest
⟵	is caused by	#	number
⟶ ⟵	is both cause and effect	%	percentage
		¶	paragraph
<	greater than	//	parallel

See how the following sentence can be rephrased with an abbreviation:

With this product, the teenage market is greater than the adult market.

teenage market > adult market

---

*Adapted from Joseph T. Straub and Raymond F. Attner, *Introduction to Business*, 4th ed. (Boston: PWS-Kent Publishing Company, 1991), p. G-9.

Words Commonly Abbreviated   Table 11-1 presents abbreviations for words and phrases that you will commonly see in textbooks and hear in lectures or discussions. Study these abbreviations; then commit them to memory.

Amongst these abbreviations you will find only four that end with a period (in., Am., ant., log.). You need to use a period after an abbreviation only if the abbreviation spells out an actual word. The period corrects the confusion. For example, "ant" without a period could be mistaken for an insect rather than an antonym.

Once you have learned these abbreviations, you will be able to take down more information during lectures and discussions. See how the following statement can be written concisely: "A large increase in advertising time usually results in greater profits." becomes "lg incr ad time usu → greater profits." Once you have memorized these abbreviations, they become easy to read and do not slow down your reading rate.

Rules to Follow When You Create Your Own Abbreviations.   Here are a few guidelines for creating your own abbreviations.

1. If the word is only one syllable, write it out. It takes about as much time to write "tax" as it does "tx."

2. When you decide to leave out letters, leave out vowels rather than consonants. You recognize a word more easily if you see the consonants. You will probably recognize the abbreviation "bkgd" as "background" because you have kept the consonants.

3. Use the first syllable of a long word if that first syllable gives you enough information to identify the word. In your history class you might use "fam" for "famine" without getting confused. But "ty" does not easily equate with "tyranny," so write out two syllables, "tyran."

4. You can sometimes use an apostrophe to delete a syllable or syllables of a word. For example, "requirement" can be written as "requir't" or "unnecessary" can be abbreviated to "unnec'y."

5. To make an abbreviation plural, add an "s" to it as you would normally add to the entire word. For example, "wds" would be the plural for "words."

6. Generally, use a number instead of writing it out. You can write "65" more quickly than "sixty-five." But "45 million" (or "45 mil") is easier to write than "45,000,000." In writing numbers, choose the method that will save you the most time.

7. Often you will be writing down a key word or a phrase several times during a lecture or discussion. Early in the lecture or discussion, make up an abbreviation for that word or term. The first time you use the term, write this abbreviation and the complete word in the

Table 11-1 *Common Abbreviations*

Quantities, Time Periods, or Geography		Conditions, Trends, or Degrees	
Word(s)	*Abbreviation*	*Word(s)*	*Abbreviation*
amount	amt	decrease	decr
centimeter	c	general(ly)	genl
century	cy	important	imp't
foot/feet	ft	include/including	incl
gram	g	incomplete	inc
inch	in.	increase	incr
meter	m	large	lg
mile	mi	logic(al)	log.
north, south, east, west	N, S, E, W	main	mn
pound	lb	major(ity)	maj
yard	yd	maximum	max
year(s)	yr(s)	minimum	min
		necessary	nec
		negative	neg
		original(ly)	orig
		positive	pos
		principal	prin
		significant	sig
		usually	usu

left-hand margin. For example, if you are studying consumer behavior in a marketing lecture, you could abbreviate consumer behavior to CB, and in your margins write: "consumer behavior = CB."

8. Quickly learn the symbols and abbreviations that your math and science instructors use. You will be regularly using these abbreviations and symbols when you read the textbook, take lecture or discussion notes, or solve problems.

9. When you edit your notes, be sure that you write out completely any abbreviated words that are not immediately clear to you. Edit your notes soon after the lecture or discussion. If you wait too long, you may not be able to decipher your abbreviations.

10. Use abbreviations even more when your instructor speaks quickly or presents a great deal of information. In these instances, you are pressed for time; using abbreviations will help you get down more information.

11. Do not overuse abbreviations. You do not want to begin reading over your notes only to find out that you do not know what the abbreviations stand for.

You may now want to complete Exercises 11.5, 11.6, and 11.7 on pages 246–248.

Concepts and Ideas		Commonly Used Words	
Word(s)	*Abbreviation*	*Word(s)*	*Abbreviation*
antonym	ant.	America(n)	Am.
compare	cf	chapter	chpt
conclusion	concl	company	co
continued	cont'd	department	dept
definition	def	each	ea
feminine	fem	mountain	mt
first, second, third	1st, 2nd, 3rd	page	p
for example	eg	pages	pp
introduction	intro	point	pt
masculine	masc	regarding	re
plural	pl	subject	subj
specific(ally)	specif		
spelling	sp		
synonym	syn		
that is, that is to say	ie		
through	thru		
versus, or against	vs		
with	w		
without	w/o		

Summary

The three most common note-taking techniques—the numeral–letter formats, indenting, and the Cornell system—are similarly organized. All place main ideas to the left of the margin and details to the right. Cornell helps you further organize your notes as you review them. Main ideas and major details are key elements to your notes. You should train yourself to be alert for details when you hear a main idea. With practice, you should be able to balance main ideas properly with major details. Do not expect to write down all of the details, only the significant ones. Try to condense whatever you hear to the *who* and the *what* of each statement.

Notes in math and science courses are structured differently. In these courses, you do more copying, mainly of solutions to problems. You should comment on the steps to a solution that you do not fully understand.

Remember to review your notes daily, making comments and corrections. Because you will be using these notes all semester, they need to be legible.

You will find that abbreviations help you to write down more information. Abbreviations are either symbols or shortened words. Memorize the most common abbreviation symbols and abbreviated words. In reviewing your notes, be sure that you write out the complete word or phrase for those abbreviations that you cannot immediately read.

Summary Box *Note-taking Techniques*

What are they?	Why do you use them?
Numeral–letter format: places main ideas (I) to the left and major details (A, B, C) to the right	To give order to your lecture and discussion notes and to separate main ideas from major details
Indenting format: places main ideas to the left and major details to the right; no numerals or letters are used.	To write down significant information from lectures
Cornell: further organizes your notes and allows you to begin studying them	To help you remember important material for exams
Math–science format: accurately lists and describes the steps necessary for solutions to problems and allows marginal comments when a step is not understood	
Abbreviations: shortened words or symbols for words or phrases	To write down more information To save time when taking notes

Skills Practice Topic: Consumer Behavior

All the exercises in this chapter deal with consumer behavior. Before you begin these exercises, answer the following questions, either individually or in small groups, to get some sense of what you already know about the field of consumer behavior:

1. What is consumer behavior?
2. What kinds of questions do you think researchers in consumer behavior ask?
3. How do you think a knowledge of consumer behavior benefits the customer?
4. Do you think consumer behavior research can really predict what a customer will buy?

Exercise 11.1
Condensing Sentences
from a Lecture

The following ten sentences are taken from an introductory lecture on consumer behavior. Your job is to read each sentence and then condense it into a phrase in which only the essential information remains. You will find that sentences from a lecture tend to be wordy, a style much different from what you normally read. Use the abbreviations "def" and "ex" where appropriate.

1. We must first define the term *consumer behavior.* Let's say it is what people do when they are involved somehow with market items—in buying, selling, or producing.

2. I want to emphasize that consumer behavior as a study is part of many other studies—that is, it is interdisciplinary, and I think it relies heavily on such fields as sociology, anthropology, and psychology.

3. How is sociology involved in the study of consumer behavior? I think in its focus on group behavior patterns, sociology helps us understand how consumers act.

4. Psychology also plays a role in our study. In its focus on the individual, psychology shows us how people typically act when they buy something. *Motivation* is an example of a psychological term that we can apply to an individual consumer's activities.

5. How do you think anthropology is related to our study of consumer behavior? Anthropology, I think, gives us a picture of the culture that determines a person's buying behavior. Ethnic preference is an example of how we use anthropological knowledge in our study of consumers.

6. Another term that we must define early in this semester is *consumer.* Let's say for now that a consumer is anyone who purchases or uses a product.

7. How should we define *purchasing*? It is a more complicated term. I want to focus on one part of its meaning today. Purchasing, on one level, simply refers to obtaining an item from someone who sells.

8. In this course we will later pursue other areas of consumer behavior—specifically where people buy particular products and how they use them. I want to explore these topics only after we have a better understanding of certain key terms.

_____

9. Other issues that I think you will find of interest in consumer behavior involve psychology and economics: how frequently people tend to purchase certain products and the decisions they use in deciding on a particular purchase.

_____

> **70%**
> (score = # correct × 10)
> Find answers on
> p. 390.

10. Finally, I want you to place yourselves in these particular explorations of consumer behavior. Analyzing how you purchase certain items will assist you in understanding your sociological, psychological, and anthropological motives.*

_____

Exercise 11.2
More Condensing of
Sentences from a
Lecture

Here are ten more sentences, again from an introductory consumer behavior lecture. Condense these sentences into phrases that pick up the significant information. Where necessary, use the abbreviations "def" and "cause."

1. Often consumer behavior scholars first look at the cultural influences of a particular group's purchasing choices. This is often defined as the macro perspective.

_____

2. In contrast, the micro perspective is often seen as what the individual in a group decides to purchase and the reasons why.

_____

3. I also want to add that an additional discipline I did not consider in the last lecture is economics. It influences consumer behavior in several ways, but particularly it shows us how an economic system like ours distributes its wealth.

_____

*Adapted from Harold W. Berkman and Christopher C. Gilson, *Consumer Behavior: Concepts and Strategies* (Belmont, Calif.: Dickenson, 1978), pp. 5–6.

4. Now I want to begin a new section to my introductory remarks on consumer behavior—its history. Did you know that consumer behavior as a serious study is very young, emerging in the late 1940s?

_____

5. Since the late forties, scholarship in consumer studies has increased tremendously.

_____

6. I think the most important cause of increased studies in our field is the many uses we have found for the computer, so that we can now project with the help of the computer what a consumer will likely do in particular situations.

_____

7. We now have several journals that study consumer behavior, and they have added a greater seriousness to our field.

_____

8. What has also been a major factor in making consumer behavior a serious study is how we have recently begun to use theory to explain how consumers behave.

_____

9. Often consumer behavior scholars study theoretical models. I would define a model in our field as the application of a certain behavioral theory to a particular problem in consumer behavior.

_____

___80%___

Ask instructor for answers.

10. I would say that the most popular study that we use to develop theoretical models is the discipline of psychology. I will be talking later on in the semester about various behavioral models that are based on psychological theory.*

_____

Exercise 11.3
Using Note-taking
Techniques on Short
Lecture Passages

Read the following lecture excerpts on the cultural and social influences on consumer behavior. After you have read and condensed the information into main ideas and major details, complete the outlines that follow. Use the Cornell System to add comments in the left-hand margin.

_____

*Adapted from Berkman and Gilson, *Consumer Behavior*, pp. 6–7.

Because you are reading an instructor's lecture, you will find some of it repetitious.

1. I want to start today's lecture by focusing on how our American culture influences what we in the United States tend to buy. From a consumer standpoint, the one aspect of our culture that seems to go beyond particular ethnic groups is our interest in purchasing material goods. This goal of wanting material wealth is also tied in to other values that seem to be American. I'm thinking about our belief in the self and our basic optimism for the future. We also seem to value order over disorder.

    I.

        A.

        B.

        C.

        D.

2. But can we really say that these values define American culture? Is there really such a thing as an American culture? In some ways Americans seem to be moving away from a focus on material wealth. And though we are not a poor country, the economic problems of the late '80s seem to make some of us question whether the American culture is still as strong as it was, say, 30 years ago. Also, some consumer scholars have argued that the American focus on self-reliance has made some Americans terrified of being alone and of facing life's problems alone. Also, many people interested in the environment have begun to question just how valuable it is to be ordered. Worded differently, we can ask: Has the order of technology created disorder for the environment?

    I.

        A.

        B.

        C.

        D.

3. There are also a great number of ethnic groups in the United States today who seem to call into question just what we mean by an American culture. African Americans and Hispanics, I think, provide a huge marketing challenge. In determining what these groups purchase, we find that many African Americans and Hispanics fit into what sociologists traditionally think is typically American. Yet in many ways we can see that their buying interests show a different set of values.

I.

   A.

   B.

   C.

4. Along with cultural questions, the student of consumer behavior must also see if class influences people's purchasing decisions. Do the values of the lower, middle, and upper classes shape what the people in each of these groups purchase? Or is this question just as difficult to answer as the question of culture and buying in the United States? Does income influence what a person buys? Or does a person's income determine what sorts of beliefs she or he holds? These are just a few of the puzzling questions that we will try to find answers to as the semester goes on.

I.

   A.

   B.

   C.

   D.

5. Another issue closely related to what people buy is where the family fits into these decisions. The family seems to have much to say about what people buy. The family gives to its members certain values. Yet purchasing decisions are also influenced by which members the product will serve. And purchasing is further complicated by who tends to be more powerful—the father, the mother, or the children. And we must also consider how these decisions change as the family gets older—I mean, as parents and children mature.

I.

    A.

    B.

    C.

    D.

Now use the indenting format to complete the following lecture material on consumer behavior and the individual. Again, use the Cornell System to add marginal comments. This time you will be given no outline format. Use a separate piece of paper to complete 6–10.

6. Now that we have talked briefly about some of the questions that consumer behavior researchers have about culture and society, we can turn to how the individual influences consumer behavior. Consumer behavior researchers begin by assuming that people learn to buy in certain ways. That is, they are not born to be a certain kind of consumer. The most important way for us to determine how an individual will react is to look at his or her past experience. Because of habit and experience, marketers try very hard to develop what they call brand loyalties, or a consumer's consistent buying of certain products.

7. Another individual factor that I want to talk a little bit about today is how perception affects what somebody buys. Marketers now realize that each person perceives a product differently. For some, price is the major concern. For others, it is the look or image that the product presents.

8. As in our discussion of class, society, and culture, an individual's choice in purchasing leads to no definite conclusions. What we do know is that the question of personality does affect what someone buys. Certain personalities tend to choose a sports car over a station wagon. A woman's personality type also helps determine the shade of lipstick she will buy.

9. Another individual factor that I want to talk about is attitude and buying. That is, how does a person's attitude affect what he or she buys? Here, marketers often try to use sports figures or actors to help sell a particular product. Marketers realize that these stars conjure up many positive and negative attitudes in the viewer. And these attitudes help sell a product.

10. Marketers have found that attitudes, unlike other parts of an individual's makeup, are difficult to change. Yet this fact in itself becomes a marketing challenge. Can a marketing campaign change a per-

70%

(score = # correct × 2, + 6 bonus points)
Find answers on pp. 390–392.

son's attitude? And can this changed attitude make an individual buy a product she would normally not buy? Researchers still do not know how effective a marketing campaign can be in changing a person's attitudes. Your reading assignment will pick up this topic in much greater detail.*

Exercise 11.4
Using Note-taking Techniques on More Short Lecture Passages

For the following three lecture excerpts on consumer behavior terminology, your job is to read each excerpt and then use the numeral–letter format to record notes. An outline is provided for these excerpts. As in Exercise 11.3, condense the information, and use Cornell to provide comments in the margins.

1. I want to introduce a few more terms today that should round out the most important terms that we will be using for this course. I want to talk a bit about micromarketing. A definition for this term is the business of marketing. Some of the areas that we will consider in micromarketing include managing a marketing campaign, researching marketing behavior, and creating profitable marketing campaigns.

   In the study of micromarketing, the most important concern is looking for new markets. The challenge today is that new markets are not that easy to come by because today's consumer tends to be more educated and less susceptible to earlier marketing strategies. With each product, marketers need to ask similar questions: Is the market young, or is the market becoming younger? Is the market ethnic or becoming culturally diverse? Marketers need to be secure in the data they receive in answer to these questions. As I have said many times before, these are not easy questions to answer.

   I. Def.:

      A.

      B.

   II.

      A.

      B.

      C.

      D.

---

*Adapted from Berkman and Gilson, *Consumer Behavior*, pp. 8–12, and Straub and Attner, *Introduction to Business*, pp. 628–629.

2. In an attempt to make their job more manageable, some marketers have looked closely at the audience that would most likely buy a particular product. The segment of the market that a marketer looks at may be very small or very large. It may be a market directed at a restricted group, like retirees interested in golfing, or a large group, like teenagers between the ages of thirteen and eighteen.

Magazine executives can tell marketers what segment of the population tends to buy their magazines. This is the population that marketers may want to target for the sale of a particular product. Magazines often provide what is called a demographic profile. What does a demographic profile consist of? It often includes the age span of the magazine audience and its average income, as well as readers' educational level. So in a strange way, marketers are finding that sometimes, if they restrict their buying population for a particular product, they are actually allowing for greater profit. Why is this so? By targeting a market well, marketers then have a better chance of attracting a greater percentage of that segment to buy their product.

I.

    A.

    B.

II.

    A.

    B.

    C.

3. I'd also like to talk about the concept of macromarketing. Macromarketing, unlike micromarketing, is concerned with consumer behavior on a larger social level. You might find macromarketers asking questions like these: How is advertising deceptive to the public? How does a particular product adversely affect the environment? How can society be trained to recycle?

In some ways, macromarketing begins with different premises than micromarketing does. I think micromarketers see the consumer as someone they need to persuade so they can sell a particular product. The macromarketer begins by assuming that the consumer is often deceived by advertisements and that his role is to help the consumer not be deceived. A healthy market comes about, I think, when macromarketers keep the micromarketers in check. What do you think?

I. Def.:

    A.

    B.

    C.

II.

    A.

    B.

    C.

Now use the indenting technique to take notes on the following two passages on the value of studying consumer behavior. This time, you are not provided with skeletal outlines. Use a separate piece of paper to complete 4 and 5.

4. Thus far I have been presenting you with an overview of our course in marketing. We have discussed important terms and important marketing concepts that we will pursue this semester. I want to talk a little bit today about the value of the study of consumer behavior. I'll try to be as brief as I can.

Because we are a capitalist society, we as a country focus a lot of our energy on consumer behavior. We have studied many reasons why consumers act the way they do and how culture and society affect their purchasing. In a way, consumer behavior studies also help sociologists and psychologists understand their fields a little better.

Let me be more specific about what I mean about the relationship between our discipline and others. When we study consumer perception, we help psychologists understand their research on perception better. And when we explore how class affects purchasing, then we help sociologists understand just what they mean by class. In this way I want you to see consumer behavior as an excellent interdisciplinary study. I'm going to be showing how our field relates to other disciplines throughout the course.

5. I also want to repeat that we have two types of consumer behavior studies: micromarketing and macromarketing. But I will be focusing on the micromarketing studies, except for a few lectures at the end of the course.

Before you can appreciate these micromarketing studies, we must go over other preliminary material. This time we'll be talking about how these studies are organized. So we'll first be looking at theories

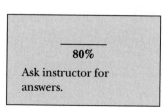

80%

Ask instructor for answers.

and models as they relate to consumer behavior. Then we'll be looking at the measurement techniques that our field uses to interpret these models. In this part of the course, we'll be learning some elementary rules about flowcharting, and we'll examine and practice some very common formulas in statistics.*

**Exercise 11.5
Writing
Abbreviations from
Memory**

Go back to Table 11-1 (pp. 234–235) to review all of the abbreviations that are listed. Then, without referring to that table, complete the following questions. Place all answers in the answer box.

Write the abbreviations for the following:

1. equals
2. greater than
3. and
4. implies
5. regarding
6. necessary
7. positive
8. increase
9. large
10. maximum

Now write the correct word or words for these abbreviations:

11. w/o
12. cf
13. vs
14. inc
15. imp't
16. prin
17. cont'd
18. #
19. ∴
20. →←

1. _____
2. _____
3. _____
4. _____
5. _____
6. _____
7. _____
8. _____
9. _____
10. _____
11. _____
12. _____
13. _____
14. _____
15. _____
16. _____
17. _____
18. _____
19. _____
20. _____

80%

(score = # correct × 5)
Find answers on p. 392.

*Adapted from Berkman and Gilson, *Consumer Behavior*, pp. 14–16, and Straub and Attner, *Introduction to Business*, p. 526.

Exercise 11.6
Making Your Own
Abbreviations

For the following twenty words and phrases relating to consumer behavior, write your own abbreviations, using the rules given on pages 233–234. Your answers may vary from those devised by other students. Discuss your answers with your instructor and classmates. Place all answers in the answer box.

1. behavior
2. advertising
3. *Wealth of Nations* (used several times)
4. social class acceptance
5. persuasiveness
6. affluence
7. competitive
8. urbanize
9. cognitive dissonance (used several times)
10. consumer behavior (used several times)
11. consumption
12. cultures
13. customers
14. industrial
15. labeling
16. law of diminishing returns (used several times)
17. perception
18. reinforcement
19. marketing
20. macromarketing (used several times)

1. _____
2. _____
3. _____
4. _____
5. _____
6. _____
7. _____
8. _____
9. _____
10. _____
11. _____
12. _____
13. _____
14. _____
15. _____
16. _____
17. _____
18. _____
19. _____
20. _____

80%

Ask instructor for answers.

Exercise 11.7
Reading and Writing
Abbreviations in
Sentences

Assume that the following abbreviated sentences on international marketing techniques are from your consumer behavior lecture notes. Your job is to rewrite each as a complete sentence, changing the abbreviations to words.

1. Mrktng bcmng an international actvty.

   _____

2. Easy to make lrg mistakes in this interntl mrkt.

   _____

3. Mny mrktrs do not undrstnd cultrl setting.

   _____

4. Anthroplgy helps cnsmr beh to undrstnd cultrs.

   _____

5. Anthrplgsts use stdy called cross-cultural resrch (CCR).

   _____

6. CCR studies how cultrs are same and diff.

   _____

7. CCR studies atts re love in cltrs.

   _____

8. CCR also works w politcl power in ea cultr.

   _____

9. CCR studies cultrl mng of color.

   _____

10. In some cultrs blk & gray = good.

    _____

Now write your own abbreviated sentences from the sentences on international marketing techniques that follow. Be sure to condense and to make up your own abbreviations when necessary.

11. Cross-cultural research has shown that the colors yellow, white, and gray are weak everywhere.

_____

12. Red and black seem to be strong colors in every country.

_____

13. Some marketers see each culture as unique.

_____

14. This belief suggests that we focus on local marketing campaigns.

_____

15. Other marketers believe in standardized marketing plans.

_____

16. These marketers believe in looking at cultural uniformity in the world.

_____

17. Therefore, they see several countries as one possible market.

_____

18. Tourism and the mass media have caused some similar marketing needs.

_____

19. These marketers see Europe as one country rather than several.

_____

20. The answers to these questions may have a positive or negative impact on each advertising campaign.*

_____

_____80%_____
(score = # correct × 10
[1–10]; answers will vary
for 11–20)
Find answers on
p. 392.

_____

*Adapted from Berkman and Gilson, *Consumer Behavior*, pp. 93–94.

Exercise 11.8
Outlining Lecture
Excerpts and Using
Abbreviations

The following lecture excerpts discuss particular markets and the strategies marketers use to sell their products to them. Use all your note-taking skills (condensing, abbreviating, and the numeral–letter format and Cornell System) to outline the first three excerpts. Use a separate piece of paper to complete 1–6.

1. We talked last time about the marketing needs of the single person. Today I want to focus on the marketing strategies used for the elderly and the poor. With the elderly, I think we need to know something about how they live and where they live. In past generations, the elderly usually lived with their children; now they often live away from them. Some live in communities for the elderly. Florida, as an example, has become a popular site for the elderly, where they live away from their children.

2. Here are some more vital statistics about the elderly. Today the elderly tend to be better educated than they were in the past. They often have greater incomes than they had in years past. They tend to be better and smarter shoppers. Also, many do some sort of part-time work. They also tend to want to enjoy their retirement years more. Therefore, you see more elderly traveling than you did in the past.

3. What are some of the markets that speak directly to the elderly? There are several, and I want you to list them in order. First, the elderly have unique housing needs. Second, their health needs are different in many ways from those of the rest of the population. Furthermore, they have a different set of insurance needs—both health and life insurance. To a degree, we can target particular foods that the elderly would tend to buy. Finally, the elderly have a unique set of travel needs. I want to emphasize that these six needs provide marketing challenges for the nineties.

    Now use the indenting and Cornell formats to outline the following excerpts on marketing strategies for the poor. Be sure to condense information and to use abbreviations where appropriate.

4. I want to turn now to another market. That is the market that concerns the poor. What are the unique needs of the poor? What is their particular profile? We know that the poor tend to spend a larger share of their income on life's necessities. These necessities include such things as food, housing, and medical care. What do you think the poor spend less on? Transportation and clothing are not areas where they spend much of their money. Researchers have also found that the poor spend a large amount of their income on sturdy items, like stoves and refrigerators. In terms of automobiles, the poor tend to buy used rather than new cars, as you would expect. In terms of furniture, the poor often buy sets of furnishings rather than individual pieces.

5. What sorts of foods do the poor often purchase, and how do they pay their bills? Of course, they tend to buy low-cost food. They often look for low-cost fresh items rather than prepackaged foods, especially in rural areas. They rarely buy more expensive convenience foods. What about credit? More and more people are using credit cards, but the poor tend to use credit and installment buying more often than the middle and upper classes do. Some researchers have even shown that poor families often have a credit debt that is twice that of higher-income families.

6. Finally, what can we say about the shopping behavior of the poor? Some of these statistics are surprising, I think. Poor urban people tend to pay more—not less—for products than those who live in wealthier areas. Also, there are fewer supermarkets in the poor urban areas for shoppers to choose from. The poor also tend not to be shrewd shoppers. They often listen to what their family members, friends, or the media say rather than looking into programs that provide reduced rates or reading newspaper ads carefully. Also, the poor often shop in areas close to their homes because transportation is often harder to come by for them. Therefore, their consumer options tend to be restricted.*

> Answers will vary. Ask instructor for sample answers.

Exercise 11.9
Taking Notes on a
Longer Lecture
Passage and Using
Abbreviations

The following is a longer lecture excerpt on consumer behavior and social responsibility. Your job is to take notes on this passage. Use the indenting and Cornell formats, condense information where necessary, and abbreviate where appropriate. After you have taken your notes, give the lecture an effective title.

Title: _____

(1) In this part of the course, I want to talk about issues that have not concerned us up to now. How does consumer behavior relate to ethics? That is, how should consumer behaviorists be concerned with treating the consumer correctly? I want to talk specifically about the key consumer issues relating to ethics: truth in marketing, product quality, and product safety. I will talk about each separately, then come to some conclusions about this issue of ethics and consumer behavior, both for the consumer and for the marketer and producer.

(2) Marketers have an obligation to be honest in their presentation of a product. The Federal Trade Commission monitors advertisements to ensure that they are not fraudulent. The Commission has uncovered and put a stop to many mail-order frauds. Recently, the question of packaging and labeling has become an important concern. For example, what does it mean for a product to be low in fat or low in cholesterol? What does it mean for a product to be fat-free? The Federal Trade

---

*Adapted from Berkman and Gilson, *Consumer Behavior*, pp. 133–135, 136–138.

Commission has now written specific requirements that spell out what these packaging statements mean, and marketers and producers are going to have to follow these regulations.

(3) The next issue that consumers need to consider is how reliable a product is. What can a consumer do if a product fails to operate as promised, or if a product becomes a hazard? Consumers need to read what the warranty promises. Often the warranty insists that consumers either exchange a product or get a refund. Particularly when consumers buy an expensive item, they need to see just what the warranty promises and does not promise, so they will not be surprised if the product somehow fails.

(4) What happens when the consumer is not satisfied with the warranty, or if the seller does not live up to the warranty? Does the consumer have any options? The customer can go to court and sue. But this process is lengthy and can prove to be expensive.

(5) Some companies have responded to consumer complaints in a positive way. I want to emphasize here that by serving the customer politely and honestly, many companies have increased, not decreased, their profits. So it can pay to be honest. What some companies have done is to ask customers to be very frank about their complaints.

(6) How can complaints serve both the customer and the company? An honest complaint provides useful information for the decisions a company makes in the future. Furthermore, complaints can make the company rewrite its warranties, so future customers will be even more satisfied with the product and the company. When a customer tells her family and friends that a company actually listened to her complaints and even changed policies because of her, they will often become customers of that company as well.

(7) I want to emphasize here that ethics works both ways. If there are unethical companies, so are there unethical customers. For the marketplace to work well, the company and the consumer need to respect each other. What companies and customers need to realize is that honesty on the part of both parties goes a long way to solidify long-term business dealings. I want to repeat that it does pay to be honest. Profits on the part of the producer and satisfaction on the part of the consumer can result if producer and consumer trust each other.*

Answers will vary. Find sample answers on pp. 392–393.

Exercise 11.10
Using Lecture Notes to Answer an Essay Question

Now use only your lecture notes from Exercise 11.9 to answer the following essay question. Begin with a main-idea sentence, and support it with relevant details from the lecture.

Essay question: In what ways are customers protected from fraudulent companies? In what ways can companies serve their customers even more efficiently? Be specific by using evidence from the lecture.

80%

Ask instructor for answers.

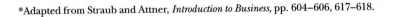

*Adapted from Straub and Attner, *Introduction to Business*, pp. 604–606, 617–618.

Follow-up on Chapter 11

Now that you have completed the exercises, it may be helpful to see how your reading on this topic has changed some of your ideas about consumer behavior. You may want to go back and reread the exercises before you answer the following questions. Answer them either in small groups or individually.

On the Topic of Consumer Behavior

1. How would you now define *consumer behavior*?
2. In what ways do you now think that a knowledge of consumer behavior can benefit marketers and consumers?
3. What are the most interesting areas of consumer behavior for you?
4. What areas would you like to study further?

On Commonly Used Note-taking Techniques

5. Of the three note-taking techniques—numeral–letter, indenting, and Cornell—which one is the most effective for you?
6. Which one of these three note-taking techniques is most difficult for you? Why is it still difficult?
7. How have these techniques helped you learn information better in your college courses?
8. What else do you still need to learn about any of these three note-taking techniques?

 **Internet Activity**

Use the Internet to do research on the topic of consumer behavior. If you have access to InfoTrac, do your research through this service. This is an activity best completed in groups of four or five. Answer the following questions as you research; then share your research with your group.

1. What information can you find on consumer behavior and the elderly?
2. What information can you find on consumer behavior and the adolescent market?
3. Discuss the procedures you used to locate information on these topics.

Visual Note-taking Techniques: Laddering and Mapping

In this chapter, you will learn about:

- The laddering note-taking technique
- The mapping note-taking technique

Now that you have studied three common note-taking techniques, you will find the visual techniques of laddering and mapping helpful. Both laddering and mapping are visual note-taking systems. You can use these two techniques best when you are editing your notes, much as you use the Cornell system when you study your notes. Laddering and mapping bring out your visual aptitude for understanding lecture, discussion, and textbook material. Remember that visualizing is an effective way of learning information that is new to you.

What Is Laddering?

Laddering is a visual note-taking system that ties main ideas to main ideas and details to details. Laddering is used best when you are editing your notes and see relationships emerging.

Here is how laddering works. Draw a solid vertical line just to the right of your main ideas. You should use a different-colored pencil or pen so that the line stands out. Then draw a perpendicular line from this vertical line to each main idea, so that the main ideas are connected. The vertical and horizontal lines should look like part of a ladder. Look at the main ideas concerning early childhood development in Figure 12-1 to see how laddering brings these ideas out.

You follow this same procedure with the details under each main idea. As it does with main ideas, laddering groups supporting details under each main idea. Place all major detail ladders under the same plane, so that your eyes see one solid vertical line for main ideas and a broken vertical line for supporting details. See how details are grouped through laddering in Figure 12-2, and how laddering brings out main ideas and major details in Figure 12-3.

By seeing how information is related visually, as in Figures 12-1 to 12-3, you have a better chance of recalling it on examinations. Laddering

The Fetus and the Newborn

Prenatal development
    beginning life as a fertilized egg
    embryo divides into many cells

Fetal development
    two months after conception
    more humanlike than embryo

Figure 12-1   *Laddering main ideas.*

Prenatal development

    beginning life as a fertilized egg

    embryo divides into many cells

Figure 12-2   *Laddering details.*

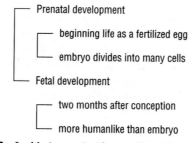

Prenatal development

    beginning life as a fertilized egg

    embryo divides into many cells

Fetal development

    two months after conception

    more humanlike than embryo

Figure 12-3   *Laddering main ideas and details.*

allows you to see main ideas and major details more easily and to group these chunks of information into units that you can more easily call to mind.

You may now want to complete Exercise 12.2 on page 264.

What Is Mapping?

Mapping is a note-taking technique that uses geometric shapes, pictures, and arrows to show the relationship of main ideas to their details. Mapping is individual. You choose your own design to show the relationship between general and specific information. The most commonly used shapes are circles, squares, rectangles, and radiating lines. Because maps are individual, they help you to retain the material more easily. Maps, also called *concept maps,* reduce large amounts of information to the essentials, so they are ideal when you study for exams.

Maps may be large or small. If they are large, they need to be put on a separate sheet of paper. If you place additional information on this page, you take away from the concept map and distort the visual picture of main ideas tied to details.

Let's say you are studying your notes in early childhood development and you come across the following statement: "Jean Piaget identified four stages in childhood development: sensorimotor, preoperational, concrete operations, and formal operations." You can map this statement in the way shown in Figure 12-4. In this map, you see childhood development as the general category, with the four stages as the distinct steps.

Let's say you want to show how the later stages in childhood development share the ability to reason logically. You can map what these stages have in common by using intersecting circles. Intersecting circles make an effective way to map similarities. See Figure 12-5.

Mapping is also effective in showing sequences. Arrows can join one step to another. If you came across this statement in your childhood development notes, how could you map it? "The sensorimotor stage begins at birth and ends at 1½ years; the preoperational goes from 1½ years to 7 years, concrete operations from 7 to 11, and formal operations 11 and above." See Figure 12-6. Do you see how this map shows both the stages and their sequence?

A map using arrows is similar to a flowchart, a visualization often used by programmers to set out the logic of their computer program. Flowcharts are now widely used by people outside programming to list the steps in a procedure. You studied flowcharts in Chapter 9. Look at Figure 12-7, which shows the responses an individual has to stimuli and how they can be conditioned, or changed. Psychologists have conducted

Childhood Development

Sensorimotor	Preoperational	Concrete operations	Formal operations

Figure 12-4   *Mapping sequential stages.*

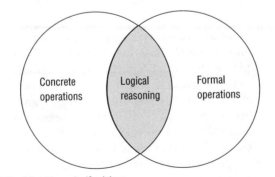

Figure 12-5   *Mapping similarities.*

Stages of Childhood Development

Figure 12-6   *Mapping a sequence.*

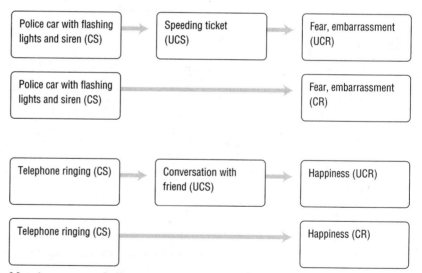

Figure 12-7   *Mapping cause-and-effect sequences. (Source: James W. Kalat,* Introduction to Psychology, *3rd ed. [Belmont, Calif.: Wadsworth, 1993], p. 282.)*

experiments studying the behaviors people cannot control—unconditioned stimuli (UCS) and unconditioned responses (UCR)—and those they can control—conditioned stimuli (CS) and conditioned responses (CR). Follow the two sets of arrows—both bottom and top—to see how

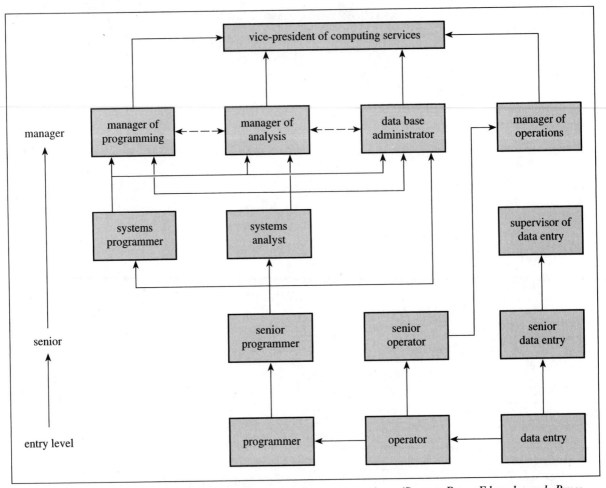

Figure 12-8 *Laddering a potential career progression. (Source: Perry Edwards and Bruce Broadwell,* Data Processing, *2nd ed. [Belmont, Calif.: Wadsworth, 1982], p. 560. Used by permission.)*

an individual can learn a particular response. Note how the bottom sets have two instead of three steps. Do you see how economically this flowchart presents the theory of stimulus and response, showing that certain stimuli can automatically create a certain emotion in an individual?

Flowcharts may also provide you with complex steps and procedures presented in a visual manner. Look at Figure 12-8, which shows the career ladder in a computer company. Follow the arrows from bottom to top, each pointing to a higher position. Also note that some arrows are joined with broken lines and point in two directions, suggesting the double career option a person at that level has.

In your own studying and note taking, you can also create larger concept maps that tie together larger chunks of information—several

Summary of Piaget's Stages of Cognitive Development

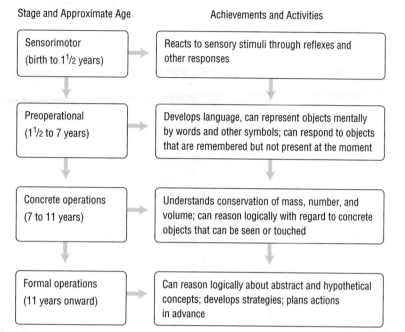

Figure 12-9   Mapping lecture notes on a sequence of stages. (Adapted from James W. Kalat, Introduction to Psychology, 3rd ed. [Belmont, Calif.: Wadsworth, 1993], p. 233.)

lectures or an entire textbook chapter. Pretend you are reviewing your notes in child development on Piaget's developmental stages, and you want to map this information. Your map could look something like the one shown in Figure 12-9. This map reduces several paragraphs into half a page, listing each developmental stage and noting its important characteristics.

More complex concept maps can also show the relationships among topics, main ideas, and supporting details. The topic is usually in the center, the main ideas branch out from the center, and details of support further branch from the main-idea branches. This concept map is often called a *line map*. See Figure 12-10. These line maps can be used to summarize an entire lecture or discussion or a complete textbook chapter.

A second way of presenting a lot of information in a concept map is through a tree diagram, or hierarchical map. The main idea is at the top of the tree, the major details branch out from the main idea, and minor details in turn branch out from the main ideas. Figure 12-11 shows the tree concept map.

A recently developed form of mapping is called a *semantic web*. Like the hierarchical map, the semantic web can condense a lot of information from an entire lecture, discussion, or textbook chapter. To create a

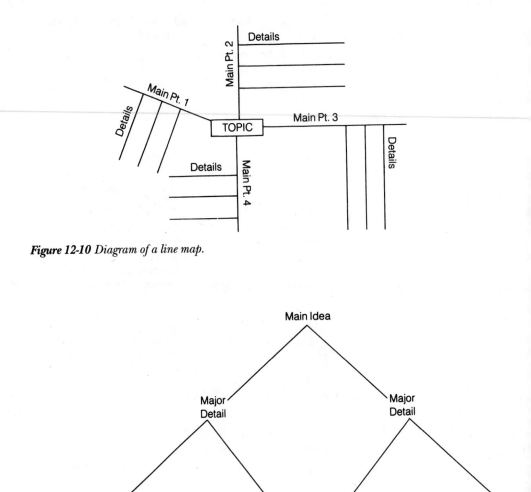

Figure 12-10 *Diagram of a line map.*

Figure 12-11 *Tree concept map.*

semantic web, you place the topic in the center and circle it. Then you radiate double lines from the center to list the subtopics, and you circle these subtopics as well. Finally, you radiate single lines from each subtopic to present the subtopic details. These details are also circled. The topic in the center of the semantic web is sometimes called the *concept,* the double-lined subtopics the *web strands,* and the single-lined details the *strand supports.* Notice in Figure 12-12 how the topic—developmental psychologist Erik Erikson's first four stages of life—is positioned in the center of the semantic web, how double lines point to the four web

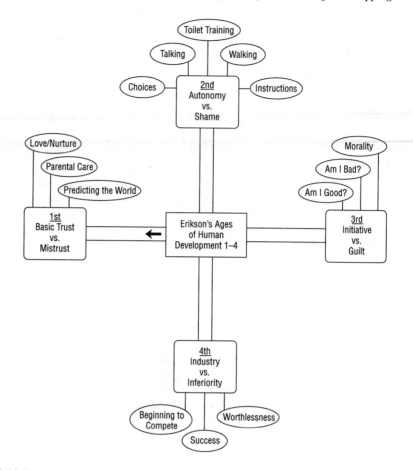

Figure 12-12 *Semantic web.*

strands, or subtopics, and how single lines point to the strand supports, or details to each subtopic. The semantic web is an effective way to see how topics you are learning relate to their subtopics and details. Semantic webs, therefore, allow you more easily to visualize and retain the parts of what you are learning.

Many students have found that these larger-concept maps, such as the flowcharts, the hierarchical maps, and the semantic webs, are effective study aids for midterm and final examinations. With these maps, students are encouraged to condense and are made to see relationships between general and specific types of material. Furthermore, the visual nature of the concept map allows students to "see" the whole and its parts when they take their exams.

Keep in mind that mapping has few rules and is for the most part individual. If you have a visual aptitude, create concept maps as you edit your notes. Even if you don't have strong visual abilities, begin using concept maps to help you review for exams, because they allow you to grasp economically a host of information.

Summary

Laddering and mapping are visual note-taking techniques. You can use them most effectively when you are editing your notes. Laddering involves placing horizontal and vertical lines next to main ideas and major details. Mapping is individualistic, allowing you to create your own shapes to illustrate relationships. Mapping also reduces information to its essentials and serves as an excellent review for exams. These two systems work best if you have a visual aptitude, but all students can benefit from using these visual techniques as study aids. Like the commonly used note-taking systems, mapping helps you see the relationships between main ideas and supporting details.

Summary Box   *Visual Note-taking Techniques: Laddering and Mapping*

What is it?	*Why use it?*
Laddering: vertical and horizontal lines join main ideas to main ideas and supporting details to supporting details. Mapping: shapes relate general and specific information; information reduced to its essentials.	To show visually how main ideas relate to major details.

Skills Practice Topic: Early Childhood Development

All four exercises in this chapter deal with early childhood behavior. Before you begin these exercises, answer the following questions, either individually or in small groups, to get some sense of what you already know about the psychology of childhood behavior.

1. How would you describe a child, from a psychological point of view?
2. What sorts of topics do you think psychologists studying children investigate?
3. What are a child's most important needs?
4. How do you think children learn to talk?

Exercise 12.1
Mapping Statements
from Lectures

The following ten statements are taken from lecture notes on infancy and childhood studies. Your job is to create, on a separate sheet of paper, a map for each statement that will show the relationship between main ideas and major details. Remember that mapping is individual, so do not expect your maps to be exactly like the ones in the Answer Key.

Infancy and Childhood

1. A child forms attachments to his parents for two important reasons: first, if his biological needs are met and, second, if his emotional needs are nourished.

2. Infants often engage in parallel play; that is, infants play at the same time, and at the same place, but independently.

3. One can identify three types of children who play: (1) the popular ones, who have many friends, (2) the rejected ones, who, as you may guess, have few other friends, and (3) the controversial ones, whom some like and others do not.

4. How do older siblings influence their younger brother or sister's behavior? They can have a positive influence by playing with them and serving as teachers for them. They can also have a negative influence. If the older sibling has emotional or physical problems, the healthy younger child may become aggressive because he has not been given enough attention by the parents and the sick brother or sister.

5. Let's talk a bit about birth order. Psychologists say that birth order affects a child in two important ways. First, every child because of her order in the family experiences the environment differently. Second, each child gets different prenatal care. By that I mean to say that the mother is in a different state of health with each child she carries.

6. There are two significant theorists in the area of early childhood development. The first is Jean Piaget—the Swiss psychologist working in the first half of this century—and the second is Erik Erikson, who was a pioneer in childhood psychoanalysis.

7. For Erik Erikson, the newborn is in a stage he calls basic trust versus mistrust. What are some of the newborn's needs at this stage? Let's put them on the board in terms of questions the child would ask if he could talk: (1) Is my world predictable? (2) Do my parents care for my needs? (3) Do my parents love or nurture me? All of these needs shape the newborn's personality, according to Erikson.

8. The second stage for Erikson is called autonomy versus shame and doubt. Autonomy simply means being able to take care of oneself. This stage is the age of the toddler—ages 1–3. The child learns to be independent or dependent as she performs the following activities: walking, talking, being toilet trained, responding to instructions, and making choices.

9. The third stage for Erikson is called initiative versus guilt, for ages 3–6. There is a major contrast between this stage and autonomy versus shame which, you will recall, is the second stage. In this third stage the child does not ask, Can I do it? as he would in stage two, but Am I good or bad? Here you will see that the child begins to develop a morality.

70%

(score = # correct × 10)
Find answers on
pp. 393–395.

Exercise 12.2
Applying Laddering
and Cornell to a
Lecture Passage

10. Let's list some of the characteristics of the fourth stage, for ages 6–12—what Erikson calls the industry versus inferiority stage. Here the child deals with questions of self-worth. They move their interests from their family to the larger society. They also begin to compete with their peers, or children their same age.*

In the following ten-paragraph lecture excerpt on Jean Piaget, you will be asked to use the indenting system to outline the material. Once you are finished, apply the laddering technique and the Cornell system to highlight the significant concepts and main ideas and major details.

This lecture continues the discussion of childhood development, focusing on Jean Piaget's four major stages of intellectual development.

Jean Piaget's Four Intellectual Stages

I want to begin my discussion today of the major intellectual stages that Jean Piaget introduced. I will be talking about them in detail, but let me introduce them now. They are: (1) sensorimotor, (2) preoperational, (3) concrete operations, and (4) formal operations. Piaget emphasized that these stages are not exact and that children develop at various rates. Some, he noted, never reach the last stage of formal-operations.

Let's begin with the sensorimotor stage. Its years are from birth to age one-and-a-half. What characterizes this stage? This is the stage of simple motor responses like sucking and grasping. The infants at this age, and this is important, respond to their surroundings, not to what they remember. Piaget emphasized that children at this stage cannot respond to what they remember; they merely respond to what they see, hear, feel, and touch at the moment. Is this maybe why we have so few memories of our early childhood?

At the end of this first period, some important changes occur. The infant begins to talk. When this happens, toddlers can begin to talk about what they do not see. This ability Piaget referred to as object permanence. Please write this term down. Infants at the end of the sensorimotor stage also begin to recognize who they are. Experiments show that babies at this time who see themselves in the mirror can recognize who they are. Often they will touch their noses as an indication that they recognize what they see in the mirror. This action seems to say: "I know

---

*Adapted from James W. Kalat, *Introduction to Psychology*, 3rd ed., pp. 247–252.

who that person is!" Also at the end of this stage, babies can show embarrassment. And this is another piece of evidence that the infant knows him or herself.

Now let's turn to the preoperational stage. It is a long stage—from one-and-a-half years to seven years, or a five-and-a-half-year span. What characterizes this stage is the tremendous development in language that the child experiences. Yet it is not the language of adults, and I want to emphasize this point. These children use many words, but they do not understand the complex meanings of many of them. Piaget talks about this use of language as reversal. Let me give you an example. If I fully understand the meaning of the word father, I know that my father also had a father. For Piaget, this means that the speaker can reverse the operations, so he calls this ability reversal. A child in this preoperational stage lacks this operation to reverse. That is, she cannot understand how her father can also be the son to someone else.

Piaget also presents another important term for this preoperational stage. He says that the child from one-and-a-half to seven is egocentric. Let's define this term. An egocentric child sees the world as being totally for himself. You can say that he cannot put himself in someone else's shoes. Piaget has shown that this egocentric state is not absolute, and he has provided examples of children who are preoperational who do show some understanding of others. In an experiment with a card having a different picture on each side, a child of three or four can say that what the adult sees on the opposite side of the table is different from what she sees.

There is another key concept that I want you to learn, and that word is conservation. In the preoperational stage, Piaget has shown that children lack the concept of conservation. What is conservation? Children do not understand that an object conserves certain properties such as number, length, volume, area, and mass. What do I mean by this? If you were to put the same volume of colored liquid in two containers, one long and thin and the other short and fat, the child would say that there is more water in the long and thin container even though he has seen the same amount of water poured from the fat container to the thin one. Because the child sees the water within a longer shape, he is sure that there is more of it than when it was in, what it appeared to him to be, a smaller container. That is the concept of conservation.

Let's now go to the concrete operations stage. Remember that this is the stage from about seven to eleven. At this time, the child begins to understand the concept of property, or conservation, which she didn't understand in the preoperational. Like all the stages, this one also does not happen all at once. So a five-year-old may know that a ball of play dough may be shaped differently but have the same mass but may not understand that water in different containers has the same volume.

Why does Piaget call this period concrete-operations? He uses this term because the child from seven to eleven likes to deal with the concrete world—sizes, shapes, and numbers. You could say that she understands all that she can sense. Yet the child at this stage has a difficult time playing with these concrete realities. If you were to ask a seven-year-old where she would like a third eye, she would likely say "Between the other two." She does not have the ability to understand the abstract abilities of seeing. Older children are much more creative with a question like this and say something like "At the back of my head so I can see what is going on behind me."

We now turn to the last Piagetian stage—formal operations, and, remember, that it happens at about age eleven, at or around the onset of puberty. In this final stage, the child is able to begin thinking in abstractions. What do I mean by abstractions? Abstractions are those thoughts that go beyond the concrete. A friend is a concrete being, but friendship is an abstraction—a concept for the idea of a friend. To abstract requires logical and systematic practices. These are practices that take a lifetime to develop. And please remember that Piaget said that not all children develop into adults who can successfully use formal-operations.

Let's look at an experiment done to identify when a child has entered the formal operations stage. The problem is to have students produce a yellow liquid from five bottles of liquid of various colors. The goal is to get the right combination of liquids. What do you think children in the concrete operations stage did? They started mixing the liquids haphazardly, picking any combination of liquids. Children in the formal operations stage are much more systematic, trying combinations with two bottles, then combinations with three. The key here is that the formal operations children approach this problem systematically; they have a set of patterned practices, which in itself is an abstraction. That is, these children realize that a system can achieve a desired goal. The concrete operations children do not appreciate the value of systematic thinking, mainly because they do not understand that the abstraction called systematic thinking can do powerful things.*

70%

Ask instructor for answers.

---

*Exercise 12.3
Mapping a Longer
Lecture Excerpt*

Your job is to read the following lecture excerpt on language learning, a continuation of the discussion of Piaget's four stages of intellectual development. As you read, take notes—condensing information and using the indenting format, laddering, and Cornell. Before you finish with your notes, write an appropriate title. Then, on a separate sheet of paper, create a concept map that includes the important points made in your notes. Remember that mapping is individual, so your map may not look like the sample one in the Answer Key. Complete your study notes in the space provided.

We are going to continue our discussion of language today. I want to start out with some interesting facts. It has been shown through solid research that a child between the ages of one-and-a-half and six learns an average of nine words per day. With each new word the child is able to explain what she experiences in greater detail. The question today is: What is it that a child needs in order to begin to acquire language, and are there stages like Piaget's that describe language development? The

---

*Adapted from Kalat, *Introduction to Psychology*, 3rd ed., pp. 229–233.

first major step in learning language is the most difficult one for an infant. He must understand that a word represents a thing. A cake—what tastes so good—is represented by that strange sound. Once he makes that connection, words make sense and become an economical way of expressing his thinking.

There are distinct stages in learning a language, what linguists call language acquisition. Infants up to six months begin by random sound-making called babbling. These sounds have no relationship to what they hear. Even deaf infants up to six months babble. By age one, infants begin to understand what they hear and can say a word or two. What do you think the first word is? It is something like "muh," or the word identifying the person closest to them—their mother. It is interesting to realize that most languages have a word similar to "muh" for Mother.

Let's now go to the child at age one-and-a-half. This little person can say about fifty words, yet she uses words in isolation. I mean to say that at this age the child cannot string words together. The baby can say "Hello" and "Mama" but usually not "Hello Mama." Most of these fifty words are nouns; some are verbs. There is some research, though, that shows children able to speak with many words at a time, but the parents often hear it as one word because it is so poorly said.

At two, the language magic begins, I would say. The toddler speaks in two- and three-word phrases. And these are not just phrases that the child has heard and is simply copying. I want to emphasize this point. For children, language is not simply copying what they hear. Language use is rather a creative process. Underline the word "creative." They make up their own phrases, their own sentences.

By age three, most children are making full sentences. But they are not usually adult sentences. The child is making up his own rules for certain language structures, especially with negatives. The child at three will often say, "I no want to go" for "I do not want to go." Here, it seems the child is making his own rule about negatives. What rule could this be? "No" before the verb makes the whole sentence negative. Parents often find these mistakes cute and do not correct them. But even if the parent did, the child would continue to make the mistake. It seems that the child needs to be ready to accept correction; and at this early age, the child cannot understand the concept of correcting his language.

By about age four, the child has mastered most of the rules of her language. Her vocabulary is still limited and develops as she gets older. And there are still a few errors in grammar and structure, but not the kinds that make understanding difficult. These young children often still cannot understand complex sentences from their parents.

I want to end with a very important concept. Language is maturational rather than experiential. Research shows that pumping lots of language into a child's head, or making the language experience rich, does not significantly improve a child's language abilities, except for maybe a slightly larger vocabulary. All children in all cultures—and this is the fascinating bit of research—mature at about the same rate and follow the same sequence I've outlined here. And there is also no research to suggest that the earlier a child talks, the smarter he is. Early

_____
80%

(Score = # of correct responses × 5)
Find answers on p. 396.

talkers and late talkers all go through the same sequence outlined in my lecture today.*

Place your lecture notes and your study map on a separate sheet of paper. Be sure to title your notes.

Exercise 12.4
Writing a Paragraph
from a Study Map

Your job is to write a paragraph from the information that you gathered in the previous lecture on language acquisition. Use only the information from your concept map to answer the following question.

> *Essay question:* In a well-organized paragraph, present the major stages in the development of a child's language. Identify the stages by age and discuss the important characteristics of each. Be sure your evidence is accurate.

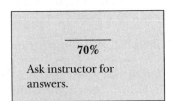

70%
Ask instructor for answers.

Follow-up on
Chapter 12

Now that you have completed the exercises, it may be helpful to see how your reading on this topic has changed some of your ideas about child psychology and development and improved your abilities in using visual note-taking techniques. You may want to go back and reread the exercises before you answer the following questions, and you may want to review the introduction. Answer the following questions either in small groups or individually.

On the Topic of Early Childhood Development

1. How do you now think children are different from adults?

2. What are some of the more interesting bits of research regarding how children acquire language that you remember from the lecture on language? Do your childhood language memories support these findings?

3. What topics in child development would you now want to study further?

On Visual Note-taking Techniques

4. Has the laddering technique helped you to organize your notes? If so, how?

5. Has the mapping technique helped you understand your notes? If so, how?

---

*Adapted from Kalat, *Introduction to Psychology*, 3rd ed., pp. 235–238.

6. Of the two techniques—laddering and mapping—which do you prefer? Why?

 **Internet Activity**

Use the Internet to do some research on early childhood development. If you have access to InfoTrac, use this research tool. Break up into groups of four or five to answer the following questions. Once you have completed your research, share your findings with your group.

1. Collect more information on Jean Piaget.
2. Collect more information on Erik Erikson.
3. Describe the procedures you used to locate your information.

PART FOUR

Study Skills Systems and Test-Taking Practices

Now that you have mastered reading and note-taking skills, you are ready to read textbook selections and be introduced to examination practices. In this part, you will learn about the SQ3R study system, which is an efficient way to read and remember textbook material. You will also learn how to take objective, essay, and math or science tests. Instructors rely on examinations to gauge how well you are doing.

CHAPTER 13

Memory Aids

In this chapter, you will learn about:

- How memory works
- Memory tips

A good memory is a key to learning. Knowing how memory is stored in the brain will give you a better understanding of how to become a more successful student. Also, in understanding how memory works, you can see how memory aids, called *mnemonic practices*, help you learn.

How Does Memory Work?

The study of the brain and learning, called *cognitive psychology*, is relatively new. All that students in this field have to work with at this time are theories, at best.

Cognitive psychologists are now suggesting that there are two kinds of memory: short-term and long-term. Everything you learn begins in short-term memory; you read or listen to something, and it enters short-term memory. Almost everything that goes into short-term memory is quickly forgotten, because forgetting is much easier for the brain than remembering. When something stays with you, it has entered long-term memory.

The best way to put information into long-term memory is through *rehearsal.* Rehearsal involves practice; with study material, that would involve rereading, discussing, summarizing, or paraphrasing. When you rehearse information, the brain records it, somewhat as a computer records bits of information on tape or chips. When you learn, the brain records the information with a physical mark on the cerebrum (the learning part of the brain). These marks are called *neural traces*, or memory grooves. Well-rehearsed information creates well-defined neural traces. If you learn something improperly, the neural trace will not be well defined, and it will probably return to short-term memory and be forgotten. Study Figure 13-1 to see how the brain remembers.

In long-term memory, information is connected through associations called *schemata.* Schema theory suggests that the more associations you can attach to a particular idea or thought, the better chance you have of understanding it and remembering it. Let's say you are studying the research on neural traces. You can develop a schema on this topic by

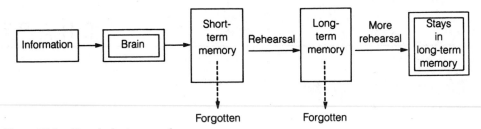

Figure 13-1   *How the brain remembers.*

reading about neural traces, by listening to someone talk about this topic, by writing about neural traces, and by discussing this topic with your peers. Each new experience with the topic of neural traces enriches your neural trace schema, or the associations connected to your knowledge of neural traces.

Forgetting works the opposite way. Even if you develop many neural traces and a rich schema on a particular topic, you have the tendency to forget this material. Researchers have shown that you tend to forget faster what you listen to than what you read or write about. Also, a negative attitude toward a topic encourages you to forget even faster. In each case of forgetting, the neural traces fade away.

How do you keep from forgetting information? How can you develop rich schemata of knowledge and retain this knowledge? To remember, you should (1) study for short periods, (2) take short rest periods between study periods, (3) review what you have learned, and (4) study different subjects in succession.

Studying for short intervals (twenty-five to fifty minutes) has several advantages. First, realize that the brain forgets more than it remembers; so if you take in less information, you have a better chance of remembering it. Remember, though, that these study periods must be concentrated. You need to reread and recite what you have read. This concentrated reading is what you will learn to do in the SQ3R system (Chapter 14).

Another characteristic of the brain is that it tends to rehearse what you have learned even after you have stopped studying. You are unaware of this rehearsal. When you read for a certain length of time, you need to take a relaxing break. Even if the break has nothing to do with what you have studied, your brain will still be rehearsing this new material. Like food being digested, new information needs to sit in the brain a while before it can enter long-term memory. Remember, though, that you need to schedule your study breaks carefully. Reading for twenty minutes and then taking a three-hour break will not train your brain to remember. If you plan to study in three intervals at night, for example, your breaks should be no more than twenty minutes long.

A third fact to know about the brain is that it tends to forget more during the first twenty-four hours after learning something than at any other time. Since you tend to forget more at first, make a point of reviewing what you have learned soon after you have read your textbook or listened to a lecture. What you review today will have a better chance of staying in long-term memory.

A final characteristic of memory is that the brain tends to forget if it is processing similar bits of information. This mental process is known as *interference*. The brain seems to take in more if two chunks of information are different. So it is wiser to study for two dissimilar courses in succession than for two similar courses. For example, you will remember more of your psychology chapter if you do some chemistry problems afterward than if you were to follow your psychology reading with reading a chapter of sociology.

Concentration Tips

Concentration can be defined simply as thinking with intensity. Of course, intense thinking is the best way to study. Apart from the optimal study area tips and goal-setting suggestions that were discussed in Chapter 2, there are several specific tips about concentrating that will improve your memory:

1. When you begin to study, don't look up or away from your study material. Each time you look out the window next to your desk or at your friends in the library, you break your intense thinking about the study material. The more you practice not being interrupted, the better your levels of concentration will be.

2. Walter Pauk, in his *How to Study in College*, offers an interesting technique to improve concentration. Each time your mind wanders, place a check on a blank sheet of paper next to your study materials. You may begin by making over twenty check marks during a study period; but if you keep up this practice, you will probably find that you have fewer occasions to make a check mark, so your concentration will be improving.*

3. Be sure you are not hungry when you study. Hunger is a very powerful distraction. If you find that you are hungry as you are studying, take a snack break; then get back to work.

4. If you are studying with concentration yet are simply not understanding what you are reading or reviewing, take a short break of two to five minutes. Then come back to the material to see if it is clearer to you—it may be. Often all you need is time for your mind to rest and digest difficult material. But if the material is still too difficult to grasp, make a note that you need to talk with a peer, a tutor, or your instructor to clear up the confusion on that particular question. Be sure to

---

*Walter Pauk, *How to Study in College*, 6th ed. (Boston: Houghton Mifflin, 1997), pp. 83–84.

continue studying, with concentration, other material you need to learn during your assigned study period. Do not let one difficult section of your study period destroy the concentration that you have achieved.

Memory Tips

From this very general introduction to learning theory, you can design certain successful learning practices. Consider the following learning hints.

1. Something learned well the first time is not easily forgotten. Study new information slowly and carefully, asking questions as you go along.

2. Relate new information to several contexts. Putting information into proper context is called *association*. The more contexts that you place information in, the more likely you are to remember this new material. If you are learning the meaning of "ostentatious," for example, it is best for you to learn both its dictionary meaning as well as its synonyms; its history, or etymology; and words related to it, such as "ostensibly," "ostentation," and "ostentatiousness." With each new context that you place the word in, you are creating more memory grooves, all of which are associated with "ostentatious."

    Similarly, the more you read in several fields, the more contexts you make, and the easier it will be for you to attach new information to them. Many composition theorists and language experts are now saying that students learn to speak and write better if they read widely. Creating several contexts seems to be central to successful learning.

3. Organize any information that you read or study into patterns, often into main ideas and major details. Organizing information into recognizable patterns is known as *categorization*. When students categorize information, they have a better chance of keeping it in long-term memory. Even if information seems disorganized, try to find an order; most information is built upon patterns.

4. Reviewing is another important way to remember. Psychological studies have shown that if you have once learned something and have forgotten it, you will have an easier time relearning it. Spaced review helps keep information in long-term memory. Don't leave your reviewing of notes and textbook markings until the night before an exam.

5. On a few occasions, you will be asked to learn a particular sequence or list that has no pattern, such as the colors in the light spectrum or the planets in the solar system. When this happens, use one of the following five mnemonic practices: a mnemonic sentence, an acronym, an abbreviation, a visualization, or a gimmick.

Mnemonic Sentences.   Your biology instructor may want you to remember the order of classifications in the animal kingdom. There is no logic to this nomenclature, so you might want to create a *mnemonic* sentence that will help you recall each term. Your job is to remember the following divisions in the animal kingdom and their proper sequence: kingdom, phylum, class, order, family, genus, and species. You note that the beginning letters for the classifications are K, P, C, O, F, G, S. Thus, to remember each term, think of a seven-word sentence whose words begin with the seven letters in the biology classifications. You might think of something like: "King Paul called out for Gus and Sam." This sentence will probably stay with you during an exam, when you need to recall this classification sequence.

Acronyms.   You use an acronym to abbreviate a phrase. *Acronyms* are made up of the first letter of each word of the phrase; these letters make an existing word or a new word. NATO, for example, stands for North Atlantic Treaty Organization, and its initial letters can be pronounced as a word. You can make up your own acronyms when you cannot use categorization to remember a particular chunk of information. For example, if you cannot remember the parts of an atom, you can create the acronym PEN to stand for "proton," "electron," and "neutron."

Abbreviations.   You can use abbreviations in a similar fashion. *Abbreviations* are made up of the first letter of each word in a phrase. Unlike acronyms, these abbreviations do not spell out a word. MVM could be your abbreviation for remembering the three planets besides Earth that are closest to the Sun: Mercury, Venus, and Mars.

Visualizations.   Another successful memory aid is called a *visualization.* In a visualization, you attach what you need to learn to something visual. You have already learned something about visualizing when you studied the spatial-geographic pattern (see Chapter 6). Here, you learned that in biology and geography courses it is helpful to see how one part of an organism or location relates to another.

Visualizing can also prove helpful in learning unrelated pieces of information; you create a picture that incorporates the information into it. For example, if you cannot remember that lapis lazuli is a semiprecious stone, you may want to invent a scene in which a queen has a beautiful stone in her lap. Note the pun on the word "lap." This scene with the jewel on the queen's lap should help you recall the first part of the word and the fact that this stone is precious, worn by queens. You should use such an elaborate visual strategy, though, only when association and categorization have failed to make the proper learning connections for you.

Gimmicks.   Gimmicks can also be used to trigger your memory when the conventional learning strategies have failed. *Gimmicks* are simply word games or tricks to help you remember; they are often used in learning to spell difficult words. If you have difficulty spelling "conscience," for example, you might remember its spelling if you learned the slogan

"There is a *science* to spelling the word *conscience*." Similarly, if you cannot remember that the noun "principal" refers to a person, you could think of your principal as your *pal*. By remembering "pal," you will no longer confuse *principal*, the person, with *principle*, the rule or belief. Instructors will often teach you these spelling gimmicks, but you may be imaginative enough to make up your own.

Summary

The brain has two storage capacities: short-term and long-term memory. As a student, it is your goal to transfer as much information as possible to long-term memory. You can place more information into long-term memory by studying in short, concentrated periods, by taking spaced study breaks, and by regularly reviewing what you have studied. You will also remember more if you relate what you have learned to several contexts (association). By studying the same material in a lecture or discussion, in your textbook, and in your study notes, you begin to see it from several perspectives. Categorization is another key learning principle; whenever possible, try to divide information into general and specific categories.

When information has no particular pattern, you may want to use verbal and visual gimmicks to learn it. Generally, though, the most effective way to learn new material is to learn it right the first time—by putting it into logical categories and associating it with what you already know about it.

Summary Box   *Memory Aids*

What are they?	Why do you use them?
Study techniques that help place information into long-term memory Three basic learning principles: (1) rehearsal, (2) association, and (3) categorization Some of the more successful memory practices: (1) concentration techniques, (2) mnemonic sentences, (3) acronyms, (4) abbreviations, (5) visualizations, and (6) spelling gimmicks	To help you retain information and easily recall it for examinations

Skills Practice

Exercise 13.1
Applying Memory
Aids to Study
Material

Your job is to use a memory aid to learn the following ten pieces of information. Your answers, of course, will vary from those of other students.

1. Think of a gimmick to help you remember the difference in spelling and meaning between *stationery* (writing paper) and *stationary* (not moving).

2. Think of a gimmick that will help you remember the difference in spelling and meaning between *allusion* (reference) and *illusion* (unreal image).

3. Think of a gimmick that will help you remember the difference in meaning between *among* (used in comparing three or more) and *between* (used in comparing no more than two).

4. Think of a gimmick that will help you remember the difference in spelling and meaning between *capital* (meaning chief, or principal) and *capitol* (meaning a building that is the seat of government).

5. Think of a visualization that will help you remember that Nimrod was a mighty hunter referred to in the Bible. Describe the scene in a sentence or two.

6. Think of an acronym that will help you remember, in order, the colors of the light spectrum: red, orange, yellow, green, blue, indigo, and violet. Remember that an acronym is a word that is made up of the first letter of each word in the series you want to learn.

7. Think of a mnemonic sentence that will help you remember, in order, the first five presidents of the United States: Washington, Adams, Jefferson, Madison, and Monroe.

8. Think of an abbreviation that will help you recall the three most populous cities in the world: Tokyo, Mexico City, and Sao Paulo.

9. Imagine that you need to remember for an anthropology class the three different kinds of societies: egalitarian, rank, and stratified. Think of an abbreviation to help you recall these three types of societies.

Answers will vary. Find sample answers on p. 397.

10. Assume that you have to learn the meaning of *zealous* (eager or passionate). Use the learning theory of association to help you recall the meaning and uses of *zealous*. Add prefixes and suffixes to this word.

**Exercise 13.2
Self-Evaluation:
Applying Memory
Tips and Theory to
Your Studies**

The following ten questions will test the learning theories that you learned in the introduction. Answer these questions as they pertain to your studies. You may want to share your answers with other students and your instructor; there are no right or wrong answers.

1. To test the theory of interference, study back to back for courses that are similar in content. What problems do you find?

2. To test the theory of interference, study back to back for courses that are different in content. What happens? Do you learn more easily?

3. To test the theory of rehearsal, read for thirty to fifty minutes, but do nothing else. Do not take notes, do not discuss the material, and do not review. Then take a ten-minute break. After the break, recite

what you remember. Is your summary complete? What information did you miss?

4. To again test the theory of rehearsal, read for thirty to fifty minutes, but this time take notes, discuss, and review. Then take a ten-minute break. Finally, recite what you remember. Is your summary complete? Is it better than the summary in question 3?

5. To test your rehearsing skills, go over your study notes, lecture and discussion notes, text markings, and concept maps for one of your classes. See which rehearsal techniques you find most helpful. In a sentence or two, discuss how the following rehearsal techniques helped you remember the material.

a. underlining: _____

_____

b. making marginal notes: _____

_____

c. summarizing: _____

_____

d. paraphrasing: _____

_____

e. making study maps: _____

_____

f. reviewing your textbook underlinings and notes: _____

_____

g. reviewing your concept maps: _____

_____

h. other techniques: _____

_____

6. In a difficult course requiring textbook reading, use the check-marking technique to improve your concentration. Try this technique for several days. In a sentence or two, discuss how or if your reading concentration improved.

7. Of the courses you are taking, choose one that requires you to memorize. Make up an acronym to help you remember a chunk of information.

8. Of the courses you are taking, choose one that requires you to memorize certain material. Make up an abbreviation or mnemonic sentence to help you learn this material.

9. Choose a course you are taking that has a difficult word you need to learn. Think of a gimmick that will help you remember either its spelling or its meaning.

Answers will vary. Ask instructor for sample answers.

10. Find another word for the course that you used for question 8. Create a visualization that will help you remember the meaning of that word.

Exercise 13.3
Applying Memory
Tips and Theory to a
Textbook Excerpt

The following excerpt is from a biology textbook. In it you will find several terms dealing with plant biology. Select five terms in this excerpt and apply a learning theory or mnemonic practice, like an acronym, abbreviation, visualization, and so on, to learn each one.

This is an exercise that is best done in groups of four or five. When you have finished, share your ways of learning these terms with the entire class.

Answers will vary.

Overview of the Plant Body

Shoots and Roots

Many flowering plants have a body plan. The aboveground parts, or **shoots,** consist of stems and their branchings, leaves, flowers, and other components. The stems are like structural beams for upright growth. An advantage of upright growth is that it favorably exposes photosynthetic cells in young stems and leaves to light. It also displays the flowers for pollinators.

The plant's descending parts are called **roots.** These specialized structures absorb water and dissolved nutrients. They typically penetrate downward and spread through the soil. Roots also anchor the plant's aboveground parts. Most roots store food as well, releasing it as required to root cells or for transport to aboveground parts.

Three Plant Tissue Systems

The stems, branches, leaves, and roots of flowering plants are similar in a key respect. Their main tissues are grouped into three systems. Their **ground tissue system** is the most extensive; its tissues make up the bulk of the plant body. The **vascular tissue system** contains two kinds of conducting tissues that distribute water and solutes through the plant body. The **dermal tissue system** covers and protects the plant's surfaces. Some tissues in these systems are simple, in that they contain one type of cell only. Parenchyma, collenchyma, and sclerenchyma fall in this category. Other tissues are complex, with highly organized arrays of two or more types of cells. Xylem, phloem, and epidermis are like this.

Meristems

Flowering plants grow at **meristems:** localized regions of self-perpetuating, embryonic cells. As they grow, stems and shoots lengthen and thicken. Increases in *length* originate at **apical meristems** located inside the dome-shaped tips of stems and roots. There, cell divisions and enlargements give rise to three primary meristems, which go on to produce the specialized tissue systems. In all, a stem or root lengthens through growth that originates at apical meristems and at meristematic tissues derived from them. This growth produces the *primary* tissues of the plant body.

Increases in diameter originate at lateral meristems, which form inside a stem or root. There are two kinds of lateral meristems: **vascular cambium** and **cork cambium.** Growth originating here produces *secondary* tissues of the plant body. Each spring, for example, primary growth lengthens a maple tree's stems, branches, and roots; and secondary growth thickens them. Some of the new cells that form during primary and secondary growth perpetuate the meristems. Others differentiate and become part of the tree's specialized tissues.

---

1. The roots and shoots of flowering plants consist of a *ground* tissue system (the bulk of the plant body), a *vascular* tissue system (which distributes water and solutes), and a *dermal* tissue system (which covers and protects plant surfaces).
2. *Primary* growth (lengthening of stems and roots) originates at apical meristems and at meristematic tissues that are derived from them.
3. *Secondary* growth (thickening of stems and roots) originates at lateral meristems, called vascular cambium and cork cambium.*

---

*Adapted from Cecie Starr and Ralph Taggart, *Biology: The Unity and Diversity of Life,* 7th ed. [Belmont, Calif.: Wadsworth, 1995], pp. 484–485.

Follow-up on Chapter 13

Now that you have studied this introduction and completed the exercises, it may be helpful to see how your abilities in using memory aids have improved. You may want to go back and review the introduction and the exercises. Then answer the following questions either individually or in small groups.

On the Topic of Memory Aids

1. How effective are you at concentrating on what you study? In what areas of concentration do you still need improvement?

2. What sorts of memory techniques seem to work best for you when you have difficulty remembering material?

3. Which course is the most difficult for you this semester? What memory aids do you plan to use to help you learn material from that course more easily?

 **Internet Activity**

Conduct some research on memory on the Internet. This assignment is best completed in groups of four or five. Answer the following questions by doing research on the following Wadsworth Web site:

Memory Theory and Techniques
http://www.psych-web.com

If you cannot access this Web site, research the Internet to find information on memory theory and techniques to answer these questions:

1. What new information on memory theory did you gather?
2. What new techniques on memory did you collect?
3. Describe the procedures you followed to locate and use this Web site.

Once you have answered these questions, go back to your group to share your responses.

CHAPTER 14

The SQ3R Study System

In this chapter, you will learn about:

- The five steps in the SQ3R study system: survey, question, read, recite, and review
- How to use these steps when study reading

Now that you have practiced locating main ideas and major details, and have used several note-taking techniques and have picked up some memory aids, you are ready to combine these skills when you study your textbook. A successful study system is the SQ3R, which gives you both reading and note-taking skills to apply as you read your textbook. The SQ3R system has been used successfully by students for a long time. Many other study systems have emerged over the years, but they all follow the essential pattern of SQ3R.

The letters in SQ3R stand for five steps: survey, question, read, recite, review. Let's look at each of these steps.

Survey

In the survey step, you preview what you intend to read. Surveying is not word-for-word reading; rather, it is selective. Surveying is a central step in study reading. Research has repeatedly shown that if you survey material before you read it, your comprehension significantly improves because you are able to predict more effectively when you read the material. In surveying, you should (1) read the titles and headings, (2) note graphics and aids, and (3) read the introduction or preface. Before you read, you should determine the length of the chapter, estimate the time it will take you to read the chapter, determine what sections you are already familiar with, and predict whether the material will be difficult or easy for you to understand. By following these steps, you establish a reading focus.

Surveying an Entire Text. When you first get your textbook, you should briefly survey all of the chapters. Consider the following suggestions for doing this.

1. Read the preface, introductory material written to the student. In the preface, the author gives reasons for writing the book, the topics covered, and suggestions for using the text.

2. Look carefully at the table of contents, which comes after the preface. See how the book is organized. Is the organization simple or complicated? Are there a few divisions or several? If there are exercises, do the explanations come before the exercises, or are all the exercises at the end of the book? Since you will be using this text all semester, you need to know the answers to these questions.

   Some textbooks have two tables of contents: one short and the other detailed. Study both of them carefully.

3. See if there is an index, the alphabetical listing of topics found at the end of the textbook. Indexes are helpful when you want to find information fast. If your textbook has an index, familiarize yourself with it so that you can use it as a study aid.

4. See if there is a glossary before the index. A glossary defines important terms used in the textbook. Instead of referring to a dictionary, you can use the glossary. Often, students do not even realize that their textbook has a glossary.

5. In some math and science textbooks, students will find an appendix, which comes before the index. In an appendix are charts, graphs, and tables that you need to use in solving problems found in the textbook.

6. In your survey of the entire textbook, you may also discover an answer key. You will often find an answer key at the end of the textbook. Occasionally, you will find an answer key at the end of an exercise or at the end of a chapter. Some keys provide all of the answers, others just some of them. This text, for example, gives answers only to odd-numbered exercises. In some math texts, the author will provide answers to the even- or odd-numbered problems within an exercise.

7. Now you are ready to get a sense of the entire textbook. Read through parts of the beginning, middle, and end of the textbook. In this way, you can determine the author's style. Is it formal or conversational? It's helpful to have some sense for the author's style before you begin reading a specific chapter.

Surveying a Chapter of Text.   Consider the following suggestions in surveying a specific chapter.

1. Study the title of the chapter. Having read the title, do you think you know anything about the subject? Has your instructor covered this topic in a lecture or discussion? Or is this a new topic for you? By answering these questions, you will give focus to your reading and improve your predicting skills.

2. At the beginning of many textbook chapters, you will find an outline or list of objectives that the author intends to address. Since this is the significant information in the chapter, read it over carefully. Also,

read the introductory paragraphs, which either summarize the chapter or introduce an interesting issue that the chapter will cover.

3. Most textbook writers divide their chapters into divisions and subdivisions. These headings are usually in boldface print or italics. Thumb through the chapter divisions. If there are no divisions, read through the first paragraph, the first sentence of the following paragraphs, and the last paragraph of the chapter. By doing this, you can determine the outline of the chapter.

4. If there are illustrations, graphs, or charts in the chapter, study them. See how this material relates to the chapter's divisions and subdivisions.

5. See if discussion or study questions come at the end of the chapter. By reading these questions beforehand, you will know what topics are most important for the author. Also, see if a bibliography is included at the end. A bibliography lists additional books that you may wish to consult after you have read the chapter.

This chapter survey should take you no more than three or four minutes, but it is time well spent. Having surveyed, you now have a better idea of what to look for in the chapter.

Question

Questions help you identify important information while you read. Sometimes you will make up a question before you read and then look for the answer. Other times you may have a study guide of questions provided by the teacher or printed at the end of the chapter so that you can think about the questions before you read or you can read a chapter part to find the answer. Since you have learned to read for main ideas and supporting details, you may wish to make up your own questions by turning various chapter headings into main-idea questions and then reading to determine the main idea and supporting details.

If you choose to make up your own questions, keep the following issues in mind: Ask yourself: (1) What is the chapter topic, and how does the author respond to this topic? (2) What are the major characteristics, steps, events, causes, or results that explain this topic? and (3) Are any terms defined?

Making up your own questions may be difficult at first, but it will provide your study reading with a necessary direction. The successful college student invariably knows the right kinds of questions to ask. Start looking at words in boldface print or italics and the first sentences of paragraphs. From this information make up your own questions. For example, if your sociology chapter prints **Deviant Roles** in boldface, you could write: "What are deviant roles?" Or if your consumer behavior chapter begins its first paragraph with "Husbands and wives influence each other's buying preferences," you could turn this statement into a question: "How do husbands and wives influence each other's buying preferences?" By the time you finish reading a textbook chapter, you may have written ten to fifteen questions and answered them.

Read   Only after surveying and questioning are you ready to read—an active skill using all of the critical reading skills you have learned. Along with your questions, you should have a pen or felt-tip marker (hi-liter). Whenever you come upon a main idea in a paragraph or a detail that supports this main idea, mark this information by either underlining or highlighting the words. But remember: *Do not underline too much.* In most cases, all you need to mark is the part of the sentence with the important or core information—material that often answers the questions you have made up. If you overmark a page of text, you will become confused when you review for an exam. And not knowing what to review, you might read the entire page over. Study Figure 14-1, which is an example of an overly marked-up textbook page.

Ten Tips for Marking Your Textbooks

1. Mark main ideas with a double underline, a curved line, highlighter, or the red end of a red-and-blue pencil. Mark only one main idea per paragraph, and mark only the key parts of this main idea. If the main ideas in a group of paragraphs are related, number them 1, 2, 3, and so on.

2. Mark major details with a single underline, hi-liter, or the blue end of a red-and-blue pencil. Look for definitions, characteristics, examples, steps, causes, or effects. Try not to underline more than two details per paragraph, and mark only the key parts of these detail sentences. If you find that the details follow a pattern, number these details 1, 2, 3, and so on.

3. For very important statements, place an asterisk (*) in the margins next to them. These askerisks will become your signal to study these important pieces of information.

4. In some cases you may want to mark both the detail and its type. If you do so, use one of the following abbreviations in the margins: *ex, cause, eff, step,* or *char.*

5. Circle the key parts of a definition if the author has not already highlighted it in boldface or italics. Remember the importance of definitions in learning a subject. You should place the abbreviation *def* in the margins to direct you to the definition when you review your markings. You may also want to write the term on one side of a 3 × 5 card and its definition on the opposite side so that, at the end of the semester, you will have collected all of the important definitions for your course on these cards. When it is appropriate, you may want to include an example along with the definition. The example will often help you remember the definition.

violation as to be another burglary (allowing for the different frequencies of these offenses). In fact, only a rather small proportion of rapes are committed by men who are specialized "sex offenders." Most rapists have committed a great variety of other crimes, and will again. Moreover, all offenders seem to "specialize" in traffic violations and in having auto accidents.

Def. These patterns are referred to as (offender versatility:) "Offenders commit a wide variety of criminal acts, with no strong inclination to pursue a specific criminal act or a pattern of criminal acts to the exclusion of others" (Gottfredson and Hirschi, 1990).

Learn this definition

The Criminal Act

By now you will have drawn some conclusions about the typical criminal act. First of all, you may have noticed that people seldom *work* at crime. Few burglars have developed any special skills for forcing doors or windows or wiring around alarm systems—they simply break things, or move on to an easier target. Few embezzlers maintain false accounts in order to shield a long-term pattern of theft—most just steal from the cash register (usually on impulse); dip into petty cash; pad their expenses; or take home tools, supplies, or products belonging to their employers. Few robbers invest time studying a target and planning how to maximize their take.

This leads to the observation that criminal acts involve *short-range choices,* that they tend to occur on the spur of the moment. Crimes are committed so close to the offender's home because offenders will not invest the time and effort to go far afield. And they frequently occur in response to perceived opportunities of the moment: a rape in response to observing a woman asleep with her window open; a robbery in response to entering a convenience store for cigarettes and seeing that the clerk is alone. It also is the case that criminal attempts very frequently are frustrated by momentary impediments; many robberies fail to take place because of a sudden increase in the number of people on the street or because police arrive for a coffee break at an all-night restaurant.

Find the important figures in this table

Table 7-3 *Homicides per 100,000 Population for Selected Nations*

Nation	*Homicide Rate*
Jamaica	21.5
Netherlands	14.4
Barbados	11.7
Botswana	11.5
Sri Lanka	11.1
Russia	9.9
United States	**9.4**
Finland	7.8
Sweden	6.9
Italy	6.5
Canada	**5.4**
Denmark	4.3
Israel	4.0
Portugal	3.9
Bulgaria	3.9
Hungary	3.1
Switzerland	3.1
Germany	3.0
Norway	2.5
Austria	2.2
Poland	2.0
Singapore	1.7
Japan	0.9

Source: United Nations World Crime Survey, 1994.

This also lets us see that most criminal actions are *brief* in duration. Moreover, the *rewards are small and fleeting.* The monetary rewards are almost always small and soon spent; robbers frequently spend all of their take within a few hours. However, it is important to see that whatever rewards are produced by a crime, they usually are *immediate.* The murderer silences an immediate source of irritation, be it a crying infant, an insolent buddy, or an uncooperative robbery victim. The rapist gains immediate sexual gratification. The burglar gains a VCR, a piggy bank full of coins, or some liquor—now.

What are the criminal's rewards?

Examples of immediate rewards

Most crimes are *easy* to commit and very *simple* in design. Nearly anyone willing to commit them can do so with little or no preparation. But, even more important, most criminal acts are *exciting.* They involve the thrill of risk and danger as well as the rush that some gain from having domination over victims.

Consider this other important point

A risk is a thrill

Figure 14-1 *Textbook page overly marked up. (Source: Rodney Stark,* Sociology, *7th ed. [Belmont, Calif.: Wadsworth, 1998], p. 173.*

6. If a sentence is particularly difficult to understand, even after rereading it and attempting a paraphrase, place a question mark in the margin. When you review, you will be alerted to what you did not understand.

7. Do not include too many written comments in the margins. Those you do include can go anywhere in the margins—top or bottom, left or right. But you should reserve these comments for short summaries of important points, paraphrases of difficult sentences, and inferences that you make. For example, if you note that one main idea or supporting detail is more important than others, you might want to write in the margin: "Most important main idea," or "Most important supporting detail." Some students find their marginal comments more important than their underlinings.

8. Do not begin marking your chapter right away, because once you have marked something you will have a hard time erasing it. Read through several paragraphs first. Then go back to underline main ideas and supporting details. Often in rereading, you can more easily pick out the important parts of a paragraph. In fact, you may want merely to mark some of the most important points in pencil as you read and then mark in detail during the recite step, discussed in the next section.

9. Be consistent with your markings. Use the system just outlined, or make up your own. Some students find that they are more comfortable with comments and summaries in the margins, whereas others use their own personal symbols. Just be sure that you employ the same underlining symbols and abbreviations throughout the textbook. Otherwise, when you review, you will not be able quickly to separate main ideas from supporting details. Some students learn better from their underlinings, others from their comments. Try out all of these suggestions and any of your own techniques to determine which ones help you learn best.

10. Think of textbook markings as *active* reading. Your markings should be your signals that you understand the form and content of the chapter. If you mark passively, you will not retain the important points made in the chapter. In Figure 14-2, you will see an example of a successfully marked-up textbook page.

Even if you follow methodically the preceding ten suggestions for marking a chapter, sometimes you will not completely understand what you have read. Almost everyone has to reread all or part of a textbook chapter sometime during the semester. In fact, research shows that most students retain only about 50 percent of textbook material the first time they read it. If a chapter is difficult, you may want to put it aside after you have read it once, and reread it in a day or two. Often, if you reread difficult material after it has "settled" for a while, you will find the material more accessible.

Jamaica highest, Japan lowest, u.s. high

Table 7-3 *Homicides per 100,000 Population for Selected Nations*

Nation	Homicide Rate
Jamaica	21.5
Netherlands	14.4
Barbados	11.7
Botswana	11.5
Sri Lanka	11.1
Russia	9.9
United States	**9.4**
Finland	7.8
Sweden	6.9
Italy	6.5
Canada	**5.4**
Denmark	4.3
Israel	4.0
Portugal	3.9
Bulgaria	3.9
Hungary	3.1
Switzerland	3.1
Germany	3.0
Norway	2.5
Austria	2.2
Poland	2.0
Singapore	1.7
Japan	0.9

Source: United Nations World Crime Survey, 1994.

violation as to be another burglary (allowing for the different frequencies of these offenses). In fact, only a rather small proportion of rapes are committed by men who are specialized "sex offenders." Most rapists have committed a great variety of other crimes, and will again. Moreover, all offenders seem to "specialize" in traffic violations and in having auto accidents.

Def. These patterns are referred to as *offender versatility:* "Offenders commit a wide variety of criminal acts, with no strong inclination to pursue a specific criminal act or a pattern of criminal acts to the exclusion of others" (Gottfredson and Hirschi, 1990).

6 key characteristics: study

The Criminal Act

1 By now you will have drawn some conclusions about the typical criminal act. First of all, you may have noticed that people seldom *work* at crime. Few burglars have developed any special skills for forcing doors or windows or wiring around alarm systems—they simply break things, or move on to an easier target. Few embezzlers maintain false accounts in order to shield a long-term pattern of theft—most just steal from the cash register (usually on impulse); dip into petty cash; pad their expenses; or take home tools, supplies, or products belonging to their employers. Few robbers invest time studying a target and planning how to maximize their take.

2 This leads to the observation that criminal acts involve *short-range choices,* that they tend to occur on the spur of the moment. Crimes are committed so close to the offender's home because offenders will not invest the time and effort to go far afield. And they frequently occur in response to perceived opportunities of the moment: a rape in response to observing a woman asleep with her window open; a robbery in response to entering a convenience store for cigarettes and seeing that the clerk is alone. It also is the case that criminal attempts very frequently are frustrated by momentary impediments; many robberies fail to take place because of a sudden increase in the number of people on the street or because police arrive for a coffee break at an all-night restaurant.

3 This also lets us see that most criminal actions are *brief* in duration. Moreover, the *rewards are small and fleeting.* 4 The monetary rewards are almost always small and soon spent; robbers frequently spend all of their take within a few hours. However, it is important to see that whatever rewards are produced by a crime, they usually are *immediate.* The murderer silences an immediate source of irritation, be it a crying infant, an insolent buddy, or an uncooperative robbery victim. The rapist gains immediate sexual gratification. The burglar gains a VCR, a piggy bank full of coins, or some liquor—now.

Criminal seeks immediate gratification.

5 Most crimes are *easy* to commit and very *simple* in design. Nearly anyone willing to commit them can do so with little or no preparation. But, even more important, most criminal acts are *exciting.* 6 They involve the thrill of risk and danger as well as the rush that some gain from having domination over victims.

Thrill involves domination.

Figure 14-2 *Textbook page appropriately marked up. (Source: Rodney Stark,* Sociology, *7th ed. [Belmont, Calif.: Wadsworth, 1998], p. 173.*

Recite

Having read and marked the important parts of your chapter, you are now ready to write what you have learned. In the recite step of the SQ3R system, you summarize what you have read. This step is critical, because it shows you how much material you have understood and remembered.

When you begin to recite, read for a short period of time—approximately ten minutes. During this time, mark the passage and make marginal comments. Some students have found that they can read and mark only one chapter subsection at a time, often just answering the question they have made up from the subtitle. No matter how small a part of the chapter you have read, close your textbook after you have reviewed your underlining and commentary in the margins. Then, in the section of your notebook designated for study-reading notes, take notes on what you read, using any note-taking format you are comfortable with. Title and date each study-reading entry, as in the following example:

The Criminal Act pp. 173–174   *10/12/98*

Some students have found that they can more successfully mark what they have read during this recite step. They often mark some material during the read step with pencil; then during their recite, they use pen or highlighter to underscore main ideas and major details and make marginal comments.

You may want to use the Cornell note-taking system when you recite. If you do, write the section title, pages, and date on the top line. To the right of the vertical, summarize the main idea and supporting details of the section without looking back at the book. Leave spaces to make corrections and additions to your notes. Then look back at the chapter to see if you omitted anything important, and edit your notes. These notes will be useful study tools for exams. You can fold the notes on the vertical, read the topic or question to the left of the vertical and attempt to answer it from memory. Reread and recite until recall is accurate.

Look at how the Cornell system effectively summarizes and quizzes the student on material she has underlined regarding criminal behavior. Note how this student has formulated questions in the margin in anticipation of the exam she will take on this material.

Criminal Act 173–174   *10/12/98*

Learn definition of <u>offender versatility</u>	Def.: offender versatility: criminal offender commits a variety of acts with no desire to commit just one crime
What are the six characteristics of criminal behavior?	<u>6 key characteristics of criminal acts</u> (1) crime not carefully thought out. (2) Criminal chooses from a short-range list. (3) Criminal acts are brief. (4) Criminal rewards are momentary. (5) Crimes have simple designs. (6) Crimes are exciting for criminal.

Key point regarding domination	Criminal enjoys the domination he feels over his victim.

In the beginning, your reciting notes may not be very efficient. With the first few sets of notes, you may have to review your textbook to see if your notes are both accurate and thorough. As the semester progresses, extend your study-reading sessions from ten to fifteen minutes, then from fifteen to twenty. By the end of the semester, you should be able to study read for fifty minutes and accurately recite what you have read. Even the best students can effectively do only one hour of concentrated reading of textbook material at one sitting.

With particularly difficult chapters, you may want to break up your reading into shorter sessions. If you do this, you may even want to write out some short, specific goals to complete. Look at the following goals for reading an economics chapter:

1. Read for ten minutes, or complete one page of the chapter on military spending.
2. Summarize this page.
3. Break for five minutes.
4. Read for ten more minutes, recite, and take another five-minute break.

Once you have completed your reading notes, it is wise to review them. As you reread your notes and quiz yourself, you may also want to make concept maps out of the material. A carefully designed concept map is a helpful study aid just before an exam.

Review

Review is the final step in the SQ3R system. You will study this step thoroughly in Chapters 15 and 16 on test-taking procedures. For now, just remember that to review is your insurance that you will remember what you worked hard to learn. When you review, you (1) study your lecture and discussion notes, (2) reread your text markings, (3) review your study-reading notes, and (4) study your concept maps or design concept maps for what you have read, tying more and more of the material together. You should now be able to predict the sorts of questions you will be asked on exams. Write your predicted exam questions in your notebook. You should not review only on the night before the exam. You need to review throughout the semester. You will retain more of the reading material if you edit and review your notes after every study-reading session. This will help you do a better job of taking class lecture and discussion notes and participating fruitfully in class discussions. Then review all your markings and your study-reading notes one week before a major exam. Predict exam questions, and use memory aids, as explained in Chapter 13, when you need to memorize particularly difficult material. Cramming may help you pass a test, but it will not help you retain the material.

Some instructors have added an additional step to the SQ3R, changing it to SQ4R, or "review again." They believe that reviewing is very important and often not completed with only one review step, so they consider many reviews to be necessary. Research has shown that almost no one can retain all textbook information in one careful reading; thus, reviewing again is not a sign of a learning problem, but what most students need to do in order to retain most of the textbook material they study.

Other study-skills professors, like Walter Pauk, refer to a different fourth R: to "reflect" (*How to Study in College,* 6th ed. [Boston: Houghton Mifflin, 1997], pp. 253–256). After reviewing, students are encouraged to think about what they have learned. Not just reciting, reflecting asks students to connect their textbook material to what they already know, to evaluate its importance to their own learning and to their understanding of the topic they are studying. It may be that a topic you have studied in your textbook is so interesting that you want to do further library research on it. Reflecting allows you to add meaning to your studying and to be more creative with what you have learned, not just to become proficient in reciting what you are asked to learn.

Some of the questions you might ask when you reflect on what you have study read include the following:

1. How is this material new to me?
2. Why is this material important for me?
3. How is this material like material that I already know?
4. Is there anything about this material that I would like to research further?

Summary

The SQ3R is a study system for use when you read your textbooks. The S stands for survey—taking a general look at your reading task. Q involves questioning—writing key questions whose answers will help you understand the reading. The first R is read, where you mark up key points and make accurate inferences. In the second R—recite—you summarize what you have read. This step is critical, because it tells you what you have learned. The last R stands for review. Here, you go over your markings and notes to retain what you have learned. Often it is necessary to review the material several times before you can say you know it. At this point, you may also want to reflect on how this new textbook material relates to what you already know.

The SQ3R is a sensible study-reading system. By using the SQ3R, you approach your study reading in an orderly fashion—surveying, questioning, reading, reciting, and reviewing.

Summary Box   *The SQ3R Study System*

What is it?	*Why do you use it?*
A systematic approach to reading textbook material S = survey Q = question R = read R = recite R = review	To understand textbook material To retain textbook material To take better notes in lecture class To ask intelligent questions in class To participate in class discussion about the chapter To recall material for exams To integrate this new material into what you already know

Skills Practice

Exercise 14.1
Underlining from
Textbook Excerpts

Following are three excerpts on the topic of environmental studies. Your job is to survey each excerpt and write at least two questions in the margin. Then in each paragraph, double-underline the main idea and single-underline one or two major details, or use any marking system that is comfortable for you. Be sure to mark only the important parts of the main ideas and major details.

1. Can Scientists Prove Anything?

In a word, no. *Scientists can disprove things, but they can never prove anything.* To win us over to their particular viewpoint, people often say that something has or has not been "scientifically proven." Either they don't understand the nature of science, or they are trying to mislead us by falsely implying that science yields absolute proof or certainty.

Instead of certainty or absolute truth or proof, scientists speak of degrees of probability or uncertainty. Scientists might predict that if we do a certain thing, then (based on the data, hypotheses, theories, and laws underlying the processes involved) there is a high, moderate, or low probability that such and such will happen.

The goal of the rigorous scientific process is to reduce the degree of uncertainty as much as possible. However, the more complex the system being studied, the greater the degree of uncertainty or unpredictability about its behavior.*

---

*From G. Tyler Miller, Jr., *Living in the Environment*, 10th ed. (Belmont, Calif.: Wadsworth, 1998), p. 54.

2. What Is Technology?

Science is a search for understanding of the natural world. In contrast, **technology** involves developing devices, processes, and products designed to control the natural world—primarily for the benefit of humans—by improving our efficiency, our chances for survival, our comfort level, and our quality of life.

In many cases, technology develops from known scientific laws and theories. Scientists invented the laser, for example, by applying knowledge about the internal structure of atoms. Applied scientific knowledge about chemistry has given us nylon, pesticides, laundry detergents, pollution control devices, and countless other products. Applications of theories in nuclear physics led to nuclear weapons and nuclear power plants.

Some technologies, however, arose long before anyone understood the underlying scientific principles. For example, aspirin, extracted from the bark of a willow tree, relieved pain and fever long before anyone found out how it did so. Similarly, photography was invented by people who had no inkling of its chemistry, and farmers crossbred new strains of crops and livestock long before biologists understood the principles of genetics. In fact, much of science is an attempt to understand and explain why various technologies work.

Science and technology usually differ in the way the information and ideas they produce are shared. Many of the results of scientific research are published and distributed freely to be tested, challenged, verified, or modified. In contrast, many technological discoveries are kept secret until the new process or product is patented. The basis of some technology, however, gets published in journals and enjoys the same kind of public distribution and peer review as science.*

3. What Is Environmental Science, and What Are Its Limitations?

Environmental science is the study of how we and other species interact with one another and with the nonliving environment (matter and energy). It is a *physical and social science* that integrates knowledge from a wide range of disciplines including physics, chemistry, biology (especially ecology), geology, meteorology, geography, resource technology and engineering, resource conservation and management, demography (the study of population dynamics), economics, politics, sociology, psychology, and ethics. In other words, it is a study of how the parts of nature and human societies operate and interact—a study of *connections* and *interactions* (see inside front cover of this book).

There is controversy over some of the knowledge provided by environmental science, for much of it falls into the realm of frontier science. One problem involves *arguments over the validity of data*. There is no way to measure accurately how many metric tons of soil are eroded worldwide, how many hectares of tropical forest are cut, how many species become extinct, or how many metric tons of certain pollutants are emitted into the atmosphere or aquatic systems each year. Sometimes the

---

*From G. Tyler Miller, Jr. *Living in the Environment,* 10th ed., pp. 55–56.

estimates of such quantities may err (either way) by as much as a factor of two or more.

We may legitimately argue over the numbers, but the point environmental scientists want to make is that the trends in these phenomena are significant enough to be evaluated and addressed. Such environmental data should not be dismissed because they are "only estimates" (which are all we can ever have). This, however, does not relieve investigators from the responsibility of getting the best estimates possible and pointing out that they *are* estimates.

Another limitaiton is that *most environmental problems involve so many variables and such complex interactions that we don't have enough information or sufficiently sophisticated models to aid in understanding them very well.* Much progress has been made during the past 50 years (and especially the past 25 years), but we still know much too little about how the earth works, about its current state of environmental health, and about the effects of our activities on its life-support systems (and thus on humans and other forms of life).*

> Answers will vary. Find sample underlinings on pp. 397–399.

Exercise 14.2
More Underlining
from Textbook
Excerpts

Here are three more excerpts from a textbook on psychology. Again, survey each excerpt and write at least two questions in the margin. Then double-underline main ideas and single-underline major details, and mark only the important parts, or use any system that is comfortable for you.

1. Psychiatry

Psychiatry is the branch of medicine that deals with psychological and emotional disturbances. To become a psychiatrist, you would first earn an M.D. degree and then take an additional 4 years of residency training in psychiatry. Psychiatrists and clinical psychologists provide similar services for most clients: They listen, ask questions, and provide advice. For clients with more serious problems, psychiatrists are authorized to prescribe drugs such as tranquilizers and antidepressants. Because psychologists are not medical doctors, they cannot prescribe drugs. Many clinical psychologists favor a change in the law to enable clinical psychologists with extra training to prescribe drugs. That proposal is highly controversial, and its eventual fate is hard to predict.

(Does psychiatrists' ability to prescribe drugs give them an advantage over psychologists? Not always. Ours is an overmedicated society. Some psychiatrists habitually treat anxiety and depression with drugs, whereas a psychologist would try to treat the problems by changing the person's way of living.)

Several other kinds of professionals also provide help and counsel. Psychiatric nurses and psychiatric social workers have an undergraduate or master's degree in nursing or social work plus additional training in care for emotionally troubled people.†

---

*From G. Tyler Miller, Jr. *Living in the Environment,* 10th ed., p. 56.
†From James W. Kalat, *Introduction to Psychology,* 4th ed. (Pacific Grove, Calif.: Brooks/Cole, 1996), p. 11.

2. Psychology

Occupational Settings in Psychology

Psychologists work in many occupational settings. A little over one-third work in academic institutions—colleges, universities, and medical schools. Almost 40% work in health-provider settings—independent practices, hospitals, and clinics. Others work in business, government, guidance and counseling centers, and public school systems. Those who work in business help companies make decisions about hiring, promotions, training of workers, and job design. Those who work in school systems help teachers deal with discipline problems and underachieving students.

Women and Minorities in Psychology

For a long time, academic psychology, like most other academic disciplines, was populated mostly by men. Women students were not encouraged to seek a Ph.D. degree; those who did were rarely offered employment at the most prestigious colleges, universities, or research institutions. Today, well over 50% of all graduate students in psychology are women, and the percentage of women among psychologists is high and growing.

Minorities also constitute a growing percentage of psychologists, though the total number is still small. According to a 1988 survey in the United States, African Americans, Hispanics, Asian Americans, and other ethnic minorities combined received 11.4% of the doctorates awarded in clinical psychology. That percentage is low compared to most other academic fields. Many graduate schools are taking active measures to attract more applications from minority students who would like to become psychologists (Hammond & Yung, 1993).*

3. Psychology Approach

The Quantitative Psychology Approach

Any useful study of natural phenomena must be based on careful measurements. **Quantitative psychologists** measure individual differences and apply statistical procedures to determine what their measurements indicate. In fact, nearly all psychologists take measurements and apply statistical procedures; quantitative psychologists are those who concentrate more on mathematics and generally give less attention to the theoretical interpretations.

To measure individual differences, psychologists have devised tests of IQ, personality, interests, and attitudes, most of them requiring pencil-and-paper answers. Once they have devised a test, they must determine whether or not it measures what it is supposed to measure.

Tests in psychology only measure; they do not explain. For example, once we determine that a particular child has a low IQ score, we can predict that the child will have trouble in school. The test score does not, how-

---

*Adapted from James W. Kalat, *Introduction to Psychology,* 4th ed., pp. 13–14.

Answers will vary. Ask instructor for sample underlinings.

ever, tell us *why* the child is performing poorly—either on the test or in school. One child may perform poorly because of visual or auditory impairments, another because of a poor educational background, yet another because he or she does not read or speak English. Measuring individual differences is a first step toward explaining them, but it is only a first step.*

***Exercise 14.3
Applying the SQ3R
System on a Textbook
Excerpt***

In this exercise, you will be reading a longer excerpt from a sociology textbook on race and ethnic groups. You will be asked to survey, make up questions, read, recite, and review. When you have completed these five steps, you will be asked to answer some questions that will demonstrate how well you comprehended the excerpt.

A. Survey.   Give yourself one minute to survey the following excerpt, noting: (1) the titles and subtitles, (2) words in italics or boldface print, and (3) any graphs or tables. If you have extra time, begin reading the first paragraph or two. When your time is up, answer the questions that follow without looking back at the excerpt.

Racial and Ethnic Inequality and Conflict

Race

(1) A **race** is a human group with some observable, common biological features. The most prominent of these is skin color, but racial groups also differ in other observable ways such as eyelid shape and the color and texture of hair. They also differ in subtle ways that are not visible, such as blood type. Although race is a biological concept, racial differences are important for intergroup relations solely to the extent that people attach cultural meaning to them (van den Berghe, 1967). Only when people believe that racial identity is associated with other traits such as character, ability, and behavior do racial differences affect human affairs. Historically, racial differences have typically been associated with cultural variances as well, because persons of different races were usually members of different societies. Race, then, has usually been an accurate indicator of who is and who is not a stranger.

(2) Major trouble arises when different racial groups exist within the same society and people still assign cultural meanings to these physical differences. For one thing, members of one racial group usually cannot escape prejudice by "passing" as members of another racial group, although many light-skinned blacks can and do pass as whites. While an Italian could change his name to Robert Davis, join the Presbyterian Church, and deny his true ancestry, people cannot as easily renounce their biology.

(3) This does not mean, however, that racial differences must always produce intergroup conflict. Biological differences may be unchangable, but by themselves they are not important. It is what we *believe* about

---

*From James W. Kalat, *Introduction to Psychology*, 4th ed., p. 14.

Table 14-1   *Primary* Ethnic Ancestry of Americans of European Descent*

	Number (in 1,000S)	Percent of Total Population
German	57,947	23.3
Irish	38,736	15.6
English	32,652	13.1
Italian	14,665	5.9
French	10,321	4.1
Polish	9,366	3.8
Dutch	6,227	2.5
Scotch-Irish	5,618	2.3
Scottish	5,394	2.2
Swedish	4,681	1.9
Norwegian	3,869	1.6
Russian	2,953	1.2

Source: Statistical Abstract of the United States, 1996.
*Making up at least 1 percent of the total U.S. population.

these differences that matters. And what we believe can change. The notion of a society that is color-blind simply refers to a society in which no cultural meanings are attached to human biological variations.

Ethnic Groups

(4) **Ethnic groups** are groups whose cultural heritages differ. We usually reserve the term for different cultural groups within the same society. By themselves, cultural differences are not enough to make a group an ethnic group. The differences must be noticed, and they must both bind a group together and separate it from other groups. As Michael Hechter (1974) put it, an ethnic group exists on the basis of "sentiments which bind individuals into solidarity groups on some cultural basis."

(5) The 1990 census asked Americans their primary ancestry. Table 14-1 shows the distribution of persons who reported a European nation as their ancestry, omitting those making up less than 1 percent of the total population. Germans are the largest ancestry group in the United States, including nearly one American in four. Next largest are the Irish and the English, followed by the Italians and the French (many of the latter came via Canada). However, identifying oneself in terms of ancestry is not the same as maintaining an ethnic identity. Consider the nearly 15 million Americans of Italian ancestry. Some of them can speak Italian, many cannot. Some like Italian food, some do not. Some are Roman Catholic, some are not. But the existence of an Italian American or Italian Canadian ethnic group does not simply depend on such cultural factors. What is important is that some of these people *think of themselves as sharing special bonds*—of history, culture, and kinship—with others of

Italian ancestry. This makes them members of an ethnic group. But persons of Italian ancestry who do not identify themselves with their Italian heritage are not members.

(6) Wsevolod Isajiw (1980) has pointed out that ethnic groups are "involuntary" groups in that people don't decide to join one as they might decide to join a fraternity or sorority. Rather, people are born into an ethnic group. However, unless they live within the confines of a relatively strict caste system, people often make a voluntary choice about *continuing* to belong to an ethnic group. In fact, as noted in Chapter 2, a substantial proportion of North Americans of Italian ancestry are not part of an Italian ethnic group (Alba, 1985). This is hardly limited to persons of Italian ancestry. After careful analysis comparing the 1990 census data with those of 1980, Stanley Lieberson and Mary C. Waters (1993) found a substantial shift away from naming a European ancestry group and a very great increase in the proportions giving their ancestry as "American." They concluded that "If this holds in future decades, it would mean a growing ethnic population of 'unhyphenated whites.'"

Cultural Pluralism

(7) For a long time, people believed that intergroup conflicts in North America would be resolved through *assimilation:* As time passed, a given ethnic group would surrender its distinctive cultural features and disappear into the dominant American or Canadian culture. At that point, people would no longer think of themselves as "ethnic," nor would others continue to do so.

Today many once formidable intergroup conflicts have been resolved in North America. Yet the ethnic groups in question, mostly European, did not disappear. True, their ethnic identity differs from that of their forebears. Typically, they have lost their native language and their bonds with the old country. But their present culture retains some elements of the old—religious affiliation, for example—while integrating a new heritage based on the special experiences of the group in the United States or Canada (Glazer and Moynihan, 1970). The important point is that conflict vanished not because noticeable differences disappeared but because the differences became unimportant. Such conflict resolutions are called *accommodation,* not assimilation. The growth of mutual interests between conflicting groups enables them to emphasize similarities and deemphasize differences.

(8) When intergroup conflict ends through accommodation, the result is ethnic or cultural *pluralism:* the existence of diverse cultures within the same society. That the United States is no longer a Protestant nation but rather a nation of Protestants, Catholics, and Jews, as well as followers of other faiths (plus nonbelievers), demonstrates cultural pluralism.

(9) Obviously, accommodation and assimilation are not the inevitable outcomes of intergroup conflict. Conflict has sometimes been resolved by the *extermination* of the weaker group, as happened with the Jews in Nazi Germany, Catholics in Elizabethan England, Indians in the Caribbean and on the North American frontier, Armenians in Turkey,

and various tribal minorities in black Africa today. Intergroup conflicts have also led to the *expulsion* of the weaker group. For example, Jews have often been expelled from nations, and Europeans were expelled from Japan in the sixteenth century. Following World War II, Pakistan expelled Hindus, India expelled Muslims, and Uganda expelled both Pakistanis and Indians, while Vietnam has driven out several hundred thousand Chinese. Finally, intergroup conflicts have been stabilized by the imposition of a **caste system,** whereby weaker groups are prevented from competing with the stronger, and through *segregation,* whereby a group is inhibited from having contact with others.

(10) The history of the New World contains all of these methods of resolution: Groups have been assimilated, accommodated, exterminated, expelled, and placed in a low-status caste. This variety, plus the persistence of intense intergroup conflicts, makes the United States and Canada extremely important in the study of intergroup relations. North America is a huge natural laboratory for examining the dynamics of such conflicts and useful means for overcoming them.

(11) Such an examination inevitably arouses our emotions. When we examine the history of prejudice and discrimination in North America, we cannot—nor should we—avoid anger and frustration. However, it would be tragic if we let these feelings prevent us from appreciating the extent to which hatred has been overcome, for the erosion of bigotry is also a prominent feature of North American history. The study of this erosion can teach us much about how present problems may be resolved.

(12) In reading the chapter you should also keep in mind that prejudice and discrimination are not peculiar to North America. These problems are as old as human history and exist throughout the modern world.

(13) Table 14-2 helps put the subject of prejudice into a properly international perspective. More than half of South Koreans and nearly half of Indians would not want foreigners living next door. Prejudice against foreigners is relatively high in most nations of eastern Europe. In contrast, few Americans and Canadians object to foreign neighbors. The second column in the table reveals that huge majorities of people in India and Turkey would object to having Jewish neighbors, as would a third in Slovenia, Nigeria, and Bulgaria, and about a quarter in Japan, Romania, Czechoslovakia, and Portugal. Contrast this with only 6 percent in Canada and 5 percent in the United States who say they would not like to have Jewish neighbors. Notice too that in many nations there is considerably more prejudice against Muslims than against Jews—50 percent of Slovakians, 41 percent of Bulgarians, 21 percent of Norwegians, and 20 percent of Germans don't want Muslim neighbors. Canadians (11%) and Americans (14%) also are less willing to live near Muslims than near Jews. To see a similar table on unwillingness to have persons of a different race living next door, see Chapter 19.

(14) These days, efforts to assess prejudice must overcome the reluctance of some respondents to admit their negative feelings about other groups (itself a sign that prejudice its receding). So, sometimes the ques-

Table 14-2   *"On This List of Various Groups of People, Could You Please Indicate Any That You Would* Not *Like To Have as Neighbors."*

Nation	Foreigners (%)	Jews (%)	Muslims (%)
South Korea	53	—	21
India	48	86	31
Slovenia	40	37	38
Czech Republic	34	17	46
Slovak Republic	34	27	50
Bulgaria	34	30	41
Latvia	31	9	26
Romania	30	28	35
Nigeria	28	34	24
Turkey	28	59	—
Hungary	22	10	18
Belgium	21	13	26
Austria	20	11	14
Mexico	**18**	**19**	**19**
Japan	17	28	29
Belarus	17	21	24
Estonia	17	13	21
Germany	17	8	20
Norway	16	9	21
Lithuania	15	18	34
France	13	7	18
Chile	12	16	12
Denmark	12	3	15
Italy	12	11	12
Great Britain	12	7	17
Russia	11	13	15
Portugal	10	19	18
United States	**10**	**5**	**14**
Spain	9	10	12
Sweden	9	6	17
Iceland	8	7	12
Netherlands	8	3	13
Canada	**6**	**6**	**11**
Finland	5	5	6
Ireland	5	6	13
Brazil	4	—	—
Argentina	2	6	6

Source: Prepared by the author from the *World Values Survey, 1990–92.*
Note: — Not asked.

tions are phrased to maximize negative responses. For example, rather than asking people whom they *dis*trust, survey researchers ask how much they trust them. Thus, respondents in the most recent World Values Survey were asked, "I now want to ask you how much you trust various groups of people: Could you tell me how much you trust . . ." It is more acceptable for Americans to say "not very much" when asked this question about Canadians, for example, than to answer how much they distrust their neighbors to the north.

1. The chapter excerpt is broken into three important topics.

   a. true
   b. true

2. The excerpt does not use italics for emphasis.

   a. true
   b. false

3. The excerpt makes use of boldface print.

   a. true
   b. false

4. The first table that appears in the excerpt shows:

   a. various races in the United States
   b. various ethnic ancestors of United States residents
   c. the number of residents at the poverty level in the United States
   d. the number of residents above the poverty level in the United States

5. The second table concerns:

   a. the most popular ethnic groups in the United States
   b. the most popular religions in the United States
   c. which ethnic groups prefer to live next to other ethnic groups
   d. where Jews and Muslims live in the world

---

1. _____

2. _____

3. _____

4. _____

5. _____

_____

80%

(score = # correct × 20)
Find answers on p. 399.

B. Question. Now go back to the excerpt and, from the title, subtitles, and italics, write five questions that this excerpt raises.

1. _____

2. _____

3. _____

4. _____

5. _____

Answers will vary. Find
sample answers on
pp. 399–400.

C. Read and Recite. Begin study-reading from the beginning of the excerpt to the end of paragraph 6, underlining main ideas and major

---

*From Rodney Stark. *Sociology,* 7th ed., pp. 274–8.

details. Then close the book and recite, using the indenting format. Finally, apply the Cornell note-taking system to your notes and study the material.

Answers will vary. Find sample outline on p. 400.

Now study the rest of the excerpt, entitled "Cultural Pluralism," and follow the same procedures as those you used to read and recite the first half of the excerpt.

Answers will vary. Find sample outline on p. 401.

Now look back at your outlines. From them, make up a concept map that ties all the information together.

D. Review.   Now study your underlinings, outline, and concept map. When you think you have learned the most important points of the excerpt, answer the following questions without looking back.

Examination: Race, Ethnic Groups, and Cultural Pluralism

Directions: Choose the letter that correctly answers the following ten questions. Place all of your answers in the answer box.

1. What is the most prominent racial feature?

   a. hair
   b. shape of eyelids
   c. physical size
   d. skin

2. A color-blind society is one in which:

   a. race is seen as an important factor
   b. ethnic identity is seen as an important factor
   c. biology is seen as an important factor
   d. importance is not placed on biological differences

3. Ethnic groups tend to:

   a. join people and separate out others
   b. only join people
   c. only separate out other people
   d. dissolve very easily

4. The largest ancestry group in the United States is the:

   a. British
   b. Germans
   c. Irish
   d. Italians

5. The important factor in one's identificaiton with an ethnic group is:

   a. a common language
   b. a common food
   c. a common religion
   d. an individual's belief that he has much in common with this ethnic group

6. It has been shown that people:

   a. cannot get out of the ethnic group they are born into
   b. often choose to stay or leave the ethnic group they are born into
   c. dislike admitting to being part of an ethnic group
   d. tend to give a strong ethnic identity to their children

7. Pluralism occurs when:

   a. ethnic groups lose their identity
   b. ethnic groups are in conflict
   c. ethnic groups settle their conflict
   d. ethnic groups accept one common religion

8. An example of cultural pluralism occurred when the United States accepted the Protestant faith as its dominant religion.

   a. true
   b. false

9. The caste system:

   a. allows for cultural pluralism
   b. prevents weaker groups from amassing power
   c. is an example of accommodation
   d. none of these

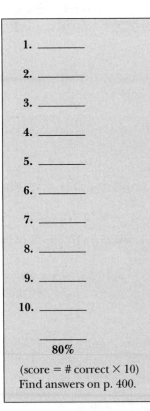

1. _____

2. _____

3. _____

4. _____

5. _____

6. _____

7. _____

8. _____

9. _____

10. _____

_____
80%

(score = # correct × 10)
Find answers on p. 400.

10. North America is an interesting area for sociologists to study because:

    a. many ethnic groups have settled there

    b. so few cultures seem to have ethnic conflicts there

    c. Canada settles its ethnic problems differently than does the United States

    d. there are few non-Christians living there

***Exercise 14.4
Writing a Paragraph
Using SQ3R***

Review one more time your text markings, study notes, and concept map for the textbook excerpt in Exercise 14.3. When you can remember the important points in this excerpt, close your book, put away your notes, and answer the following essay question.

> *Essay Question:* In an organized paragraph, discuss three ways that an ethnic group can become part of or be separated from another group. Begin with a topic sentence.
>
>   Use the following outline to jot down the important points you want to make in your paragraph.

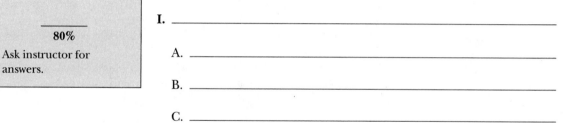

I. _____

    A. _____

    B. _____

    C. _____

In the shaded box:

80%

Ask instructor for answers.

***Follow-up on
Chapter 14***

Now that you have studied this introduction and completed the exercises, it may be helpful to see how your abilities in using the SQ3R study system have improved. You may want to review the introduction and the exercises you completed. Then answer the following questions either individually or in small groups:

On the SQ3R Study System

1. What about the SQ3R system is effective in your study-reading?

2. What about the SQ3R system is still difficult for you to apply to your textbook reading?

3. Are you now able to underline and comment on your textbook chapters effectively? What about underlining and marking is still difficult for you?

4. What about textbook reading is still difficult for you?

 **Internet Activity**

Use the Internet to do more research on study-reading textbooks. Break up into groups of four or five to answer the following questions using the following Wadsworth Web site; then return to your groups with your information:

How to Read Your Textbook More Efficiently
http://www.psych-web.com

If you cannot access this Web site, research the Internet to find information on textbook reading to answer these questions:

1. What new information on reading textbooks did you find?
2. Does any of this information differ from what you learned in the introduction to this chapter on SQ3R?
3. Describe how you located the information you selected.

CHAPTER 15

Suggestions for Taking Objective Tests

In this chapter, you will learn about:

- Objective tests
- How to prepare for objective tests: multiple choice, true–false, and matching

So far you have learned to read your textbook critically, take notes from your textbook and from lectures and discussions, and use memory aids when you cannot remember information. You use all of these skills when you prepare for an exam. In most courses, how well you do on exams determines how well you do in the course.

You will be taking two kinds of exams: objective and essay. Each type of exam requires a different set of practices. This chapter looks at objective tests.

What Are Objective Tests?

For objective tests, you often need to have learned many details and understood the basic concepts. You will have little or no writing to do, because objective exams are often machine-scored. Usually they require you to mark the correct response from among two to five choices on the answer sheet. Objective tests typically follow three formats: multiple choice, true–false, and matching. You will study each type later in this introduction.

How Do You Prepare for Objective Tests?

If your economics instructor announces that you will be taking a 100-question multiple-choice exam the following week, how should you study for it? Cramming the night before, of course, goes against the principle of learning effectively through spaced intervals. Preparing for a 100-question exam should take you three to five days.

If this period, you should first review your textbook markings. You should be looking for highlighted main ideas and supporting details. You should then read your marginal comments, which often give insights not stated in the textbook. If you come upon any new insights or want to underline additional information, do so at this time.

Third, review your study-reading notes. These notes will likely repeat much of what you studied in your textbook, but reading the same information from a new perspective will provide an additional context for you to remember the material. Fourth, review your lecture and discussion notes, underlining key points and making marginal comments, as you did in your textbook. Study especially carefully those parts of your notes that are not mentioned in your textbook.

You may choose to make a study sheet that combines lecture, discussion, and study notes. After you have reviewed your lecture and discussion notes and your study notes, you may find that the information you have read and the information you have heard is similar, slightly different, or substantially different. Also, you may find that one concept in your textbook is not mentioned at all in any lecture or discussion, or vice-versa. It is effective to jot down the key term or concept in the left-hand column, then in the middle column to write a summary of your reading notes, and in the right-hand column a summary of your lecture notes that pertain to that term or concept. As you complete this sheet, you will be able to see how much and what kind of information you have learned from each source. You will also be able to determine where you know a lot about a particular concept or term and where your knowledge is incomplete. Look at how Figure 15-1 combines textbook and lecture information on the issue of allergies, from an introductory biology class.

As you study your lecture and study notes, you will come across definitions that you need to remember. Put these terms on 3 × 5 cards, with the term on the blank side of the card and the definition on the lined side. Whenever it is appropriate, make a note after your definition showing how one term is similar to or different from another that you have studied. The night before the exam, study these cards carefully. Divide your cards into two piles as you study—those terms that you know and those that you don't. By the end of the night, you need to have all of your cards in the "I know" pile. Your cards should look like the one in Figure 15-2, which defines "net national product." Some students prefer to write these definitions on a sheet, with the term on the left side of the page and the definition to the right, as in the following list of economic terms:

Term	Explanation
net national product (NNP)	gross national product without depreciation
gross national product (GNP)	sum of government purchases, consumption, investments, and exports
national income (NI)	net national product without indirect business taxes

Terms/Concepts	Reading Notes	Lecture Notes
Allergy A. Definition:	Secondary immune response to harmless substance	
B. Characteristics:		1. Response can occur suddenly
	2. Some are born with allergic response	
		3. Caused by emotions, stress, weather changes
	4. Can be life-threatening	
		5. Wasp or bee venom can be fatal
C. Ways to cure:	1. Antigen: antibody to allergy	
		2. Larger doses administered over time

Figure 15.1 *Study sheet combining lecture, discussion, and study notes. (Adapted from Walter Pauk,* How to Study in College, *6th ed. [Boston: Houghton Mifflin, 1997], pp. 279–280.)*

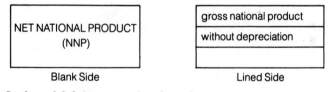

Blank Side   Lined Side

Figure 15-2 *Study card defining* net national product.

The only problem with such a study sheet is that you cannot verify that you have learned the term, as you can with the cards. On your sheet, you cannot separate the "I knows" from the "I don't knows."

You may also want to create more elaborate cards called *visual cards.* They are similar to the 3 × 5 cards you studied previously, but on the back they also present a visual explanation of the concept or word. As you have learned, visualizing is another powerful way to learn new material, because it engages the visual centers of the brain. Look at how the soil layers in an environmental studies course are named, defined, and visually portrayed in the visual card in Figure 15-3.

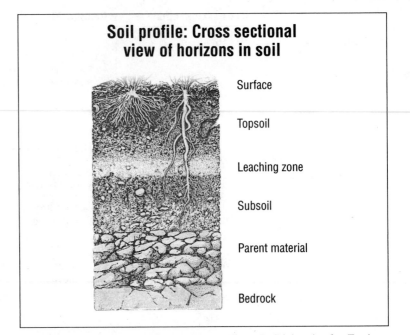

Figure 15-3 *Visual Card: Soil profile. (Adapted from G. Tyler, Jr.,* Living in the Environment, *7th ed. [Belmont, Calif.: Wadsworth, 1998], p. 311.)*

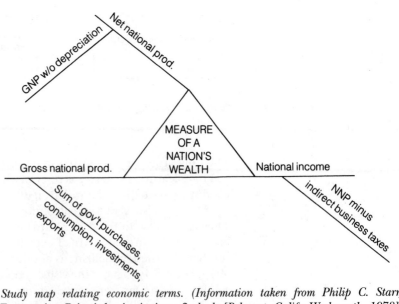

Figure 15-4 *Study map relating economic terms. (Information taken from Philip C. Starr,* Economics: Principles in Action, *2nd ed. [Belmont, Calif.: Wadsworth, 1978], pp. 174–175.)*

Along with note cards, study sheets, and visual cards, you should also design concept maps. Look at how the concept map in Figure 15-4 inter-relates the economic terms previously mentioned. The visual nature of the concept maps may help you remember these terms more easily.

Another very effective way to prepare for an examination is to devise organizational charts. Organizational charts are efficient ways to organize study material with few words and in a small amount of space. In Chapter 6, you learned about the major organizational patterns used to organize material that you read and study. Of these patterns, cause–effect, problem–solution, comparison–contrast, thesis–support, and description work nicely into organizational charts. Look at how the following organizational chart* uses the descriptive pattern to characterize the various types of psychological approaches. See how the chart is clearly divided up into psychological approaches and their descriptions:

Psychological Approach	*Description*
Quantitative	Measures individual differences
Biological	Studies nervous system, genetics, hormones
Cognitive	Studies thought and knowledge
Social	Examines behavior in social context
Clinical	Treats emotional trouble

Similar organizational charts can be created to condense information on the following psychological issues: contrasting behavioral psychology with cognitive psychology, listing the possible causes of schizophrenia, proposed psychological solutions to teenage drug use, and evidence showing that psychotherapy is unsuccessful. Organizational charts are best used when you have finished studying your textbook material and your notes and you want to organize the material into small, easily learned units of information.

Finally, you should carefully read any instructor handouts. These often present important material, and your instructor may even design questions from them. Also, if your instructor has provided you with a syllabus, you may want to review the titles for all the class meetings to see how the topics relate to each other. If the syllabus does not have titles, review the titles that you have given the lectures and discussions.

If you have the time, it is often helpful at this point to condense all that you have reviewed: lecture and discussion notes, study notes, lecture and study notes sheets, cards, and concept maps. You should try to place all of the most important information on just one sheet that follows the Cornell note-taking system, with questions on the left and responses on the right. Walter Pauk refers to these sheets as *advanced summary sheets*

---

*James W. Kalat, *Introduction to Psychology*, 3rd ed. (Belmont, Calif.: Wadsworth, 1993), p. 14.

Memory

1. <u>Key terms</u>
   A. Ebbinghaus approach

   B. Information processing
      model

Testing memory with nonsense syllables	
First stored as short-term memories, later processed as long-term memories	

2. <u>Important questions</u>
   A. What are the characteristics
      of memory capacity?
   B. What happens when you
      forget?
   C. What are the various kinds
      of memory?

   Short term: 7 items
   Long term: large, not easily measured
   Caused by interference from similar
   items and decay over time
   Working, reference, semantic,
   episodic

3. <u>Possible essay question</u>
   What are the ways to ensure
   long-term memory?

   1. To regard something as important
      or interesting
   2. To relate material to other,
      familiar material
   3. To form cues that link memory to
      when we first learned it

Figure 15-5   *Advanced summary sheet on the subject of memory.*

(*How to Study in College*, 6th ed., p. 319). This sheet will require that you select the most important pieces of information to focus on. You will be reflecting on all of the material you have studied and evaluating what is most important and what is less important. Look at how the advanced summary sheet in Figure 15-5 is used to condense and evaluate study material on a memory unit in a psychology course.

The night before the exam, concentrate on concepts that emerge from this advanced study sheet. Never cram for details the night before an exam.

How to Answer Multiple-Choice Questions

Multiple-choice questions are the most commony used objective questions. In the multiple-choice format, a question or statement is posed; this section is called the *stem*. Three to five choices follow that either answer the question or complete the statement. It is up to you to eliminate the incorrect choices and find the correct one. Look at the following multiple-choice question on Sigmund Freud:

stem   1. According to Freud, the three parts of human consciousness are

choices
   a. the ego, the id, and the libido
   b. the id, the alterego, and the ego
   c. the id, the ego, and the superego
   d. the child, the adult, and the parent

If you know something about Freudian psychology, you know that the correct answer is c. You either write c on your answer sheet or darken c on your answer grid.

Hints on Taking Multiple-Choice Exams

1. Read the stem with each choice as if it were a separate true-false statement. (In the previous example you would have read, "According to Freud, the three parts of the human consciousness are the ego, the id, and the libido.") Then determine whether this statement is true or false.

2. If you determine the statement to be false, draw a line through it (if your instructor allows you to mark on the exam), as in the following:

   1. According to Freud, the three parts of the human consciousness are

      a. ~~the ego, the id, and the libido~~

   By crossing out, you eliminate choices. You also save yourself time by preventing your eyes from returning to incorrect choices.

3. Continue to eliminate incorrect choices until you find the correct answer. In some difficult questions, two choices may appear correct to you. If this happens, reread the stem to pick up any shades of meaning in the words; then reconsider the two choices. Look at the following question on short-term memory, from which two choices have already been eliminated:

   2. The best example of the use of short-term memory is

      a. reciting key points in reading material
      b. repeating a phone number just told to you
      c. ~~understanding what categorization means and using this information on an essay exam~~
      d. ~~remembering the name of a friend whom you have not seen for eight years~~

   You can eliminate c and d, because both are examples of information that has been in long-term memory for a long time. Both a and b, however, refer to recently learned information. In rereading the stem, note that the question is asking for the *best* example of short-term memory. Reciting helps put information into long-term memory, so b is the best answer. You need to use your best skills in logic and critical reading when you come upon two choices that both seem correct.

4. Question choices that include absolute terms of qualification, such as "always," "never," and "only." Choices using these terms are frequently incorrect because they need to be true in every case, and

few statements are always true. Look at the following question on categorization:

> 3. Which statement best describes categorization?
>
>   a. Categorization and association are never both used to learn new information.
>   b. Categorization is always used to learn disorganized information.
>   c. Categorization is an unsuccessful learning technique.
>   d. Categorization is an effective learning technique used by students in several disciplines to learn new material.

You would be correct in omitting both a and b as correct answers, because the qualifiers "never" and "always" insist that these statements be true in every case. If you can think of one exception for each choice, you can eliminate that choice. You are then left with c and d. Knowing that categorization is a basic learning principle, you would choose d as the correct answer.

5. Look for choices that give complete information. Although incomplete answers may not be false, they do not qualify as acceptable choices. Study this question on rehearsal:

> 4. Which statement gives the best definition of rehearsal?
>
>   a. Rehearsal is a learning process involving rereading.
>   b. Rehearsal is a learning process involving rewriting.
>   c. Rehearsal is a learning process that helps put information into long-term memory.
>   d. Rehearsal is a learning process that may use all of the senses to place information into long-term memory.

Although choices a, b, and c are all partially correct, choice d is like the main idea for the three preceding choices, so it is the best choice.

6. Read the stem carefully for the terms "not," "except," and "but." These words completely change the meaning of the question. If you skip over these terms, you may know the answer, yet still choose incorrectly. Consider the following question on rehearsal:

> 5. As a learning process, rehearsal includes all of the following activities except
>
>   a. rereading
>   b. reciting
>   c. discussing
>   d. reading

Note how the word "except" reverses the question, asking you to choose the activity that does not involve rehearsal. Choice d is that activity. If you had overlooked "except," you could have chosen a, b, or c—all acceptable rehearsal activities.

7. Be careful to read all of the choices, especially those that say "all of these," "both a and b," or "none of these." Instructors who carefully design multiple-choice questions often make "all of these" or "both a and b" correct choices. "None of these" frequently serves as a filler choice, when the test maker has run out of interesting choices. Look at the following question on neural traces and see how the option "both a and b" is thoughtfully designed as the correct choice:

6. A neural trace is

   a. a mark on the cerebrum
   b. also called a memory groove
   c. only induced by drugs
   d. both a and b

Had you not read all of the choices, you could have marked a as the correct choice.

8. With multiple-choice questions, make educated guesses. If you can eliminate two of the four choices, you have a 50 percent chance of choosing the correct answer. Be sure that your instructor or the test does not penalize you for guessing. Some standardized tests do. Even if there is a guessing penalty, if you have narrowed your choices down to two, make an educated guess. If you cannot eliminate two or more of the choices, don't spend too much time on that particular question. If there is no guessing penalty, make your choice quickly and move on to the next question. If there is a guessing penalty and you cannot narrow your choices down to two, leave that answer blank.

Many instructors criticize multiple-choice exams, saying that the best indicator of what a student knows is an essay exam. Although this is a valid point, multiple-choice questions are the most frequently used type of objective question on standardized tests. You will be taking such tests in your college career, so you need to have an efficient set of practices for taking them.

You may now want to complete Exercise 15.1 on page 319.

How to Answer True–False Questions

True–false questions are also popular on objective exams. Unlike multiple-choice questions, which may have up to five choices, true–false questions have only two. Your chance of being correct is always 50 percent. Instructors emphasize details when they design true–false questions; so when you study for a true–false test, you need to look carefully at the details.

Hints on Taking True–False Exams

1. For a statement to be true, each part must be true. One detail in the statement can make the entire statement false. When you read a true–false statement, look for the following: the "who," the "what," the "why," the "when," the "where," and the "how much." The answer to each of these questions must be correct for you to mark the entire statement true. Look at the following true–false question on Jean Piaget, and see if it correctly answers the "who," the "what," and the "when":

> Jean Piaget made some revolutionary discoveries about child behavior during the nineteenth century.

The "who" (Jean Piaget) and the "what" (child behavior) are correct, but the "when" is not. Piaget did his research during the twentieth century.

Study the key parts of this statement on the Los Angeles School District:

> With 48 percent of its 490,000 students Spanish-speaking, the Los Angeles School District continued to search for competent bilingual teachers in 1987.

With this question, the "who," the "what," and the "when" are correct. The Los Angeles School District was concerned with hiring more bilingual teachers in 1987. But the "how many" is incorrect; the correct enrollment for this school district in 1987 was 590,000. Because this one bit of information is incorrect, you must mark the entire question incorrect.

2. Like multiple-choice questions, true–false questions also may use qualifiers such as "never," "always," and "only." These qualifiers frequently make the statements false. On the other hand, less definite qualifiers, like "often," "may," "many," "most," "frequently," and "usually," tend to make the statement true. Read the following true–false statement on association:

> The memory technique of association is always used when you learn a new word.

Although association is successfully used in vocabulary learning, it is not always used. The word "always" makes this statement false. If you can think of one case in which the statement is untrue, then the statement is false. But see how a less inclusive qualifier can make the same statement true:

The memory principle of association is often used when a student learns new words.

The word "often" allows for the statement to have some exceptions. Because of the flexibility that "often" gives this statement, you can mark this statement true.

3. In designing true–false questions, instructors frequently match terms with inappropriate definitions. So in preparing for a true–false test, be sure that you know your definitions and your people. Read this example on categorization:

Categorization involves placing a word in several contexts in order to remember it. Association, not categorization, is the process of placing a word in several contexts.

The test maker consciously exchanged "association" with "categorization." If you did not know the meaning of both words, you may not have chosen the correct answer.

You may now want to complete Exercise 15.2 on page 321.

How to Answer Matching Questions

Of the three kinds of examination questions, matching questions are the hardest to answer correctly by guessing. In answering matching questions, you need to know the information very well. In the matching format, you are given a list of words in one column and a list of explanations of these words in a second column, often to the right of the first list. It is your job to match correctly the word with the explanation.

Hints on Taking Matching Exams

1. Look at both columns before you begin answering. Are there terms in one column and definitions in another? people in one column and descriptions of them in another? people in the left column and quotations in the right column? What pattern do you detect in the following example from learning theory?

1.	neural trace	a.	a process of placing information into several contexts to ensure retention
2.	rehearsal	b.	a process of transferring information from short-term memory to long-term memory
3.	association	c.	a physiological mark on the cerebrum storing a bit of information

In this set, terms are on the left, definitions on the right.

2. With each correct match, cross out the term and the explanation of it (if your instructor does not plan to reuse the test). In this way, you save time by not rereading material that you have already cov-

ered. Look at how crossing out is used for the following matching questions.

__c__	1. ~~neutal trace~~	a. a process of placing information into several contexts to ensure retention
_____	2. rehearsal	b. a process of transferring information from short-term memory to long-term memory
_____	3. association	~~c. a physiological mark on the cerebrum storing a bit of information~~

3. If the information in the right-hand column is lengthy, begin reading in this column first. Read the explanation; then match it with the appropriate term. You save time by not rereading the lengthy explanations.*

You may now want to complete Exercise 15.3 on page 323.

How to Take Objective Tests

Here are some suggestions for taking an objective test:

1. Read over all of the directions carefully. Know what you need to do.

2. Plan your time. If your test has three parts—true–false, multiple-choice, and matching—divide your exam hour into equal time allotments. Check your watch so that you do not stay on any one section of the exam for too long.

3. Read through the questions quickly to determine the difficulty level of the exam.

4. Answer the easiest sections first. Since you have a better chance of getting the easier questions right, do not wait until the end of the hour to answer them.

5. Do not spend too much time on any one question. If you are unsure about an answer, make an educated guess. Then place a mark to the left of the question so that if you have time, you can go back to it.

6. Check your numbering so that the number on your answer sheet corresponds to the number on your exam booklet. Students often place a correct answer on the wrong number of their answer grid and get the question wrong.

7. If possible, leave five to ten minutes at the end of the exam to review your answers. Check for carelessness. Change only those answers you are reasonably sure are incorrect. Do not change a guess; more often the guess is correct and the correction is not.

---

*James Shepherd, *College Study Skills* (Boston: Houghton Mifflin, 1990), p. 247.

Summary

There are three major types of objective tests: multiple-choice, true–false, and matching. Each type of question requires a different set of practices. The multiple-choice question is the most commonly used objective question. With multiple-choice and true–false questions, you can make educated guesses; matching questions, on the other hand, leave little room for guesswork. With matching questions, you need to know names and definitions well.

Multiple-choice questions are frequently used on entrance and professional exams. Thus it is important to develop a successful set of practices for answering them.

Summary Box   *Objective Tests*

What are they?	How do you take them?
Examinations, frequently machine-scored, that test the breadth of your knowledge on a subject Three most common types: multiple-choice, true–false, and matching	Multiple-choice: learn to eliminate incorrect answers; cross them out and consider other choices True–false: look for statements that are absolute; they are frequently false Matching: see how the columns are organized; with each match that you make, cross out the statement in one column and the name or term in the other

Skills Practice

Exercise 15.1
Answering Multiple-
Choice Questions

Read the following text excerpt about sleep stages. Underline important points and make marginal comments. After reading, recite either by taking notes or by making a concept map. When you think you know the material, answer the five multiple-choice questions that follow. Before you answer these questions, you may want to refer to pp. 312–315 in the introduction to review the practices to use when answering multiple-choice questions.

Stages of Sleep

In the mid-1950s, Michel Jouvet, a French scientist, discovered that brain activity and body activity vary from time to time during sleep. While trying to record the very small head movements that a severely brain-damaged cat made while asleep, he found periods in which its brain was relatively active even though its muscles were completely relaxed. Further research indicated that such periods occur not only in brain-damaged cats but also in normal cats (Jouvet, Michel, & Courjon, 1959). Jourvet referred to these periods as *paradoxical sleep.* (A paradox is an apparent self-contradiction.) The paradox is that such sleep is very light in some respects but very deep in other ways. The brain is active, and the body's heart rate, breathing rate, and temperature fluctuate substantially (Parmeggiani, 1982). In these respects paradoxical sleep is very light. And yet most of the muscles, especially the large muscles involved in posture and locomotion, are very relaxed. In these respects paradoxical sleep is deep.

At about the same time that Jouvet discovered paradoxical sleep, American researchers William Dement and Nathaniel Kleitman (1957a, 1957b) observed that in one recurrent stage of human sleep, the sleeper's eyes move rapidly back and forth under the closed lids. They referred to this stage as **rapid eye movement (REM) sleep.** (All other stages of sleep are known as **non-REM,** or **NREM, sleep.**) Almost at once investigators realized that REM sleep is the same as paradoxical sleep. When Dement and Kleitman awakened people during REM sleep, the sleepers usually reported that they had been dreaming. Apparently, the rapid eye movements were external indications of an internal event; for the first time, it became possible to undertake scientific studies of dreaming.

Sleep Cycles During the Night

Sleep researchers have identified four stages of sleep: After we fall asleep, we progress from stage 1 sleep, in which the brain remains fairly active, through stages 2, 3, and 4. Researchers can detect the stages by recording brain waves with electrodes attached to the scalp. A device called an **electroencephalograph,** abbreviated **EEG,** measures and amplifies slight electrical changes on the scalp that reflect patterns of activity in the brain. An awake, alert brain produces an EEG record with many short, choppy waves. In sleep stages 1 through 4, the brain produces an increasing number of long, slow waves. These large waves indicate *decreased* brain activity. They grow larger from one stage to the next because a larger proportion of the active neurons are active at the same time. During wakefulness, by contrast, the neurons are out of synchrony and their activities nearly cancel each other out, rather like a crowd of people talking at the same time.

After we have reached stage 4 of sleep, we gradually move back through stages 3 and 2 to stage 1 again. A normal young adult cycles from stage 1 to stage 4 and back to stage 1 again in about 90 to 100 minutes. Then he or she repeats the sequence, again and again, all through the night.

During the first part of the night, stages 3 and 4 predominate. Later in the night, the duration of stages 1 and 2 increases. Except for the first occurrence of stage 1 (when the person is just entering sleep), REM periods replace most of the stage 1 periods.*

---

*James W. Kalat, *Introduction to Psychology,* 4th ed., pp. 188–189.

Directions: Choose the correct letter to answer the following questions. Place all answers in the answer box.

1. Paradoxical sleep is a stage in which

    a. the brain is active
    b. the muscles are relaxed
    c. both a and b
    d. neither a nor b

2. REM stands for

    a. roving eye movement
    b. rapid eye movement
    c. relaxed eye movement
    d. relaxed eye muscle

3. How many stages of sleep are there?

    a. two
    b. three
    c. four
    d. five

4. For humans, the sleep cycle lasts for:

    a. 60–80 minutes
    b. 90–100 minutes
    c. 100–120 minutes
    d. 140–160 minutes

5. REM seems to replace which sleep stage(s)?

    a. 1
    b. 1 and 2
    c. 2 and 3
    d. 2, 3, and 4

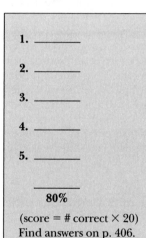

1. _____

2. _____

3. _____

4. _____

5. _____

80%

(score = # correct × 20)
Find answers on p. 406.

Exercise 15.2
Answering True–
False Questions

Read the following textbook excerpt on the stages of sleep and dreaming, continuing the discussion of sleep in Exercise 15.1. Underline the important points and make marginal comments. After reading, recite either by outlining or by making a concept map. When you think you have learned the information, answer the five true–false questions that follow. You may want to refer to pp. 315–317 of the introduction to review the practices to use when answering true–false questions. Remember that true–false questions often test your knowledge of details.

Sleep Stages and Dreaming

Dement's early research indicated that people who were awakened during REM sleep usually reported they had been dreaming but that people who were awakened during any other period seldom reported dreaming. So, for a time, REM sleep was thought to be almost synonymous with dreaming. However, later studies found a fair amount of dreaming during non-REM sleep as well. Non-REM dreams, however, are less vivid, less visual, less bizarre, and less likely to be experienced as something really happening. We can describe these experiences as dreams if we wish, or we can simply classify them as thoughts.

The link between REM sleep and highly vivid dreams enabled sleep investigators to determine with fair accuracy whether or not someone was dreaming. Scientific progress frequently depends on an improved way of measuring something; in this case, a method of measuring dreaming enabled researchers to answer some basic questions.

For example, does everyone dream? People who claim they do not dream have been taken into the laboratory so that researchers could examine brain waves and eye movements. The people who claimed not to dream had normal periods of REM sleep. If awakened during one of these periods, they reported dreams (to their own surprise). Apparently, these people dream as much as anyone else; they simply forget their dreams faster.

Another question: How long do dreams last? Before the discovery of REM sleep, this was an unanswerable question; now, suddenly, researchers had a method to answer it. William Dement and Edward Wolpert (1958) awakened people after REM periods of various durations and asked them to describe their dreams, if any. A person awakened after 1 minute of REM sleep usually would tell a brief story; a person awakened after 5 minutes of REM sleep usually would tell a story about 5 times as long, and so on. Evidently, dreams take place in "real time." That is, a dream is not over in a split second; if it seemed to last several minutes, it probably did.*

Directions: Read the following statements. Write A for true and B for false. Place all answers in the answer box.

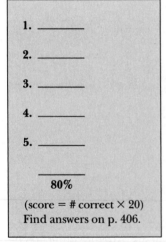

1. _____

2. _____

3. _____

4. _____

5. _____

_____
80%
(score = # correct × 20)
Find answers on p. 406.

1. Dreaming only occurs during REM sleep.
2. It has been shown in the laboratory that everyone does not dream.
3. People who claim that they do not dream do not have REM sleep patterns.
4. A one-minute dream in real time seems to last an hour in dream time.
5. Research shows that dreams do not take place in real time.

Exercise 15.3
Answering Matching
Questions

Read the following excerpt, which defines *insomnia*. Underline important points and make marginal comments. After reading, recite either by outline or by making a concept map. When you think you know the

---

*James W. Kalat, *Introduction to Psychology*, 4th ed., pp. 189–191.

material answer the five matching questions that follow. You may want to refer to pp. 317–318 of the introduction to review the practice to use when answering matching questions.

Insomnia

The term **insomnia** literally means "lack of sleep." However, we cannot usefully define insomnia in terms of the number of hours of sleep. Some people feel well rested after 5 or 6 hours of sleep per night; others feel poorly rested after 8 or 9. Furthermore, many people who seek help for their insomnia greatly underestimate how much they sleep. Some of the insomniacs who have been studied in sleep laboratories get to sleep almost as fast as other people and accumulate almost a normal amount of sleep per night. However, when they are awakened, even from stage 4 sleep, they claim that they were not asleep! Evidently they are getting many hours of sleep without feeling rested. Many of these same people report feeling "much better rested" after a night when they took sleeping pills, even though the sleeping pills increased their total sleep time by only about half an hour (Mendelson, 1990). In short, insomnia is a subjective condition. *A complaint of insomnia indicates that the person feels poorly rested at the end of the night.* By this definition, about one third of all adults have occasional insomnia and about one tenth have serious or chronic insomnia (Lilie & Rosenberg, 1990).

It is convenient to distinguish three main types of insomnia: People with onset insomnia have trouble falling asleep. Those with termination insomnia awaken early and cannot get back to sleep. Those with *maintenance insomnia* awaken frequently during the night, though they get back to sleep each time. In many cases, onset insomnia and termination insomnia are related to a circadian rhythm that is out of synchrony with the outside world. At 11:00 P.M. a person with onset insomnia may feel as if it were still only 6:00 P.M. At 2:00 A.M. a person with termination insomnia may already feel as if it were 7:00 A.M. In such cases, therapy is a matter of trying to readjust the circadian rhythms so that the person can feel sleepy and wakeful at the normal times.

In addition to an out-of-synch circadian rhythm, we can identify many other causes of insomnia (Kales & Kales, 1984). People sometimes have trouble sleeping because of noise, worries, uncomfortable temperatures, use of various drugs including alcohol, indigestion, and miscellaneous other problems. Overuse of tranquilizers can also become a cause of insomnia. That statement may be surprising, because people often take tranquilizers as a way of *relieving* insomnia. Tranquilizers do induce sleep and help people get a restful sleep. The problem is, no pill exerts its effects for exactly the period of time that someone wanted to sleep. Some tranquilizers produce brief effects that wear off before morning, so the person awakens early (Kales, Soldatos, Bixler, & Kales, 1983). Others have effects that last too long, so the person remains sleepy for part of the next day.

An additional problem with tranquilizers is that a consistent user may come to depend on them to get to sleep (Kales, Scharf, & Kales, 1978). When such a person tries to sleep without taking a pill, he or she

<table>
<tr><td>

1. _____

2. _____

3. _____

4. _____

_____
75%
(score = # correct × 25)
Find answers on p. 406.

</td></tr>
</table>

may experience more severe insomnia than the original insomnia the pill was supposed to relieve.*

Directions: Match a letter from column B with the appropriate number in column A. Place all answers in the answer box.

Column A	Column B
1. insomnia	a. trouble falling asleep
2. onset insomnia	b. awakens frequently during the night
3. termination insomnia	c. awakens early and cannot get back to sleep
4. maintenance insomnia	d. lack of sleep

Follow-up on Chapter 15

Now that you have studied this introduction and completed the exercises, it may be helpful to see how your abilities in taking objective tests have improved. You may want to review both the introduction and the exercises. Then answer the following questions either individually or in small groups.

On Taking Objective Tests

1. Of the three types of objective questions—multiple-choice, true–false, and matching—which is the easiest for you to answer?

2. Of these three types of objective questions, which is the hardest for you to answer? Why?

3. Which test-taking suggestions that you have learned in this chapter are you now successfully applying to the tests you are currently taking?

4. What information about objective tests do you still need to understand better?

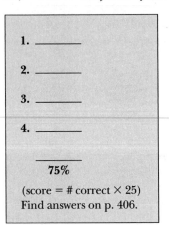 **Internet Activity**

Do some research on the Internet to further your understanding of objective tests. This assignment is best completed in groups of four or five. Access the following Web site to see what new information you can gather. As you research this Web site, answer the following questions. Then return to your group with your information.

University of California, Berkeley, Student Learning Center
http://128.32.89.153/CalRENHP.html

---

*James W. Kalat, *Introduction to Psychology,* 4th ed. (Pacific Grove, Calif.: Brooks/Cole, 1996), p. 195.

If you cannot access this Web site, research the Internet to find information on taking objective tests to answer these questions:

1. What new information on the multiple-choice test did you gather?
2. What new information on the true–false test did you gather?
3. What new information on the matching test did you gather?
4. Describe the procedures you used to access this Web site.

CHAPTER 16

Suggestions for Taking Essay Exams and Math or Science Tests

In this chapter, you will learn about:

- How to prepare for an essay exam
- The two major kinds of essay questions: the short-answer essay question and the extended essay question
- How to prepare for a math or science test
- How to take a math or science test

Essay exams are different in many ways from objective tests. Unlike objective tests, which ask you to remember many details, essay exams make you choose main ideas and major details from a large body of material and then form an organized response. When you are writing an essay question, you need to recall main ideas and major details quickly. Problem-solving questions in math and the sciences are similar to essay questions. The major difference is that instead of using words, you are using numbers and symbols. In both an essay exam and a math or science problem, you need to use skills in logic and organization. Unlike objective exams, the best essay and math or science exams ask you to generate important information yourself.

How to Prepare for an Essay Exam

When preparing for an essay exam, you again need to review your textbook underlinings, textbook comments, study-reading notes, lecture and discussion notes, organizational charts, and concept maps. (See the section in Chapter 15 titled "How to Prepare for Objective Tests.") Instead of trying to remember many details, as you would in preparing for an objective test, for an essay exam you need to concentrate on significant main ideas and details of support. Your job is to reduce a great deal of information into its significant points. This may not be easy for you at first.

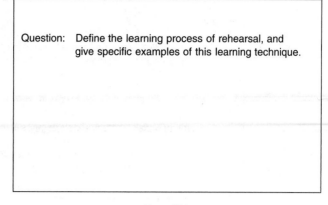

Question: Define the learning process of rehearsal, and
            give specific examples of this learning technique.

Front Side

Figure 16-1   *Front of a study card, with an essay question.*

If your instructor has provided you in advance with several possible essay topics, find information in your study material to answer them. If your instructor does not provide you with questions, check to see whether there are discussion questions at the end of your textbook chapters. Find the ones that you think are most important, and then locate information that would best address each question. As you study, you should formulate your own essay questions from topics that you think are important. You can often design your own essay questions from the divisions and subdivisions of your textbook chapters or from the lecture and discussion titles in your syllabus or lecture notes.

After you have reviewed your notes and underlinings, write the three or four most likely essay topics on a separate sheet of paper or on the blank side of 5 × 8 note cards. These sheets and cards are similar to those mentioned in Chapter 15 for preparing for an objective exam. On the back side of the paper or the lined side of the card, answer the question, giving pertinent main ideas and major details. Use a numeral–letter or indenting format. Don't write this information in paragraph form at this time. Save your more thorough sentence writing for the essay exam itself. The cards or sheets of paper should look something like what is shown in Figures 16-1 and 16-2.

Once you have completed the study sheets or cards, turn each over to the question side to see if you can orally respond to the question. See if you can quickly remember the main idea and the necessary supporting details. If it is hard for you to remember the supporting details, use a memory aid. "RWD" is an abbreviation that you could design to remember "rereading, writing, and discussion"—the details for the essay question in Figure 16-1. Review these cards or sheets until you can respond promptly to each question. A key to doing well on an essay exam is being able to recall main ideas and accurate details with ease.

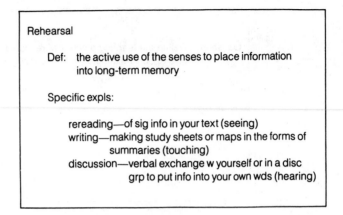

Back Side

Figure 16-2   *Back of a study card, answering the question.*

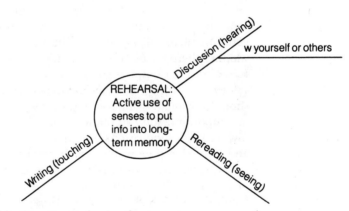

Figure 16-3   *Concept map showing the answer to an essay question.*

Concept maps are also good tools to use when you study for essay tests. Figure 16-3 shows how the information on rehearsal can be neatly arranged into a concept map. If you had several terms to learn associated with rehearsal, you could effectively learn them all in an organizational chart.

How to Read an Essay Question

Having studied well for your essay test, you are now ready for the questions. Understanding the intent of the question is as important as being prepared for the exam. Study the following key terms, which are commonly used in essay questions, and learn how they are used.

Words That Ask for Retelling of Material

summarize, survey, list, outline

If these words appear in your question, you are being asked to give only the important points. You should not concentrate on many details or on analyzing any one point in depth.

Sample question: List the major stages in the development of the human fetus.

To answer this question well, you should list each step in the fetal development of the child. You should then briefly comment on each stage, but you do not need to discuss the relationship of one stage to another or the importance of any of these stages.

Words That Ask You to Make Inferences

discuss, explain

These are two of the most frequently used words in essay questions. They ask you to give the "why" of an argument. You must carefully choose those details that clarify your main idea.

Sample question: Discuss four reasons for the entry of the United States into World War II.

In this question, you need to choose those examples that account for the United States's entry into World War II. These reasons are often your own, so be sure to include terms of qualification when you are presenting opinions—words like *may, might, likely, it is suggested,* and so on. See pp. 162–163 for a more thorough list of qualifiers.

A Word That Asks You to Define

define

Define usually asks you for a short answer, no more than three or four sentences. You are not asked to analyze, just to give the term's major characteristics. Just as a dictionary definition is concise, so should your response be concise.

Sample question: Define prejudice as used in sociology.

Here you are being asked to explain prejudice from a sociological perspective. You are not being asked to list its various meanings or to explain its history. Your focus should be on how prejudice relates to sociology.

Words Showing Similarities and Differences

compare, contrast

Compare means to show both similarities and differences. To avoid confusion, some instructors use the phrase "compare and contrast." *Contrast* used singly means to show differences. With contrast questions, you are treating opposite sets of information, so use transitions of contrast: *unlike, conversely,* and so on. With strict comparison questions, you are treating similar sets of information; here, use transitions of similarity, such as *likewise, similarly,* and so on. See p. 108 for a more thorough list of transitions of comparison and contrast.

> *Sample question:* Compare and contrast the attitudes of Presidents Clinton and Bush regarding social welfare programs.

In this question, you need to cite programs and legislation from both administrations that show similarities and differences.

Words That Ask You to Critique

analyze, examine, evaluate

Questions using these words are asking you to express a point of view. When you evaluate, you must even judge the merit of your topic. The details you choose are important because they present the bulk of your argument. Critique words are often used in essay questions in the humanities—literature, art, music, film—where you are asked to judge the value of a poem, a painting, or a film. These questions can be difficult because you are being asked to do more than summarize.

> *Sample question:* Analyze the major characters in Dickens' *Great Expectations.* Are these characters successful?

This question is asking you to choose characters in the novel whose actions and traits make them believable. Ultimately, you are judging the success of Dickens' characters. So you need to choose carefully those details that demonstrate Dickens' success or failure in rendering character.

A Word That Asks You to Take a Stand

defend

Defend is often used in speech topics or in essay questions in political science or history. With defend questions, you take a definite stand, presenting only evidence that supports this position. In this sense, defend questions ask you to ignore evidence that goes against your position.

> *Sample question:* Defend the premise that nuclear arms will one day lead to nuclear holocaust.

In answering this question, you should discuss only how nuclear arms are a threat to peace. If you suggested that nuclear arms are a deterrent to war, you would weaken your argument.

A Word That Shows Connections

trace

Trace is mainly used in history essay questions where you are asked to discuss a series of events and show their relationship to one other. Again, you need to be selective in choosing details that support the connections you see.

> *Sample question:* Trace the development of labor unions in the United States from 1900 to the present.

In this question, you need to choose the important figures and events that led to the formation of unions in the United States; you also need to show how events or individuals influenced other events or individuals.

A Word That Asks You to Relate a Concept to a Personal Experience or to a Specific Situation

apply

In questions that ask you to apply what you know, you need to show that you understand the concept well by seeing it through a particular experience or event. Application questions are often asked in composition, literature, and psychology courses.

> *Sample Question:* Apply the concept of the tragic hero to Willy Loman in Arthur Miller's *Death of a Salesman*.

Here you need to show that you understand what a tragic hero is in general terms, then relate this general understanding to specific events in the character development of Willy Loman. In answering application questions, you can show how the event conforms well or does not conform well to the concept.

Words That Ask for Important Information

significant, critical, key, important, major

In most subjects, instructors use these words to guide you in presenting only meaningful evidence. These terms subtly ask you to distinguish the significant from the insignificant. An instructor using these words will often criticize your essay if you fail to choose the important evidence.

> *Sample question:* Discuss three key factors that led to the Great Depression in the United States.

Your instructor may have discussed ten factors, but you are asked to discuss only three. Here, you need to review the ten factors to determine which three have priority. This is difficult to do because you are both summarizing and evaluating information.

Kinds of Essay Questions

Three basic types of essay questions are used on exams: those that ask for a short answer, the short essay, and the extended essay. Each type requires a different set of practices.

The Short-Answer Question. In the short-answer question, you are asked to respond in a phrase, a sentence, or several sentences. In a one-hour exam, you can expect to answer up to twenty short-answer questions. The key to doing well is to be as concise and specific as you can. In biology and geology courses using short-answer questions, instructors are often looking for the breadth and accuracy of your knowledge, not your writing style. Ask your instructor whether you need to answer the short-answer questions in sentences. If the answer is no, answer in phrases; you will be able to write more during the hour. In contrast, in an English course your instructor will probably want you to answer the short-answer questions in complete sentences that are correctly punctuated.

Look at the following short-answer question and study the response, which received full credit.

Question: Name and identify the three branches of the federal government.

Answer:

1. legislative: makes laws; made up of House and Senate
2. executive: sees that laws are carried out; President
3. judicial: sees that laws are enforced; Supreme Court and other federal courts

This student has presented accurate information in an organized way. Beside each government branch, the student describes the activity, then names the person or agency responsible.

Now see how this same question is answered poorly.

Question: Name and identify the three branches of the federal government.

Answer:

1. legislative: works on laws; made up of two houses
2. executive: the President
3. judicial: courts

This student has not presented the information in an organized way or with enough detail. Although the student names the legislative branch, "works on laws" is vague. With the executive branch, the student names the President but does not describe the function. With the judicial branch, the Supreme Court is not specifically named, nor does the student mention the Court's function.

The Short-Essay Question.   The short-essay question asks you to write an organized paragraph of several sentences. In an hour, you should be able to answer up to five such questions. Your goal when writing the short-essay answer is to present your main idea or thesis right away, and then present accurate details of support. These details must follow logically from your main idea. If you have completed the writing assignments in this book, you are familiar with how a convincing paragraph is put together.

Read the following short-essay question and the response, which received full credit.

Question: Discuss the three major characteristics of human language.

Answer:

Human language has three qualities that distinguish it from animal communication. First, human language uses a limited number of sounds that produce thousands of utterances. Second, human speech is not imitative. The human being can generate a sentence never heard before.

Finally, human language can discuss what is not there. Human beings can discuss the past and future as well as the present.

Do you see how the student directly addresses the question? The main-idea sentence comes first, stating that there are three characteristics of human language. Then the sentences of support discuss these characteristics. The student has used the transitions "first, second, and finally" to direct the reader to these three characteristics.

Now consider this second response, which is both poorly organized and less detailed.

Question: Discuss the three major characteristics of human language.

Answer:

Human language has three qualities. Human language uses few sounds. Also, human language uses sentences. Humans can also discuss what is not there. Philosophers have spent centuries discussing what language is all about.

Note how the main-idea sentence is too general, so the student makes no attempt to distinguish human language from animal language. Note how the second detail sentence, "Also, human language uses sentences," does not discuss how the human being can generate sentences that have never before been uttered. This supporting detail does not directly address the uniqueness of human language. Note how the last sentence, "Philosophers have spent centuries discussing what language is all about," introduces an entirely new topic, so the paragraph loses its focus.

The Extended-Essay Question.   You will often be asked to write on only one topic during a one-hour exam. Obviously, your instructor is expecting you to write more than one paragraph during this hour. In an hour, you should be able to write several organized paragraphs. This type of essay response is known as the extended essay.

In structure, the extended essay resembles the short essay. The main idea of the paragraph becomes the first paragraph, or introduction, of the extended essay. The detail sentences of the paragraph then each become separate paragraphs. Together, these paragraphs are referred to as the *body*. Unlike the short essay, the extended essay has a concluding paragraph, called the *conclusion*, which often summarizes the key points of the essay. Look at Figure 16-4, which shows the structure of the extended essay and states the purpose of its three parts.

The extended essay is difficult to write well at first because you must successfully use several organizational skills. Start by committing the information in Figure 16-4 to memory so that each essay you write has a recognizable introduction, body, and conclusion. Also, begin using transitions to join sentences and to hook one paragraph to another. By using such transitions as *for example* and *to conclude*, you will give additional

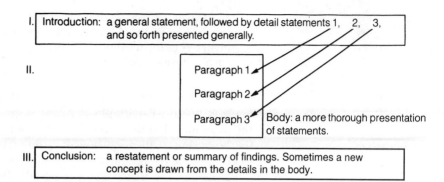

Figure 16-4   *Diagram of an extended essay.*

order to your essay. In Chapter 6, on organizational patterns, there are lists of several transitions that you may want to review and use in your extended essays.

Read the following extended essay question and response. See if you can locate the introduction, the body, and the conclusion, and note how transitions are used.

Question: Discuss the three major functions of religion.

Answer:

(1) Every society has a religion of some sort. Although the beliefs and expressions of religion vary from one culture to another, three basic functions emerge when you study all religions. For one, religion helps clarify the unexplained. Second, religion helps reduce anxiety among its followers. Third, religion helps give order to society.

(2) Every culture has tried through religion to answer such questions as where the universe came from and where we go after death. Western religions explain their origin in the Book of Genesis. In this book, we learn that one God created parts of the universe and the world on separate days. Eastern religions see many gods as creating the universe. Western religions believe that human souls live after death, whereas Eastern religions such as Hinduism believe that human beings are reincarnated into other beings after death.

(3) Prayer seems to be part of all religions. In each culture, prayer seems to relieve anxiety. In many African cultures, tribesmen perform rituals to help crops grow or to cure the sick. Prayer in Western cultures works similarly. Western priests often ask their parishioners to pray for the health of their sick loved ones. In each case, prayer becomes an outlet to relieve anxiety.

(4) Finally, religion has an important ordering effect on society. Religious services almost always accompany births, baptisms, marriages, and deaths. And the faithful are invited to witness these events. Such group activities give to the members of the religion a sense of community. Just think of how many wars have been fought over religious beliefs, and you will realize how closely tied religion is to social structure.

(5) In conclusion, it is clear that religion still plays an important role in human life. Through the ages religion has helped explain the mysteries of the universe, comforted people in their grief, and given to each culture a set of social rules.

Note how paragraph 1 presents the three issues that the essay intends to discuss. Paragraphs 2, 3, and 4 give the necessary support for the main idea that religion is found in every society. Each paragraph in the body centers its discussion on a separate function of religion. Nowhere in these paragraphs does the discussion lose its focus.

Note also the transitions that signal different sections of the essay: "for one," "second," and "third" in paragraph 1, and "in conclusion" in paragraph 5. Finally, note that the conclusion summarizes the major points made in the essay.

If you want to study other acceptable models of the extended essay, read some of the longer passages that appear at the end of most exercise sections in this book. These longer passages are often modeled after the extended essay.

Now consider how this same question is answered in a disorganized way. Look at this essay to see what is lacking in the introduction, the body, and the conclusion.

Question: Discuss the three major functions of religion.

Answer:

(1) Religion has been used to explain the unexplainable. Each culture has certain creation myths and beliefs about an afterlife. There are many similar creation myths in Western and Eastern religions.

(2) All cultures seem to pray. Prayers help people's problems. People pray in various ways throughout the world. The end is always the same.

(3) Religion has a purpose in society. Many social functions are somehow related to religion. People get together and feel a bond. That is another important function of religion.

Did you note that this essay has no introduction? If you did not have the question before you, you would not know what question this essay was trying to answer. Furthermore, the evidence is vague. In the body, creation myths are mentioned, but no specific creation myths of East and West are discussed. Similarly, the relationship between social functions and religion is presented, but no rituals such as marriage and funerals are introduced. An instructor evaluating this essay would mark it down for its lack of direction and relevant details.

In the next section of this chapter, which analyzes math and science problems and tests, you will see parallels to what you have just learned about essay tests.

You may now want to complete Exercise 16.1 on page 341.

How to Prepare for a Math or Science Test

As in preparing for exams in other courses, for a math or science test you will be studying lecture notes, textbook underlinings and comments, and study notes. The study notes are usually solutions to problems. Before you begin studying for your math or science test, see if your instructor has provided you with some sample problems. Also, be sure you know whether you will be allowed to look at your textbook or notes during the test.

You should spend a week reviewing all important material. Because the last class session before an exam in math and science courses is usually a review, it would be helpful if you had done most of your studying before this session. In this review session, you will have the opportunity to ask questions that may have come up during your studying.

When you study, spend most of your time reviewing the problems and solutions shown in your textbook, completed in lecture, discussion, and study notes, and done as homework. Trace the logic used to solve each problem. While you are reviewing, use note cards to write down important theorems, laws, formulas, and equations. Know these cards well, because you will probably need to recall this information quickly on the exam.

Look at the sample study card in Figure 16-5, from a chemistry study review. Note that the name of the formula is listed on the blank side, and the formula itself and a sample solution using the formula are on the lined side. Using the blank side of the card, you can test yourself to see whether you can recall the variables of the formula.

When it is possible to design a concept map of math and science information, do so. Since math and science courses build from one lecture to another, seeing connections among units is most helpful; concept maps often help you see these connections more easily. Figure 16-6 shows how the metric system is presented via a concept map. In this map, the units of measure become progressively larger as your eyes move clockwise.

You can also efficiently learn this material on the metric system by devising an organizational chart like the following:

Formula for obtaining volume

Blank Side

Volume of a cube =
length × width × height
(L) × (W) × (H)
Ex:
4 cm × 4 cm × 4 cm = 64 cubic
centimeters or 64 cm³

Lined Side

Figure 16-5   *Study card from a chemistry study review.*

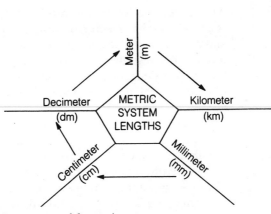

Figure 16-6   *Concept map of the metric system.*

Metric System Measures

Unit	Size
millimeter	.001 meter
centimeter	.01 meter
decimeter	.1 meter
dekameter	10 meters
hektometer	100 meters
kilometer	1000 meters

Once you have made these study cards, concept maps, and organizational charts, choose three to five problems that you have never done and that will probably be on your test. Complete each problem, and time yourself. If you have difficulty moving from one step to another, try to figure out your confusion. Go back to your notes and textbook.

If your instructor allows crib notes, or notes that list certain formulas and rules, write these out neatly. But do not use these notes as a crutch. Crib notes should be used when you need to use a formula or theorem that is hard to remember.

The night before the exam, do not cram. Just go over your study cards and maps.

How to Take a Math or Science Test

Instructors in math or science generally score an exam by looking at the steps that you used to arrive at a solution. They are often more interested in the way you solved the problem than in the correct answer.

Before you start solving a problem on your test, be sure you know what is being asked of you. The two most commonly used words on math and science tests are *solve* and *prove*. Both words ask you to present the logic of your solution, not just give an answer. Look at the following question on the metric system and its solution.

Question: How many kilograms are there in 2543 grams?

Detailed Solution	*Vague Solution*

1. 1 kg $= 1000$ grams $\dfrac{2543}{1000} = 2.543$

2. kg $= \dfrac{g}{1000}$

3. kg $= \dfrac{2543}{1000}$

4. kg $= 2.543$

5. 2.543 kg

Do you see how you can easily follow the pattern of thought in the first solution? Step 1 shows the conversion, step 2 the formula, and steps 3 and 4 the procedures used to solve the equation. The second answer does not present any of these steps and so does not explain why 1000 is to be divided into 2543.

Hints to Use in Solving Math or Science Problems

Use these steps to solve math or science problems on homework or on exams.

1. Read the question carefully. Determine the unknown. If you have to, write out the unknown in the margin. In the previous solution, kg is the unknown.

2. Reread the question to determine the known quantities. In the previous solution, 2543 grams is the known. You may want to write out the known in the margin as well.

3. Then figure out what the problem is asking you to do.

4. Write out the formulas or equations you need to solve the problem. In the example, the needed formula is 1000 g = 1 kg. Then plug your knowns into the formula, and solve for the unknown.

5. When you arrive at an answer, check it by rereading the question. Is it reasonable? In the example, 254,300 kg would be illogical, because you know that kilograms are heavier than grams. You can often spot a simple computational error, such as multiplying when you should have divided, by rereading the question with your answer in mind.

6. If you cannot solve the problem, list the formulas that you know can be used to solve it. Most instructors give partial credit.

You may now want to complete Exercise 16.2 on page 343.

Hints for Taking Math, Science, or Essay Tests

Here are some tips for taking all the kinds of examinations discussed in this chapter.

1. Read the directions carefully. Know how many questions you have to answer and the point value assigned to each question.

2. Read through each question, underlining such key words as *analyze, solve,* and *major.*

3. Answer the easiest questions first.

4. Jot down a brief outline of what you intend to say for each question or a list of equations you need to use in solving each problem. With these phrases and formulas, you will be able to structure your answers. They will also help you if you draw a momentary blank during the exam.

5. Plan your time wisely. If you are to answer two essay questions or two problems during the hour, be sure to start the second question or problem halfway through the hour.

6. When writing the essay or solving the problem, use only one side of the paper and leave margins. If you want to add information, you can put it either in the margins or on the back side of the paper.

7. If you are pressed for time, list the equations that you intended to use or an outline of the rest of your answer. You will probably get partial credit by including these abbreviated responses.

8. Save at least five minutes at the end of the exam time to review for errors in computation or in spelling, punctuation, and diction.

9. With essay exams, do not expect to write the perfect essay. Your goal is to present accurate information in an organized way.

Summary

Unlike objective tests, which ask you to remember many details, essay tests ask you to present the important points of what you have studied in an organized way and to reduce what you have learned to its essentials. This process of evaluating all that you have studied to find the significant points may be difficult at first. The three most commonly used essay exams are the short-answer exam, the short-essay exam, and the extended-essay exam.

Math and science questions are like essay questions; for both, you must present information in a logical way. In place of words, math and science tests use numbers and symbols. Instructors are often looking not just for the correct answer but for how you arrived at your answer.

Effective writing skills and the ability to solve math and science problems are skills that employers are coming to value more and more. Two of your more important goals in college should therefore be to develop efficient writing and problem-solving skills.

Summary Box   *Essay Exams and Math or Science Tests*

What are they?	*How do you do well on them?*
Essay exams: ask for organized responses on material that you have studied; can be short answer, short essay, or extended essay	By reducing information to its essentials By presenting accurate information in an organized way
Math or science tests: ask you to use numbers and symbols to solve a problem in a logical way	By determining known and unknown quantities By choosing correct formulas By showing the steps that you used to arrive at your answer

Skills Practice

Exercise 16.1
Answering Short-
Essay Questions

Read the following excerpt on Martin Luther King, Jr., from a sociology textbook. Underline the important points, and make marginal comments. After reading, recite what you have learned, either by taking notes or by creating a concept map. When you think that you know the information well, answer the essay question that follows. You may want to reread pp. 333–334, on the short essay.

Martin Luther King, Jr.: The Power of Protest

The civil rights movement invented new techniques for minorities to gain power and influence in American society. *Mass protest* is a technique by which groups seek to obtain a bargaining position for themselves that can induce desired concessions from established powerholders. It is a means of acquiring a bargaining leverage for those who would otherwise be powerless. The protest may challenge established groups by threatening their reputations (unfavorable publicity), their economic position (a boycott), their peace and quiet (disruption of daily activities), or their security (violence or the threat of violence). The protest technique appeals to powerless minorities who have little to bargain with except their promise *not* to protest.

The nation's leading exponent of *nonviolent* protest was Dr. Martin Luther King, Jr. Indeed, King's contributions to the development of a philosophy of nonviolent, direct-action protest on behalf of African Americans won him international acclaim and the Nobel Peace Prize in 1964. King first came to national prominence in 1955, when he was only twenty-five years old; he led a year-long bus boycott in Montgomery, Alabama, to protest discrimination in seating on public buses. In 1957 he formed the Southern Christian Leadership Conference (SCLC) to provide encouragement and leadership to the growing nonviolent pro-test movement in the South.

In 1963 a group of Alabama clergymen petitioned Martin Luther King, Jr., to call off mass demonstrations in Birmingham, Alabama. King, who had been arrested in the demonstrations, replied in his famous "Letter from Birmingham Jail":

> You may well ask, "Why direct action? Why sit-ins, marches, etc.? Isn't negotiation a better path?" You are exactly right in your call for negotiation. Indeed, this is the purpose of direct action. Nonviolent direct action seeks to create such a crisis and establish such creative tension that a community that has constantly refused to negotiate is forced to confront the issue. It seeks to so dramatize the issue that it can no longer be ignored. . . .
>
> One may well ask, "How can you advocate breaking some laws and obeying others?" The answer is found in the fact that there are *unjust* laws. I would be the first to advocate obeying just laws. One has not only a legal but a moral responsibility to obey just laws. Conversely, one has a moral responsibility to disobey unjust laws. . . .
>
> One who breaks an unjust law must do it *openly, lovingly* . . . and with a willingness to accept the penalty. I submit that an individual who breaks a law that conscience tells him is unjust, and willingly accepts the penalty by staying in jail to arouse the conscience of the community over its injustice, is in reality expressing the very highest respect for law.

Nonviolent direct action is a technique requiring direct mass action against laws regarded as unjust, rather than court litigation, political campaigning, voting, or other conventional forms of democratic political activity. Mass demonstrations, sit-ins, and other nonviolent direct-action tactics often result in violations of state and local laws. For example, persons remaining in offices, halls, or buildings after being asked by authorities to leave ("sit-ins") may be violating trespass laws. Marching in the street may entail the obstruction of traffic, "disorderly conduct," or "parading without a permit." Mass demonstrations often involve "disturbing the peace" or refusing to obey the lawful orders of a police officer. Even though these tactics are nonviolent, they do entail *disobedience to civil law.*

Civil disobedience is not new to American politics. Its practitioners have played an important role in American history, from the patriots who participated in the Boston Tea Party, to the abolitionists who hid runaway slaves, to the suffragists who paraded and demonstrated for women's rights, to the labor organizers who picketed to form the nation's major industrial unions, to the civil rights marchers of recent years. Civil disobedience is a political tactic of minorities. (Because majorities can more easily change laws through conventional political activity, they seldom have to disobey them.) It is also a tactic attractive to groups wishing to change the social status quo significantly and quickly.

The political purpose of nonviolent direct action and civil disobedience is to call attention or "to bear witness" to the existence of injustices. Only laws regarded as unjust are broken, and they are broken openly, without hatred or violence. Punishment is actively sought rather than avoided because punishment will further emphasize the injustices of the law. The object of nonviolent civil disobedience is to stir the conscience of an apathetic majority and to win support for measures that will eliminate the injustices. By accepting punishment for the violation of an unjust law, persons practicing civil disobedience demonstrate their sincerity. They hope to shame the majority and to make it ask itself how far it will go to protect the status quo.*

Essay question: In your own words, define *nonviolent direct action.* Then list three actions that would be considered examples of this nonviolent protest. Finally, explain Martin Luther King's understanding of nonviolent direct action.

80%

(score = # correct × 10)

Find answers on p. 406.

Exercise 16.2
Answering Problem-
Solving Questions

Read the following excerpt on exponents. Underline the important points, and make marginal comments. After reading, recite what you have learned, either by taking notes or by creating a concept map. When you think that you know the information well, solve the following problems. You may want to refer to pp. 339–340 in the introduction to review the practices to use in solving math or science problems.

Exponents

Any decimal number can be multiplied by 10 raised to some power or exponent. Examples are 1×10^2, 1×10^{-6}, and 9.8×10^4. A *positive* power or exponent of 10 indicates how many times the number must be *multiplied* by 10. For example, 1×10^2 is read as "one times ten to the second power," and it is equal to $1 \times 10 \times 10$ or 100. Often 1×10^2 is written as 10^2, with it understood that it is multiplied by 1. Some other examples are

$$10^1 \text{ or } 1 \times 10^1 = 1 \times 10 = \mathbf{10}$$
$$10^5 \text{ or } 1 \times 10^5 = 1 \times 10 \times 10 \times 10 \times 10 \times 10 = \mathbf{100{,}000}$$
$$6 \times 10^6 = 6 \times 10 \times 10 \times 10 \times 10 \times 10 \times 10 = \mathbf{6{,}000{,}000}$$

A *negative* power or exponent of 10 indicates the number of times a number is *divided* by 10. For example,

$$10^{-2} \text{ or } 1 \times 10^{-2} = \frac{1}{10^2} = \frac{1}{10 \times 10} = \frac{1}{100} = \mathbf{0.01}$$

$$10^{-4} \text{ or } 1 \times 10^{-4} = \frac{1}{10^4} = \frac{1}{10 \times 10 \times 10 \times 10} = \frac{1}{10\,000} = \mathbf{0.000\,1}$$

$$8.3 \times 10^{-9} = \frac{8.3}{10^9} = \frac{8.3}{10 \times 10 \times 10 \times 10 \times 10 \times 10 \times 10 \times 10 \times 10}$$

---

*Thomas R. Dye, *Power and Society*, 6th ed. (Pacific Grove, Calif.: Brooks/Cole, 1993), pp. 252–253.

$$= \frac{8.3}{1\,000\,000\,000} = \textbf{0.000 000 008 3}$$

The sign of the exponent is reversed when a power of 10 is moved from the numerator to the denominator and vice versa. For example,

$$\frac{1}{10^{12}} = 1 \times 10^{-12} \text{ or } 10^{-12} \quad \text{and} \quad 6 \times 10^{-4} = \frac{6}{10^4}$$

To convert a number in exponential form to its decimal equivalent number, move the decimal point in the exponential form one place to the *right* for each *positive* power of 10 and one place to the *left* for each *negative* power of 10. This works because each positive power of 10 multiplies the number by 10 and moves the decimal point one place to the right. Similarly, each negative power of 10 divides the number by 10 and moves the decimal point one place to the left. For example,

$$1 \times 10^1 = 1\,0\_ \quad (\textit{move decimal point one place to the right})$$

Note that when the decimal point is not shown, it falls at the end of a number.

$$6.409 \times 10^2 = 6\,4\,0\,.9 \qquad (\textit{move the decimal point 2 places to the right})$$
$$1 \times 10^{-3} = 0\,.0\,0\,1 \qquad (\textit{move the decimal point 3 places to the left})$$
$$5.6 \times 10^{-6} = 0\,.0\,0\,0\,0\,5\,6 \quad (\textit{move the decimal point 6 places to the left})$$

Note that for numbers less than one a zero is always placed to the left of the decimal point to show its location clearly.*

Problem: Convert the following three numbers in exponential form to their decimal equivalents. Show all your work. Follow the same procedure used to determine decimal equivalents that you just studied in the excerpt.

66%

Ask instructor for answer.

1. 6.409×10^2

2. 1×10^{-3}

3. 5.6×10^{-6}

Follow-up on Chapter 16

Now that you have studied this introduction and completed the exercises, it may be helpful to see how your abilities in taking essay exams and math/science tests have improved. You may want to review both the introduction and the exercises you completed. Then answer the following questions either individually or in small groups.

---

*G. Tyler Miller, Jr., *Chemistry: A Basic Introduction*, 4th ed. (Belmont, Calif.: Wadsworth, 1987), p. 21.

On Taking Essay Exams and Math or Science Tests

1. What is it about preparing for essay exams that is still difficult for you?
2. What is it about preparing for math/science exams that is still difficult for you?
3. Which types of essay exam questions are still difficult for you to answer?
4. Betewen objective tests and essay exams, which are easier for you to complete? Why?

Internet Activity

Do some research on the Internet on solving mathematics problems. This exercise is best completed in groups of four or five. Locate the following Web site to answer the questions that follow. Then return to your groups with your responses.

> Understanding Mathematics
> http://www.math.utah.edu/~alfeld/math.html

If you cannot access this Web site, research the Internet to find information on solving math/science problems to answer these questions:

1. List three new techniques that you learned to solve mathematics problems by studying this Web site.
2. In what ways is the information in this Web site similar to what you already learned about math/sciences problems in this chapter?
3. Describe the procedures you used to access this Web site.

Applying SQ3R to Textbook Material

The three reading selections in Part Five are excerpts from college textbooks; the first two are excerpts from chapters, and the last one is an entire chapter. In each selection, you will be applying all the skills you have studied in previous parts of this book. If you do well on the examinations on these three selections, you should be adequately prepared for the kinds of tests you will be taking in most of your college courses.

Study Reading 1

Global Warming

Vocabulary (words not defined in this excerpt)

greenhouse gases: Gases in the earth's lower atmosphere that trap heat near the earth's surface.
troposphere: Innermost layer of the atmosphere.
photosynthesis: Complex process that takes place in the cells of green plants by which oxygen and carbohydrates are produced.

This excerpt from an environmental science textbook discusses the issues surrounding global warming, that is, whether or not it is a problem, and which elements in the environment affect it. This excerpt relies mostly on three organizational patterns: definition, cause–effect, and spatial–geographic. Read over the following suggestions; they should help you learn this information more easily.

1. Study the cause–effect statements carefully, since this is how the bulk of this excerpt is organized. Most of the cause–effect statements relate to whether or not global warming exists. Be sure you can identify both cause and effect. If you do not remember the characteristics of the cause–effect pattern, refer to pp. 102–103.

2. Read over the defintions carefully. Mark the key words and phrases that explain these terms.

3. Some of what is said in this excerpt can be visualized. Study the one illustration carefully to see how ocean water travels. Also, when particular parts of the world are mentioned, be sure you have a sense for where those areas are. If you do not remember the spatial–geographic pattern, refer to p. 106.

4. Because of this excerpt's reliance on the cause–effect structure, your best way to remember much of this information is to design concept maps to illustrate various natural processes that relate to global warming. When you are reviewing the material, you may want to design a few concept maps that explain the major cause–effect patterns related to global warming.

5. Before you take the test on this excerpt, you should not only know the meanings of the key terms but also be able to explain the important cause–effect patterns that underlie global warming.

A. Survey

Take three minutes to survey this chapter excerpt. Read the title of the excerpt, the titles of the various sections, and any terms that are highlighted. Also, study the one illustration and the one graph to see how they relate to the excerpt. Finally, if time permits, read through the first and last paragraphs of the excerpt to get a sense of its style and difficulty level.

When you have finished with your survey, answer the following questions without looking back at the excerpt. Place all of your answers in the answer box.

Global Warming or a Lot of Hot Air? How Serious Is the Threat?

G. Tyler Miller, Jr.

Will the Earth Really Get Warmer?

(1) There is much controversy over whether we are already experiencing global warming, how warm temperatures might be in the future, and the effects of such temperature increases. One problem is that many of the past measurements and estimates of the earth's average temperature are imprecise, and we have only about 100 years of accurate data. With such limited data, it is difficult to separate out the normal, short-term ups and downs of global temperatures (called *climate noise*) from an overall rise in average global temperature.

G. Tyler Miller, Jr. Living in the Environment, *10th ed. (Belmont, Calif.: Wadsworth, 1998), pp. 370–373.*

(2) Scientists have also identified a number of factors that might amplify (positive feedback) or dampen (negative feedback) a rise in average atmospheric temperature. These factors influence both how fast temperatures might climb and what the effects might be on various areas. Let's look more closely at the possible effects of such factors.

How Do Changes in Solar Output Affect the Earth's Temperature?

(3) Solar output varies by about 0.1% over the 11-year and 22-year sunspot cycles—and over 80-year and other, much longer cycles. Sunspots occur when strong solar magnetic fields periodically protrude through the sun's surface and slightly increase the sun's energy output.

(4) In 1995, solar physicist Judith Lean at the Naval Research Laboratory estimated that solar warming accounted for roughly half of the global warming taking place between 1860 and 1970 and about one-third of the warming since 1970. Other studies suggest that sunspot cycles may account for only 10–30% of the warming during the past century. Two 1992 studies concluded that the projected warming power of greenhouse gases should outweigh the climatic influence of the sun over at least the next 50 years.

How Do the Oceans Affect Climate?

(5) The world's oceans might amplify global warming by releasing more CO_2 into the atmosphere (positive feedback) or might dampen it by absorbing more heat (negative feedback). We know that the oceans currently help moderate tropospheric temperature by removing about 29% of the excess CO_2 we pump into the atmosphere (negative feedback), but we don't know if they can absorb more. If the oceans warm up enough, some of the dissolved CO_2 will bubble out into the atmosphere (just as in a glass of carbonated ginger ale left out in the sun), amplifying and accelerating global warming (positive feedback).

(6) Global warming could be dampened if the oceans absorbed more heat, but this depends on how long the heat takes to reach deeper layers. Recent measurements indicate that deep vertical mixing in the ocean occurs extremely slowly (taking hundreds of years) in most places because water density increases with depth, inhibiting mixing of different layers.

(7) There is also concern that deep ocean currents could be disrupted. At present, these currents (driven largely by differences in water density and winds) act like a gigantic conveyor belt, transferring heat from one place to another and storing carbon dioxide in the deep sea (Figure 14-6). In the Atlantic Ocean, the resulting enormous amount of heat transported northward from tropical waters accounts for Europe's unusually warm climate relative to its latitude.

There is concern that global warming could halt this thermal conveyor belt by reducing the density and salinity of water in the North Atlantic. If this loop should stall out, evidence from past climate changes indicates that this could trigger atmospheric temperature changes of more than 5°C (9°F) over periods as short as 40 years (positive feedback).

(8) Research reported in 1995 suggested that the nitrogen content of the oceans is decreasing. If levels of this nutrient (which supports the growth of photosynthesizing phytoplankton) are dropping, as the oceans warm they will tend to absorb less CO_2. This would enhance global warming by increasing the rate of CO_2 buildup in the troposphere.

How Do Water Vapor Content and Clouds Affect Climate?

(9) Changes in the atmosphere's water vapor content and the amount and types of cloud cover affect climate. Warmer temperatures would increase evaporation and the water-holding capacity of the air and create more clouds. Significant increases in water vapor, a potent greenhouse gas, could enhance warming (positive feedback).

(10) Predicting the net effect of additional clouds on climate is difficult. They could have a warming (positive feedback) or cooling (negative feedback) effect depending on whether it is day or night and on their type (thin or thick) and altitude. During the day clouds are reflective and have a cooling effect; at night they have an insulating effect and lead to warmer temperatures. In general, high and thin (cirrus) clouds have a warming effect; low and thick clouds have a cooling effect. Scientists don't know which of these factors might predominate or how cloud types and heights might vary in different parts of the world as a result of global warming.

How Might Changes in Polar Ice Affect Climate?

(11) The ability of the earth's surface (land, water, or ice) to reflect light is its **albedo**. Dark-

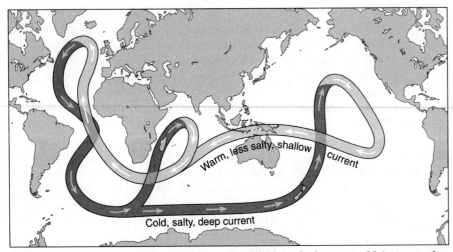

Figure 14-6 *This loop of ocean water stores carbon dioxide in the deep sea and brings warmth to Europe. It occurs when ocean water in the North Atlantic is dense enough (because of its salt content and cold temperature) to sink to the ocean bottom and well up in the warmer Pacific (helping cool that part of the world). Then a shallower return current aided by winds brings warmer and less salty—and thus less dense—water to the Atlantic, which can then cool and sink to begin the cycle again. If this heat conveyor belt or loop should stall out because of a drop in density of ocean water in the North Atlantic (possibly from changes caused by global warming), massive climate changes over much of the earth's surface could occur within only a few decades. Models indicate that this oceanic conveyor belt would return, but only after hundreds of thousands of years.*

colored surfaces (land and water) absorb heat from sunlight and warm up. Light-colored or shiny surfaces (polar ice caps and high, thin clouds) remain cool because they reflect back into space much of the sunlight that hits them.

(12) Because of their high albedo, the Greenland and antarctic ice sheets act like enormous mirrors reflecting sunlight back into space without adding to the heating of the earth. If warmer temperatures melted some of this ice and exposed darker ground or ocean, more sunlight would be absorbed. This decrease in the earth's albedo would accelerate global warming. Then more ice would melt, further amplifying the rise in atmospheric temperature (positive feedback).

(13) On the other hand, the early stages of global warming might increase the amount of the earth's water stored as ice. Warmer air would carry more water vapor, which could drop more snow on some polar glaciers, especially the gi-

gantic antarctic ice sheet. If snow accumulated faster than ice was lost, the ice sheet would grow, reflect more sunlight (higher albedo), and help cool the atmosphere (negative feedback). However, this cooling could get out of hand. As the climate cools, more ice is formed, further increasing the earth's albedo—a positive feedback system that could lock the earth into a global cooling cycle and perhaps lead to a new ice age within a thousand years.

How Might Air Pollution Affect Climate?

(14) Climate can also be affected by air pollution, primarily *aerosols* (tiny droplets and solid particles) released or formed in the atmosphere from volcanic eruptions and human activities. Projected global warming might be partially offset by aerosols because they reflect some of the incoming sunlight back into space. This negative feedback from increased air pollution is beneficial in

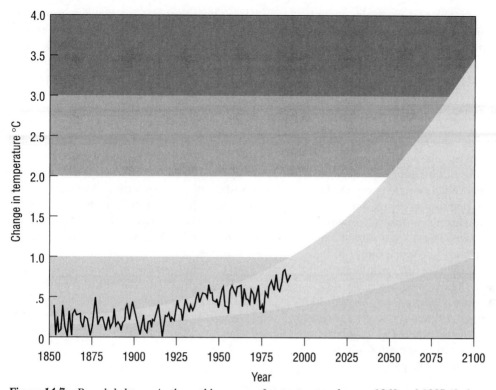

Figure 14-7 *Recorded changes in the earth's mean surface temperature between 1860 and 1995 (dark line). The curved gray region shows global warming projected by various computer models of the earth's climate systems. Note that the climate model projections roughly match the 0.3–0.6°C (0.5–1.1°F) recorded temperature increase between 1860 and 1995. Current models indicate that the average global temperature wil rise by 1–3.5°C (1.8–6.3°F) sometime during the next century. However, this projection assumes that air pollution from sulfate aerosols will continue to increase and exert a slight cooling effect— despite the fact that sulfur emissions have leveled off since 1990. The projected warming shown here could be overestimated or underestimated by a factor of two. (Data from U.S. National Academy of Sciences and National Center for Atmospheric Research)*

terms of global warming (Figure 14-7) but harmful in terms of vegetation and human health.

(15) It is hypothesized that SO_2 and tiny particles in the troposphere attract enough water molecules to form condensation nuclei, which leads to increased cloud formation. The resulting clouds have a high albedo and thus reflect more incoming sunlight back into space during daytime. During daytime this helps counteract the heating effects of increased greenhouse gases. Nights, however, would be warmer because the clouds would still be there and prevent some of the heat stored in the earth's surface (land and water) during the day from being radiated back into space.

(16) Because about 90% of SO_2 emissions (which can be transformed in the atmosphere to aerosol droplets of sulfuric acid and particles of sulfate salts) occur in the heavily industrialized northern hemisphere, this portion of the globe may undergo cooling that could offset or delay global warming. These pollutants may explain why most recent warming in the northern hemisphere occurs at night. Climate expert Thomas Karl at the National Climatic Data Center estimates that currently the United States is about

1°C (1.8°F) cooler because of aerosols formed from SO_2 emissions.

(17) A similar cooling effect may be occurring in the southern hemisphere from particles in smoke emitted by large-scale burning of rain forests, grasslands, agricultural waste, and wood (used for heating and cooking). These aerosol emissions in both hemispheres may help explain why global warming observed to date is only about one-half of that projected by earlier climate models that did not include this effect.

(18) But these interactions are complex. Pollutants in the lower troposphere can either warm or cool the air, depending on the reflectivity of the underlying surface. These contradictory and patchy effects, plus improved air pollution control, make it unlikely that air pollutants will counteract projected global warming very much in the next half century. Aerosols also fall back to the earth or are washed out of the atmosphere within weeks or months, while CO_2 and other greenhouse gases remain in the atmosphere for decades to several hundred years.

(19) These aerosols are major components of acid deposition (commonly known as *acid rain*), which slows forest growth and weakens or helps kill many trees. This reduces the ability of trees to absorb some of the CO_2 we are putting into the atmosphere and could accelerate global warming (positive feedback).

(20) We could maintain or increase levels of aerosol air pollutants to offset possible global warming. However, because these pollutants already kill hundreds of thousands of people a year and damage vegetation (including food crops), they need to be and are being reduced. The models used to project the temperature increases in Figure 14-7 assume that sulfate aerosol levels will continue to rise. However, if current and projected SO_2 emissions in developed countries continue to fall, they could offset projected increases in such emissions in developing countries—leading to higher temperatures than those shown in Figure 14-7.

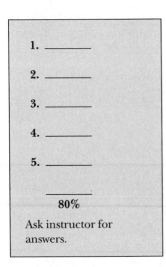

1. _____

2. _____

3. _____

4. _____

5. _____

_____
80%

Ask instructor for answers.

1. This chapter excerpt makes use of

    a. boldface print
    b. italics
    c. underlining
    d. both a and b

2. The one illustration shows how

    a. warm the ocean is
    b. cold the ocean is
    c. cold and warm ocean water are transported
    d. deep the ocean floor can get

3. A topic that will *not* be covered in this excerpt is

    a. solar output
    b. oceans and climate
    c. water vapor and clouds
    d. overpopulation and pollution

4. This excerpt makes use of some chemical formulas.

    a. true
    b. false

5. The title of this excerpt suggests that global warming

    a. may exist
    b. definitely exists
    c. definitely does not exist
    d. is definitely not a serious problem

B. Question

Having surveyed this excerpt, make up five questions that you will answer as you study read. Use the chapter title, subdivision titles, and italicized terms to help you to make up these questions. Write your questions in the spaces provided.

1.

2.

> Ask instructor for
> sample questions.

3.

4.

5.

C. Read and Recite

1. After you have composed these five questions, you can begin study reading. Underline important points and make marginal comments. Remember not to underline too much. Read paragraphs 1–10. Afterward, on a separate sheet of paper, recite what you have read, using the Cornell note-taking system. When you have finished, go back to these ten paragraphs to see if your summary is complete and accurate.

2. Now read paragraphs 11–20. Follow the same procedures as you did for paragraphs 1–10: Recite on a separate sheet of paper, and then return to these paragraphs to see if your summary is complete and accurate. Make any necessary additions to your summary.

D. Review

Now you are ready to review all of your material. Read over text underlinings, marginal comments, and your two summaries. You may also want to make concept maps from some of this material. Finally, go back to your original five questions to see if you can answer them without any help.

Examination: Global Warming

Directions: Give yourself fifty minutes to complete the following questions. Be sure to budget your time to answer all three parts: matching, multiple choice, and short essay.

I. Matching: Match up the following terms with the appropriate definitions. Each term should be matched up to only one definition. Place the letter of the correct definition in the answer box next to the appropriate number. (24 points)

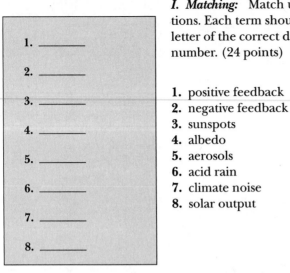

1. positive feedback
2. negative feedback
3. sunspots
4. albedo
5. aerosols
6. acid rain
7. climate noise
8. solar output

a. amount of energy the sun produces
b. acid depositions in the atmosphere's water
c. the ability of the earth's surface to reflect light
d. moderation of global warming
e. acceleration of global warming
f. sun's energy increased when its magnetic fields protrude
g. tiny droplets and solid particles
h. normal ups and downs of global temperature

1. _____
2. _____
3. _____
4. _____
5. _____
6. _____
7. _____
8. _____

II. Multiple Choice: Choose the letter that correctly completes each question or statement. Place all answers in the answer box. (36 points)

9. How many years of accurate data concerning weather change do scientists currently have?

   a. 50 years
   b. 100 years
   c. 150 years
   d. 200 years

10. Sunspots allow for

   a. a decrease in the sun's energy output
   b. a slight increase in the sun's energy output
   c. a significant increase in the sun's energy output
   d. no change in the sun's energy output

11. How can the oceans serve to amplify global warming?

   a. by producing less oxygen in the atmosphere
   b. by producing more oxygen in the atmosphere
   c. by producing less carbon dioxide in the atmosphere
   d. by producing more carbon dioxide in the atmosphere

12. There could be less global warming if the oceans

   a. lost some of their salt content
   b. gained more salt content
   c. gave up more heat
   d. absorbed more heat

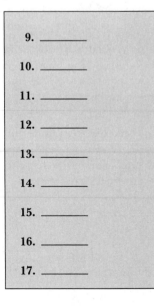

9. _____
10. _____
11. _____
12. _____
13. _____
14. _____
15. _____
16. _____
17. _____

13. As the nitrogen content of the oceans decrease,

    a. the oceans absorb less carbon dioxide
    b. the oceans absorb more carbon dioxide
    c. there is less global warming
    d. global warming is not affected

14. Low and thick clouds tend to

    a. heat the environment
    b. cool the environment
    c. prevent rain
    d. prevent snow

15. Dark-colored surfaces on the earth tend to

    a. absorb heat
    b. remain cool
    c. collect water vapor
    d. stay dry

16. Aerosols tend to

    a. heat the environment
    b. stay in the environment for hundreds of years
    c. prevent cloud formation
    d. cool the environment

17. Aerosols tend to be a major component in

    a. the vegetation in Greenland
    b. the vegetation in Antarctica
    c. carbon dioxide
    d. acid rain

70%

Ask instructor for answers.

III. Short Essay: Certain aspects the environment affect global warming in contradictory ways. In an organized paragraph, discuss how the following three features of the environment can both heat up the environment and cool it down: (1) clouds, (2) the earth's surface, and (3) the world's oceans. (40 points)

Study Reading 2

Atoms and Molecules

This chapter excerpt is from a chapter entitled "Elements, Compounds, Molecules, and Ions" in a college chemistry text. The style is straightforward, but this simplicity is deceiving. You may need to reread many of the sections in order to master them and to use this knowledge in solving specific problems. Use the following suggestions to master the material in this excerpt.

1. Read the definitions carefully, underlining or circling important parts. You need to know what each term in this excerpt means, so read to understand every part of each definition.

2. Much of what is described in this excerpt requires your spatial–geographic abilities. You may want to reread the section on the spatial–geographic pattern on p. 106, since you will be asked to visualize the various parts of an atom and the ways atoms combine.

3. Read carefully for the relative sizes of protons, neutrons, nuclei, and electrons and for the electrical charges that each exhibits.

4. By the time you have finished the excerpt, you should be able to recall, without help, the meanings of the terms. You should also be able to visualize the various parts of an atom and understand how their electrical charges are interrelated.

A. Survey

Take three minutes to survey the chapter excerpt. Read the excerpt title, the titles of each section, the terms and statements that are highlighted, as well as the summary at the end of the excerpt. If time permits, begin reading the first several paragraphs of the excerpt.

When you have finished, answer the following questions without looking back at the excerpt. Place all of your answers in the answer box.

Atoms and Molecules

G. Tyler Miller, Jr.

Structure of Elements: Atoms and Molecules

(1) Cut a piece of pure copper in half and then cut one of the halves in half. Repeat this subdividing process again and again. Could you theoretically go on cutting the material forever, or would you eventually reach some basic structural unit of an element that is "uncuttable"?

(2) According to the **atomic theory of matter,** the basic structural unit of any chemical element and thus all matter is an *atom* (from the Greek *atomos,* meaning *uncuttable*). An **atom** is the smallest possible piece or particle of an element that can exist and still have the properties of that element. Using a powerful electron microscope, scientists have been able to take pictures of atoms of several of the larger elements such as uranium. In these pictures, the individual atoms appeared as fairly spherical, fuzzy shapes. Because the atoms of most elements are too small to be seen by the microscopes available today, atoms are normally represented by enormously magnified spheres showing their relative sizes. Figure 3.1 shows a greatly magnified mental model of the structure of a piece of solid copper metal, which is trillions and trillions of minute, spherical atoms of copper packed close together. The atoms of different elements differ primarily in their relative size and properties, and sometimes in the way they are packed together. Atoms shown in Figures 3-1 and 3-2 are about 40 million times larger than their actual sizes.

G. Tyler Miller, Jr. Chemistry: A Basic Introduction, *4th ed. (Belmont, Calif.: Wadsworth, 1987), pp. 60–64.*

(3) The basic structural units for most elements are individual atoms. Two or more atoms of a few nonmetal elements, however, can link together to form a more complex structural unit called a **molecule**—a group of two or more atoms of the same or different elements that have combined chemically and that are held together by attractive forces called *chemical bonds.* Molecules can also be the building block units for a number of *compounds* when two or more atoms of different elements combine, as discussed later in this chapter. Because all molecules can be broken down by chemical means into atoms, the atom is still the most fundamental building block unit for all matter.

(4) Molecules formed by the combination of two atoms of the same or different elements are called **diatomic molecules** (*di-* means *two*); those consisting of a combination of three atoms are called **triatomic molecules** (*tri-* means *three*); and those formed by a combination of four or more atoms are called **polyatomic molecules** (*poly-* means *many*). The seven elements that can exist as diatomic molecules and the two elements that can exist as polyatomic molecules at 20.0°C and a pressure of 1 atmosphere are shown in Figure 3-2. Notice that all of these elements are nonmetals.

Chemical Formulas

(5) A chemical formula is a shorthand representation of a molecule or compound in which each element present is represented by its chemical symbol and the number of atoms of each element in the molecule or compound is represented by a *subscript* placed after the symbol for each element. When no subscript appears, it is understood that this represents one atom. Thus,

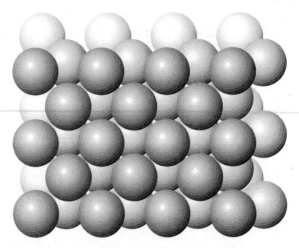

individual copper atom   array of copper atoms packed together

Figure 3-1   *Model of a sample of solid copper as a gigantic number of minute, spherical atoms packed together in a regular, repeating pattern. Models of the atoms shown in this figure are about 40 million times larger than the actual size of copper atoms.*

a diatomic molecule of the element hydrogen can be represented by the chemical formula H_2 (read as "H-two"). The subscript 2 indicates that there are two atoms of hydrogen chemically combined to form a hydrogen molecule.

(6) Figure 3-2 shows seven nonmetal elements that can exist as diatomic molecules. Atoms of a smaller number of elements can form polyatomic molecules. Two examples shown in Figure 3-2 are phosphorus, which can form P_4 (read as "P-four"), and sulfur, which can form S_8 (read as "S-eight"). Unfortunately, the fact that some elements can exist as diatomic molecules and polyatomic molecules can cause confusion. For example, in referring to the element hydrogen, it is not always clear whether this means H or H_2.

3.2   Modern Atomic Theory: An Overview

Atomic Structure: Protons, Neutrons, and Electrons

(7) An atom is the smallest particle or structural unit of an element that can exist and still have the properties of that element. However, for almost 100 years scientists have gathered evidence that atoms have an internal structure and are composed of three major types of subatomic particles called *protons, neutrons,* and *electrons,* as discussed in Chapter 4.

(8) Although atoms are often represented as tiny hard balls (Figure 3-2), they are mostly free space. This results from the fact that most of the mass of an atom is concentrated in an extremely small and very dense core at the center, called the **nucleus.** The nucleus contains one or more subatomic particles called **protons** (represented by the symbol *p*) and one or more subatomic particles called **neutrons** (represented by the symbol *n*). The one exception to this is a type of hydrogen atom that has one proton and no neutrons in its nucleus; this is discussed later in this section.

(9) Each proton has a single positive electrical charge (1+ or +), and each neutron is neutral with no electrical charge (0 charge). Thus, the overall electrical charge on the nucleus of an atom is positive with the total positive charge equal to the number of positively charged protons in the nucleus. For example, the nucleus of

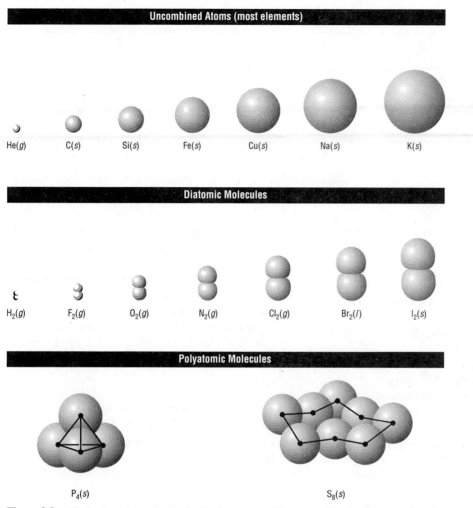

Uncombined Atoms (most elements)

He(*g*)   C(*s*)   Si(*s*)   Fe(*s*)   Cu(*s*)   Na(*s*)   K(*s*)

Diatomic Molecules

$H_2(g)$ $F_2(g)$ $O_2(g)$ $N_2(g)$ $Cl_2(g)$ $Br_2(l)$ $I_2(s)$

Polyatomic Molecules

$P_4(s)$ $S_8(s)$

Figure 3-2   *The basic structural units for the elements are either uncombined atoms or molecules formed by the chemical combination of two or more atoms of an element. Physical states of these elements at 20.0°C and 1 atm are given in parentheses with solids represented by (s), liquids by (l), and gases by (g).*

a carbon atom with six protons ($6 \times 1 +$) and six neutrons (6×0 charge) has a total positive charge of 6+.

(10) Somewhere outside the atom's tiny nucleus there are one or more subatomic particles called **electrons** (represented by the symbol *e*) whizzing around in constant motion. Each electron has a single negative electrical charge ($1-$ or $-$). The number of negatively charged electrons outside the nucleus is equal to the number of positively charged protons inside the nucleus.

Table 3-3   *Characteristics of Subatomic Particles*

Name of Particle	Symbol	Position in Atom	Relative Electrical Charge	Mass (in g)	Relative Mass (in amu*)	Approximate Relative Mass (in amu*)
Proton	p or p^+	Inside nucleus	1+	1.6726×10^{-24}	1.00728	1
Neutron	n or n^0	Inside nucleus	0	1.6750×10^{-24}	1.00867	1
Electron	e or e^-	Outside nucleus	1−	9.1095×10^{-28}	0.00055	0

$$\frac{\text{number of protons}}{\text{inside the nucleus}} = \frac{\text{number of electrons}}{\text{outside the nucleus}}$$

For example, an atom of carbon with six positively charged protons and six neutrons inside its nucleus has six negatively charged electrons somewhere outside its nucleus.

(11) Because neutrons have no electrical charge, and there is one proton with a 1+ charge for each electron with a 1− charge, *the atom as a whole is electrically neutral—it has no overall electrical charge.* For example, a carbon atom with six protons (6 × 1+ = +6) and six neutrons (6 × 0 = 0) in its nucleus and six electrons (6 × 1− = −6) outside its nucleus has an overall electrical charge of zero (+6 + 0 −6 = 0). Atoms of the 108 known elements differ in the number of protons, neutrons, and electrons they contain, as discussed later in this section.

(12) Table 3-3 summarizes some of the properties of the three major types of subatomic articles. For convenience, chemists have set up a relative scale of mass in atomic mass units (amu), which is discussed later in this section. On this relative scale, the approximate mass of a neutron is 1 amu, that of a proton is also 1 amu, and that of an electron is only 0.00055 amu, approximately 0. Because the electrons contribute practically nothing to the mass of the atom, you can see why most of the mass of an atom is concentrated in its nucleus.

(13) According to modern atomic theory, all that can be said about the electrons in an atom is that they are in rapid constant motion somewhere outside the nucleus. You can obtain a crude, greatly magnified mental model of an atom by imagining a spherical cloud with a diameter of about 2 km (1.25 mi). At the center of the cloud hidden from view is a grape representing the nucleus. Flying around somewhere inside this large cloud and also out of sight are one or more tiny gnats representing electrons.

Atomic Size

(14) It is important to keep in mind that atoms are incredibly small. The area of the period at the end of this sentence could hold 10^{18} typical atoms. This many atoms is approximately equal to the number of people populating 1 billion planets like the earth, with each planet containing 5 billion people. Although the diameter of an atom is extremely small, the diameter of its nucleus is typically 100,000 times smaller. This explains why most of the atom is free space with one or more extremely small electrons in constant motion somewhere outside the nucleus.

(15) Summary of Modern Atomic Theory

1. Atoms of the 108 known elements have an internal structure consisting of one or more subatomic particles called *protons (p), neutrons (n),* and *electrons (e).*

2. Most of the mass of an atom is concentrated in a tiny positively charged center core called the *nucleus* with a diameter about 100,000

times smaller than the diameter of the entire atom.

3. The nucleus of an atom contains one or more protons *(p)*, each with a single positive electrical charge (1+ or +), and one (except for one type of hydrogen atoms) or more neutrons *(n)*, each with no electrical charge (0 charge).

4. The total positive charge on the nucleus is equal to the number of positively charged protons found in the nucleus.

5. One or more electrons *(e)*, each with a single negative electrical charge (1− or −), are in constant motion somewhere outside the nucleus.

6. The number of negatively charged electrons outside the nucleus is equal to the number of positively charged protons inside the nucleus so that the atom as a whole has no overall electrical charge.

7. An atom is mostly free space because the volume of the nucleus and the electrons outside the nucleus are extremely small relative to the overall volume of the atom.

8. Atoms of the 108 known elements differ in the number of protons, neutrons, and electrons they contain.

1. This excerpt makes use of
   a. boldface print
   b. italics
   c. illustrations
   d. all of these

2. The illustrations
   a. show what atoms look like
   b. show what molecules look like
   c. show what a uranium atom looks like
   d. both a and b

3. The table in this excerpt
   a. presents the physical properties of metals
   b. presents the physical properties of nonmetals
   c. presents the chemical properties of metals
   d. lists the characteristics of subatomic particles

4. It appears that in this excerpt you learn something about
   a. the structure of atoms
   b. the structure of molecules
   c. atomic theory
   d. all of these

5. Which topic will *not* be covered in this excerpt?
   a. chemical formulas
   b. atomic size
   c. diatomic molecules
   d. the periodic table

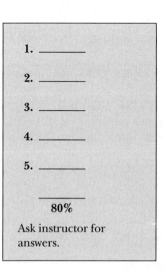

1. _____

2. _____

3. _____

4. _____

5. _____

_____
80%

Ask instructor for answers.

B. Question

Having surveyed the chapter excerpt, write five questions that you intend to answer when you study read. Use the chapter title, section titles, and boldface print to formulate your questions. Write your questions in the space provided.

1.

2.

3.

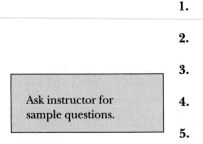

4.

5.

C. Read and Recite

With these questions, you are ready to begin study reading. Use your best underlining and commenting skills, underlining sparingly and making marginal notes on important terms and formulas. Read the section titled "Structre of Elements: Atoms and Molecules." Then, on a separate sheet of paper, use the Cornell note-taking system to recite what you have read. Once you have done that, read the second part of the excerpt, titled "Modern Atomic Theory: An Overview." Again recite, using the Cornell note-taking system. When you have completed your summaries, go back to the excerpt to be sure that your summaries are both accurate and complete. Make any additions to your summaries at this time.

D. Review

Now you are ready to review your underlinings, your marginal comments, and your summaries. Before you take the exam, you should know how the subatomic electrical charges relate. There will be a problem on subatomic charges on the exam.

Examination: Atoms and Molecules

Directions: Give yourself fifty minutes to complete the following questions. Be sure to budget your time.

I. Matching: Match up the following terms with the appropriate definitions. Each term should be matched up to only one definition. Place all answers in the answer box. (18 points)

1. atom
2. molecule
3. chemical bonds
4. compounds
5. diatomic molecules
6. nucleus

a. a group of two or more atoms of the same or different elements
b. two or more atoms of different elements combined
c. smallest piece of an element with properties of that element
d. small, dense core of an atom

e. molecules formed by two atoms of the same or different atoms

f. attractive forces holding atoms together

II. Multiple Choice: Choose the letter that correctly completes each question or statement. Place all answers in the answer box. (27 points)

7. A particular molecule is formed by the combination of five atoms. It is called

    a. monatomic
    b. diatomic
    c. triatomic
    d. polyatomic

8. The subscript 4 after the element oxygen (O_4) indicates that

    a. there are four oxygen atoms
    b. there are four oxygen atoms chemically bonded
    c. there are two sets of two oxygen atoms
    d. there are two sets of two oxygen atoms chemically combined

9. Atoms are mostly made up of

    a. a nucleus
    b. free space
    c. protons
    d. neutrons

10. What is the electrical charge of a neutron?

    a. positive
    b. no charge
    c. negative
    d. none of these

11. Of the three parts of an atom, which has the smallest mass?

    a. proton
    b. neutron
    c. electron
    d. nucleus

12. Which subatomic particle is in constant motion?

    a. nucleus
    b. proton
    c. neutron
    d. electron

13. How many known elements are there?

    a. 108

---

1. _____

2. _____

3. _____

4. _____

5. _____

6. _____

7. _____

8. _____

9. _____

10. _____

11. _____

12. _____

13. _____

14. _____

15. _____

  b. 98
  c. 90
  d. 80

14. Atoms of all the known elements differ in the number of

  a. electrons they contain
  b. protons, neutrons, and electrons they contain
  c. nuclei they contain
  d. none of these

15. The charge of a nucleus is

  a. positive
  b. negative
  c. neutral
  d. none of these

III. Problem Solving: Complete the following two problems. You can earn partial credit. Show all your work.

1. Draw a diagram of an atom containing one proton, one neutron, and one electron. Label each atomic part, and identify the nucleus. (25 points)

2. Copper is an element with 29 protons. (30 points)

  a. How many electrons does it have? _____ (6 points)

  b. How many neutrons could it have? _____ (6 points)

  c. What is the charge of its protons? _____ (6 points)

  d. What is the charge of its electrons? _____ (6 points)

  e. What is the overall charge of the copper atom? _____ (6 points)

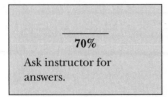

70%

Ask instructor for answers.

Study Reading 3

Social Power

Unlike the previous two textbook excerpts that you have read, this one is an entire chapter, the first chapter in a sociology textbook. Study reading it will closely resemble the activities you will engage in when you read textbooks in college. Also, instead of answering objective questions about the chapter, you will be answering essay questions.

This selection introduces and defines the key concepts examined in the textbook. Thus it relies heavily on two organizational patterns: definition and comparison–contrast. You may want to reread the sections in Chapter 6 on these two organizational patterns (pp. 104–105 and 107–109) before you start your study reading of this chapter. And you may want to review how to answer extended essay and short-answer questions.

Use the following suggestions to master this chapter's material.

1. Read carefully for definitions. See how the definitions of terms interrelate. Identify and mark the key terms.

2. Look for comparisons and contrasts in the definitions and issues that the author presents. Make marginal comments about these comparisons.

3. Read the case study carefully, as well as the summary of the chapter and the discussion questions.

4. As you study read, see how your previous reading of sociology material in Chapter 6 and your reading of business material in Chapter 5 help you understand this chapter. You may want to review the exercises in Chapters 5 and 6 after you complete the study reading of this chapter to clarify any questions about sociology or business that you may have had.

5. As you read the last section of the chapter—on ideology, race, and poverty—see whether you can apply any of your own experiences to the sociological issues that are explained.

A. Survey

Take four minutes to survey this chapter. Read the titles, subtitles, and terms in boldface and italics. Notice the chapter's special features: how the definitions are highlighted, the purpose of the case study, and the kinds of discussion questions at the end.

When you have finished, answer the questions that follow without looking back at the excerpt.

The Nature of Power

Thomas R. Dye

(1) Ordinary men and women are driven by forces in society that they neither understand nor control. These forces are embodied in governmental authorities, economic organizations and markets, social values and ideologies, accepted ways of life, and learned patterns of behavior. However diverse the nature of these forces, they have in common the ability to modify the conduct of individuals, to control their behavior, to shape their lives.

power   the capacity to affect the conduct of others through the real or threatened use of rewards and punishments

(2) *Power is the capacity to affect the conduct of individuals through the real or threatened use of rewards and punishments.* Power is exercised over individuals or groups by offering them some things they value or by threatening to deprive them of those things. These values are the *power base*, and they can include physical safety, health, and well-being; wealth and material possessions; jobs and means to a livelihood; knowledge and skills; social recognition, status, and prestige; love, affection, and acceptance by others; a satisfactory self-image and self-respect. To exercise power, then, control must be exercised over the things that are valued in society.

(3) *Power is a special form of influence.* Broadly speaking, influence is the production of intended effects. People who can produce intended effects by any means are said to be influential. People who can produce intended effects by the real or threatened use of rewards and punishments are said to be powerful.

power   based on control of valued resources

unequally distributed

exercised in interpersonal relations

exercised through large institutions

Power can rest on various resources. The exercise of power assumes many different forms—the giving or withholding of many different values. Yet power bases are usually *interdependent*—individuals who control certain resources are likely to control other resources as well. Wealth,

Thomas R. Dye, Power and Society, *6th ed. (Pacific Grove, Calif.: Brooks/Cole, 1993), pp. 4–14.*

economic power, prestige, recognition, political influence, education, respect, and so on, all tend to "go together" in society.

(4) *Power is never equally distributed.* "There is no power where power is equal." For power to be exercised, the "powerholder" must control some base values. By *control* we mean that the powerholder is in a position to offer these values as rewards to others or to threaten to deprive others of these values.

Power is a relationship among individuals, groups, and institutions in society. Power is not really a "thing" that an individual possesses. Instead, power is a relationship in which some individuals or groups have control over certain resources.

elite and masses the few who have power and the many who do not

(5) The *elite* are the few who have power; the *masses* are the many who do not. The elite are the few who control what is valued in society and use that control to shape the lives of all of us. The masses are the many whose lives are shaped by institutions, events, and leaders over which they have little control. Political scientist Harold Lasswell wrote, "The division of society into elites and masses is universal," and even in a democracy, "a few exercise a relatively great weight of power, and the many exercise comparatively little."[1]

(6) *Power is exercised in interpersonal relations.* Psychologist Rollo May wrote that "power means the ability to affect, to influence, and to change other persons."[2] He argued that power is essential to one's "sense of significance"—one's conviction that one counts for something in the world, that one has an effect on others, and that one can get recognition of one's existence from others. Power is essential to the development of personality. An infant who is denied the experience of influencing others or of drawing their attention to its existence withdraws to a corner of its bed, does not talk or develop in any way, and withers away physiologically and psychologically.

(7) *Power is exercised in large institutions*—governments, corporations, schools, the military, churches, newspapers, television networks, law firms, and so on. Power that stems from high positions in the social structures of society is stable and far-reaching. Sociologist C. Wright Mills observed: "No one can be truly powerful unless he has access to the command of major institutions, for it is over these institutional means of power that the truly powerful are, in the first instance, powerful."[3] Not all power, it is true, is anchored in or exercised through institutions. But institutional positions in society provide a continuous and important base of power. As Mills explained:

> If we took the one hundred most powerful men in America, the one hundred wealthiest, and the one hundred most celebrated away from the institutional positions they now occupy, away from their resources of men and women and money, away from the media of mass communication that are now focused upon them—then they would be powerless and poor and uncelebrated. For power is not of a man. Wealth does not center in the person of the wealthy. . . . To have power requires access

to major institutions, for the institutional positions men occupy determine in large part their chances to have and to hold these valued experiences.[4]

Power and the Social Sciences

social science   the study of human behavior

(8) *Social science* is the study of human behavior. Actually, there are several social sciences, each specializing in a particular aspect of human behavior and each using different concepts, methods, and data in its studies. Anthropology, sociology, economics, psychology, political science, and history have developed into separate "disciplines," but all share an interest in human behavior.

(9) Power is *not* the central concern of the social sciences, yet all the social sciences deal with power in one form or another. Each of the social sciences contributes to an understanding of the forces that modify the conduct of individuals, control their behavior, and shape their lives. Thus, to fully understand power in society, we must approach this topic in an *interdisciplinary* fashion—using ideas, methods, data, and findings from all the social sciences.

Anthropology

anthropology   the study of people and their ways of life

(10) *Anthropology* is the study of people and their ways of life. It is the most comprehensive of the social sciences. Some anthropologists are concerned primarily with people's biological and physical characteristics; this field is called *physical anthropology*. Other anthropologists are interested primarily in the ways of life of both ancient and modern peoples; this field is called *cultural anthropology*.

culture   all the common patterns and ways of living that characterize society

(11) *Culture* is all the common patterns and ways of living that characterize society. The anthropologist tries to describe and explain a great many things: child rearing and education; family arrangements; language and communication; technology; ways of making a living; the distribution of work; religious beliefs and values; social life; leadership patterns; and power structures.

(12) Power is part of the culture or the way of life of a people. Power is exercised in all societies, because all societies have systems of rewards and sanctions designed to control the behavior of their members. Perhaps the most enduring structure of power in society is the family: power is exercised within the family when patterns of dominance and submission are established between male and female and between parents and children. Societies also develop structures of power outside the family to maintain peace and order among their members, to organize individuals to accomplish large-scale tasks, to defend themselves against attack, and even to wage war and exploit other peoples.

(13) In our study of power and culture, we shall examine how cultural patterns determine power relationships. We shall also examine patterns of authority in traditional and modern families and the changing power role of women in society. We shall examine the origins and development of power relationships, illustrating them with examples of soci-

eties in which power is organized by family and kinship group (polar Eskimos), by tribe (Crow Indians), and by the state (the Aztec empire). Finally, as a case study, we shall look at the controversy over "sociobiology"—that is, the extent to which genetics or culture determines behaviors.

Sociology

sociology the study of relationships among individuals and groups

(14) *Sociology* is the study of relationships among individuals and groups. Sociologists describe the structure of formal and informal groups, their functions and purposes, and how they change over time. They study social institutions (such as families, schools, churches), social processes (for example, conflict, competition, assimilation, change), and social problems (crime, race relations, poverty, and so forth). Sociologists also study social classes.

social stratification the classification and ranking of members of a society

(15) All societies have some system of classifying and ranking their members—a system of *stratification*. In modern industrial societies, social status is associated with the various roles that individuals play in the economic system. Individuals are ranked according to how they make their living and the power they exercise over others. Stratification into social classes is determined largely on the basis of occupation and control of economic resources.

Power derives from social status, prestige, and respect, as well as from control of economic resources. Thus, the stratification system involves the unequal distribution of power.

(16) In our study of power and social class, we shall describe the stratification system in America and explore popular beliefs about "getting ahead." We shall discuss the differing lifestyles of upper, middle, and lower classes in America and the extent of class conflict. We shall examine the ideas of Karl Marx about the struggle for power among social classes. We shall describe the differential in political power among social classes in America. Finally, we shall explore the ideas of sociologist C. Wright Mills about a "power elite" in America that occupies powerful positions in the governmental, corporate, and military bureaucracies of the nation.

Psychology

psychology the study of the behavior of people and animals

(17) *Psychology* may be defined as the study of the behavior of people and animals. Behavior, we know, is the product of both "nature and nurture"—that is, a product of both our biological makeup and our environmental conditioning. We shall examine the continuing controversy over *how much* of our behavior is a product of our genes versus our environment. There is great richness and diversity in psychological inquiry. For example, *behavioral psychologists* study the learning process—the way in which people and animals learn to respond to stimuli. Behavioral psychologists frequently study in experimental laboratory situations, with the hope that the knowledge gained can be useful in understanding more complex human behavior outside the laboratory.

Social psychologists, on the other hand, study interpersonal behavior—the ways in which social interactions shape an individual's beliefs, perceptions, motivations, attitudes, and behavior. Social psychologists generally study the whole person in relation to the total environment. *Freudian psychologists* study the impact of subconscious feelings and emotions and of early childhood experiences on the behavior of adults. *Humanistic psychologists* are concerned with the human being's innate potential for growth and development. Many other psychologists combine theories and methods in different ways in their attempts to achieve a better understanding of behavior.

personality   all the enduring, organized ways of behavior that characterize an individual

(18) *Personality* is all the enduring, organized ways of behavior that characterize an individual. Psychologists differ over how personality characteristics are determined—whether they are learned habits acquired through the process of reinforcement and conditioning (behavioral psychology), products of the individual's interaction with the significant people and groups in his or her life (social psychology), manifestations of the continuous process of positive growth toward "self-actualization" (humanistic psychology), the results of subconscious drives and long-repressed emotions stemming from early childhood experiences (Freudian psychology), or some combination of all these.

(19) In our study of power and personality, we will examine various theories of personality determination in an effort to understand the forces shaping the individual's reaction to power. Using a Freudian perspective, we shall study the "authoritarian personality"—the individual who is habitually dominant and aggressive toward others over whom he or she exercises power but is submissive and weak toward others who have more power; the individual who is extremely prejudiced, rigid, intolerant, cynical, and power-oriented. We shall explore the power implications of B. F. Skinner's ideas of behavioral conditioning for the control of human behavior. To gain an understanding of humanistic psychology's approach to power relationships, we shall examine Rollo May's formulation of the functions of power for the individual and Abraham Maslow's theory of a "hierarchy of needs." Finally, in our case study, we shall describe the startling results of an experiment designed to test the relationship between authority and obedience.

Economics

economics   the study of the production and distribution of scarce goods and services

(20) *Economics* is the study of the production and distribution of scarce goods and services. There are never enough goods and services to satisfy everyone's demands, and because of this, choices must be made. Economists study how individuals, firms, and nations make these choices about goods and services.

(21) Economic power is the power to decide what will be produced, how much it will cost, how many people will be employed, what their wages will be, what the price of goods and services will be, what profits will be made, how these profits will be distributed, and how fast the economy will grow.

(22) Capitalist societies rely heavily on the market mechanism to make these decisions. In our study of economic power, we shall explore both the strengths and weaknesses of this market system, as well as the ideas of economic philosophers Adam Smith and John Maynard Keynes. In addition, we shall consider the role of government in the economy, which has increased over the years. We shall then turn to an examination of America's vast wealth—how it is measured, where it comes from, and where it goes. We shall examine the relationship between wealth and the quality of life, which are not always equivalent things. We shall also examine the concentration of corporate power in America. Finally, in our case study, we shall discuss the power of the corporate managers, the "CEOs," and whether they use that power to benefit the stockholders or themselves.

Political Science

political science the study of government and politics
authority the legitimate use of physical force

(23) *Political science* is the study of government and politics. Governments possess *authority*, a particular form of power; that is, the legitimate use of physical force. By *legitimate*, we mean that people generally consent to the government's use of this power. Of course, other individuals and organizations in society—muggers, street gangs, the Mafia, violent revolutionaries—use force. But only government can legitimately threaten people with the loss of freedom and well-being to modify their behavior. Moreover, governments exercise power over all individuals and institutions in society—corporations, families, schools, and so forth. Obviously the power of government in modern society is very great, extending to nearly every aspect of modern life— "from womb to tomb."

(24) Political scientists from Aristotle to the present have been concerned with the dangers of unlimited and unchecked governmental power. We shall examine the American experience with limited, constitutional government and the meaning of democracy in modern society. We shall observe how the U.S. Constitution divides power, first between states and the national government, and second among the legislative, executive, and judicial branches of government. We shall examine the growth of power in Washington, D.C., and the struggle for power among the different branches. We shall also explore competition between political parties and interest groups and popular participation in decision making through elections. Finally, in our case study "Political Power and the Mass Media," we shall examine the growing power of television in American politics.

History

history the recording, narrating, and interpreting of human experience

(25) *History* is the recording, narrating, and interpreting of human experience. The historian recreates the past by collecting recorded facts, organizing them into a narrative, and interpreting their meaning. History is also concerned with change over time. It provides a perspective on the present by informing us of the way people lived in the past. History helps us understand how society developed into what it is today.

(26) The foundations of power vary from age to age. As power bases shift, new groups and individuals acquire control over them. Thus, power relationships are continuously developing and changing. An understanding of power in society requires an understanding of the historical development of power relationships.

(27) In our consideration of the historical development of power relationships, we shall look at the changing sources of power in American history and the characteristics of the individuals and groups who have acquired power. We shall describe the people of power in the early days of the republic and their shaping of the Constitution and the government it established. We shall discuss Charles Beard's interpretation of the Constitution as a document designed to protect the economic interests of those early powerholders. We shall also discuss historian Frederick Jackson Turner's ideas about how westward expansion and settlement created new bases of power and new powerholders. We shall explore the power struggle between northern commercial and industrial interests and southern planters and slave owners for control of western land, and the Civil War, which resulted from that struggle. In addition, we shall explore the development of an industrial elite in America after the Civil War, the impact of the depression on that elite, and the resulting growth of New Deal liberal reform. In a brief case study, "Reconstruction and Black History," we shall examine how history occasionally overlooks the experiences of powerless minorities and later reinterprets their contributions to society. Finally, we shall undertake a brief historical study, "Vietnam: A Political History," which argues that despite military victory, this war was "lost" through failures of America's political leadership.

Social Sciences and Social Problems

(28) Social problems—the major challenges confronting society—include ideological conflict, racism, sexism, poverty, crime, violence, urban decay, and international conflict. These problems do not confine themselves to one or another of the disciplines of social science. They spill over the boundaries of anthropology, economics, sociology, political science, psychology, and history—they are *interdisciplinary* in character. Each of these problems has its *historical* antecedents, its *social* and *psychological* roots, its *cultural* manifestations, its *economic* consequences, and its impact on *government* and public policy. The origins of these social problems, as well as the various solutions proposed, involve complex power relationships.

interdisciplinary study the use of theory, methods, or findings from more than one social science

Ideological Conflict

(29) Ideas have power. Indeed, whole societies are shaped by systems of ideas that we call *ideologies*. The study of ideologies—liberalism, conservatism, socialism, communism, fascism, radicalism—is not a separate social science. Rather, the study of ideologies spans all the social sciences, and it is closely related to philosophy. Ideologies are integrated systems

ideology an integrated system of ideas that rationalize and justify the exercise of power in society

of ideas that rationalize a way of life, establish standards of "rightness" and "wrongness," and provide emotional impulses to action. Ideologies usually include economic, political, social, psychological, and cultural ideas, as well as interpretations of history.

(30) Ideologies rationalize and justify power in society. By providing a justification for the exercise of power, the ideology itself becomes a base of power in society. Ideology "legitimizes" power, making the exercise of power acceptable to the masses and thereby adding to the power of the elite. However, ideologies also affect the behavior of the elite, because once an ideology is deeply rooted in society, powerholders themselves are bound by it.

(31) In our study of power and ideology, we shall first explore the ideology of *classical liberalism*—an ideology that attacked the established power of a hereditary aristocracy and asserted the dignity, worth, and freedom of the individual. Classical liberalism and capitalism justify the power of private enterprise and the market system. Whereas classical liberalism limits the powers of government, *modern liberalism* accepts governmental power as a positive force in freeing people from poverty, ignorance, discrimination, and ill health. It justifies the exercise of governmental power over private enterprise and the establishment of the welfare state. In contrast, *modern conservatism* doubts the ability of the governmental planners to solve society's problems; conservatism urges greater reliance on family, church, and individual initiative and effort.

(32) We shall then look at ideologies that have influenced other societies. *Fascism* is a power-oriented ideology that asserts the supremacy of a nation or race over the interests of individuals, groups, and other social institutions. *Marxism* attacks the market system, free enterprise, and individualism; it justifies revolutionary power in overthrowing liberal capitalist systems and the establishment of a "dictatorship of the proletariat." *Socialism* calls for the evolutionary democratic replacement of the private enterprise system with government ownership of industry.

We shall describe the current crisis of communism and the reasons for its collapse in eastern Europe and the former Soviet Union, and communism's unpopularity among the Chinese people. We shall also record the recent historic events of democratic movements in communist nations and shall provide a case study. "The Rise and Fall of Communism in the Former Soviet Union."

Racial and Sexual Inequality

(33) Historically, no social problem has challenged the United States more than racial inequality. It is the only issue over which Americans ever fought a civil war. We shall describe the American experience with racism and the civil rights movement, which brought about significant changes in American life. We want to understand the philosophy of that movement, particularly the "nonviolent direct action" philosophy of Nobel Peace Prize winner Dr. Martin Luther King, Jr. We shall describe the recent successes of blacks in acquiring political power. However, we shall

also examine continuing inequalities between blacks and whites in income, employment, and other conditions of life in the United States. Our case study describes the political rise of Douglas Wilder, the nation's first black governor. In addition, we confront sexism in American life, particularly in the economy. And we shall examine the arguments both for and against government efforts to assure "comparable worth" in the labor market. We shall describe the successes and failures of the women's movement in recent years and examine the constitutional status of abortion laws. Finally, we shall examine the controversy over "affirmative action" and "reverse discrimination" and its implication for how America is to achieve real equality.

Case Study

Bertrand Russell: Power Is to the Social Sciences What Energy Is to Physics

(34) Bertrand Russell (1872–1970), English philosopher and mathematician, is regarded as one of the twentieth century's greatest thinkers, mainly because of his contributions to mathematics and symbolic logic. However, Russell possessed a great breadth of interest that included history, economics, and political science, as well as education, morals, and social problems. He received the Nobel Prize in literature "in recognition of his many-sided and significant authorship, in which he has constantly figured as a defender of humanity and freedom of thought." He summarized his views about the importance of power in society in a book significantly entitled *Power: A New Social Analysis.**

(35) First of all, power is fundamental to the social sciences:

The fundamental concept in the social sciences is power, in the same sense in which energy is the fundamental concept in physics.

(36) Second, the desire for power as well as wealth motivates people:

When a moderate degree of comfort is assured, both individuals and communities will pursue power rather than wealth: they may seek wealth as a means to power, or they may forgo an increase of wealth in order to secure an increase of power, but in the former case as in the latter their fundamental motive is not economic. . . .

(37) Third, power takes many forms:

Like energy, power has many forms, such as wealth, armaments, civil authority, influence on opinion. No one of these can be regarded as subordinate to any other, and there is no one form from which the others are derivative. The attempt to treat one form of power, say wealth, in isolation can only be partially successful. . . . To revert to the analogy of physics: power, like energy, must be regarded as continually passing from any one of its forms into any other, and it should be the business of social science to seek the laws of such transformations.

(38) Finally, power produces social change:

Those whose love of power is not strong are unlikely to have much influence on the course of events. The men who cause social changes are, as a rule, men who strongly desire to do so. Love of power, therefore, is a characteristic of the men who are causally important. We should, of course, be

---

mistaken if we regarded it as the sole human motive, but this mistake would not lead us so much astray as might be expected in the search for causal laws in social science, since love of power is the chief motive producing the changes which social science has to study.

Poverty and Powerlessness

powerlessness a social-psychological condition of hopelessness, indifference, distrust, and cynicism

(39) The American economy has produced the highest standard of living in the world, yet a significant number of Americans live in poverty. We shall observe that poverty can be defined as *economic hardship* or as *economic inequality* and that each definition implies a different governmental approach to the problem. Poverty can also be defined as *powerlessness*—a social-psychological condition of hopelessness, indifference, distrust, and cynicism. We shall then discuss whether or not there is a culture of poverty—a way of life of the poor that is passed on to future generations—and what its implications for government policy are. We shall describe government efforts to cope with poverty and discuss whether or not some government policies encourage poverty. We shall focus special attention on homelessness in America. Finally, we shall examine the future of the Social Security program in a look at "Senior Power."

Crime and Violence

a problem of democratic government to protect its citizens without violating individual liberty

(40) Governmental power must be balanced against *individual freedom.* A democratic society must exercise police powers to protect its citizens, yet it must not unduly restrict individual liberty. We shall explore the problem of crime in society, the constitutional rights of defendants, the role of the courts, and the relationship between drug use and crime. We shall also describe briefly the history of violence in American society and the continuous role that violence has played in American struggles for power. We shall summarize social-psychological explanations of violence, violence as a form of political activity, and violence as an aspect of lower-class culture. Finally, we shall examine the arguments for and against the death penalty as society's ultimate sanction.

Urban Life

(41) A variety of social problems affect the quality of life in the United States. The solution to these problems, if there is any solution, depends in great part on how government chooses to exercise its powers. We shall explore the growth of urban and suburban populations in the United States. We shall also explore the social patterns of urban life—the characteristic forms of social interaction and organization that typically emerge in a large metropolis—and the socioeconomic conflicts between cities and suburbs. We shall observe how our nation's communities are governed. We shall focus special attention on the social and economic problems of the inner city and how the concentration of social

problems can make them worse. Finally, we shall present a case study, "Community Power Structures," to compare power structures in different cities.

International Conflict

(42) The struggle for power is global. It involves all the nations and peoples of the world, whatever their goals or ideals. Nearly 200 nations in the world claim *sovereignty:* authority over their internal affairs, freedom from outside intervention, and political and legal recognition by other nations. But sovereignty is a legal fiction; it requires power to make sovereignty a reality. Over the years nations have struggled for power through wars and diplomacy. The struggle has led to attempts to maintain a fragile balance of power among large and small nations, as well as to attempts to achieve collective security through the United Nations and other alliances. Despite its internal problems, Russia remains a nuclear "superpower," together with the United States. In our discussion of the international system, we shall describe the nuclear "balance of terror" and the "triad" of weapons that maintains this balance. We shall describe the history of the Strategic Arms Limitations Talks (SALT) between the United States and the Soviet Union, the Intermediate-Range Nuclear Forces (INF) Treaty, and the major reductions in nuclear forces agreed to in the Strategic Arms Reduction Talks (START) Treaty. The collapse of communism in eastern Europe brought an end to the Soviet-dominated Warsaw Pact and changed the balance of power in Europe. We shall describe the NATO alliance and speculate on the future of the new Europe. The United States continues to face challenges around the world; we shall describe various regional mini-balances of power, notably in the Middle East. Finally, we shall observe the continuing need for U.S. military power in our case study. "American Military Power: Desert Storm."

sovereignty authority over internal affairs, freedom from outside intervention, and recognition by other nations

Notes

1. Harold Lasswell and Abraham Kaplan, *Power and Society* (New Haven, Conn.: Yale University Press, 1950), p. 219.

2. Rollo May, *Power and Innocence* (New York: Norton, 1977), p. 20.

3. C. Wright Mills, *The Power Elite* (New York: Oxford University Press, 1956). p. 9.

4. Ibid., p. 10.

About This Chapter

Power in society is not just an abstract concept or a convenient focus for academic exercise. Nor is power something that is located exclusively in the nation's capitals. Power is very much a real factor that affects the lives of each of us. We experience it in some form in our families, in school, and at work; we feel its effects in the grocery store and on the highway. And we each react to it in characteristic ways. Our aim in this chapter was to understand just what power *is*. We also saw why it provides us with a useful perspective from which to gain a unified view of the social sciences and the social problems that concern us all.

Now that you have read this chapter, you should be able to

- define power in society and describe its characteristics;

- define the area of study of each of the social sciences, as well as their common focus, and discuss how each relates to power in society;

- identify the major social problems that the social sciences study and explain why they are interdisciplinary in nature and how they relate to power.

Discussion Questions

1. How would you define power? What characteristics of power deserve to be discussed in any definition of power?

2. Consider the power relationships that directly and indirectly affect your life. On the basis of your experiences and observations, assess the validity of these statements by Bertrand Rus-

sell: "The fundamental concept in the social sciences is power, in the same sense in which energy is the fundamental concept in physics. . . . When a moderate degree of comfort is assured, both individuals and communities will pursue power rather than wealth. . . . Love of power is the chief motive producing the changes which social science has to study."

3. Identify and briefly define the area of study of each of the social sciences. Discuss how you would study power from the perspective of each of these disciplines.

4. What is meant by the *interdisciplinary* study of social problems?

5. Choose two of the following social problems and briefly explain how they involve power: (a) racial and sexual inequality, (b) poverty, (c) crime and violence, (d) international conflict.

---

1. How are boldface print and italics used?

2. What is the case study generally about?

3. What types of questions are asked in the "Discussion Questions" section?

4. What are the three basic parts of this chapter?

80%

Ask instructor for answers.

---

5. Why do you think the various disciplines that you have studied in this textbook—business, sociology, anthropology—are introduced in this chapter?

B. Question

Having surveyed the chapter excerpt, write five questions that you intend to answer as you study read. Use the chapter title, section titles, italicized words and phrases, or any other feature of this chapter to formulate your questions. Answer these questions as you read the chapter.

1.

2.

Ask instructor for sample questions.

3.

4.

5.

C. Read and Recite

With these questions, you are ready to begin study reading. Use your best underlining and commenting skills, making marginal notes on important terms and comparisons. Then on a separate sheet of paper, recite what you have read, and apply the Cornell note-taking system. When you have completed your summary, go back to the excerpt to be sure that your summary is both accurate and complete. Make changes to your summary and to the main points you highlighted by using the Cornell note-taking system.

Read and summarize paragraphs 1–27 first. Then read and summarize paragraphs 28–42.

D. Review

Now you are ready to review your underlinings, your marginal comments, and your summaries. You may want to make concept maps that organize this material even more clearly.

Examination: Social Power

Directions: Give yourself two class sessions (100 minutes) to complete the following essay questions. Be sure to budget your time. Write all of your answers on separate sheets of paper or in a blue book.

I. Definitions: In a few sentences, define the following sociological terms. (25 points)

1. power

2. elite

3. social stratification

4. authority

5. sovereignty

II. Short Essay: Answer each question in an organized paragraph. (25 points)

6. Discuss the specific ways that the study of sociology differs from the study of psychology. (13 points)

7. Discuss the specific ways that the study of sociology differs from the study of political science. (12 points)

III. Extended Essay: In an essay of at least five paragraphs, define *ideology* and *ideological conflict.* Then explain two conflicts in ideology—for example, Marxism versus fascism and conservatism versus liberalism. Finally, choose *one* of the following three social issues and show how it has been treated differently by different ideologies: (1) women, (2) African Americans, or (3) the American poor. For example, discuss how the American poor are understood differently by a conservative ideology and by a liberal ideology. Your response may incorporate your own experiences or what you have previously studied about this issue. (50 points)

70%

Ask instructor for answers.

Answer Key

Answers have been provided for most odd-numbered exercises. Ask your instructor for the answers to all even-numbered exercises, the essay questions, several short-answer questions, and the study reading selections in Part Five.

Chapter 4
Locating the Main
Idea

Exercise 4.1

1. a **2.** d **3.** imp **4.** imp **5.** a **6.** a **7.** a **8.** a **9.** d **10.** imp

Exercise 4.3

Your wording may differ, but your answers should be essentially the same as these:

1. the Industrial Revolution
2. the effects of the Industrial Revolution on the farms
3. how the new inventions were run
4. the results of the new inventions on the farmer
5. machines in the early 1900s
6. how the machines of industrialization affected human life
7. industrialization's effect on the environment
8. the negative effect of industrialization on the environment
9. how industrialization affected society
10. the negative effects of industrialization on society
11. the city's effect on the environment
12. the city's negative effect on the environment
13. the Industrial Revolution's effect on the economy
14. the increased costs caused by the Industrial Revolution
15. the overall effects of the Industrial Revolution
16. the positive and negative effects of the Industrial Revolution
17. the Industrial Revolution and nature
18. the Industrial Revolution making human beings superior to nature
19. the superior attitude toward nature
20. questioning what this superior attitude means for human beings and nature

Exercise 4.5

1. d **2.** c **3.** b **4.** b **5.** a

**Chapter 5
Locating Major and
Minor Details**

Exercise 5.1

1. a, b, e	**5.** a, c, d	**8.** a, b, d
2. a, b, d	**6.** a, b, c	**9.** a, c, d
3. a, b, c	**7.** a, d, e	**10.** b, c, d
4. a, c, e		

Exercise 5.3

1. MN	**11.** MA	**21.** MN	**31.** MA
2. MA	**12.** MI	**22.** MA	**32.** MA
3. MI	**13.** MN	**23.** MI	**33.** MN
4. MA	**14.** MA	**24.** MI	**34.** MA
5. MN	**15.** MA	**25.** MN	**35.** MI
6. MA	**16.** MI	**26.** MA	**36.** MA
7. MA	**17.** MA	**27.** MA	**37.** MN
8. MA	**18.** MA	**28.** MI	**38.** MA
9. MN	**19.** MA	**29.** MN	**39.** MA
10. MA	**20.** MN	**30.** MA	**40.** MI

Exercise 5.5

1. c **2.** a **3.** b **4.** d **5.** c

6. any of the following: American farmers and businessmen did much business in England, **or** Americans often exchanged precious metals and agricultural products with England for finished products, **or** Most of American business was structured on the cottage system, where goods were made at home.

7. The Industrial Revolution changed the way Americans produced goods.

8. any of the following: Large machines were used, and workers moved from their homes to their factories, **or** The reaper allowed for more grain to be planted or harvested, **or** The telegraph and railroad allowed material to be sold and moved more quickly.

9. American business must be sensitive to changes in the market and must change accordingly in order to be competitive.

10. minor detail, "that is"

**Chapter 6
Identifying
Organizational
Patterns**

Exercise 6.1

1. fact	**5.** fact	**9.** thesis	**13.** a
2. thesis	**6.** fact	**10.** fact	**14.** d
3. fact	**7.** thesis	**11.** a	**15.** d
4. thesis	**8.** fact	**12.** d	

Exercise 6.3

Your answers should be essentially the same as these, although your wording may differ. Each definition has two parts, each counting 5 points.

Term	General Category	Examples
1. conflict theory	studies why people disagree	crime
2. deduction	logical process moving from general to specific	women's discrimination
3. demography	study of population	movement of Mexicans to California in the 1990s
4. empirical study	observer gathers data	how American men greet
5. field research	observing in natural setting	political rallies
6. hypothesis	conclusion drawn from intuition or observation	criminals as society's victims
7. induction	conclusion reached by studying data	New Yorkers' attitudes toward taxes
8. population	group meriting study	students in community colleges
9. random selection	selecting data by chance	random numbering
10. social interaction	how a person directs social responses	conversation

Exercise 6.5

1. DEF or C-C	**6.** DEF
2. C-E	**7.** C-E
3. SEQ	**8.** DEF
4. C-C	**9.** C-E
5. SEQ	**10.** C-C

Exercise 6.7

1. d

2. d

3. d

4. c

5. c

6. Factors other than money are involved in determining social status.

7. Some prestigious jobs are doctor, scientist, and Supreme Court justice—none of which makes a huge salary.

8. thesis–support

9. Spiritual and intellectual possessions are also valued by society.

10. thesis–support

Chapter 7
Summarizing and
Paraphrasing

Although your responses to the excerpt on pp. 134–135 may differ, they should be similar to these:

(1) Who were the Nacirema? How did they live? What accounted for their extreme ideology of remaking the natural environment? Why did they disappear? What can we learn from a study of their culture?

(2) **Anthropology,** the comparative study of human societies and cultures, provides some answers to questions like these. The aim of anthropology is to describe, analyze, and explain the different ways of life, or cultures, through which human groups, or societies, have adapted to their environments. Anthropology is comparative in that it attempts to understand both similarities and differences among human societies, in both the past and the present. Only by the study of humanity in its total variety can we understand the origins and development of our species.

(3) Anthropologists study our species from its beginnings several million years ago right up to the present. We study human beings as they live in every corner of the earth, in all kinds of physical environments. Some anthropologists are now trying to project how human beings will live in outer space. It is this interest in humankind throughout time and in all parts of the world that distinguishes anthropology as a scientific and humanistic discipline. In other academic disciplines, human behavior is studied primarily from the point of view of Western society. "Human nature" is thought to be the same as the behavior of people as they exist in the modern industrial nations of Europe and the United States.

(4) Human beings everywhere consider their own behavior not only right, but natural. For example, both "common sense" and Western economic theory see human beings as "naturally" individualistic and competitive. But in some societies, human beings are not competitive, and the group is more important than the individual. Anthropologists see the Western idea of "economic man"—the individual motivated by profit and rational self-interest—as the result of the particular socioeconomic and political system we live in. It is not an explanation of the behavior of the Arapesh hunter in New Guinea, who makes sure he is not always the first to sight and claim the game, so that others will not leave him to hunt alone (Mead 1963:38). In anthropology, more than any other discipline, concepts of human nature and theories of human behavior are based on studies of human groups whose goals, values, views of reality, and environmental adaptations are very different from those of modern, industrial Western societies.

(5) In their attempts to explain human variation, anthropologists combine the study of both human biology and the learned and shared patterns of human behavior we call culture. Other academic disciplines focus on one factor—biology, psychology, physiology, or society—as the explanation of human behavior. Anthropology seeks to understand human beings as whole organisms who adapt to their environments through a complex interaction of biology and culture.*

I. Anthropology

A. Definition: comparative study of human societies and cultures.
B. Three basic aims: describe, analyze, and explain different cultures' adaptation to environment.

---

*Serena Nanda, *Cultural Anthropology*, 4th ed. (Belmont, Calif.: Wadsworth, 1991), p. 5.

C. How anthropology is different from other disciplines: interest in humankind throughout time and all over the world.

D. Two studies anthropology combines: human biology, culture

Exercise 7.1

Score your answers to the five questions, not the underlinings, which will probably differ from this sample underlining. Just check to see that the main ideas have been correctly underlined.

The Functions of Religion

The Search for Order and Meaning

(1) One of the most important functions of religion is to give meaning to and explain those aspects of the physical and social environment that are important in the lives of individuals and societies. Religion deals with the nature of life and death, the creation of the universe, the origin of society and groups within the society, the relationship of individuals and groups to one another, and the relation of humankind to nature. Anthropologists call this whole cognitive system a cosmology, or world view. Human societies create images of reality, often in symbolic ways, that serve as a framework for interpreting events and experiences, particularly those that are out of the ordinary. These "different realities" emerge as a way of imposing order and meaning on the world within which humans live and of giving humans the feeling that they have some measure of control over that world.

(2) Science and religion, which are often opposed in Western thought, are similar in that both involve "the quest for unity underlying apparent diversity; for simplicity underlying apparent complexity; for order underlying apparent disorder; for regularity underlying apparent anomaly" (Horton and Finnegan 1973). But where science provides explanations that are open to new data and explicitly acknowledges a possibility of various alternatives, religious systems tend not to be open to empirical testing.

(3) The separation between religion and science in our own society corresponds to our sharp separation of the supernatural and the natural. In other societies, these two concepts are less sharply separated. The supernatural can be seen as part of the natural and as intervening in all aspects of life. Thus, the kin group includes both living relatives and dead ancestors; power and leadership are often believed to have divine origins; rules of behavior are given divine sanction; and breaches are punished by the gods. The success of even ordinary undertakings in the physical world is ensured by enlisting the help of supernatural powers. Natural disasters, illness, and misfortune are believed to be caused by extrahuman or supernatural spirits. Natural and supernatural, human and natural, past, present, and future may be perceived as a unity in a way that violates the logic of Western thought. This makes it difficult for us to understand many non-Western religions and accounts for our eth-

nocentric labeling of them as "irrational," "contradictory," or the products of faulty thinking.

(4) **Reducing Anxiety and Increasing Control** Many religious practices are aimed at ensuring success in carrying out a wide variety of human activities. Prayers and offerings are made to supernatural beings in the hope that they will aid a particular individual or community. Rituals are performed to call on supernatural beings and to control forces that appear to be unpredictable, such as those in the natural environment upon which humans depend for survival. One of the widespread practices used to control supernatural forces is magic. Although magical practices exist in many societies, magic seems to be more prominent in those in which there is less predictability in the outcome of events and thus less feeling of being in control of the social and physical environment. In the Trobriand Islands, for example, magic is not used for ordinary canoe trips within the lagoons, but only when the Islanders undertake the long-distance and dangerous canoe trips to other islands in their kula trade. Magic is also prevalent in sports and games of chance.

(5) Even if magic cannot "work" from the standpoint of Western science, it may be effective in achieving results indirectly, mainly by reducing the anxiety of the individuals and groups that practice it. This reduced anxiety allows them to proceed with more confidence, and the confidence may lead to greater success. Where technological advance and science are able to increase predictability and control over events and human relations, magic tends to become less important.

(6) **Maintaining the Social Order** Religion has a number of important functions that either directly or indirectly help maintain the social order and the survival of a society. To begin with, religious beliefs about good and evil are reinforced by supernatural means of social control. Thus, religion is a powerful force for conformity in a society. Furthermore, through myth and ritual, social values are given sacred authority and provide a reason for the present social order. Religious ritual also intensifies solidarity by creating an atmosphere in which people experience their common identity in emotionally moving ways. Religion is also an important educational institution. Initiation rites, for example, almost always include the transmission of information about cultural practices and tradition.

(7) By supporting the present social order and defining the place of the individual in society and in the universe, religion also provides people with a sense of personal identity and belonging. When individuals have lost a positive identity, or when life has no meaning because of the disintegration of a traditional culture, religion can supply a new and more positive identity and become the basis for a new adaptation. Religion can also provide an escape from reality; in the religious beliefs of an afterlife or the coming of a Messiah, powerless people who live in harsh and deprived circumstances can create an illusion of power through the manipulation of religious symbols. Religion in these circumstances is an outlet for frustration, resentment, and anger and is a way of draining off energy that might otherwise be turned against the social system. In this way, religion indirectly contributes to maintaining the social order.

(8) In summary, religion has both instrumental and expressive functions. The instrumental aspect of religion has to do with actions performed in the belief that, if people do certain things, they can influence the course of natural or social events to their advantage. The expressive aspect of ritual refers to the ways in which religious symbolism is used to express ideas about the relation of humans to nature, self to society, or group to group. In its expressive aspect, religion is an important force for social integration.*

1. c **2.** b **3.** a **4.** b **5.** b

Exercise 7.3

Here is one correct way to underline this excerpt:

Kinds of Beliefs: Animism and Animatism

(1) A basic distinction in types of religious beliefs is that between animism and animatism. **Animism** is the belief that not only living creatures but also inanimate objects have life and personality; these supernatural persons are referred to as spirits, ghosts, or gods. Such beings are believed to behave as people do: They are conscious, they have will, and they feel the same emotions as human beings feel. Such spirits may reside in features of the physical environment, such as trees or stones, or they may reside in animals. In hunting societies—for example, the Lele of Africa and the Inuit—the spirits of animals are worshipped because it is believed that a hunt will be successful only if an animal allows itself to be killed. Souls, which may also reside in human bodies, are believed to be able to leave the body at will, temporarily during sleep or permanently as in death. Spirits or souls that leave the body at death turn into ghosts, which come in a variety of forms and relate in various ways to the living in different cultures.

(2) The distinction between a spirit and a god is mostly one of scale. A god is a supernatural being of great importance and power; a spirit is a lesser being. **Polytheism** is the term used for a religion with many gods, and **monotheism** refers to a religion with only one god. Whether a religion is polytheistic or monotheistic is not so clear-cut in real cultures, however. In so-called polytheistic religions, the many gods may be just so many aspects of the one god. In India, for example, it is said that there are literally millions of gods; yet even an uneducated Indian will understand that in some way (which does not confuse him or her, though it may confuse us), these are all aspects of one divine essence.

(3) The Nuer are another culture in which the distinction between the Great Spirit and lesser spirits is fuzzy to the outsider. The Nuer, of course, have no difficulty in understanding the different contexts in which different aspects of the Great Spirit are invoked. E. E. Evans-Pritchard (1968) describes a ceremony held to end a blood feud. All the

---

*Nanda, *Cultural Anthropology*, pp. 361–363.

speakers, representing both clans and including the Leopard Skin chief, addressed the various gods: Great Spirit, spirit of the sky, spirit of our community, spirit of the flesh (this refers to the divine power of the Leopard Skin chief), and spirit of our fathers. Each clan representative appealed to God not only as God but also as God in relation to the group he represented. The Leopard Skin chief referred to God in his special relation to his religious role as mediator, as well as to the priestly lineage he belonged to.

(4) Just as in polytheistic religions, in which all gods and spirits may be reflections of one god, so in monotheistic religions, the one god may have several aspects. In the Roman Catholic religion, for example, there is God the Father, the Son, and the Holy Ghost, in addition to a number of lesser supernatural spirits such as the saints, ghosts, the devil, and the souls of people in heaven, hell, and purgatory, as well as the souls of those living on earth.

(5) **Animatism** is the belief in an impersonal supernatural power. *Mana* is perhaps the most widely known term for this power. **Mana**, or supernatural power, may be inherent in the universe but may also be concentrated in individuals or in objects. We have seen earlier that Polynesian chiefs had a much higher degree of mana than ordinary people did. Mana is the key to success, but it can also be dangerous. That is why the belief in mana is so frequently associated with an elaborate system of taboos, or prohibitions. Mana is like electricity; it is a powerful force, but it can be dangerous when not approached with the proper caution.

(6) A cross-cultural approach seems to indicate that mana, or power, is often found in those areas (spatial, temporal, verbal, or physical) that are the boundaries between clear-cut categories. Hair, for example, is believed to contain supernatural power in many different cultures (remember the Old Testament story of Samson and Delilah). Hair is a symbol of the boundary between the self and the not-self. It is both part of a person and can be separated from the person. Hence its ambiguity and its power. Doorways and gates are also familiar symbols of supernatural power. They separate the inside from the outside and can thus serve as a symbol of moral categories such as good and evil, pure and impure. Because these symbols of boundaries contain supernatural power, they are frequently part of religious ritual and are surrounded by religious taboos.*

Although your wording will likely differ, most of the information in your outline should be essentially like this one:

I. Animism def: All objects, living and dead, are alive.

    A. Hunters worship animals because they believe animal soul must allow animal to be killed.

    B. Souls can leave body and turn into ghosts.

---

*Nanda, *Cultural Anthropology*, pp. 367–369.

II. Polytheism versus Monotheism

    A. Polytheists believe in many gods.

    B. Monotheists in one god.

    C. The distinction between monotheism and polytheism not clear in India and Nuer culture.

    D. The distinction between monotheism and polytheism not clear in Catholic religion.

III. Animatism def: Belief in power that is not in the form of a person.

IV. Mana—term for animatistic power.

    A. Both powerful and dangerous.

    B. Usually represented in objects that are on the boundary of the particular object, like hair on a human or the door of a temple.

    C. Characterized by many taboos and rituals.

    C. Allows you flexibility in dealing with life's uncertainties

    D. Gives you a value system in interpreting ethics, politics, and the arts

Exercise 7.5

Wording may vary, but paraphrases should be essentially the same as these. Take partial credit where you think it is appropriate.

15. The Aztecs were warlike mainly because war allowed commoners to improve their place in society and gave them rights in feasts where human flesh was eaten.

18. The Aztecs believed that eating human flesh was more a sacred than a physical act because it brought people closer to the gods.

21. By giving food to the gods and people in sacrifice, the Aztecs believed that everyone in their culture was reborn.

24. Sanday and Sahlins believe that politics, economics, and war relations encouraged the eating of human flesh; they do not agree with Harner that it was a purely physical act, considering his ideas too simple and too influenced by American economic thought.

31. What has been discussed does not prove that one belief is better than another, but it shows how anthropologists explain religion by studying the particular society's culture and religion.

Chapter 8
Reading and
Listening for
Inferences

Exercise 8.1

You may want to go back to the paragraphs marked *V* to see how they could be made more credible.

1. D **2.** V **3.** D **4.** V **5.** V **6.** D **7.** V **8.** D **9.** D **10.** V

Exercise 8.3

Wording may vary, but the information should be essentially the same as in the following answers. You may take partial credit where you think it is appropriate.

1. A "miracle" is an event that goes beyond human abilities. The author is suggesting that Mozart's accomplishments were almost unbelievable in their quality and genius.
2. To "astonish" is to shock. The author is expressing extreme surprise at Mozart's ability to compose at the age of five.
3. "Phenomenal" suggests exceptional abilities. Again, this word suggests that Mozart's musical abilities were superior.
4. "Impossible" suggests that something cannot be done. In regard to Mozart, this word again suggests his surprising greatness.
5. "Unfathomable" suggests that one cannot fully grasp something; in regard to Mozart, this word suggests the complexity of his musical abilities.
6. "Disastrous" suggests great hardship and suffering. This word shows how destructive Mozart's personal life was to his career.
7. A "giant" is someone who is extremely large; this word shows how important Mozart was perceived as a musician in relationship to others.
8. To "explore" is to travel and study carefully; this word suggests how carefully Mozart examined and used various types of classical music.
9. "Indelible" means that something cannot be erased or destroyed. It suggests that Mozart's music will endure.
10. A "genius" is one with exceptional talents, and the word aptly describes Mozart's musical abilities.

Answers to the question about the mood of this excerpt on Mozart will vary but should approximate this one:

All the words about Mozart's musical talent are strongly positive. The one word about his personal life, disastrous, is strongly negative, showing how different Mozart's life was from his musical contributions.

Exercise 8.5

Wording may vary, but the answers should be essentially the same as those that follow. You may want to use the following scoring formula: score = number correct × 33.

1. Beethoven's accomplishments after he became deaf are astonishing and show his musical genius.

2. Mendelssohn was a versatile musician—accomplished musician, conductor, and concert organizer. Mendelssohn had a keen understanding of music and the musical needs of his people.

3. Chopin had a desire to leave his country of Poland to seek friendships with the great artists in Europe. He seemed keenly interested in those artists who were highly talented and had interesting personalities.

Chapter 9
Reading Graphs,
Charts, and Tables

Exercise 9.1

1. d **2.** c **3.** b **4.** b **5.** d **6.** b **7.** c **8.** b **9.** b **10.** c

Chapter 11
Commonly Used
Note-taking
Techniques: Numeral–
Letter, Indenting,
and Cornell

Exercise 11.1

Your wording may differ, but the condensed information should be essentially the same as shown here. You may take partial credit.

1. Def.: what people do when they buy, sell, or produce a product
2. Consumer behavior interdisciplinary, relying on sociology, anthropology, and psychology
3. Consumer behavior related to sociology in its focus on group behavior
4. Psychology shows how a person acts when purchasing a product—ex: motivation
5. Anthropology shows how culture determines buying—ex: ethnic preference
6. Def. consumer: anyone purchasing or using a product
7. Def. purchasing: getting an item from a seller
8. Later in course focus on where people buy and how they use products
9. Relationship between psychology and economics: how often people buy a product and why
10. Seeing yourself as consumer helps you understand yourself anthropologically, sociologically, and psychologically

Exercise 11.3

Your phrasing may differ from what is shown here, but the information should be essentially the same. Be sure that main ideas are separated from major details. Give yourself 2 points for each correct entry and partial credit where you think it is appropriate. Do not include Cornell commentary in your scoring.

What are basic American beliefs?

1. I. How American culture affects purchasing

    A. Interest in buying material items
    B. Belief in self
    C. Optimism
    D. Order

2. I. Is there an American culture?

Comments on current American culture

    A. Movement away from material wealth
    B. Is it still optimistic?
    C. Self-reliance makes some afraid of being alone
    D. Is order valuable?

3. I. Ethnic groups questioning American culture

What is the influence of the ethnic market?

    A. African-Americans and Latinos huge marketing challenge
    B. Some fit into American mold
    C. Some of their buying interests different

4. I. How class influences purchasing

Key questions regarding class and purchasing

    A. How do lower, middle, and upper classes shape buying?
    B. Is class question difficult, like culture question?
    C. Does income influence buying?
    D. Does income influence beliefs?

5. I. Relationship of family and purchasing

How does family relate to purchasing?

    A. Family seems to have much to say
    B. Family gives certain values
    C. Which family member will product serve?
    D. Who is more powerful: father, mother, children?
    E. Purchasing decisions change as family gets older

6. Individual's influence on consumer behavior

Def. "brand loyalty"

    People learn—are not born to buy in certain way
    Consider past experience
    Def. brand loyalty: consistent buying of a product

7. How perception affects purchasing

How is perception related to buying?

    Each of us perceives products differently
    For some, price important
    For others, look or image important

8. Determining purchasing choice has no definite answers

No definite conclusions regarding buying

    Personality has effect on purchasing
    Ex: sports car versus station wagon buyer, shade of lipstick person buys

9. Attitude and buying

How sports stars and actors sell products

    Sports figures or actors help sell product
    Stars provide positive and negative images
    Attitudes help sell product

10. Attitudes difficult to change

Key challenge: changing
purchasers' attitudes

A marketing challenge
Can marketing campaign change attitudes?
Can changed attitudes change buying patterns?
Researchers still unclear

Exercise 11.5

1. =	**11.** without
2. >	**12.** compare
3. + or &	**13.** versus
4. ⊃	**14.** incomplete
5. re	**15.** important
6. nec	**16.** principal
7. pos	**17.** continued
8. incr	**18.** number
9. lg	**19.** therefore
10. max	**20.** is both cause and effect

Exercise 11.7

You may take partial credit for your answers to 1–10. Answers will vary
for 11–20.

1. Marketing is becoming an international activity.
2. It's easy to make large mistakes in this international market.
3. Many marketers do not understand cultural setting.
4. Anthropology helps consumer behavior to understand cultures.
5. Anthropologists use a study called cross-cultural research.
6. Cross-cultural research shows how cultures are the same and different.
7. Cross-cultural research studies attitudes regarding love in cultures.
8. Cross-cultural research also works with political power in each culture.
9. Cross-cultural research studies the cultural meaning of color.
10. In some cultures black and gray are good.
11. CCR resrch shows yllow, whte, gry, weak evrywhre
12. Red & blk strng clrs in ev country
13. Some mrktrs see ea cltr unque
14. ⊃ focus on local mrktng techs
15. othrs believe in stndrdzd mrktng plans
16. These mrktrs believe in cltrl uniformty in wrld
17. Sev cntrys as 1 mrkt
18. Toursm and mass media → sim mrktg needs
19. Mrktrs see Europe as 1 cntry
20. Answrs have pos or neg impct on ad campgn

Exercise 11.9

Here are sample responses. Your approach may differ.

Consumer Behavior and Ethics (Consumer Behavior = CB)

3 key ethical considerations

How is CB rel to ethics? Consider:
  Trth in mrktng
  Prdct quality
  Prdct safety

What is role of FTC?

Mrktrs obliged to be hnst
  Fdrl Trade Comms monitors ads (FTC = Federal Trade Commission)
  Mny mail order frauds FTC has uncovrd
  Pckgng and labeling impt concern
    Ex: what is fat-free prdct?
      FTC has made spec rqrmts

Consumers' role re product reliability

Prdct reliability
  What can consmr do if prdct a hazard?
    Read warranty (W = warranty)
      Exchange prdct or get rfnd
  W/expnsve prdct, see what W promises

What if W is bad?
  Consmr can go to court
    expensive and lngthy

Respndg to complaints in pos way
  Being honest, cmpnys incr profits
  Pays to be hnst
  Some compnys ask cstmrs to be frank re prdct

How can cmplnts be effctv?
  Provide useful info
  Cmpnys can rewrite Ws
  Fmlys and frnds oftn go to honest cmpny

How does ethics work 2 ways?

Ethics wrks 2 ways
  Both unethical cstmrs and unethical cmpnys
  Cstmrs and cmpnys need to wrk togethr
  Hnsty goes a long way
  Pays to be honest → profits for cmpny and satisfctn for cstmr

***Chapter 12
Visual Note-taking
Techniques:
Laddering and
Mapping***

Exercise 12.1

Answers will vary. Take credit if you think your concept maps clearly show the relationship between main idea and major details.

1.

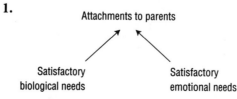

2.

Parallel Play

At same time	At same place	Independently

3.

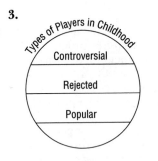

Types of Players in Childhood

Controversial

Rejected

Popular

4.

Influence of older siblings on younger siblings

Positive   Negative

Teach them to play	Serve as teachers	Can make them more aggressive

5.

Birth order makes child

Have different prenatal care

Experience environment differently

6.

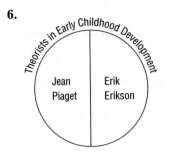

Theorists in Early Childhood Development

Jean Piaget | Erik Erikson

7.

Questions in Erikson's Stage:
Basic Trust versus Mistrust

1	2	3
Is my world predictable?	Do my parents care for my needs?	Do my parents love me?

8.

Activities in Autonomy versus Shame and Doubt

Stage

| Walking | Talking | Toilet training | Following instructions | Making choices |

9.

Intuitive versus Guilt ≠ Autonomy versus Shame

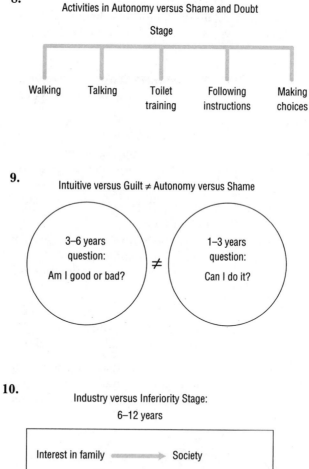

3–6 years question:

Am I good or bad?

≠

1–3 years question:

Can I do it?

10.

Industry versus Inferiority Stage:
6–12 years

Interest in family ⟹ Society

Competition ⟹ With peers and friends

Self Worth

Exercise 12.3

Your wording will vary from that shown here, but your answers should be essentially the same. Be sure that main ideas are clearly separated from major details. The concept map that accompanies this outline is only an example. Score only your outline, not the study map.

Stages in Language Development

List major characteristics of each of the five stages.

Two key questions about language
    How does a child learn language?
    Are there stages?

From birth to 1 year
    up to six months—babbling: "random sounds"
    at one, understanding begins.
    first word, "muh."
Age 1½
    50-word vocabulary
    Several words can be joined as one word.

What is meant by creative?

Age 2
    2–3 word phrases
    toddler not copying language
    important to note that language is a creative process—child
        creates entirely new sentences

Age 3
    full sentences
    Child makes up own language rules.
        Ex: "I no want to go."
    does not often understand parent correcting grammar errors

Age 4
    mastered most grammatical rules
    vocabulary still growing
    A few grammatical errors remain.

Important concept: maturational

Key to remember that language is maturational
    All children follow the same stages in language learning.
    early talkers not necessarily smarter

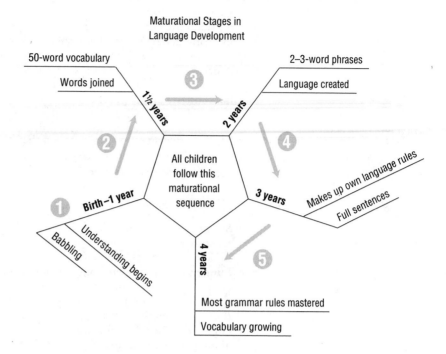

Maturational Stages in
Language Development

1. Birth–1 year — Babbling, Understanding begins
2. 1½ years — 50-word vocabulary, Words joined
3. 2 years — 2–3-word phrases, Language created
4. 3 years — Makes up own language rules, Full sentences
5. 4 years — Most grammar rules mastered, Vocabulary growing

All children follow this maturational sequence

Chapter 13
Memory Aids

Exercise 13.1

Here are possible answers:

1. Station*ary* refers to cold and warm air fronts. "Air" rhymes with "ary."
2. People who have illusions may be psychologically **ill**.
3. **Between** means that no more than two items are compared, and b is the second letter of the alphabet.
4. Capit**ol** buildings are usually **old**.
5. Hunters carry spears and **rods**. I see a hunter with a **rod** in his hand chasing an animal.
6. Roy G. Biv (a name)
7. We Are Just Mighty Mice.
8. MTSP
9. ERS
10. zeal, zealously, zealot, zealousness

Chapter 14
The SQ3R Study
System

Exercise 14.1

The following are examples of correctly underlined and marked passages. Your underlinings may differ.

1. Can Scientists Prove Anything?

What can scientists do?

In a word, no. *Scientists can disprove things, but they can never prove anything.* To win us over to their particular viewpoint, people often say that something has or has not been "scientifically proven." Either they don't understand the nature of science, or they are trying to mislead us by falsely implying that science yields absolute proof or certainty.

Instead of certainty or absolute truth or proof, scientists speak of degrees of probability or uncertainty. Scientists might predict that if we do a certain thing, then (based on the data, hypotheses, theories, and laws underlying the processes involved) there is a high, moderate, or low probability that such and such will happen.

What is the goal of science?

The goal of the rigorous scientific process is to reduce the degree of uncertainty as much as possible. However, the more complex the system being studied, the greater the degree of uncertainty or unpredictability about its behavior.*

What Is Technology?

What is technology?

Science is a search for understanding of the natural world. In contrast, **technology** involves developing devices, processes, and products designed to control the natural world—primarily for the benefit of humans—by improving our efficiency, our chances for survival, our comfort level, and our quality of life.

In many cases, technology develops from known scientific laws and theories. Scientists invented the laser, for example, by applying knowledge about the internal structure of atoms. Applied scientific knowledge about chemistry has given us nylon, pesticides, laundry detergents, pollution control devices, and countless other products. Applications of theories in nuclear physics led to nuclear weapons and nuclear power plants.

Some technologies, however, arose long before anyone understood the underlying scientific principles. For example, aspirin, extracted from the bark of a willow tree, relieved pain and fever long before anyone found out how it did so. Similarly, photography was invented by people who had no inkling of its chemistry, and farmers crossbred new strains of crops and livestock long before biologists understood the principles of genetics. In fact, much of science is an attempt to understand and explain why various technologies work.

How do technology and science differ?

Science and technology usually differ in the way the information and ideas they produce are shared. Many of the results of scientific research are published and distributed freely to be tested, challenged, verified, or modified. In contrast, many technological discoveries are kept secret until the new process or product is patented. The basis of some technology, however, gets published in journals and enjoys the same kind of public distribution and peer review as science.†

---

*From G. Tyler Miller, Jr., *Living in the Environment*, 10th ed. (Belmont, Calif.: Wadsworth, 1998), p. 54.
†From G. Tyler Miller, Jr. *Living in the Environment*, 10th ed., pp. 55–56.

3. What Is Environmental Science, and What Are Its Limitations?

What is a good definition of environmental science?

Environmental science is the study of how we and other species interact with one another and with the nonliving environment (matter and energy). It is a *physical and social science* that integrates knowledge from a wide range of disciplines including physics, chemistry, biology (especially ecology), geology, meteorology, geography, resource technology and engineering, resource conservation and management, demography (the study of population dynamics), economics, politics, sociology, psychology, and ethics. In other words, it is a study of how the parts of nature and human societies operate and interact—a study of *connections* and *interactions.*

There is controversy over some of the knowledge provided by environmental science, for much of it falls into the realm of frontier science. One problem involves *arguments over the validity of data.* There is no way to measure accurately how many metric tons of soil are eroded worldwide, how many hectares of tropical forest are cut, how many species become extinct, or how many metric tons of certain pollutants are emitted into the atmosphere or aquatic systems each year. Sometimes the estimates of such quantities may err (either way) by as much as a factor of two or more.

We may legitimately argue over the numbers, but the point environmental scientists want to make is that the trends in these phenomena are significant enough to be evaluated and addressed. Such environmental data should not be dismissed because they are "only estimates" (which are all we can ever have). This, however, does not relieve investigators from the responsibility of getting the best estimates possible and pointing out that they *are* estimates.

Why are environmental problems difficult to study?

Another limitaiton is that *most environmental problems involve so many variables and such complex interactions that we don't have enough information or sufficiently sophisticated models to aid in understanding them very well.* Much progress has been made during the past 50 years (and especially the past 25 years), but we still know much too little about how the earth works, about its current state of environmental health, and about the effects of our activities on its life-support systems (and thus on humans and other forms of life).*

Exercise 14.3

A. Survey

1. a **2.** b **3.** a **4.** b **5.** c

B. Question (answers will vary)

1. What is the definition of *race?*
2. What is the definition of *ethnic groups?*

---

*From G. Tyler Miller, Jr. *Living in the Environment,* 10th ed., p. 56.

3. What is the definition of *cultural pluralism?*
4. What is the caste system?
5. What does the table on foreigners, Jews, and Muslims suggest about group behavior?

C. Read and Recite *(answers will vary)*

Race and Ethnic Groups (pp. 279–299)

Def.: race	Race: human group with observable, common biological features
	Accurate indicator of who belongs and does not belong
	Race belief are taught and can change
Def.: color-blind	Color-blind society: no cultural meanings are attached to race
Def.: ethnic groups	Ethnic groups: groups whose cultural heritages are different
	Individuals in ethnic groups bound together
	Germans largest American ancestry group
Key point about ethnic group	Individual determines if he is part of an ethnic group
	More people giving their ancestry as American

Cultural Pluralism (pp. 299–301)

Def.: assimilation	Assimilation: ethnic group surrendering its cultural features to the larger group
Def.: accommodation	Accommodation: developing shared interests among groups in conflict
Def.: cultural pluralism	Cultural pluralism: different cultures existing within the same society
4 ways to resolve group conflict	Ways to resolve group conflict:
	extermination
	expulsion
	caste system: weaker groups cannot compete with stronger
	segregation
	North America important sociological area of study because there are so many ethnic groups
	Prejudice seems to be in all cultures and countries

D. Review

1. d 2. c 3. a 4. b 5. d 6. b 7. c 8. b 9. b 10. a

Compare the following sample concept map and marked-up excerpt with yours.

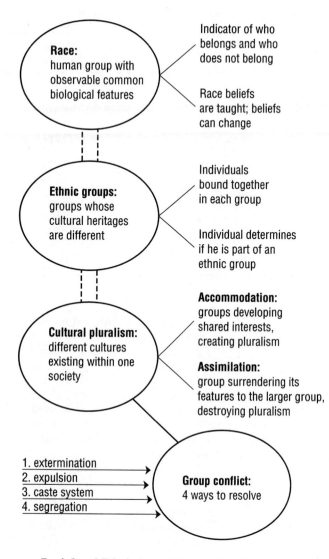

Race:
human group with
observable common
biological features

Indicator of who
belongs and who
does not belong

Race beliefs
are taught; beliefs
can change

Ethnic groups:
groups whose
cultural heritages
are different

Individuals
bound together
in each group

Individual determines
if he is part of an
ethnic group

Cultural pluralism:
different cultures
existing within one
society

Accommodation:
groups developing
shared interests,
creating pluralism

Assimilation:
group surrendering its
features to the larger group,
destroying pluralism

1. extermination
2. expulsion
3. caste system
4. segregation

Group conflict:
4 ways to resolve

Racial and Ethnic Inequality and Conflict

Race

def: race

(1) A **race** is a human group with some observable, common biological features. The most prominent of these is skin color, but racial groups also differ in other observable ways such as eyelid shape and the color and texture of hair. They also differ in subtle ways that are not visible, such as blood type. Although race is a biological concept, racial differences are important for intergroup relations solely to the extent that people attach cultural meaning to them (van den Berghe, 1967). Only when people believe that racial identity is associated with other traits such as character, ability, and behavior do racial differences affect human affairs. Historically, racial differences have typically been associated with cultural variances as well, because persons of different races were

Important point

Table 14-1   *Primary* Ethnic Ancestry of Americans of European Descent*

	Number (in 1,000s)	Percent of Total Population
German	57,947	23.3
Irish	38,736	15.6
English	32,652	13.1
Italian	14,665	5.9
French	10,321	4.1
Polish	9,366	3.8
Dutch	6,227	2.5
Scotch-Irish	5,618	2.3
Scottish	5,394	2.2
Swedish	4,681	1.9
Norwegian	3,869	1.6
Russian	2,953	1.2

Source: Statistical Abstract of the United States, 1996.
*Making up at least 1 percent of the total U.S. population.

usually members of different societies. Race, then, has usually been an accurate indicator of who is and who is not a stranger.

(2) Major trouble arises when different racial groups exist within the same society and people still assign cultural meanings to these physical differences. For one thing, members of one racial group usually cannot escape prejudice by "passing" as members of another racial group, although many light-skinned blacks can and do pass as whites. While an Italian could change his name to Robert Davis, join the Presbyterian Church, and deny his true ancestry, people cannot as easily renounce their biology.

(3) This does not mean, however, that racial differences must always produce intergroup conflict. Biological differences may be unchangable, but by themselves they are not important. It is what we *believe* about these differences that matters. And what we believe can change. The notion of a society that is color-blind simply refers to a society in which no cultural meanings are attached to human biological variations.

Ethnic Groups

(4) **Ethnic groups** are groups whose cultural heritages differ. We usually reserve the term for different cultural groups within the same society. By themselves, cultural differences are not enough to make a group an ethnic group. The differences must be noticed, and they must both bind a group together and separate it from other groups. As Michael Hechter (1974) put it, an ethnic group exists on the basis of "sentiments which bind individuals into solidarity groups on some cultural basis."

(5) The 1990 census asked Americans their primary ancestry. Table 14-1 shows the distribution of persons who reported a European nation as their ancestry, omitting those making up less than 1 percent of the total population. Germans are the largest ancestry group in the United

key point

Def.: color-blind

Def.: ethnic groups

States, including nearly one American in four. Next largest are the Irish and the English, followed by the Italians and the French (many of the latter came via Canada). However, identifying oneself in terms of ancestry is not the same as maintaining an ethnic identity. Consider the nearly 15 million Americans of Italian ancestry. Some of them can speak Italian, many cannot. Some like Italian food, some do not. Some are Roman Catholic, some are not. But the existence of an Italian American or Italian Canadian ethnic group does not simply depend on such cultural factors. What is important is that some of these people *think of themselves as sharing special bonds*—of history, culture, and kinship—with others of Italian ancestry. This makes them members of an ethnic group. But persons of Italian ancestry who do not identify themselves with their Italian heritage are not members.

key to ethnic identity

(6) Wsevolod Isajiw (1980) has pointed out that ethnic groups are "involuntary" groups in that people don't decide to join one as they might decide to join a fraternity or sorority. Rather, people are born into an ethnic group. However, unless they live within the confines of a relatively strict caste system, people often make a voluntary choice about *continuing* to belong to an ethnic group. In fact, as noted in Chapter 2, a substantial proportion of North Americans of Italian ancestry are not part of an Italian ethnic group (Alba, 1985). This is hardly limited to persons of Italian ancestry. After careful analysis comparing the 1990 census data with those of 1980, Stanley Lieberson and Mary C. Waters (1993) found a substantial shift away from naming a European ancestry group and a very great increase in the proportions giving their ancestry as "American." They concluded that "If this holds in future decades, it would mean a growing ethnic population of 'unhyphenated whites.'"

Def.:
involuntary
group

Cultural Pluralism

(7) For a long time, people believed that intergroup conflicts in North America would be resolved through *assimilation:* As time passed, a given ethnic group would surrender its distinctive cultural features and disappear into the dominant American or Canadian culture. At that point, people would no longer think of themselves as "ethnic," nor would others continue to do so.

Def.:
assimilation

Today many once formidable intergroup conflicts have been resolved in North America. Yet the ethnic groups in question, mostly European, did not disappear. True, their ethnic identity differs from that of their forebears. Typically, they have lost their native language and their bonds with the old country. But their present culture retains some elements of the old—religious affiliation, for example—while integrating a new heritage based on the special experiences of the group in the United States or Canada (Glazer and Moynihan, 1970). The important point is that conflict vanished not because noticeable differences disappeared but because the differences became unimportant. Such conflict resolutions are called *accommodation,* not assimilation. The growth of mutual interests between conflicting groups enables them to emphasize similarities and deemphasize differences.

Def.:
accommodation

(8) When intergroup conflict ends through accommodation, the result is ethnic or cultural *pluralism:* the existence of diverse cultures within the same society. That the United States is no longer a Protestant

Def.:
cultural
pluralism

Table 14-2   *"On This List of Various Groups of People, Could You Please Indicate any That You Would Not Like to Have as Neighbors."*

Nation	Foreigners (%)	Jews (%)	Muslims (%)
South Korea	53	—	21
India	48	86	31
Slovenia	40	37	38
Czech Republic	34	17	46
Slovak Republic	34	27	50
Bulgaria	34	30	41
Latvia	31	9	26
Romania	30	28	35
Nigeria	28	34	24
Turkey	28	59	—
Hungary	22	10	18
Belgium	21	13	26
Austria	20	11	14
Mexico	**18**	**19**	**19**
Japan	17	28	29
Belarus	17	21	24
Estonia	17	13	21
Germany	17	8	20
Norway	16	9	21
Lithuania	15	18	34
France	13	7	18
Chile	12	16	12
Denmark	12	3	15
Italy	12	11	12
Great Britain	12	7	17
Russia	11	13	15
Portugal	10	19	18
United States	**10**	**5**	**14**
Spain	9	10	12
Sweden	9	6	17
Iceland	8	7	12
Netherlands	8	3	13
Canada	**6**	**6**	**11**
Finland	5	5	6
Ireland	5	6	13
Brazil	4	—	—
Argentina	2	6	6

Source: Prepared by the author from the *World Values Survey, 1990–92.*
Note: — Not asked.

nation but rather a nation of Protestants, Catholics, and Jews, as well as followers of other faiths (plus nonbelievers), demonstrates cultural pluralism.

(9) Obviously, accommodation and assimilation are not the inevitable outcomes of intergroup conflict. Conflict has sometimes been resolved by the *extermination* of the weaker group, as happened with the Jews in Nazi Germany, Catholics in Elizabethan England, Indians in the

Caribbean and on the North American frontier, Armenians in Turkey, and various tribal minorities in black Africa today. Intergroup conflicts have also led to the *expulsion* of the weaker group. For example, Jews have often been expelled from nations, and Europeans were expelled from Japan in the sixteenth century. Following World War II, Pakistan expelled Hindus, India expelled Muslims, and Uganda expelled both Pakistanis and Indians, while Vietnam has driven out several hundred thousand Chinese. Finally, intergroup conflicts have been stabilized by the imposition of a **caste system,** whereby weaker groups are prevented from competing with the stronger, and through *segregation,* whereby a group is inhibited from having contact with others.

Def.:
caste
system

(10) The history of the New World contains all of these methods of resolution: Groups have been assimilated, accommodated, exterminated, expelled, and placed in a low-status caste. This variety, plus the persistence of intense intergroup conflicts, makes the United States and Canada extremely important in the study of intergroup relations. North America is a huge natural laboratory for examining the dynamics of such conflicts and useful means for overcoming them.

(11) Such an examination inevitably arouses our emotions. When we examine the history of prejudice and discrimination in North America, we cannot—nor should we—avoid anger and frustration. However, it would be tragic if we let these feelings prevent us from appreciating the extent to which hatred has been overcome, for the erosion of bigotry is also a prominent feature of North American history. The study of this erosion can teach us much about how present problems may be resolved.

(12) In reading the chapter you should also keep in mind that prejudice and discrimination are not peculiar to North America. These problems are as old as human history and exist throughout the modern world.

Interesting
fact

(13) Table 14-2 helps put the subject of prejudice into a properly international perspective. More than half of South Koreans and nearly half of Indians would not want foreigners living next door. Prejudice against foreigners is relatively high in most nations of eastern Europe. In contrast, few Americans and Canadians object to foreign neighbors. The second column in the table reveals that huge majorities of people in India and Turkey would object to having Jewish neighbors, as would a third in Slovenia, Nigeria, and Bulgaria, and about a quarter in Japan, Romania, Czechoslovakia, and Portugal. Contrast this with only 6 percent in Canada and 5 percent in the United States who say they would not like to have Jewish neighbors. Notice too that in many nations there is considerably more prejudice against Muslims than against Jews—50 percent of Slovakians, 41 percent of Bulgarians, 21 percent of Norwegians, and 20 percent of Germans don't want Muslim neighbors. Canadians (11%) and Americans (14%) also are less willing to live near Muslims than near Jews. To see a similar table on unwillingness to have persons of a different race living next door, see Chapter 19.

(14) These days, efforts to assess prejudice must overcome the reluctance of some respondents to admit their negative feelings about other groups (itself a sign that prejudice its receding). So, sometimes the questions are phrased to maximize negative responses. For example, rather

than asking people whom they *dis*trust, survey researchers ask how much they trust them. Thus, respondents in the most recent World Values Survey were asked, "I now want to ask you how much you trust various groups of people: Could you tell me how much you trust . . ." It is more acceptable for Americans to say "not very much" when asked this question about Canadians, for example, than to answer how much they distrust their neighbors to the north.

**Chapter 15
Suggestions for
Taking Objective
Tests**

**Chapter 16
Suggestions for
Taking Essay Exams
and Math or Science
Tests**

Exercise 15.1

1. c **2.** b **3.** c **4.** b **5.** d

Exercise 15.3

1. d **2.** a **3.** c **4.** b

Exercise 16.1

Your wording will differ, but the information should be essentially the same as shown here. You may want to use the following method for calculating a score.

1. Take 4 points for defining nonviolent direct action as a peaceful action—through means other than legal action, political campaigns, and voting—by a large group to change a law seen as unjust by that group.

2. Take 3 points for mentioning these three activities: demonstrations, sit-ins, and boycotts.

3. Take 3 points for noting that Dr. King saw nonviolent direct action as a loving way of creating concern in a community for an unjust issue. King believed that all laws must be analyzed for their moral content, so that a law may be violated if the group considers it immoral.
Here is a sample paragraph receiving all 10 points:

> Nonviolent direct action is a peaceful activity by one or several people to change a law that is seen as unjust. This peaceful action does not rely on the courts, political campaigns, or voting to achieve its goal. Examples of nonviolent direct action include sit-ins, demonstrations, and boycotts. Dr. Martin Luther King, Jr., saw nonviolent direct action as the best way for a community to change an unjust law. King realized that some laws were considered constitutional but were, in fact, immoral. In these cases, King believed that an immoral law should be violated through nonviolent direct action.

---

*From Rodney Stark. *Sociology*, 7th ed., pp. 274–8.

Index